This is a work of fiction inspired by the true events of the author, Loki Keeler.

The book you hold in your hands would be a lot different without the help of Roma: writer, ruthless editor, hired gun, friend and confidant. We did it, brother.

D1738406

Disclaimer:

This work of fiction contains characters and events that are products of the author's imagination. Any resemblance to actual persons, living or dead, or events is purely coincidental. The author acknowledges the distinction between reality and the created narrative, and all characters are fictional and do not represent real individuals. Reader discretion is advised.

Glitter only shines when it's in the light

CHAPTER ONE

I wake up Friday afternoon with a handful of rubber bands, small empty baggies, and scattered glitter in my back pocket minutes before my shift. Stress hitting me like an electric shock when I see the clock, I stumble out of bed to throw on gold pants, a white and black fur coat down to my ankles, and enough glitter to make a disco ball jealous.

You'd think this would catch looks from nearby pedestrians as I walk the five blocks of warehouse after warehouse down a dirty Bushwick street, but they don't care. They know NYC is full of freaks, and just being a few blocks from the craziest club in the city they know where I'm headed.

I walk through the door at 5:15pm, two hours before doors open. My call time is 6:15, but one of the only ways to not die of a heart attack during a stressful 12-hour shift is to come in even earlier and put some extra prep in. Sure, I could come in later—as the manager I do all the scheduling—but why kill myself when I can just torture myself instead.

Besides, with the surprising news I received Monday, I don't think I can handle any extra chaos at the moment.

Tonight's events are "The Foreplay" and "Love House," our monthly sexy theater show and party, which means there will be plenty of action and lots of extra tech and setup to make it happen. I walk through the Front Room and take note of my surroundings. The house lights are on (bright, white working lights) as Amar, one of the four owners, is finishing setup for yet another one of his wildly creative and perverted experiences. The long wooden bar along the wall to the right, the bathrooms across the room, and the nook, diagonal from the entrance, with black leather couches and a ten-foot tall face with silver-disco skin, are activated. With the lights on it's easy to see every scattered crack in the black and white tiled floor and the small rips in the shimmering disco fabrics hung all along the walls.

For tonight, Amar, standing just over six feet tall with dark bronze skin and wearing a red silk robe with a black dragon on the back, designer black jeans, black boots and smeared makeup, plans on having our local alcoholic pirate, Carlos Surfista, handcuffed and bent over a small table covered with plates of grilled rare steak while wearing women's laced lingerie and silicone titties. For an added twist, Amar has precariously hung a feather from the ceiling with a clear fishing line perfectly positioned near Carlos' very exposed anus so the patrons can have some tickling fun, if they so desire.

To my right, on a massive projector screen behind the bar, Amar is screening one of his amazing vintage pornos. These films aren't your run-of-the-mill, boring and misogynistic pornos. No. They're the art pieces with apparently limitless costume budgets, actual plots, and linear storylines that somehow sensibly explain the scenes of Egyptian pharaohs having sex with Catholic nuns. I haven't the slightest clue where he finds these gems, but rumor has it Amar owned one of New York City's best sex shops back in the day, so maybe leftover stock. Regardless, all the coked up clowns backstage and myself agree they are amazing.

Supermodel #1, Amar's personal office intern, is the only person who doesn't like the films. She's wearing lingerie and rehearsing her dancing for the night on the bar positioned in front of the screen by swaying her body like a cobra listening to a snake charmer. She always appears to be having the time of her life—it's part of the job—but beneath the veneer she's more frustrated than a cat in a bath. Not only is she not trying to block the viewing of the porno, but she's deftly avoiding stepping on the eight large glass bowls of fruit, three cash registers, and, of course, chocolate fountain. A tough job for anyone to do with a smile. She deals with it by inhaling three shots of cheap tequila served to her by Oliver, the Australian bar manager who's as serious as water is dry, before the shift.

Look towards the center of the room and you will see Sandra, or Supermodel #2. She's sitting in a tub of red water wearing only nude colored panties. It's as if a bunny walked right off a Playboy cover, came to the club, took off most of her clothes and sat in this very tub. She's very kind, approachable, and will feed you raspberries if you say hi to her.

For the last activation in this room, we have the two women dominatrices and their male sub in the nook area. He's a hot guy, not too smart, and always ends up in some crazy situation. Each time I walk by he is either licking someone's shoe, getting electrocuted, having something stuffed up his ass, or all three at the same time. I worry about the guy, but everytime I look over he seems to be enjoying himself.

You never know what Amar's wild imagination will come up with next. Early on in my career Amar made me famous by tying a saltshaker to my cock and making me a star of one of his art pieces, but we'll get to that later.

From a quick glance this room seems under control. I take a peek through the gold doors that lead to the patio, no one is there, it's clean and quiet. *Perfect,* I think to myself.

I make my way to the office by cutting through the Theater. The Theater is about four times the size, with a ceiling twice as high, as the Front Room. Luscious red carpets cover the floor and various sized red pillows are strewn about for sexy comfortability around a large, central, steeldeck platform. Looking up I see Dreams, a black, versatile performer and one of our resident drag queens, and other performers tech-ing (rehearsing with lights and sound) their acts. They are all flying through the air. Some on straps, others on silks. To the right, above the long Theater bar, are two performers wearing underwear as protective as a piece of floss dancing in the suspended, golden, stripper cage. Across the room is production, the ones who physically set up everything and pull the ropes behind the scenes during the events. They're in all black installing human sized, LED flowers on the stage while communicating with drill bits between their teeth.

Zoe and Lada, the two founders and part owners of this madhouse, are yelling at the performers and tech team, constructively sharing what they love and hate.

"The blue lights were a good idea but this act needs something warm and sultry! Give me orange and red!" Zoe yells up to Nasty, the lighting designer (LD) and type of dude you would find on ten hits of acid at a heavy metal concert, in the raised tech booth, opposite to the stage.

"Cold linguini baby!" Nasty replies.

"Cold what? The lights, Nasty. The lights! Are you alright today? You seem off?" Asks Zoe.

"I'm fine. Here we go," replies Nasty. He presses a few buttons and within seconds the room is bathed in a different, warmer light. Zoe, standing tall with black heels and a tight black dress down to her upper thighs that makes her curly, tangerine hair pop, loves it.

"When dancing in the cage you need to hit the audience with a pose every rotation. Think spin and hit. Spin and hit! Yes!" Lada screams out while clapping to the beat of her words. Lada is wearing a glimmering, black underwear and bra combo that matches her slightly taller black heels and dark hair.

I look at my phone. It's 5:19. Time to get working.

The office is secretly tucked away upstairs, behind one of the elevated go-go platforms in the theater. Black curtains hide it from sight. There's a secret staircase stage left which takes you to a platform above and behind the stage. I walk up and follow a dark corridor to the office door. The other option is a ladder in the greenroom backstage that leads to a trap door in front of the office entrance, but if we're not open yet I tend to take the stairs to give the performers their space.

I punch in the code on the lock and open the door. The office is a swimming pool of confetti from the night before.

Deep breath, Loki, I tell myself to prevent a pre-shift meltdown.

These days a large portion of my life entails cleaning up everyone's various messes here at the club and it's driving me to the edge. Tonight could be the night I tip over.

I sit in a black office chair, blow yellow and red confetti off my desk and computer keyboard, and log in. Next to me on a different computer is Juicy, the fourth and final owner, smoking a cigarette and so engrossed in his work that he doesn't even look over at me. The way the cigarette hangs from his lip and his wide, blank eyes are staring into the screen, I wouldn't be surprised if he's been on that computer answering emails and running operations for twelve hours straight. Knowing his work ethic, I wouldn't put it past him.

I open my mouth to ask how he's doing, but no words come out. It's difficult to carry on pretending things are business-as-usual after our conversation a few days ago.

Whatever. Time to get going.

Now to the three steps of office prep:

Step 1—Check any last minute emails and texts for new information about the night's events and make a game plan accordingly. Tonight we have a new performer, which means paperwork to fill out. Amar said he'd send his assistant, Victor, to get pizzas for the bottle service tables, so I won't have to. The DJ who'll be spinning later tonight requested coconut water, so I will need to send the barbacks to Zana, the airport-priced, organic grocery store next door for Brooklyn gentrifiers, to purchase some. And it's Daisy's last shift which means we need to do a big surprise for her. I grab my phone and text Koochy, lead stage manager and clown extraordinaire, to scheme up something spectacular.

Step 2—Set up the reports for the night. With every event there are several crucial reports to be filled out, filed, and shared as needed. There's the Tip Sheet, which helps me to calculate the tips for all the bartenders, barbacks, hosts and bottle servers and a Daily Management Report (DMR) that provides an event summary for all the managers and owners. These files can't be finished until after the event is over, but information such as online ticket presales, who will be working, and contract info for the event can be filled in within 20-30 minutes. Better to do this part before the night begins rather than when you're stuck dealing with hundreds of people in line because half the door team is doing bumps in the tech booth or giving blowjobs in the costume closet.

Step 3—Grab the five magical items: a few thousand dollars for the cash registers, a stack of free-drink tickets, my radio earpiece, the ticket scanners and iPad counter for the door, and five printed event memos with info on performances and DJs to be placed in employee areas.

It's 6:02. Let's hit it.

I run across the Theater, hopping over plush pillows while narrowly dodging naked performers' heels, which are flying through the air as they tech their acts. Dreams has a penchant for six-inch black heels, and I've personally witnessed the damage they can inflict on an unsuspecting face. It's not pretty, and something I don't need at the beginning of my shift.

The radios are in the kitchen. I grab them and begin to distribute them, along with the event memos to—

I hear singing. I immediately head back to the Theater, leaving the walkies behind, utterly forgotten—the legendary Kate Cummings is practicing the songs she will perform tonight. When Kate Cummings sings, you stop, watch, and listen. A white Beyonce with her thick, toned physique and angelic singing voice, Kate is one of those people who should be famous but isn't for some reason. Not yet, anyway. She is worth much more than what our budget allows us to offer, but she loves our artistic radicalism and is down to take a pay cut to work with us.

I stare shamelessly, jaw to the floor, as Cummings rehearses a song that melts my soul. I'm hypnotized by her voice and her legs, the flesh of her beautifully thick thighs practically bursting from their fishnet prison. *Please marry me, I*—and everyone watching—think as this goddess rehearses.

The bag of cash hangs from my right fist, forgotten. I don't care that I need to get going. If I've learned anything here, it's the little things that prevent me from going insane at this point.

When Kate's last note trails off, I snap out of my trance and head to the Front Room. I disperse the cash between the bar, door, and coat check, nestled in the back of the patio.

It's 6:15, one hour before doors. The barbacks have all arrived; black-and-blue-bagged garbage bins have been dispersed around the club and they're in the kitchen cutting up limes and making pre-batched cocktails. *Perfect.*

The coat check girls, the wives and friends of the barbacks, are late as usual. The only reason I don't give them a hard time about it is because they make me home-cooked Mexican delights that are so delicious I would sell a kidney for a second portion.

Time to set the vibe.

Because the Front Room and Patio will open at exactly 7:15 while the theater will stay closed until the show begins at about 8:15, it's imperative to focus on those areas first. To start, I replace the bright lights in both areas with sultry, red, mood lights. Next I switch on the massive eyeballs hung over the 2.5 meter tall, wooden Theater doors. The eyes, about one cubic meter and stricken with red veins, emit volcanic lights and commence blinking, each eyeball at a different speed. Then I turn on all the LED candles meticulously placed around the space.

Here at the club we use plastic candles because, like everything else in this place, they need to be what I call "night-child-proof". I've learned that running a nightclub is like running a daycare for adults. Everything needs to be child-proofed, or the "children" will find a way to destroy the thing in question and hurt themselves in the process. Once we left the fire hydrant outside its box in the Onyx Room, our small rave cave at the far back corner of the outside area, during one of our monthly gay parties, Bad Behavior. Well, a perfectly lovely fellow got his hands on it and gleefully discharged the red canister into the cuddle puddle of hairy men rolling around back there. Fun as it was, nobody stopped him, and he managed to keep spraying fire retardant gas until the thing was completely empty, making the room appear like twenty bears were swimming in shaving cream. Michelle, our cleaning guy, was real happy about that one the next day.

Back to my pre-doors process. I throw on a Satori playlist—slow, deep house with dark, chanting undertones—before the lights and sound are set. Food is to follow. As part of the The Foreplay event there are dozens of plates of bite-sized hors d'oeuvres that need to be set before doors open: strawberries and grapes, classic bruschetta, cheesy mushroom ravioli on skewers, and the crowd pleasing (unless if you're a vegetarian like me) medium-rare steak.

I look in the kitchen. Chef's there with his assistant, prepping. At this point I've worked with Chef long enough to know not to bother him during his prep. Even though I'm the boss, Chef will come at me with a butcher's knife if I stick my head in the kitchen while he's working. Typical chef behavior when the front-of-house managers check up on them—which doesn't mean I shouldn't—but by now I trust him enough to leave him alone. I ask what he wants to drink, bring him the Diplomatico and Coke he always wants, and move on.

Now for the holiest of sanctuaries: the bathrooms. Where hundreds of intoxicated humans urinate inaccurately, experience ecstasy induced-defecation, vomit uproariously, repeatedly snort powders, and curiously partake in small orgies throughout the night. A party bathroom can either be an unforeseen adventure or a traumatic nightmare for anyone, especially if you're on acid. Just ask any Burner for a Porta-potty story and prepare to be amazed.

Through the disco corridor on the far side of the bar in the Front Room we have two unisex, multiple occupancy bathrooms. One has gold tiles, shimmery gold spray painted doors, bedazzled stalls with multicolored gems, and a large mirror that is mostly used for makeup and cocaine. The other has black and white tiles, four armed mannequins coming out of the walls, one basic stall and three white urinals. This one is mostly used for handjobs and cocaine.

On the right side of the stage in the Theater we have three themed, private restrooms. First is a hand painted, sci-fi, comic book bathroom with images of aliens in UFOs and a wolfman having sex with a platinum blonde. Next we have an ocean bathroom with seashells covering every inch of the walls and a dim light emitting from the fish tank. Then, lastly, we have a Yes House memorabilia bathroom that used to be a gold Hindi themed bathroom until a Hindi pointed out how disrespectful it is to shit and do drugs with images of religious deities.

Even though it's not my job, I thoroughly check all five bathrooms, making sure they are spotless, the trash cans are empty, the toilets are flushed, and the toilet paper is stocked. God forbid a bathroom runs out of toilet paper during peak hours. If a staff member is nowhere to be found, that's me having to awkwardly cut in front of 50 sweating, drugged out, impatient, half naked humans to resolve the issue.

6:45; thirty minutes before doors. Security, bartenders, and the door staff begin to arrive. Nearly everyone comes in five minutes early these days, but it sure didn't used to be like this. It took me being a real hardass and meting out punishment. Back in the day our staff of drag queens and clowns would roll in half an hour late, half a gram bag of blow in their nose, ready to party. I should have expected it, trying to manage a group of recalcitrants. Mr. Grandma, variety show producer and clown extraordinaire, has the biggest cast of talented clowns in the whole city, and he'll even tell you, "Never. Hire. Clowns."

I check in with Harlequin, the door girl, standing just over five feet tall with short dark hair and a butt the size of Twin Peaks. She's wearing a conservative outfit consisting of a black thong, two pieces of black tape over each nipple, and glitter. I give her the iPad, ticket scanners, and starting cash. I make sure she knows tickets at the door are $80, we have room for 20 more tickets to be sold, and there's no table service. This is all info she should already know, but since the name of the game is minimizing errors I don't leave it up to chance.

"How are you?" I ask out of generosity before running off.

"Well I have no money, I'm ugly, and I'm about to turn thirty. So I'm great!" Harlequin replies, flashing a big smile.

"Oh c'mon. You're beautiful. Why do you keep saying that?"

"Nobody loves me!" Harlequin replies, throwing her head back and her hands over her heart.

"We love you and that's all that matters. See you soon." I say before walking out to the street.

On the sidewalk outside I relay the same event information to Crius, a large Nicaraguan man from the Bronx and our head of security, who has already set up the two opposing lines with red stanchions. I also let him know that the owners are expecting a couple of VIPs, people who should be shown right in, no line. He smiles and says "copy," which I love. No matter how much information I throw at Crius, he listens carefully, absorbs, and confirms that he understands.

Standing beside security are the Consenticorns. That's right; Consenticorns. They are our mobile consent monitors that wear light up unicorn horns and roam our sexy parties, making sure everyone is behaving. If anyone looks dehydrated, they get them water. If anyone is misbehaving, they let security or myself know about it right away. Having a large public party of a sexual nature creates an immense amount of liability. Perverts and sex offenders, people taking unauthorized videos, people being too intoxicated—there is a galaxy of potential issues—and we take a lot of action to foresee and prevent them. Security can't be everywhere at once, so that's where the consenticorns come in.

Our parties are costume mandatory, so tonight if you're not wearing hot fetish gear, the consenticorns won't let you in. Every party is better when everyone participates (especially if the theme is underwear), and it's essential for sexy parties. This helps prevent voyeurs and creeps not in the scene from making participants uncomfortable with their distanced stares.

After the costume approval comes the extensive consent speech at the door, laying out the laws of the land: "No pictures at any time. No touching without an absolutely enthusiastic 'YES!' If it's not a 'yes' or a 'fuck yes', it's a 'no'. Drink water. The bathrooms are gender neutral. And there's no harassment, discrimination or violence of any kind. If you see or experience something, let a staff member know and we will help you!" If anyone complains about you breaking these rules, you're out. We believe the victim here. It's the only way to keep these parties safe, and the consenticorns play a major role.

. I take a quick look. The consenticorns are ready to go. I make sure the street and sidewalk in front of the club are clean and check on coat check again. They are here and set up. *Perfect.* I collect my delicious Mexican food that's perfectly placed in the plastic tupperware like it came from Grubhub and briskly walk (which is actually a six minute mile pace) to the bar. Oliver emerges his lean, six-foot tall frame from the bathroom with nose sniffles and a nose that looks like it was stuffed in a snowman.

"Ready mate? It's another day in paradise!" Oliver remarks upon seeing me.

I'm working with A-class management here.

It's 7:10, five minutes before doors, and the Front Room performers are nowhere to be found, naturally. My job mostly consists of herding cats, so this is nothing new. I run to the kitchen to drop off my Mexican food then head backstage. The narrow corridor is packed with performers. Some are hurriedly finishing up their eyelashes and doing their face makeup while the rest are drinking Rosé and gossiping about how often Dreams' wig falls off during her performances. "We're opening now!" I yell, as I hustle the Front Room entertainers into position.

Drinks are thrown down as near naked bodies in various colored heels (except for Carlos Surfista, who holds on to both of his drinks) scurry across the Theater towards the Front Room. Once the artists are where they need to be I sprint to the kitchen and yell down the hall for the barbacks: "Armando, Jesus, Santiago!" Within seconds they appear and we grab all the plates of food in the kitchen and distribute them throughout the Front Room. I look at my phone: it's 7:14. I glance at Oliver and the other bartender and they nod. I turn to Harlequin, she nods as well. It's 7:15 as I walk out the front doors. On the sidewalk there's a line full of gorgeous creatures stretching to the corner. They're wearing coats that conceal their leather, their fur, their feathers, their lace... they're ready to play their dirty little hearts out.

I exchange a look with security and the consenticorns.

"Yes House is open," I say with a mischievous smile.

Then the night begins.

C H A P T E R   T W O

Four years before that night at Yes House, I was a 21-year-old poster boy for California hippiedom: a massage therapist living out of a converted van in San Francisco, finishing up college. My luscious mane of dark brown hair with natural highlights (most prominent in the curly tips) complimented the Om tattoo that took up the entire left side of my chest. It might as well have been a bullseye for the yoga army, who were dismayed to discover my strong disliking of yoga and most things New Age and hippie. Growing up surrounded by the woo woo culture of the San Francisco Bay Area had left me jaded.

Frustration was pulsing through my veins as I was on the call. "I can't believe you didn't come to visit me again." I said with disdain into the telephone.

"I tried, I promise! I was just tired," replied my Father.

Of course. Tired. There was always a reason. My whole life he's always had a reason.

I was just back from my first Burning Man and had become *that* guy, the stereotypical first-burner who won't shut up about the whole thing. It was extraordinary, unworldly, heart-exploding. "Life-changing" was an understatement. It's a brutal desert filled with 70,000 polyamorous, drugged out, caring, extreme weirdos and hundreds of art projects, some worth millions of dollars, for you to play with. Add on a gifting economy where everything is free, even the most pessimistic non-believers become converts. I left with an insatiable desire for more.

The only thing I regretted was the bitter taste left in my soul from my father's yet-another neglect. He was there, too. I was camping with friends while he spent the Burn on another section of the Playa (what we called the ancient dried up lake bed on which the event takes place) with my half-brother, Mando. Mando and I were never too close as he grew up with our father and I grew up with my mother. He is ten years older, too, and the age difference played a role.

Twice I traveled through the blistering hot desert sun to visit their camp and see them both. Ecstatic joy rushed through me as the three of us met in this magical place.

"Dad! Let's go on an adventure together. A bike ride through the city or to see some art!" I said on my first visit there.

The Puerto Rican man in his mid sixties with a scrunched face and a couple teeth missing grumbled in his chair. He was *tired*. "I'll come find your camp and we'll go on an adventure later, I promise," my Father said.

He didn't come. The next day I rode my bike over the chalky, alkaline desert a second time, again to ask if he'd go on an adventure with me. I got the same response, the same promise. Again, the same result. And again, he let me down.

Growing up I saw my father once a month—if I was lucky. It was easier to see him on a consistent monthly basis when I was a teenager and he was in prison—wasn't so easy to use the ol' "out of town" excuse at that point. Now, though, I was just starting to realize that my whole life I chased his love like a child reaching for a helium balloon flying into the clouded sky. I always believed I was going to reach that balloon one day, despite how obvious it was to everyone that it would never happen.

Between chasing my father's elusive love and running away from my mother's overbearing care and affection, I was left to find my own, new family.

That's what I loved about Burning Man. I've been to big parties before, with lots of people hanging at the beach or someone's house, drinking, enjoying… but this was different. It felt like everyone I made friends with was family. Real or not, the feeling made it so for me. For the first time, for most of the time I spent in that desert bacchanalia, I felt whole.

I needed more of that feeling. Fortunately, about one month after the desert debauchery some cities in the US had a post-Burn event called Decompression, so for one evening I was able to dive back into that fantasy culture.

Flying on acid and skipping through the crowd of costumed San Franciscans, I felt at home. I hadn't known there were people as wild and wacky to the core as me, yet here they were, a massive international community, many of them residing in my very own neighborhood. I was trying to take all this in while lying in the grass. I loved these freaks even though I didn't even know them.

It was nearing dark. To my right the sun fell behind the skyline, leaving the sky pink behind the painted silhouette of the city. On the grass a woman was attempting to do a headstand in front of her friends. I watched as she got closer to full vertical with every attempt, adding to the suspense by yelling, "Ohhh, Ohhhhhhh, Ohhhhhhhhhhhhhh!" A man in their group yelled through the almost-dark, "Get over here! You seem fun!"

I leaped up and sprinted over faster than a California fire engulfs an untended field. Within seconds I was fully immersed in a 15-person cuddle puddle of total strangers. More accurately, I was the stranger, but this didn't last. I was instantly accepted, embraced as a friend, as one of them.

We exchanged names. They expressed gratitude and joy at my joining them. I was in love with these weirdos, yet surprised a group of people like this could exist. It felt as if I was seeing a new color. I may have been rushing things, but for the first time in my life I felt I had a family in my hometown.

"We're going to Xavier's later!" The message fluttered around like a bird as we cuddled.

Introduce yourself to Xavier so you can go to his house later! I kept telling my lysergically altered acid brain.

Normally this would be very easy, but performing the most basic of tasks while on acid can be extremely difficult. Just the mental effort of figuring out how to stand up, stumble yourself towards the bathroom, and urinate can be exhausting.

"I'm going to head out in five minutes." I heard Xavier say from somewhere in the gloom. Xavier is of average height, has tan skin, and was wearing jeans, a stylish black coat, a top hat and spectacles.

Fuck. Come on acid brain. Go say hi. Open your mouth, and release the words. Hello. It's not that hard!

Before my brain could stop winding up Xavier spoke again. "Alright, I'll see you guys at my place later!"

Oh shit, it's now or never. I jumped up, got his attention and said, "Hey Xavier! I'm Loki."

Xavier stopped and looked at me. "I know… You've literally introduced yourself three times in the last 10 minutes."

My mouth was frozen open as I stood there dumbly.

He just giggled and said, "don't worry about it, I'm excited to see you later tonight."

Embarrassed, but ultimately relieved, I smiled. He walked away and I began to look for a hole in the Earth that I could crawl into and die.

Shortly after Xavier left we got up off the grass and made our way to his apartment in Berkeley. Walking beside me was Rico, one of the dudes from the cuddle puddle, a loveable Scandinavian-Canadian. He was six-foot four with a big scruffy beard and buck teeth. You looked at him and smiled—not meanly, it's just that he had such a disarming look to him. Rico had the apartment right next to Xavier's, so they both lived directly above Rico's kava bar, BulaBula. All night we migrated from Rico's to Xavier's to the closed kava bar, cavorting like sugar-high monkeys. We danced the love story night away, falling for each other over and over. Looking back, the connection might have had something to do with all the MDMA we took, but we were meant to be together, regardless. Those beautiful smiling faces at the brunch table the next day are forever burned deep into my memory.

Fast forward a few days. I'm driving back and forth from the city to Berkeley every day to hang out at the kava bar with Rico, Xavier, and the rest of the gang. Within a month I was bartending at the place. A year later we were going back to Burning Man, but this time together. Xavier, Rico, and I were inseparable.

My second Burn I camped with Xavier and Rico's crew. The camp name was Chewbacca, like the Wookie character in Star Wars. It was made up of our California crew and a group of New York City degenerates who worked with Xavier's brother and cousin, the co-owners of a crazy theater and nightclub called Yes House. I had never heard of it before, but Xavier painted a picture so vivid I could close my eyes and almost feel the bass thumping in my chest and the hot bodies pressed against me.

The days leading up to the Burn Xavier told colorful tales of the owners and what happened in their venue. His cousin Amar grew up working with cattle on a kibbutz, a collective community focused on agriculture, in Israel. He saved enough money to leave the Kibbutz by catching poisonous snakes and selling them to a nearby university. Apparently, when nothing was going to plan at the club and everyone was panicking, only Amar remained calm, giving wise directions. This mythical creature never needed sleep, was utterly unaffected by substances, and successfully ran multiple businesses in NYC—just to share some of the Legend of Amar. This, along with the fact that he put up most of the money to get the club off the ground, was supposedly why all the performers called him "Dad."

Then we have Xavier's brother, Juicy. He was a man in his early 30s with already graying hair due to the amount of stress he dealt with during the first couple years of the business opening. Although pinned as a maverick from his coworkers, his hard working and team building work ethic shone above all and earned him the title of the "glue of the business."

Another owner was Lada. The beautiful Muscovite who did some growing up in upstate New York was a shaken up champagne bottle with a loose cork. A mad genius and circus extraordinaire, legend had it that when left alone for a day without anything to do, she'd have a zipline with back-flipping, electric guitar playing drag queens flying through the venue by sunset. Dangerous? You bet. Aware of the danger? Hell, yes. Did that ever stop her? Never.

Last but not least was Zoe. She and Lada were childhood best friends from upstate New York and a seemingly perfect duo, whether organizing parties or performing together. Zoe was known as one of the most bubbly and charming humans you'd ever meet, always quick with a contagious smile. If her exceptional circus performances didn't get you to fall in love with her, her winning personality would.

It was these stories and images that circulated through my mind as I made my way back to the dusty wonderland where it all started.

~~~

Speeding with the windows down and Rufus Du Sol blaring out the speakers; the adrenaline was overwhelming. My heart was beating three times faster than the bass. Every breath surged an electric stimulation through every molecule in my body. I was alive.

Hours flew by as I soared through the night. The sun was rising over the desert horizon as I neared Black Rock City, the only city that exists for only one week out of the year. The Craigslist hitchhiker in my passenger seat, who swore an oath to stay awake with me during the drive through the night, had slept for seven and a half hours of the eight hour stint. Him waking up by my abrupt sunrise howling out the window was a satisfying retribution.

We were here. Deep in the desert where dust whirled through the air and magic became reality.

We arrived Tuesday morning and cruised right through the empty, desert entry road into the city of madness. Most of the city was heading for sleep at 7:30am. Chewbacca was regrouping after a wild night for a breakfast party.

In a small kitchen, consisting of a couple gas stovetops and held up by a few metal poles and tarps, a near 50 year old, tall Israeli man wearing a king's robe and makeup looking like it was done by a blind clown on acid, was making shakshuka. Beside him was a man dressed in a full-body lobster outfit pretending to help, but is just repeatedly inhaling nitrous out of a whipped-cream cracker. Managing the situation was a topless woman wearing a viking horn necklace and a twelve-inch strap-on dildo asleep in a camping chair. Bon appetit.

"Hey, I'm Loki. I'll be camping with you this year. I'm a friend of Xavier's," I said as I reached out my hand, shaking from the residual adrenaline.

"What's up? I'm Amar," responded the man in the king's robe. He smiled, and gave me a quick, piercing stare. It felt as if he was viewing all the events that had happened in my life within those few seconds. I understood why Xavier said some called him The Godfather.

The next day I was sitting on a circle of Moroccan pillows in the back of a box truck with Amar, still in the king's robe, and his friend Jayce, wearing shorts and a sombrero. Amar and his friend spoke only Hebrew as we sat in the sauna of a truck. Twenty minutes went by without me understanding a word until Jayce finally turned to me and asked, "so what's your story? What do you want to do?"

Caught off guard by the sudden switch in languages, I hesitantly responded, "Well... I now work at Rico's kava bar and would like to open up my own someday. I love the community aspect of it, and would be happy to just create another community even if it didn't make much money."

Amar jerked back. "What do you mean not make money?" he cried in a cold, raspy voice. "The most important aspect of a business is to stay open, which means you have to make money. If your business fails then your community fails!" He chuckled. "You don't even know how to spell business!"

Rejection slapped me across the face as I sank into my red, feathery pillow. I didn't know how to respond. Jayce tried to back me up and said maybe it could be gratifying to sustain a business that is community based but didn't make much profit. Amar was still in disbelief. Amar owned Yes House and many other businesses. I just had dreams.

The multi-colored LEDs, dancing fire, and bumping music raged on throughout the nights. With all the excitement around I picked up some old habits.

When I met Juicy he was wearing pink from head to toe: sneakers, jeans, fluorescent belt, blazer, chain, and clip-on earrings—all pink. He had a lean frame and a silver 5 o'clock shadow that accentuated his olive skin. I asked him for a cigarette. Without flinching he gave me two. A couple hours later while I was rolling on ecstasy in a 200-meter LED sound wave tunnel deep in the dark desert I asked for another. Again two more appeared without hesitation.

It wasn't until sunrise at Bubbles & Bass when I watched Juicy go up to the DJ and try to trade some champagne in exchange for a headlining gig at Yes House that I realized that he was actually Xavier's brother Juicy. I couldn't believe someone as loose as this guy was trusted to make toast, let alone run a major business.

Within five days Juicy provided me with 100 cigarettes, and was the person I bonded with the most. I was grateful for the chivalry, and wasn't sure if I would ever be able to repay the guy.

Sitting around the orange embers as they flickered bright in the night sky, I watched the magic unfold. The owners and staff of Yes House danced freely, cooked family meals, and laughed together. A guy with strong shoulders, a slight gut, and brown, curly hair stood on the dusty street with a small posse of clowns as they screamed at people walking by if they wanted to buy cold linguini.

Juicy ran up to the man sitting in a red chair next to me, gave him a tight squeeze, and followed up with a big kiss on the man's cheek. The man cackled in response, then reached up and squeezed Juicy back.

The rest held each other as brothers and sisters while staring up at the galaxies of stars. Juicy ran off to join them.

"If this is the team, then what is the club like?" I asked the man sitting in the red camping chair next to me, now slowly smoking a cigarette, eyes lost in the fire.

He glanced at me for a second then returned his gaze towards the flames. "Imagine a bunch of circus mermaids on acid flying around a warehouse made of glitter. That's Yes House," said the man. His voice was drier than stone. We introduced ourselves. His name was Dan Rockies. He was a born-and-bred New Yorker, and the opening bar manager for the club. These were his first days off since the club opened almost a year ago.

As I listened to Dan I stared into the burning embers of the fire, pondering the simultaneous creation and destruction of the flames. It was what was happening with these people in front of me. Every moment seemed to be a new dance, memory, and creative endeavor. Moving on from the last moment, and experiencing the new one.

"This is my roommate, Strom," said Dan, introducing the man next to him and snapping me out of my ponder. I remembered

Strom because he shamed me for—living up to my reputation—asking where he was from three times already. He's also a native New Yorker.

I waved at Strom and he dryly smiled back at me. His expression remembered my forgetfulness. "What's your role with Yes House," I asked.

"Ha. I don't work there. Although, sometimes I help Juicy count cash at the end of the night, depending on how hard he partied. That, and the after-hours of course." Replied Strom. He added that he and Dan Rockies were throwing the after-hours parties for the YES (Yes House) staff two to four times a week from 4am - noon. This would be after Dan already worked twelve hours at the club, of course.

Strom continued on, giving me the basic history scoop on Yes House. It was founded by two girls from upstate New York, Zoe and Lada, and had three iterations. The first iteration started nearly ten years prior in a small NYC apartment, where they would throw wild and eccentric parties until some hanging pants caught fire in the kitchen and burnt the place down. Then YES 2.0 evolved into an underground warehouse operation in Bushwick, Brooklyn. Here Zoe and Lada would throw more illegal, eccentric parties, host shows, and present outlandish circus performances to their growing community. Finally, it wasn't until after this underground warehouse was shut down that Zoe and Lada teamed up with Juicy and Amar to create the third, and first legal, iteration of Yes House. Being open then for less than a year, it had already become a smashing success and one of New York City's wildest night clubs.

My eyes were locked on Strom as I heard this story. His words were illuminated by the orange glow of the fire.

CHAPTER   THREE

It's 7:15 and the ready-to-play patrons start pouring through the doors. For the first time in two hours I take a second to stand still and watch. My heart is pounding like a gorilla on the bongos. Opening the doors is generally the most stressful part.

I stand by Harlequin at the register and make sure everything is going smoothly. For The Foreplay and all our early events we only have one door staff on duty rather than the usual four during the 10pm night events. After IDs are checked by Crius outside on the sidewalk, people are ushered inside where they meet Harlequin and a security guard at a desk with a golden shimmery tablecloth. Harlequin is in charge of scanning tickets, receiving payments for tickets, or checking in the patrons as guest-list, then stamping them on their inner wrist for entry. Stamp options include "Daddy," "Glitter Bitch," "Drink Water," and the like. Once stamped, the security guard allows entry into the rabbit hole. The only difference with the team of four door staff during the night events is that tickets and guest list are scanned, checked-in, and stamped by the extra staff outside before they are ID'd in the line.

Despite the initial bottleneck of guests, the flow is steady: the tickets are scanning correctly, guest-list is swiftly checked in, cash is flowing appropriately, etc.

7:18. I walk outside and take a look at the line. Most of the first rush is already inside, and the Consenticorns are consenting the last group. I come a bit closer and secretly listen in. The Consenticorns get a proper training before their shift, so no one really monitors, but since I'm a micromanaging control freak that takes it upon himself to ensure that everyone has the best experience, I spy on them.

The Consenticorns make sure everyone has a kinky outfit, explain our enthusiastic consent policies, and describe some of the key features of the club, such as the water stations and gender neutral restrooms. I'm pleased to hear them doing it a bit differently, improvising, but getting the main points across. *Perfect.*

7:25, I walk back inside. Another rush of people has just arrived and the Front Room is starting to fill up. People are enjoying the delicious bites while playing with all the interactive displays: some are feeding Sandra, the bunny in the tub, raspberries, others are tickling Carlos Surfista's laced booty, and folks in the nook are taking turns getting spanked by the dominatrices. Again, *perfect.*

"Loki!!"

I turn around to see a couple wearing an X-rated butler and maid outfit. It's the first one of the night: *Club friends.* They have been coming for years, always dressed up and always with a positive attitude. They are infatuated with the club and our staff—they can't stop talking about it every week. I have even given them BFF cards, black cards that allow free entry into every party. I truly love these two, and just like with so many of my other deep, club-only friendships, I don't know their names.

"Hey!" I say as I walk over and embrace them, genuinely happy to see them. They squeeze their near-naked bodies against me as if we were best friends that hadn't seen each other for years.

We do the small talk thing, how we are, what's new, etc. Our closeness warms my heart, but I can't remember their goddamn names and this makes me uncomfortable. And now we've known each other for too long for me to ask them. It would break their hearts and make them feel like our relationship is a lie, but just as with other forgotten name friendships, I have to keep it going. The truth is, when you work in nightlife there are only so many names you can remember. I see a thousand faces a night and meet at least fifty new people every day. During my shift I process hundreds of pieces of information which need to be stored for just a short time before being forgotten forever. I've rewired my brain to let information flow in and out, so that I can receive new information right away. It's great for high-stress work, but terrible for names.

7:33. Plates of food are disappearing faster than usual. I walk away mid-sentence with the maid and butler—they are used to it by now—grab all the empty plates and run them into the kitchen. Chef, a seasoned veteran, is guzzling down his second Diplomatico and Coke beside the new plates ready to go out. I grab them and let him know everything is going quicker than at previous The Foreplay events. It takes me several trips of squeezing through the costumed crowd, holding plates above everyone's heads, to restock the Front Room with yummies.

Looking around, everything is going well. The bar is smooth, the door is flowing, and the vibe is sexy. The place is filling up quickly, though. The Front Room comfortably fits 150; 100 if we're trying to keep it spacious and sexy. I check the guestlist and ticket sales, and see that we're expecting 200 attendees instead of the usual 130. Some members from our management team must have added a whopping 70 extra people to the guestlist without me noticing. Fuck.

Deep breath, Loki. All will be okay, I tell myself, not believing it in the slightest. I rush over to Harlequin and blurt out, "stop selling tickets. Ticket holders only."

She nods and gives me a double take. "You okay? You look worse than me."

"I'm fine," I say, sweat dripping down my forehead, "just a bit busy."

Harlequin tilts her head, looking through my words. I must have the poker face of a two-year old. The nature of this job demands that you never freak out, that you just roll with the punches, but when you're teetering on the edge of a full meltdown—composure is a scarcity.

I look at my phone. It's 7:45. I run to check on the Theater. Performers are still tech-ing acts, staff are all over the place, and there are purses and belongings littered on the seats. I can't even begin to explain how: One, annoying this bag bullshit is since we go over it every single fucking day, and two, stressful it is that no one but me seems to care about opening on time. But, as I said, it's time to roll with the punches. I communicate to Zoe, the stage manager, and tech team that the front is filling up quickly and we have an unprecedented 200 expected attendees. We need to open ASAP. They are totally with me, but still have two more acts to tech, which simply can't be rushed.

I yell, for the 500th time in my tenure here, "I'm moving everyone's personal belongings backstage!" I grab makeup kits, purses, bookbags, jackets, whips, a cell phone and one dildo and run backstage.

Backstage is a tiny, well-lit hallway with a long ledge along a wall-sized mirror. It used to be the dining area for our hole-in-the-wall falafel restaurant. A door on one side opened to the theater while a door on the other side opened to the falafel shop. When Falafel House was still open, we'd close that door around 5pm when the performers would arrive. This sharing of the space worked surprisingly well, except for the occasional mishap: a random customer looking forward to their uneventful meal would accidentally open the door to be greeted with the sight of ten naked people putting on fake eyelashes and self-inserting butt plugs. The shawarma sandwich would first be forgotten then dropped altogether, splattering lamb upon their feet. Sandwich or not, they got their money's worth.

Fuck. Backstage is always the most crowded for The Foreplay and Love House. A space that comfortably fits eight performers now has twenty crammed into it. I squeeze through with my armful of their personal belongings, profusely apologizing as I bump everyone, and dump everything into an empty corner. "I moved all the things from the theater to back here!" I announce.

"*That's* where I left that thing!" exclaims my ex girlfriend as she retrieves the dildo and calmly goes back to finishing her makeup. I'm pretty sure that the dildo is for the Shadow Box, a play area for the patrons that my ex is just monitoring, but either way I try not to think about it.

The radio earpiece in my left ear comes to life and I hear the head of security, Crius', slightly accented voice, "Loki, Loki, I need you at the front. Not an emergency."

"Copy," I respond, before making my way to the front. The Front Room is packed, and except for the fruit, all the food is gone. The guests are tip-toeing through a crowded room from plate to plate, frowning disappointment at each stop. My body is put through the electric chair; the unsatisfactory experience of the guests directly reflects upon the service I'm providing.

I make my body into a piece of paper and squeeze through the crowd, hoping that whatever situation Crius is involved in will be resolved quickly.

Outside, Crius is standing next to a smelly, out of shape man who looks to be in his late 30s. Turns out he's dropping off a bartending resume. I'm in luck: this will be quick. His vibe is as toxic as his stench, radiating tension and awkwardness. I grab the resume. "Thanks! We'll be sure to check this out and get back to you."

I run back inside and chuck the resume into the nearest trash bin, then head to the kitchen. *Fucking rookie.* Even if he had been a wonderful candidate with a great vibe, he was dead in the water from the get-go. A word of advice: if you're applying for a job in nightlife, don't come at night! We are fucking busy. Come in the light of day and someone will be much kinder and gracious with their time.

I grab more food from the kitchen and put the plates out in the Front Room. The plates are swarmed upon like paparazzi on a celebrity. It looks like a vampire's feast as bright-red steak juice drips from the mouth of a tight-waisted, ample featured blonde, wearing a revealing black masquerade outfit, down her chin and along her exposed breasts.

It's 8:02. Show time. I run to the Theater and tell the stage manager (SM) we gotta open or the Front Room is going to burst. Generally, it's the SM's job to open the Theater, but he doesn't know how full the Front Room is, so sometimes I let them know to hurry it up. They're finished tech-ing and ready. Production closes the red stage curtains and hangs the 100-pound, hollowed steel, crescent-moon apparatus over the bar as Leche, the Brazilian sound guy who's more relaxed than a sloth after smoking a joint, flips on Love to Love You Baby by Donna Summer. I make eye contact with the lighting designer, the sound guy, and the SM. All thumbs up. At 8:05 I open the Theater doors, the floodgates, and 200 gorgeous, nipple-clamp wearing humans pour inside.

Everyone excitedly takes their seats to wait for the show. I go to the kitchen and collapse onto a couple milk crates. Head back, eyes closed, I take ten deep breaths. My bass drum heart beat slows down as the tightness in my chest begins to loosen up. If I continued breathing like this for a few more minutes I would settle right down, but I'm too anxious about all the things that could be going wrong, so I wipe the sweat off my face and head back to the Front Room. Sometimes it kills to care.

With the guests in the Theater, the Front Room performers started their break. *Perfect.* I gather the empty plates and bring them to the kitchen. Chef, having to wake up at 4am to open the prep for the Falafel shop the next day, has left. For the rest of the night his assistant is in charge of the kitchen. Normally this would be fine, but we have many more attendees than usual, so it might be problematic. I tell him to prepare as many plates of food as possible and to use every last crumb we have. I can already tell we don't have enough food for the intermission, but we will make do. Somehow we always manage.

8:15. The show has begun. I can hear Kate Cummings's voice from the Theater, warming up the crowd. I quickly check the scene in the Patio and the line outside. Everything is calm; a couple is smoking cigarettes and speaking Russian in the Patio and Cirius is out front, alone, smoking a cigar. I head back through the kitchen and stand at the far back corner of the Theater. With everyone seated and the guest-list standing up by the tech booth the room is full but not overcrowded. I spot Zoe sitting with a friend in a booth. I walk over to them and in an over-the-top French accent say, "Bonjour madame. Today on the menu we have Veuve and Veuve Rosé. Perhaps madame desires une glass?" Zoe smiles, and tells me she will have a bottle of the rosé, in a French accent far superior to mine. I step back in the kitchen and yell out, "Jesus! Can we please get a Veuve Rosé at 106?" He nods, and then I step back into the dark Theater.

Ms. Cummings, wearing a white corset and a white thong so small it's nearly nonexistent, has the crowd mesmerized. She is singing her heart out as a naked woman, attached to Kate Cummings by a tangled net of string, twists and flows around her. It is elegant, artistic, and hot. Straight men, bisexuals, and lesbians are lusting for Kate; straight women are reconsidering their life choices, and gay men, well, couldn't give two shits. They do recognize her unearthly beauty and scream, "queen!" and, "yaaaas girl!" Beyond that? What are you gonna do, they like the penis, and that's that.

Much to everyone's delight, Kate Cummings is the host of the show, so we'll get to see a lot of her. As the crowd cheers and whistles at the end of the performance I sneak backstage to climb up the secret ladder to the office.

Hidden behind and above the stage, I see everyone is on point. The assistant stage manager is pulling apparatus lines while the tech team is pulling off their lighting and sound cues with precision. The performers are in look and ready to go as the stage manager is closing the curtain and communicating to the next performers face-to-face and the tech team via headset. The host is working the crowd, occasionally glancing at the SM to see if the next act is ready. Damn, I'm proud of these guys. What used to be an anxiety inducing, wildly uncoordinated circus production is now a slightly stressful and well organized show! I remember the days in the not-so-distant past when the stage managers and Lada would have regular meltdowns backstage. Glad those days are behind us. Mostly...

It's 8:32. About twenty minutes before intermission. In the office I type up my managerial notes in the DMR: "Doors on time 7:15pm, Theater 8:05pm, show 8:15pm. More people than ever before for The Foreplay led to food shortage and an overcrowded front room. We opened Theater doors earlier than planned to accommodate. Kate Cummings rocking the hosting..."

I open the safe and grab a few bills to buy the DJ's coconut water. On second thought, I reach in and take a couple more just in case Amar shit's the bed on the pizzas he promised. I close the safe door, spin the wheel, and peer past the curtain. The crowd is a sea of shocked faces, eyes wide, hands covering mouths. Cross and Die are on stage. Sideshow time.

They look like they walked out of a poster for the Coney Island Circus. They're a couple, and the big bald man with a mustache, covered in tattoos, wearing a red-and-white-striped leotard is staple-gunning his girlfriend, an equally badass babe with dark-witch vibes, in black thigh-highs, garters, and a pin-striped corset to match her beau. He puts half a dozen staples into the flesh of her exposed ass, the gun emitting a dry ka-thwack every time, then muscles her around and spanks her with his phone-book sized hand. When he's done, her ass is redder than a stop sign on Wycliff Avenue. For the finale, he flips her over and places a cinder block on top of her smooth white stomach, then smashes it with a ten-pound sledgehammer. The crowd flinches back as the impact breaks the block and sends fragments of cement onto the stage.

From my office perch above and behind the stage, I just smirk. I've seen the performance at least twenty times, so I'm more or less desensitized to it, but the crowd's reaction is priceless. It reminds me of the good ol' days, when I, too, would sit on the edge of my seat, wide-eyed with shock and a healthy dose of fear after such a display. Now the "abusive" couple is just another of hundreds of great acts on the Yes House stage.

"Loki Loki, I need you at the front." I hear from the radio. 8:49, intermission is in a couple minutes. I climb down the ladder, run through the side of the Theater and cut through the kitchen, shouting orders at the barbacks who are leisurely eating their taco dinners.

"Armando, Jesus, Santiago! Let's get this food out now!" They take a hurriedly last bite of their carnitas and spring into action, helping me get the beautifully plated bites to the Front Room with seconds to spare.

"Performers! Positions! Now!" I scream out. The entertainers throw their drinks onto the bar and get into place. Carlos Surfista's silicone titties bounce out of their laced container as he scurries to return to his handcuffed position while Supermodel #1 sighs, throws back another shot, and jumps back on the bar.

"Relax! Play! Get kinky and have a drink! We'll be back soon after the intermission!" I hear Kate announce from the stage. The crowd is still talking about the last performance as they spill out of the Theater and pour into the Front Room. I run outside to meet Crius. Hopefully this time it's as quick as with the would-be bartender.

It's not. In fact, this one is a lot more tricky. Jose has denied entry to one of our regulars due to an altercation during his last visit. To make matters more complicated, this dude and I have one of those club friendships I described earlier, and he requested to talk to me personally. Let's call him Georgy (since, like with that couple, I don't actually remember his name). Georgy is extremely upset, shaking with anger, barely keeping himself from losing it completely. It doesn't help that it's freezing out here and he's wearing only leather plants and a black tank top. I'm giving Georgy my full attention, but all I can think about is the food running out inside.

Georgy begins to explain what went down last time and how he's the victim here. He tells me that he and his girlfriend were having a great time at our Love House event, dancing, being silly, when he took out his phone and started videotaping her. This other chick sees the phone and freaks the fuck out, Love House being a strict no-phones event and all. She attacks him and wrestles the phone from his hand, but Georgy's not having any of it. A bit of pushing and shoving ensues, Georgy reclaims his phone, and gets the hell out of there. The phone-snatching woman proceeds to inform security on the "creepy old white guy," and they escort him out.

I hear him out calmly, trying not to stare at the horns about to burst through his forehead. These things need to be dealt with diplomatically. The person needs to feel heard and supported, but also I need to know the truth. Generally speaking, these stories tend to be exaggerated. I listen closely and make direct eye contact. Someone's body language can really tell you whether someone is telling the truth or not. Unfortunately, the truth usually presides in between both accounts of the stories anyways.

Shivering, I tell Georgy, "Okay, thanks. Let me speak to Crius a minute." I turn to my head of security. "So what happened the night of?"

Crius has written and video testimonies from the accused and the accuser the night of. The big Nicaraguan man lays it out for me, professionally and unbiased. A woman told a member of the security team that she saw Georgy videotaping somebody dancing, took his phone, and reminded him of the event's no-phone policy. She claimed that Georgy then put her in a choke hold and didn't let her go until she dropped the phone. After hearing her account of the incident, security escorted Georgy out of the club. Jose took video testimonies from both Georgy and the choked lady, then politely informed him that while he didn't have to go home, he could no longer be at Yes House.

As expected, it's not exactly the same story, and who really knows what the whole truth is? Likely something a bit different from either account. It sounds like Georgy was just having some harmless phone fun with his partner, not being a creep or anything, but I can see how it escalated when this other woman got involved. There is the no-phone policy to think about, though; as well as the club's always-believe-the-victim rule (this just keeps things safer, we find).

I thank Crius and turn back to Georgy. He seems more angry than before. The situation sucks. Georgy's here all the time, and all he ever does is dance with his girlfriend. Literally, that's it. It's almost weird. I will walk by them at the beginning of the night, and three 3 hours later they will be in the same exact spot, still dancing, into nothing and nobody but each other.

Regardless, I had to make a decision. The fact is, it doesn't matter if someone is a regular. Hell, I don't care if they have a standing weekly dinner party with the four owners: if they break policy, they're out. "Georgy. Unfortunately, from what I've heard I can't let you back in tonight. I'm not sure what the truth is, but I'd like to set up a meeting with our consent team and an owner to figure it out. We will also refund your ticket for tonight."

Georgy's face turned into a hot air balloon painted redder than roses. He was suddenly livid and his voice rose. "I'm a routine customer! I've spent thousands here! I thought this was the Yes House. This is just the House of Bullies! Just a bunch of bullies here! C'mon, Loki. Are you going to do this to me?"

I can't afford to stick around for the guilt trip, not with a full house and a heap of responsibilities on the other side of that door. "Sorry, Georgy. We will chat soon." I run back inside, head down. It's never fun looking your friend in the eye and having to lay down the law. Even if you don't remember their name. In fact, it fucking sucks.

CHAPTER FOUR

Xavier and I always hung out at his place, being more spacious than my van and all. I would just walk up the two flights of stairs from the kava bar and show up at his door, unannounced. It was a small, studio apartment with Moroccan tassels and colorful fabrics hung along the walls. I would sit in one of the two wooden chairs positioned by the only window of the apartment and listen to the wild stories he repeated from his brother about Yes House. There were tales of eating sushi off beautiful naked models, epic clown battles on stage, and mini orgies in the hottub.

One day we were sitting around the apartment, steaming mugs of coffee in hand, when Xavier's phone rang. It was his mom, calling from Queens. He hit the green button on the iPhone screen and put it on speaker. "Xavier," said his mother in her nasally Jewish-mom-from-New-York voice, "I just wanted you to know that the Mayor came to Yes House and sat with your brother to abolish the Cabaret Law." We cracked up, barely containing our laughter until after she hung up. Not that the news was funny, but her delivery was priceless.

The stories didn't seem to end, it was just never-ending pandemonium and joy over there. Apparently it wasn't for everyone, though. Xavier and I read Dan Rockies' facebook post out loud, describing his mental state during one of the parties. It read, "I was so tired of parties. So tired of costumes, gin and tonics, explaining the liquor laws of NYC, anyone who had ever been to Burning Man, the idea of fire safety, silks, trapezes, swings, basically anything back lit and definitely house music. I was tired of generic parties, drugs, alcohol, guys fumbling and failing to discern the difference between a five and a fifty because the mushrooms they were on were better than they were on mushrooms. I was exhausted from facilitating, from enabling, from encouraging…"

The post was sincere, but I knew there was more to Dan's attitude than Yes House. I remembered the night by the fire, his melancholy, the times people in camp would say hey to him and he wouldn't even look up. Dan could be a grumpy dude. Dan's post definitely had more to do with his own attitude than the work he was doing. I was sure of it. *How could something so blissful be so withering*? I thought to myself.

I heard new stories every week for months. Before I knew it, it was early summer. Two things happened: I graduated from college and learned from Xavier that Juicy had hit a rock bottom and spontaneously decided to get sober. He had been working himself to death, and at 33 had a nearly full head of gray hair to show it. His way of dealing with the stress of running Yes House was to self-medicate with booze.

Xavier, while sad and concerned about his bro, was ultimately relieved. He knew not drinking would really improve his life.

It did for me, anyways. An alcoholic by the age of 12, I got myself in a lot of trouble over the years. Spending my 18th birthday in jail for a DUI wasn't pleasant. Nor was having a closer relationship with a toilet than with my father. But it wasn't until I spent a week in county jail that I really learned my lesson.

"Welcome to West Side!" says a compact but solid white dude as he throws a muscular arm around my neck. A warm greeting from a warm gentleman as I take my first steps inside the concrete cell block. He looks pretty much like an extra in any modern movie or TV show about prison: a tattooed bodybuilder. "We're going to take great care of you! Nothing to worry about as long as you just follow a few tiny rules: don't talk to niggars, don't eat with niggars, don't drink with niggars, and don't sit with niggars."

My reality just became an American History X nightmare. The previous night my friend and I got wasted and involved in a silly petty theft. We thought it was funny at the time. The police did not. They slapped me with a few felony charges and locked me behind metal doors. Now, this was my world.

Growing up I visited my father in prison. He always explained it as a civil place where people were just trying to finish their time without getting into any more trouble. When I was young I believed him. Now I was quickly becoming aware of all the details he left out.

My cellmate was Ray Pork, also known as "Ray-P" or the "Head White" as the others called him. He was a tall, bald, out of shape man with a goatee and four one-inch scars on his cheeks and forehead. Like many of the inmates, he was covered head-to-toe in tattoos and sentenced for six months due to a parole violation. A lot of the guys had been in and out multiple times, seemingly unable to stay out for longer than a couple months before returning.

Ray gave me the rundown on the place as we stood in our concrete, closet sized cell, containing two bunk beds and us. "There's four groups here: The Whites, Hispanics, Brothers and Others. We don't associate with the other races. If you have—wait, you got any jelly beans, addies, anything like that?" I didn't fully understand the question, but assumed he wasn't talking about chewy candy. I shook my head. Ray sighed a bit. "Damn. I'd kill for some uppers right now. I'm making some jail wine under my bed. In here we just call it 'wine'—ha! Where was I? Oh, right, fighting with the niggars. If you have an issue with somebody from another group, you come to me first, you understand? You don't wanna go off half-cocked and start a race war. How it works is, let's say you get into a thing with a black guy—hey, no problem, it happens, what are you gonna do? You come to me, I go to the 'Head Black,' we hash it out and set up a time for you and his guy to fight. With me so far? Everyone will know about the fight and it's, what do you call it, legitimacy. This way nobody will jump in, though there'll be plenty of cheering. After it's over, the guards will send you to a different cell block. Or the infirmary. Got it?"

The only thing I "got" was nauseous and terrified by the idea of having to fight another inmate, black or otherwise, during a sanctioned timeslot, but I just nodded, feeling kind of numb.

I climbed to the top bunk and lay on my inch-thick mattress. The metal bed frame protruded through the mattress and stabbed at my back as I began to fully comprehend this alternate reality I was suddenly a part of. I hated everything around me. I hated the hospital-bright, white fluorescent lights illuminating the white walls. I hated the mattress, thinner than a fancy yoga mat. I hated these Neo-Nazi jail politics that now governed me. I hated my bile-puke-yellow jumpsuit. Hottest burning was the hate I had for myself. I wondered how long I would be in this shit hole for.

The U.S. legal system gives everyone a court date within 72 hours of being arrested, but you don't find out until you're in jail that the law only applies to business days. That means weekends don't count, which means that if you get popped on a Friday night, guess what—no court date until the following Wednesday or Thursday.

I was arrested Friday night.

Hopelessness settled in as I pressed my face against the cold, metal bars of my cell and stared at the uniformed guards pacing the twenty-foot-wide corridor between cells. The brass keys dangling from their utility belts were a physical reminder of my captivity. I looked around for a friendly face, but only found scars and eyes full of hate.

A buzzer sounded.

"Everyday at three we exercise in the yard. It's mandatory, but easy. Let's go," said Ray Pork.

Our yard consisted of a basketball court, a small workout area with free weights and a bench press in the corner, and a large, green, grassy lawn. The grass was surprisingly well kept. Each of the ten cell blocks had an exact replica of our yard, separated by a twenty-foot fence topped with a tight coil of barbed wire.

"Get into position, boys!" screamed an inmate. The Whites quickly arranged themselves into a square on the grass, evenly spaced apart. "Jumping jacks, and let's make 'em loud!"

All of the other inmates were glaring at us. Not only from our yard, but the neighboring yards too. *Why is everyone staring at us? They must see this everyday? I thought to myself.*

"1, 2, 3, WHITE! 1, 2, 3, WHITE!" yelled the whites.

I was in a sixth grade PE class—the Adolf Hitler edition.

Head down, I began to jump and bring my hands over my head as my feet landed wide, but I refused to count off. I looked up to see everyone was still staring at us. The shirtless black men on the basketball court were shaking their heads and looking directly at me. Not that I believed in him much, but I was sure God was also watching, planning my judgment day, and forewarning the Devil of my imminent arrival.

On Monday I spoke to my assigned lawyer over the phone. He gave it to me straight, telling me that one of two things was going to happen. Either the judge was going to reduce my charges to a misdemeanor and let me go, or they would keep the felony charges and sentence me to the maximum sentence of 1.5 years—to be served in the jail I was currently in.

I sank deeper into the wall next to the payphone. With the phone pressed tightly against my ear, I closed my eyes and fell into the silence. Another day of those white supremacy jumping-jacks was a death sentence. Another year and a half of this? I couldn't even fathom it.

My lawyer said my court date was set for Wednesday. I slouched against the wall, whispered my thanks and hung up the phone. There was a line of yellow-jumpsuited inmates behind me, all waiting to use the phone. I walked past them with my head down, went to my cell and went to bed.

The next day I went through the motions like a zombie. Woke up to screaming guards at 6am, ate breakfast, listened to Ray Pork's revolutionary, future plans for the Whites, read whatever novel I could get my hands on, begrudgingly did my Nazi exercises, and slept as much as possible. Unconsciousness was the only solace available to me.

It was Tuesday night. I was alone, laying on my pencil-thin mattress, staring at the ceiling. My cellmate was "dealing with some business" in another cell somewhere.

I reflected on my life. Drinking got me here, just like it got me into most of my trouble over the years.

Because my dad wasn't around, I had chosen a different role model, an older cousin. His name was Brett, he was 17 years-old, and boy did he love to party. He seemed so cool to my

12-year-old self. I wanted to be just like him. Of course now I realized that Brett had substance issues. At 19, I did, too, and here I was.

But no more.

I didn't want to stay in jail. I didn't want Ray Pork to become my best friend. Something had to change. I sat up in bed, my head inches from the cement ceiling, and announced, "God, the Universe, Buddha, beam of benevolent energy—whoever you are—If you get me out of this, I promise I will stop drinking!"

My vow was met with silence. I'm not sure if I expected some cinematic clap of thunder or beam of light, but I lay back down and placed my hands over my chest, feeling the rise and fall of my breaths, and fell into the deepest slumber I had since being arrested four days before.

The next day my yellow jumpsuit made me cringe. It was a loathsome experience wearing it in front of a judge, a group of random citizens, and my mother. The judge, a white man with a scrunched, wrinkly face that frowned on top of a black silk gown, barely looked up from the papers on his podium to look at me. I was just another face, another yellow jumpsuit.

The judge spoke. From all the legal jargon I began to understand what he was saying. I couldn't believe it: I was going to walk. I got the misdemeanor, and not only that, but he let me sign up for a program to expunge it off my record. Halle-fucking-lujah!

My mouth was open and air was in my lungs, but no words came out. I just smiled, placed my hand over my heart, and gave a short bow before walking out of the courtroom.

From that day forward, I kept up my end of the bargain. Four years later, sitting in Xavier's apartment, I hadn't had a drop of booze. I had to experience something terrible before I made that decision. My rock bottom was the jail, the yard, The Whites. It's what kept me off the bottle. I hoped Juicys rock bottom would do the same for him.

Fast forward to a week before the Burn and all this was far from our thoughts, though, as we stepped out of his building onto the sunny sidewalk of Berkeley. We hopped in the back of Rico's silver Nissan Altima and cruised down University Avenue, headed to the pier for a sailing adventure gifted to us by a kava client.

Suddenly, Rico dropped the bomb: "Loki, I'm selling my half of the business."

The news landed like a punch to the gut. My clear, seemingly utopian life just got flipped upside down. Now I had to find the next thing and had not a hint of where to start.

The next few days before the Burn brought no clarity. Rico was packing up his apartment and preparing to embark on a journey. At the time of Rico's announcement there were five employees at BulaBula, only two of which had worked there as long as I had. Dante, a tall and black version of Mr. Clean, quit immediately. Clam, a petite Filipina, also quit. She then broke up with her lesbian fiance, decided she wasn't a lesbian after all, and started dating our now former boss Rico. She was also in Rico's apartment, preparing to embark on an adventure with him.

All this meant that if anyone was going to be managing BulaBula, it would be me. Before hearing Rico's news, I would have killed to manage the kava bar. Now, with the family separated, I was unsure of what I wanted. Step up and become the leader of the BulaBula community, or move on and start fresh at something new? It was a question I couldn't get off my mind, one that needed an answer, and soon.

I took this question with me to the place where time was relative, and I frequently didn't know what the day of the week was. Where Mad Max met Planet of the Apes then lit up like Tron, complete with a Daft Punk soundtrack. I was wearing a rainbow bandana over my nose, blue gas-station sunglasses over my eyes, and a skin-tight, zebra leotard. A pirate ship aglow with LED lights rolled in front of the setting sun as dust whipped across my body.

I was back at the Burn.

At camp there were old faces and new. Amar was back; Juicy was not. He stayed behind in New York so his partners, Zoe and Lada, could have a turn at the debaucherous mayhem.

"I'm Zoe," said the woman with curly, orange hair. It matched the color of the spitting campfire flames we were sitting next to. I introduced myself. We began sharing stories from our previous Burns. She, like all the owners of Yes House, had been to

Burning Man many times, and it changed the way they partied, created art, and saw the world: without limits.

Zoe told me she not only loved the outlandish art here, but the brains behind it. It wasn't just the oak tree constructed from an elaborate galaxy of LED bulbs that got her off—it was also the madness behind the piece. The art was great, but the artist was everything to her.

We were surrounded by art cars, which were reconstructed school buses usually designed in some sort of themed decor and with a stage built on the roof. To our left was one: a twenty-foot tall octopus made of scrap steel. Its tentacles started from its midsection, went down towards the ground then up as high as its head. Each tentacle shot flames into the sky. Lada bicycled closely around it with an enormous smile stretched across her face. She bounced back and forth between the different art cars like a pinball. There was never a dull or peaceful moment with her—only pure excitement. Follow her around, and you'd find yourself in the craziest situations, surrounded by the most interesting individuals, at the wildest parties.

Despite the endless excitement all around me—from the massive dance parties in the desert to the debauchery at camp—for me, letting loose wasn't a possibility. I felt disconnected from the whole. There were 70,000 people playing around me, yet I felt alone. I could have been receiving a dusty blowjob on top of a unicorn golf cart during Tycho's sunrise set, yet I felt uninspired. Sometimes it didn't matter how amazing a party was. You just couldn't escape. There's someone you need to speak to. There's something you need to take care of. You have something on your mind.

I watched the Yes House family dance around me at camp while I felt lost and reflected on my situation at home. The BulaBula community had an amazing vibe and was my only consistent family, but maybe it was time to move on to another community? *Maybe I could join the Yes House family?*

Unlikely, I thought.

The next day the sun was relentless in a cloudless sky. I was covering under the shade of camp, hoping to survive the heat. Then a ubiquitous sound came from every direction.

Tink! Tink! Tink! Tink! People were hastily hammering stakes into the ground. Tent structures sailed across the sky as costumed humans chased after them. I couldn't see five feet in front of me.

A storm had rolled in. It was a white-out: a thick and dangerous dust storm. Winds, full of debris, whipped through the air at 60 miles per hour, dragging with it anything not tied down to the ground.

Generally, there are two things you can do during a storm like this: take cover inside a tent or another sturdy structure, or ride your bike into the fierce winds like a mad-man. Today I chose the latter.

I slowly rode out into the unknown, only able to see the ground immediately in front of my front tire. In the far distance I heard music coming from various sound systems as people danced and partied, almost in defiance of this wild desert phenomenon. I steered away from the music and pedaled into the storm.

After ten minutes of riding, over the sound of my creaking bicycle, I heard voices like ghosts in the wind, never seeing their owners. I kept going into the desert until I could no longer hear or see any sign of human activity, only the angry storm.

When I stopped I was completely alone. I kicked down the squeaky kickstand, parked my bike and walked a few steps away. I stood still and felt the storm rage on, the wind and dust flying around as if a helicopter was hovering above me. The storm reflected perfectly the turbulence in my mind.

It had been four years since I addressed the Divine beings from that jail cell bunk. It was time to call them again. I dropped to my knees, threw my hands into the whirling air, and screamed into the desert storm, "God! Atheist Lord! Whatever you are! Please give me a sign! Should I stay in Berkeley and run BulaBula, or take a chance and move on to something new?"

My words seemed to soar away into the storm faster than I screamed them. I sat there, alone, feeling the weight of humility just as I had four years ago, to the very day.

About a minute had passed when I heard the creaking of a bicycle. Thinking it was mine I spun around, but there it sat, where I left it.

The creaking got louder. A silhouette appeared out of the near-white of the sandstorm, taking form as a man, a nomad from a post-apocalyptic future, riding a vintage bicycle towards me. This far away from "civilization," I must had been the first person he had seen in some time.

He saw me on my knees and stopped. After getting off the bike he took off his goggles and face mask, revealing a middle-aged face and a kind smile. I looked up at him expectantly. He squatted down on his heels in front of me and said, "Hey man, life is tough. Sometimes you just gotta go for it. Really, you just have to take a chance and go for it man!"

A moment passed and he nodded, then got back on his bicycle. Then just like the very words I loudly pleaded into the storm, he disappeared into the desert.

"Wow". I chuckled. "Well that's a fucking sign if I ever saw one."

As I rode back I wondered if he was real or if I made the whole thing up. The storm started to let up, which made navigating easier, and by the time I was back at camp it had ceased.

The first person I saw was Jayce, the other Israeli in the truck with Amar and me a year ago. I hopped off my bicycle, letting it fall on the ground, and ran up to him. "Jayce, hey man, I got a question for ya. Do you think there's room for me at Yes House?"

"Are you kidding me?" he said, "of course there's room for you. You're family! All you gotta do is show up." Responded Jayce with arms wide.

And just like that, I had decided: I was moving to New York City to work at Yes House. Feeling like a kid again, I spent the next five minutes jumping up and down through camp like a bunny in a field, spending more time in the air than on the ancient lakebed beneath my feet.

I ran over and to Xavier to tell him about my mystical desert encounter and the resulting revelation, and the conversation with Jayce.

"Loki. You know Jayce can't hire you, right?" replied Xavier.

Fuck. My excitement dropped. I knew that Jayce couldn't give me a job—he didn't even really work there himself—but was too wrapped up in celebrating my new life to consider this minor detail. "You're right," I told Xavier, "give me one minute."

With my heart beating out of control, I ran over to Amar.

Amar, that crazy motherfucker, was sitting by himself in a camping chair in the blazing afternoon sun, wearing a black long-sleeve shirt, black sunglasses, and black jeans. He was alternating between taking long drags off a cigarette and cracking his neck side to side.

I ran over to him. "Amar! Amar! Is there room for me? At Yes House?" I spat out.

He took two drags off his cigarette before slowly tilting his head to look at me. "Well... Sort of... During Halloween, yes, but otherwise, I'm not so sure. It's hard to say. Maybe."

Well, not the most confidence boosting response, but fuck it: There was a chance, and a chance was all I needed.

When I got back to Berkeley I gave BulaBula my two weeks notice. Fourteen days later I drove to New York City.

CHAPTER FIVE

The accumulation of body heat hits me like a pillow to the face as I step inside the Front Room. I step around the register and look down at Harlequin's iPad on the way in. It's 9:05 p.m. and we did ten door sales. That's ten more than we're meant to have inside, but the owners will be happy for the extra 800 smackers in their pockets. At intermission, walking through the Front Room is like trying to navigate Times Square on New Year's Eve. I can't move two inches in any direction without inadvertently breaking up a makeout session. Despite our keeping the Theater doors open at intermission to prevent overcrowding, nearly everyone has packed into the Front Room for snacks and spankings. There are two people still in the Theater, canoodling on a heart-shaped pillow. The man is big enough to play on the defensive line for the 49ers, has shoulder-length cornrow braids, and is wearing leather underpants that don't leave much room to the imagination. His playmate is one of our Consenticorns, a tiny woman in a hot-pink bob wig. She's still wearing her lit up horn which, I might add, is roughly half as long as the clearly discernible erection in big man's undergarments.

By the time I come back to the Front Room, the plates, which minutes before were piled high with yummies, look like they have been licked clean. I weave and squeeze through the mingling mass collecting them, then head to the kitchen.

"That's everything," says Chef's assistant as he sharpens his favorite knife, indicating the last few decorated plates of steak and fruit set on the counter.

"Copy that," I sigh. I grab them, balancing two on my forearms, and distribute them in the Front Room before making myself a drink behind the bar. Seltzer with lemon on the rocks. My go-to drink, one of twenty I will have during a shift.

I hear Kate Cummings' voice from the Theater. "You know what really turns me on?" She's back on the mic and the second half of the show has begun. The Front Room begins to empty as everyone slowly makes their way back to their seats, flirting and laughing every step of the way. *Thank God.* I need some chill time.

I head to the Front Room bar. Oliver, Carlos Surfista and I shoot the shit for ten minutes, chatting about people we've been hooking up with, horrible customers, and retirement dreams. Oliver's share consists of retiring and starting a miniature golf business in Vermont.

I check the time. It's 9:20. Final entry allowed for the early event is at 9:30, which means I need to close the front doors in ten minutes, but in the meantime I pop back into the Theater to check out some of the show.

Sparrow is performing. They are a duo of female aerialists, possibly the best in the city. Built like Olympic gymnasts, these gorgeous creatures glide through the air with a power and grace that would raise the eyebrows of a Cirque du Soleil scout. World-class talent, right here in a warehouse in Bushwick. The crowd oohs and awes, without fully grasping how much talent, strength, and practice a performance of this caliber requires.

9:30. The show is supposed to end now, but is running late. Production staff standby, awaiting The Flip. This is when the manager and production staff begin to transform the event and space from show to party. The next hour will be the most stressful of the night. Once the show ends the staff will herd all the guests into the Front Room, close the Theater doors, and turn on the work lights in the Theater. Once the lights are on, the staff and production team immediately commence running in different directions and yelling across the space to communicate with each other like it's a meltdown in a nuclear power plant. Giant metal apparatuses fly in the air, fabrics are strung up from the ground to the ceiling, all fans and AC units are turned on to cool the place down, and the sound of power tools roar through the Theater as the party continues in the Front Room. Many new staff members—door, tech, bar, bottle service, coat check, security, and performers—arrive for their shifts. Mayhem would be an understatement. We somehow finish a three hour job in thirty to sixty minutes. Adrenaline pumps through our veins like lightning in clouds. For our souls, it's detrimental, yet it's my favorite time of the night. As much as I hate the stress, in a way I'm addicted to the rush of it all. *There's no stress like YES.*

The show is running late, but I get a move on. I do my NYC walk through the kitchen and straight to the door register. Harlequin has the cash wrapped up and ready for me. I grab the brick-sized packet and run into the kitchen to count it. *Five, six, seven, eight,* I say in my head as twenty dollar bills waterfall from my hand. The money is good. I stuff it in my back left pocket. "Armando, Jesus, Santiago!" I yell, "let's clear the Front Room!" The barbacks come stampeding down from the upstairs kitchen. We grab all the plates and break down the tables with lightning speed. Within five minutes the room is clear and ready for a party.

9:38. I walk outside to meet with the door, security, and consent teams. It's vital to clearly discuss the flow of the night before doors reopen at 10 for Love House.

"Crius, close the doors."

"Copy that," Crius replies.

I turn to Nina, the Consenticorn manager. "Is the new team here, prepped and ready to go? They all know that costumes are mandatory, and if someone's not looking absolutely fabulous they're not getting in?"

"One person is late, but besides that we're ready," she says.

"Copy," I reply. Consenticorns are basically volunteers, so I can't really unleash my wrath upon them for being late. I bite my tongue and move on.

Tacks is our dinosaur of a door manager. The father of an O.G. YES regular, he's 60, mostly bald (but insists on bleaching the few strands of hair he has left), and can barely operate a telephone.

Why, you might ask, do we have a senior citizen running the door of New York City's wildest nightclub? I often ask the same question, too, despite knowing the answer. It's because Juicy is fed up with the high-risk/high-reward nature of a drag queen doing it.

For years our last gatekeeper and everyone's first real taste of Yes House was Mrs. Miss, and whether it was your first or 100th time entering the club, your jaw dropped. Just picture being greeted by a six-and-a-half-foot-tall drag queen in a homemade ensemble of head-to-toe flowing fabrics, jewelry, and platform shoes. Top it off with a wig the size of your torso framing an immaculately made-up face (Mrs. Miss' mirror time before work? Three hours) and you have someone who'd give the contestants on Ru Paul's Drag Race a run for their money. Thing is, though, the customer's experience was completely dependable on Mrs. Miss' mood.

The door is a tough job. In the sweltering heat of summer or in the snow blown nights of winter, you're out there. And if that weren't enough, you're guaranteed ten unpleasant issues a night. Tickets are sold out and someone wants in? It's your job to say no. Someone bought a ticket for the wrong night, *and* they don't speak English? You deal with it. One girl in a 20-person bachelorette party forgot her ID? Good fucking luck getting out of that one alive. A gaggle of Frenchies is morally opposed to paying the cover? Or how about a clearly too-intoxicated friend of the owner wants in? "But it's my birthday!" (this you'll hear twenty times a night.) *Jesus Fucking Christ*. As the door, you're it. You're the last thing between the outside world and the best night of someone's life, and people are not shy about taking their shit out on you.

You might be able to do this for a night. Shit, you might be able to do it with kindness and grace for a few nights in a row. But how about a month? A year? Probably not as long as you think, anyway. So there's the burnout factor. Plus, which everyone in the industry knows, drag queens have superpowers, and you do not want to experience their wrath—especially after you've accused one of losing your nonexistent ticket. Once properly provoked, a drag queen will break you down into an unsalvageable puddle of barely recognizable human scraps before you can say, "fake eyelashes." They are wittier, quicker, and more dramatic than you. You will not walk away from the altercation a victor. This is all fine and good, but even if the customer is a belligerent imbecile, we are in the experience industry and Juicy want's a professional pacifier, not a sharp-tongued fighter.

Personally, I think Juicy is nuts (the drag queen lashouts were my favorite part of the night), but I pretend I agree and move on.

I throw words at Tacks with the speed of a seasoned auctioneer. "Tacks, there is a very large group still in there from the early event, so no sales until we reopen the Theater. In fact, slow the line down for the first 30 minutes to prevent overcrowding. Tonight is our sexy party—no sales all night unless their outfits are absolutely amazing from head to toe. There are a few tables and a large guestlist, it's all on the app. You good?"

"Sounds good," he replies in his raspy voice. "I'm gathering the stamps and electronics now. We'll be ready to go by ten." He's calm, and his smile crinkles his big nose and deepens the wrinkles in his face. He radiates a happy grandpa's warmth.

All set at the door. It's 9:45, though, and time is ticking. On my speedy way to the kitchen I stop at the serving station, a grand title for a four-by-four nook that barely fits a POS computer, a small fridge of Veuve and Dom Perignon, and a locked wooden case of top shelf booze bottles. The host and two servers are already here, waiting for our table service meeting. I stay in the hallway outside the server station to avoid spooning my employees.

Lacera, the sword-swallowing viking with torpedos for breasts and black streaks racing down her blonde hair, is the host. Her role is to meet the table reservations at the door, sell tables to the people waiting in line, collect the table's ID and credit card, and seat them. When she's not seating or selling tables she's supposed to be at the door helping Tacks check-in ticketed guests. She's good at her job—sweet talks the high rollers and always looks fabulous—but isn't a great communicator and is afraid of confrontation. That's why it's imperative that she is super clear on the details for the night. Later on she won't ask questions and is sure to mess up if any uncertainty arises. If she's not, she won't ask questions to clarify and will mess up later.

Our bottle boy, Romeo, is also at the meeting. He used to be Beyoncé's private waiter at a restaurant in the West Village. A talented server who's infatuation with theater has provided him with an exceptional talent for improv. He was once waiting on a table of Casamigos execs visiting the club. Management forgot to tell him that and he just thought they were some random well-dressed dudes. Looking at the menu, one of them asked if we served the Don Julio 1942 listed in the top-shelf section. We were, which put us directly in breach of our verbal contract with Casamigos to serve exclusively their tequila for bottle service. Romeo knew none of this, but immediately picked up on something being off about the man's curiosity. He snatched the menu from his hands, gave it a cursory glance, laughed by way of apology, and tore it up on the spot. "Whoops, where did this come from?—we haven't used this menu in years!"

The second server tonight is Krystal. She's literally a supermodel, a blonde who gets more bottle orders from guys (and a few girls) than anyone else. She doesn't fit the stereotypical model-blonde type, though. Krystal will throw on the red nose, act as an eccentric buffoon for all to see, then immediately change character to discuss the most modern psychological theories on human behavior with you. She plays the clown, the royal princess, and the sophisticated educator.

I'm all brisk business right out of the gate. "Alright I don't have much time so let's make this quick. Table 110 (the nook in the Front Room) will not be used tonight. We have three reservations. Dimitri is a 15-top birthday so let's put them at 101 and 102. Adam is a baller regular who wants Don Julio 1942 right off the bat. Let's give him 103 and 104 with extra attention. Lastly, Stephanie is a prepaid bachelorette—your favorite! She's an 8-top who wants to be near the action, so let's give them 106. Give the tables extra care and birthday love tonight, please. There's fruit and pizzas upstairs. Are we good?"

Fuck. Pizzas. I forgot to check.

"Yayyyy!" Romeo screams, throwing his arms in the air.

"Lacera, you good?" She looks me in the eye and nods. She seems confident, so I end it there.

I run to the upstairs kitchen and check the freezer. *God dammit.* No pizzas, of course. I swear, Amar keeps only half of his promises. To be fair, though, he only remembers half of them. Some days he's amazing: I'll give him a list of ten things to fix around the club, including repairing the AC unit and reflooring the Onyx Room, and everything will be done and perfect before we open the next day. Other days I'll ask him to tighten a couple screws under the bar, and it won't get done for two weeks. Today he forgot the pizzas.

"Jesus!" I yell. As soon as he appears, out of breath, I throw a wad of money at him. Pizzas, and coconut water for the DJ—corre!" Jesus barely has time to wipe the sweat off his forehead before grabbing the cash and taking off. I send up a silent prayer to God and barbacks everywhere. I truly love them. In times of high stress, they are pound for pound my most valuable employees.

9:51. I race to the office. The Theater is still full because the show is running late, as usual. It's the final act and the audience is on the edge of their seats, squeezing their pillows for dear life.

On stage it's as if the final scene of a Disney film took a terrible twist. Standing proud under the blue lights is a tall man with a buzzed head and heavy eye-shadow. He's wearing a blue, ankle-length poncho with fifty-plus teddy bears sewn into the cloth. With every step the bears dance and jump about.

Also on the stage is a low, round platform, rotating slowly. It's covered with a black cloth and there are several pillows covered with baseball bat print pillowcases. Amongst the pillows on all fours is a short, skinny man in a sheer blue negligee. As poncho guy lip-syncs to a rising opera aria, he gazes up at him with star-struck eyes.

The tall man stops behind the platform, "holds" a 20-second note, and plunges his arm elbow-deep into a red bucket labeled "Vaseline." He whips his arm from the bucket and the lubricant—likely off-brand KY, based on its viscosity—splashes on the people in the front row who are throwing up their hands and ducking to avoid the jelly rain.

The opera crescendos with short, fast notes as he lifts his cupped hand high for all to see. With a horrific smile of triumph and intention, he plunges his fingers, hand, wrist, and forearm into the small man's anus, whose head jerks back as his eyes roll to the back of his skull. The teddy bears continue their dance as the pitcher's hand slides in and out of the prostrate man, smooth as a spoon stirring melted butter.

When the opera piece finishes, the teddy bear creature removes himself from his accomplice. He turns toward the audience and pushes his hair off of his face, leaving streaks of lube on one side of his head. The speakers come back to life with Lady Gaga's "Bad Romance", and the tall man springs back into action, alternating between dipping his arm into the bucket and the smaller performer. This time they're both lip-syncing and snapping their heads up and down at the audience, both the head movements and the sodomist's thrusts in perfect time with the beat. The audience is stunned into silence, but the duo on the stage is just getting warmed up. The teddy bear creature begins walking around the other, slowly rotating him like a puppet to provide a 360-degree view of the gruesome scene.

The audience is now exchanging half-concerned glances, making sure this isn't some sort of sick dream. The teddy bears shift with one last thrust, the song ends, and the fister pulls his arm from the small man. The performance is over. The audience is frozen in place, mouths ajar. Some of them have wrapped their arms around themselves. A few seconds of silent stillness go before one person starts to clap. Then a second and a third join in. Someone stands. Then, all of a sudden, the audience erupts in an uproarious standing ovation. The two men on stage take a gracious bow. The curtains close on them as the crowd continues to go wild, the clapping, whistles, and screams overwhelming in the relatively small space.

Cummings jumps on the mic. "Now that's what I call a show! Wow. Thank you all for coming out! Now who's feeling a dance? Let's move to the front so we can flip this room into a dance club!" The crowd, faces still wearing stunned expressions, slowly makes its way to the Front Room.

It's 9:54, 24 minutes later from when the show was supposed to end. Time for the next part of the circus to begin.

I jump onto the stage, stepping carefully to avoid the puddles of "Vaseline", and head up to the office. After the crowd has finished migrating to the Front Room, Production closes the Theater doors and brings up the house lights. "Watch out! Dropping cage!" "Coming through, watch your back!" "Barney, get those projections set up ASAP!" shouts pingpong across the space.

In the office I drop all the cash from the door into a safe. My eyes happen on the new performer paperwork I never took care of lying in a neat pile in the center of my desk. "Fuck," I say under my breath and snatch the packet, sprinting back down. "Koochy! Great show. Here's a packet for the new performer, please get it to her now!" I toss the packet to Koochy as I run by. It's a great pass from five feet away, but he didn't know it was coming. The papers bounce off his blank face and drop to the floor. I would apologize, but I'm already squeezing through the Theater doors, not knowing if he even processed what I said.

We had cleared the tables and removed the bathtub, so even though the Front Room is full it doesn't feel packed. I mentally go through what needs to happen in the next few minutes. The front doors reopen at ten on the dot. Two new bartenders will replace the two that have been slinging drinks up to this point.

It's 9:58. I take a quick peek in the kitchen and see Jesus has come through with the pizzas. God bless him. I run into the Front Room and move quickly through the crowd, side stepping, shouldering, creating space in the mass of bodies. By the time I get to the front door and poke my head out, I'm panting. "Nina! Have the consenticorns take their time with their spiel, slow things down for the first 30 minutes."

I find my door man tinkering with gadgets at the other end of the vestibule. "Tacks! Are we ready to go?"

"We're ready," he says, cool as a cucumber.

"Let's open!" I scream, making sure security can hear me, as well.

Back in through the gold doors, I tell Harlequin we're open, and move towards the bar. The bartenders are standing by the bar, ready to go. *Thank God they're not doing bumps in the costume closet right now.* I grab the new register banks from a lock box at the end of the bar, grab the cash from the registers and the tip buckets faster than a junkie robbing a liquor store, and shove the new banks into the registers. "Take your break," I tell Daisy and Oliver, and they split.

People start pouring through the gold doors with stars in their eyes. Excitement and adventure fills the room.

Zester, Zoe's ex-boyfriend, has begun to set up his photo booth for the night. Zester is six-foot, four-inches with short brown hair and is more quirky than a clown on a unicycle. He's on time, for a change, and in different circumstances I'd be pleased. "Zester! Sorry, but I'm worried about capacity in here until the Theater opens up. Can you hold for about thirty minutes?"

"Uh, sure! Whatever works!" replies Zester. Bless his positive attitude, an invaluable trait in the night life world. I throw him some drink tickets and run off to the Theater, making myself pancake-thin to slide through the cracked theater doors.

It's 10:06. Production has gutted the Theater of all carpets and pillows, the floor is clean and lube-free thanks to the mop-wielding barbacks and the dishwasher, Leche, and the tech team is building the DJ booth. Meanwhile, the servers are in the booths setting up candles and wiping the tables down with Windex—the only cleaning solvent Amar buys (he swears it works for everything, despite it having no antibacterial agents); the decor girl is putting up sheer, red fabrics on the ledge behind the stage; Nasty is programming his party light settings for the night, and Barney is projecting psychedelic red and black shadows on the curtains hugging the wall above the ledge.

From an outsider's perspective, this scene looks like a mad-house of Looney Tunes characters—nonsensical yelling and items soaring through the room. It reminds me of when I first witnessed a busy motorbike intersection in Saigon: hundreds of bikes racing from every direction into an unlit nighttime intersection. To me, it looked like calamity and death just waiting to happen, but for the locals it was just a way of life. That's what our "flip" is: a precisely performed orchestra of mayhem.

I weave through the pandemonium and poke my head backstage to check on the performer's hospitality set-up. There should be a jug of ice water, two bottles of rosé, two bottles of champagne, and one bottle of house tequila on the end of the ledge beside the room length lit-up mirror.

Backstage I'm suddenly an innocent bystander caught in a bitter conflict between a couple of divas. Dreams is finishing her makeup, eyes wide, appraising her reflection in the mirror. "Clea, I forgot my lashes, can I borrow a pair of yours?"

Next to her, Clea puts down her makeup brushes and looks pointedly at Mrs. Miss. "No, you *can't*! Because *someone* never *returns them* at the end of the *night*!" she says, her hands adding an accusatory accent to every other word.

Utterly unperturbed by Clea, Mrs. Miss keeps looking at herself in the mirror, puckering her lips and making bedroom eyes. She takes her sweet time responding. "That's simply not true. I left them on top of your bag last night like you asked me to. It's not my fault they disappeared." This fails to mollify Clea, who goes off on a tirade of accusations.

Having zero interest in sticking around for this, I tip-toe backwards into the Theater as the arguing gets louder.

Shit. I never checked on the water and booze.

Not worth it, I think.

I rush across the stage, where tool-belted production folks are brandishing screw guns like Wild West Colt .45's, and up to the office. *Drop the bar tips into the safe and jump onto the computer,* I order myself, to keep on track, and follow my mental directions. I lock the tips away and finalize the first event's DMR and tip sheet by 10:14. I quickly look over my work and email the report.

I kick the metal cabinet to my right to propel myself into a swivel in my computer chair. On the other side of the office is a production employee setting up the Shadowbox, our most famous Love House spectacle, where fantasies come to life and orgasms are on-tap.

The shadowbox is a cloth-draped go-go dancer's cage with an easily-cleanable cushion on the bottom. When a powerful red light hits it from the inside, it transforms into a glowing red cube, and when someone is inside of such cube, everyone in the Theater sees their silhouette in razor sharp, vivid detail. After finishing with the Box, the production dude transforms half of the office into a cozy little sex den: he covers the desks, computers, safes, and money counter with black fabric, strategically places a few LED candles around the space, and lays out an array of whips, strap-ons, lubricants, and condoms. Presto change-o!

Initially, we didn't think anyone would go for it, essentially putting themselves in the spotlight for everyone to see, but oh how wrong we were. Giving people an opportunity to fuck, get spanked, and generally experiment on their own little stage, essentially, in total anonymity… has proven to be one of the best and most popular gifts we could've given them. With every party we throw we realize more and more that everybody has a bit of the exhibitionist in them, and we're happy to curate a space where they can express it in a fun, safe, and sexy way.

My previous two romantic relationships began in that box. Neither lasted longer than a year, unfortunately. I used to wonder why, until I asked myself out loud, "why does it never work out with someone I meet at a sex party?" Hearing it put that way, the answer suddenly became clear.

Back in the present, I'm standing beside the illuminated red cube and looking down at the stage. The DJ booth, a high long table protected on three sides by black plywood, is done, and Leche is setting up the DJ decks and routing the numerous cables to their connections. *Perfect.*

A text coming in vibrates my leg through the fabric of the pocket lining. The opening DJ, Arc, has arrived and is out back. "I'll be right there," I respond. I run through the emergency exit door in the small corridor between the Theater and into the green room. DJ Arc and I embrace in a tight bear hug and I feel the laptop in his hand against my back as we squeeze each other. He's six-feet tall with long, wavy black hair. It's good to see the guy. He's a super homie and a good friend that I haven't seen in a couple months.

We do a quick catch up as I bring him in through the back door. I tell him I'm doing all right, same old, same old, working myself to death. He's been busy as hell. New Yorkers… He's still dating Lesh, he tells me.

Ah, Lesh. A bonafide super babe: slender, blonde, Israeli. A nymphomaniac with brains and sex appeal in equal measure. It doesn't hurt that she wears the most revealing lingerie every time she's at the club. About a year ago she and another burning-jet-fuel-hot girl did a line of coke off my dick in the bathroom—a super fantasy moment. A month after that I couldn't bear the weight of guilt I was carrying and ended up telling Arc.

He didn't take it very well, but was ultimately relieved I told him the truth. Lesh, on the other hand, wanted to tear my fucking guts out. For months she gave me the cold shoulder at the club. She wouldn't even look at me. When we did accidentally make eye contact during that time, the flames in her eyes nearly singed my eyebrows. It was downright unsettling to be around her, but I forged a truce a few weeks ago when I hooked her up with a table and some free bottles for her birthday.

I pretend I'm not thinking back to that whole mess as Arc and I walk to the DJ booth. He looks like Assassin's Creed went to Berlin—black jeans, a black hooded shawl-jacket, and a silver chain around his neck that matches his nose ring

As per Arc's rider there are two bottles of rosé, a bottle of decent mezcal, and several waters in an ice bucket next to the turntables.

I ask him if he needs anything else.

He smiles and tells me he's all set.

I turn to the sound engineer. "Leche, are we ready to go?"

"We ready," he replies, his words barely making it past the handful of cheetos he stuffed in his mouth a moment ago.

"Arc, I'm going to open the Theater in ten minutes, can you start before then?"

"I. Am. Ready. Let's do this," responds the long haired man. He plugs in his flash drive and starts looking for the perfect entrance song as I check in with the rest of the team.

It's essential to have a thumbs up from Decor, Lighting, Visuals, Sound, Production and the Stage Manager prior to opening. Arc just started spinning, so Leche strolls to the Front Room to sync all the speakers to Arc's set. *Boom.* Backstage Koochy tells me there's no opening performance we need to wait for. *Boom Boom.* I pop back in the Theater and check in with the decor queen on the ledge above the stage, screaming over the music. She needs five minutes. *Boom, boom, boom.* From the stage I yell up at the tech booth, "you guys ready up there?" The tech team huddles for a few seconds before the lighting operator holds up an open hand: five minutes. *Boom x a million.*

It's 10:26. As I wait, feeling Arc's thundering bass in my chest, I check my phone. It's been going off like fireworks on the

Fourth of July. The Front Room is overcrowded and the Door is asking when will we open the Theater. "Soon," I text back. Amar is asking me to add his friends to the guestlist, him being technologically incapable of doing it himself. "Copy, it's good now," I respond. I have four different "friends" asking me to put them and their crew on the list. Two of them I throw on the list with a "+3," the other two I ignore. I barely know them; they only ever reach out to ask me to put them on the list. Next, Juicy lost his jacket—could I look around the club? "I'll get back to you later but ASAP," I reply. Last, I scroll through the security chat. Fifty new messages in the last hour. Fortunately, everything is all good. Just a bunch of arrival time confirmations.

     When I am working, I spend half the time running around the club, phone in hand, texting. To those who don't know I work here, I must look like that lame-o at the party, on the phone the whole time.

     "Loki, we're good to open!" screams Koochy over the loud music in the Theater. 10:29. *Perfect*, with a minute to spare.

     I look up at the tech booth to see Leche and the rest of the tech team with their thumbs up, like a cheesy vacation photo. I glance back at the decor queen and get the same response.

     "We're opening!" I yell out and run over to the Theater doors. "Opening the Theater doors," I say over the radio.

     "Copy, copy," Cirius replies.

     I take a deep breath and hold it, my sweaty palms flexing on the big wooden handles to the Theater door. I breathe out and open the floodgates.

     Let the party begin.

CHAPTER SIX

Everyday leading to my departure I was riding a high. It felt like undiluted adrenaline was pumping through my veins. The mere thought of taking on a new life in New York City was thrilling.

When I was working my final shifts at the kava bar, I obsessed over the journey, agonizing about every detail. When I wasn't working, I was preparing for it. I spent nearly all my money repairing my van so it could make the trip east without incident, the memory of an 8am breakdown on the Bay Bridge during commute still fresh in my mind.

Packing was simple. I lived in my van. I just had to pick up the last of my belongings from my mom's condo: my warmest coat, a lightweight windbreaker, a pair of brown hiking boots, and my birth certificate.

I said goodbye to my mother, friends, and the Bula community with a big heart. I was ready. Everyone said they could see it in my eyes. On the morning of September 23rd, 2017, I filled my tank at the Chevron on University Avenue, and drove away from the glistening San Francisco Bay without looking back. With my window down, long hair blowing in the wind, and Leon Bridges's "River" blasting from the speaker—the journey had begun.

It was my first cross country road trip. I definitely didn't want to rush through the experience, so I took a fairly indirect route to see friends along the way. First, I headed south to L.A., then cut over to Flagstaff, Arizona.

Arizona was beautiful—the sun glaring upon the large, red plateau rocks that slid past my window as I drove through the state. I remember playing "Home Again" by Michael Kiwanuka on repeat while gazing upon the reddish orange landscape for hours on end. This song cut me to the core. The feeling of saying goodbye to one life and moving towards some unknown future. The lyrics over the gentle arpeggio of the acoustic gave rise to my own deep emotions, allowing me to feel them. I mean, *really* feel them.

From Santa Fe to Denver, with every day and every desert town I passed I got a little closer to my new life. I spent a whole week in Colorado. I was so excited, I called Juicy and Amar everyday. I just had to tell them where I was on my journey and how much I was looking forward to seeing them again and getting involved with Yes House. Amar picked up on the first day, then ignored the rest of my calls. Juicy pretty much did the same.

I must have called them ten times, and left as many voicemails, before I even got to the East Coast. The one time we spoke they each voiced encouragement for my trip and arrival, but I could sense their wariness. I mean, let's face it: to them I was just some guy they partied with in the desert, tripping out in a literal and figurative faraway land. Now this maniac was calling them from the road after leaving his life behind, driving across the country for a job that didn't exist.

I began to second guess and question. Those midnight miles are the perfect landscape for fear-based thoughts. *Maybe this won't work out, after all,* I thought. But resolving to trust and hope for the best, I rolled on, making my way to the Big Apple.

Blasting Leon Bridges's "Coming Home" album, I cruised into Chicago… where I got my van towed on the first night. This setback cost me my entire emergency fund, leaving me with maybe enough money to afford first month's rent somewhere in the city.

I blasted through Ohio. I was getting close. Late in the night, I pulled over at a truck stop, hoping for a few hours of shuteye. All jacked up on racing nerves, though, sleep wasn't gonna happen. I just closed my eyes and rested.

I opened my eyes. 5:04am on Friday, October 6th, 2017. This was it, the final leg: twelve hours to my new life. Far from being tired, I was riding that high, my body tingling from crown to feet, every breath a lungful of possibility and anticipation.

I did some belly breathing exercises to calm down as I ate my breakfast, a spotted banana and a cold egg sandwich. Inhale for four seconds, hold for four, exhale for four, hold the breath out for four. My heart rate slowed, but my nerves were still jumping. I went outside and brushed my teeth in the brisk air, spitting white foam on the asphalt. I looked at the empty parking lot lit up bright by yellow lights on top of tall posts, the predawn sky just starting to brighten to the east.

This was it. Everything led up to this moment: the first day of my new life.

I tilted my head back and offered up a prayer to the universe for safe travels to New York City, hopped up into the driver seat, started the engine, and was off.

The sun rose, painting the plains of Ohio golden in my rearview. I followed the hypnotic, seemingly never ending broken white line dividing my lane from the one next to it. By mid-morning I was on my third styrofoam cup of gas station "coffee" and ready to drop the beat. I threw on Camp Chewbacca's playlist, a smorgasbord of heavy deep-house, and cranked the volume.

Around noon, my vision started to blur due to the near seven hours of driving. The trees on either side of the road were all dressed up in their autumn leaves, and the exuberant reds, oranges, and yellows transformed the Pennsylvania highway into a three-dimensional Van Gough painting. I glanced at the green number of the digital clock. 1:22. Next time I looked it was 3:30 and I was about to cross the George Washington Bridge from New Jersey into New York City. I thought my heart was going to beat right out of my chest. With my right hand clenched into a tight fist, I pounded the steering wheel and howled out the window. The blue haired babe driving a Beamer in the left lane looked over, unimpressed, but I had a feeling this city—New York City, not Fort Lee—encouraged such behavior.

Immediately upon crossing the bridge I realized how bad of an idea it was to drive into the city on a Friday afternoon, never having been there before, in a massive van. Navigating the congested, honking, concrete labyrinth had my eyes popping out of my skull and my tie dye tee soaked with stress-sweat in minutes. It was downright terrifying, attempting to switch lanes to a chorus of protesting honks, quick turns to the left, wrong turns to the right, not knowing where the fuck I was. I slapped myself across the face, not gently, the sound bringing me back as much as the sting in my cheek. "You got this!" I told myself. "Keep going straight. Okay, now switch lanes!" *Slap!* "Alright, wrong turn, fuck. Okay, now turn left. Stop!" *Slap!* At some point I switched to the plural. "We're okay. We can do this…"

I made it through Manhattan without any lasting mental/emotional damage, more or less. By 5 p.m. I was cruising through Brooklyn. Bushwick, the warehouse district in that borough where Yes House resides, was within reach.

I made it. I felt like a fucking yokel tourist, unable to stop swiveling my head, looking around, staring, my mouth slightly open. I drove past bars, restaurants, cafes, bodegas, and warehouses. Young, beautiful people were everywhere, walking around, smoking, laughing, living. There were enormous murals everywhere, colorful, stunning works of art fifty feet tall. Bushwick was hip and happening, not dissimilar from Oakland, another warehouse district successfully converted into a gentrified hot spot.

My hands were still shaky from the rush-hour drive across two of New York City's busiest boroughs as I finally parked my van and killed the engine. I felt my life slow pleasantly. The green signs on the corner light post informed me I was on Yefferson Street and Wycliff Avenue. I let out a sigh of relief. *I made it.*

I jumped out of the van and took in the outside of the club I had been dreaming about for so long. I was underwhelmed. It wasn't the Bellagio, that's for sure.

In front of me was a two story warehouse that looked like some massive storage container that had been left in a junkyard for too many years. Bright turquoise, it had a massive YES on it, painted in white letters. There was a hole in the wall restaurant right on the corner, part of the building, evidently. An ornate wooden sign above the door read "Falafel House." The door itself was in the middle of a painted yellow triangle. Fifty feet to the right was the entrance to the club, two golden-colored metal doors. There was a blue vestibule in front of them, cloth and clear plastic, like something you'd see at a mid-range Thai joint. This one was so dilapidated, it looked like something homeless folks would live in under an overpass. On the sidewalk, two paper coffee cups rolled lazily, leaving a trail of brown liquid on the concrete. There wasn't a soul in sight.

After all the stories, I had imagined something large and lavish, with a sidewalk outside draped with red carpets and matching velvet ropes strung between shiny brass stands. I had visions of stunning eurasian models getting out of black SUVs and runway-stepping past the perpetual line of people waiting to get in.

The establishment in front of which I now stood… was not that. Unless all the red carpets and models in stilettos were inside. Yet—according to Xavier, anyway—it had been home to some of the best NYC parties of the last decade.

Despite its shabby first impression, I hoped it would be my new home, too.

A little ways past the main entrance was a black door, an exit, I assumed. It was open and I heard voices on the other side. I took my first-ever steps into Yes House and found myself in an outdoor patio the size of a small suburban backyard. The stained concrete-and-tile floor was littered with cigarette butts. A 20-foot-tall metal wall separated the space from the warehouse next door. It was covered in fake grass and many mannequins and two fake game statues were attached to it (a hippopotamus and a rhinoceros). Against the wall, well-worn church pews ran the length of the space. There were four life-size statues of angels in the corner. White, made to look like plaster, they seemed to have stepped out of a Renaissance painting, and were a stark contrast to the three people sitting on the pews, all focused on the screens of their MacBooks. The man in the yellow sweatshirt and mushroom-print baseball cap spinning a pen between his fingers, the slender woman with long black boots and a thin smile, and the short, dark-haired woman with a slight frown all looked zonked out, probably from a full day of staring at the screen to finish their weekend deadlines.

There was a brick-red shipping container in the back corner of the space, with a wooden staircase along its side. The stairs had seen better days, load-bearing would be a stretch, but seemed to be effective enough to lead to an area fenced off with bamboo. The back of the patio connected to the rest of the building. There were two doors side by side, with a sign that said "On Air." I assumed that if everything worked properly—not an assumption I was making, at this point—the sign lit up. The door on the left was labeled Coat Check; the one on the right was evidently the Onyx Room.

A bar ran half the length of the patio, attached to the main building. Leaning against it and smoking cigarettes were Juicy and Amar.

"Hey guys, I made it!" I announced, somewhat unnecessarily.

They both looked over, eyebrows raised.

"Oh shit!" said Amar, exhaling smoke. Did it take him a second to recognize me?

"Yoooo! My dude! What's up man? You want a drink?" Juicy asked.

I refused the drink, but gave them each a hug, squeezing extra tight to make sure I wasn't dreaming, asleep behind the wheel, plowing through a corn field somewhere in Iowa.

They took the last drags off their smokes and flicked their cigarettes, despite there being at least two ashtrays on the bar and several standing butt receptacles around the patio. They walked me through another set of golden doors and proceeded to give me a tour of the venue. In the Front room, on either side of two large wooden doors were two beach ball-sized eyeballs suspended from the ceiling, complete with lids and eyelashes that closed and opened languidly. Behind the bar was a laser-cut wooden sign that read, "No blowjobs on the dancefloor." An eight-foot-tall polar bear stood in one corner, wearing a Hawaiian shirt and a fedora. His faux fur seemed to absorb the light. He had his forepaws up, either menacingly or playfully, I couldn't tell.

We continued on through the large wooden doors into a large space they called the Theater. A rehearsal was under way, and under the bright lights performers were practicing choreography, aerial moves while hanging from ropes and rings, and costume changes. There were several people dressed in all black, setting up various structures around the space. Lada was frantically looking for something she had lost, moving in a similar course to her bicycling days at Burning Man. Zoe was in a small circle of four performers changing costumes and sharing stories from previous shows. They must have been humorous because they were all smiling and laughing, Zoe's red hair bouncing as she giggled. Juicy told me they were rehearsing for the night's performance of Ketamine the Musical.

The energy was intoxicating, and I was instantly hooked. From the circus production in the Theater to whatever it was the three laptoppers were doing out back, I wanted in. I asked if there was anything I could do to help out. Juicy and Amar exchanged a look, at a loss, apparently. After a few moments Juicy said that I could sweep the Patio before they opened for the show tonight. I didn't bat an eye.

Juicy showed me where the brooms were and a few seconds later I was sweeping up a storm in the Front Room. I didn't mind the grunt work. Shit, after spending time with this crew out west and hearing all the epic stories, I would have scoured the place for a toothbrush just to be involved. It didn't hurt that I was still flying high from my drive and all those styrofoam cups of coffee.

I swept the Front Room, then the Patio. The MacBook crew paused as one, long enough to give me a who-the-fuck-are-you? look before going back to their screens.

I swept my way into the Onyx Room, where one of the all-black guys was working. He was wearing jeans and a tee shirt and pretty much looked like a roadie. He was wearing a cap with a psychedelic cat face on it and, coincidentally or not, was decorating the small, windowless room in a cat motif. I introduced myself and asked if he needed help. He selected a stuffed beanie baby from a large black plastic bag, put it on a DJ table, and finally gave me an appraising look.

"You work here?" He asked.

"Um… No, but I hope to soon." I stuttered.

Cat Hat nodded, introduced himself as Whiskers, shook my hand, and went back to work. "You can sweep this room," he said, over his shoulder, then chose another cat, this one a Siamese with a haughty look sewed on its face, and carefully placed it next to the beanie baby.

I began to sweep the Onyx Room with short, efficient strokes of the broom. The silence in the gloomy cave-like room and Whiskers and his cats became unsettling. Just to make conversation I began to share my story, focusing on Burning Man, meeting the Yes House crew, and the excitement of coming to New York on a whim.

Halfway through my story, Whiskers left the room without saying a word.

Getting into this world isn't going to be easy, I thought.

I finished sweeping, put the broom back in its place, and hung out as people started arriving. A few were dressed in the extravagant, sparkly attire from the stories I had heard, but most were wearing normal street clothes. I quickly observed that people in New York were a lot prettier than the ones in the Bay Area.

The Front Room, now a dark and sexy space compared to the bright, living room vibe it was before, started filling up. Juicy appeared and pulled me into a small hallway. I followed him through a kitchen where a man was loading dishes in a dishwasher. We passed through black curtains and emerged at a back corner of the Theater. "Sit wherever," he said, then disappeared backstage. Only the guys in black were moving about the space, putting finishing touches on the stage and adjusting the rows of folding chairs into neat lines.

Since that one drama class I took in high school, I'd never witnessed a behind-the-scenes look at a theater production. I was in awe, stars layered across my eyes, as I watched the show before the show. The production crew closed the heavy red curtain, tossed props out of a side door into a waiting truck on Yefferson Street, and flooded the Theater with red and blue light from the powerful fixtures set into the 30-foot by 20-foot truss below the ceiling.

At someone's signal, the big wooden doors were ceremoniously opened wide. I heard a booming voice from the speakers, Nasty's, I think. "Ladies, gentlemen, and everyone in between. Please take your seats!"

People poured inside and began to claim their seats, unassigned folding chairs. Within a few minutes, every one was taken. "Remember kiddos, no flash photography, and enjoy

Ketamine the Musical!" came through the speakers. This voice was Whiskers.

The lights dimmed and for a moment we were all in darkness—a spotlight suddenly illuminated a man sitting on the bar on the stage right side of the Theater. An angel with long, white, feathered wings, glowing in the light, began to sing in a heart-achingly beautiful voice. As the ethereal wordless melody filled the room he tossed small bags of white powder into the crowd.

The curtains opened on a living room—a black couch, wooden night stands, leather chairs, and standing light fixtures. Two more angels appeared and pranced around the furniture to the sweet song, eventually leaving the stage and weaving between the rows of audience. They selected a patron, seemingly at random, a man wearing jean shorts and a red Hawaiian shirt, and taking an arm on each side brought him up on stage. The three plopped down on the couch. These angels, too, had bags of white powder, which they began to sniff and offer to their guest. After several loud and exaggerated snorts, the three slumped deeper into the black cushions and began to sway side to side.

Suddenly, two eyeballs, each the size of a volleyball, rose from behind the couch and began floating around the living room. They gazed cross-eyed at the audience until the man in the Hawaiian shirt locked eyes with them. The staring contest continued for several seconds until, without warning, all the furniture on stage levitated and began to swing in different directions.

As the furniture floated and swayed, Hawaiian shirt appeared relatively calm, all considered. Then things took a turn for the (even more) bizarre. A man appeared, a lumberjacking brute of a creature, 300 pounds, easy, with an untamed beard and more tattooed skin than not. He would have looked like the leader of a motorcycle gang, were it not for the baby blue and pink two-piece cupcake outfit. In his enormous fist was a whipped cream cracker, presumably loaded with nitrous oxide. He gave the device an enthusiastic wrenching, emitting a gas-releasing sound all too common to Camp Chewbacca, put his lips on the nozzle, and inhaled the entire cartridge in one sweeping breath. Five more cupcakes appeared on stage and all six erupted into a tightly choreographed dance.

I literally would not blink for fear of missing even half a second of what was happening in front of me, and while I was completely sober, my mind refused to believe my eyes and acknowledge that so much raw magic could be made to exist on stage. After an epic dinosaur battle and a scene in which a penis and vagina engaged in a rap battle, I was in love.

The last scene was a dance party. Rufus Du Sol blared from the speakers as dinosaurs and angels flew through the air, singing from trapeze within arm's reach of the audience. The man in the Hawaiian shirt, now clearly a plant, stroked the penis rapper while the tattooed cupcake giant did The Twist with the vagina. An audience member, for real this time, was pulled up to dance. Before we fully realized what was happening, my fellow audience members and I were on our feet, knocking over chairs, to jump and dance and share the moment with the actors who created it. The black-clad production staff joined in. Nasty and Whiskers boogied away in the tech booth. Unadulterated joy spread like wildfire.

When the celebration died down the audience was ushered into the Front Room. The show was over, but a party was about to begin. I stayed in the Theater and helped fold chairs. I was gonna work whether anyone paid me to, or not.

I noticed Zoe speed-walking through the Theater towards backstage. She was barefoot, a pair of white heels dangling from her hand. I folded the chair I was holding and put it with the others on a rolling rack. "Hey Zoe!" I shouted across the Theater.

She slowed her pace, looked over, confused, managed to give me a smile after a couple seconds, then continued on her way. It wasn't the reaction I was hoping for, but at least she acknowledged my presence.

Minutes later Lada stormed by, Juul in mouth. "Hi Lada!" I said, smiling, hoping to get a warmer reception. What I got was a blank stare as she picked up the pace and put distance between us as if I was a hooded figure on a dark street asking for money, then darted out of the Theater. I put my head down and placed another chair on the rack.

The all-in-black crew pushed the chair racks out the emergency exit door on the side of the Theater and parked them on the sidewalk beside the club. With the flick of a switch, the bright work lights inside the now-empty Theater were replaced with colorful, moving beams of reds and purples. Music began blasting from the speakers, so loud I could feel my eardrums pulsate. Someone opened the Theater doors and what seemed about two hundred people poured in. In less than a minute, the whole crowd was moving, grooving, and otherwise dancing up a storm.

I weaved through the glittered tops, bell-bottom velvet pants, altered Renaissance jacks, and glossy platform shoes until I spotted Juicy by the bar. He was wearing an open white coat with decorative gold stitching and white jeans. His lean torso showed and a black rhinestone necklace hung around his neck, the triangular pendant nearly to his hairy belly button. It looked like he was having fun, dancing slowly in place. He didn't seem stressed—it didn't even look like he was working, just another party boy. I came over and we began chatting, casual at first, talking about our favorite parts of the show, all the attractive people on and offstage, yadda yadda. I then steered towards more pressing, serious matters. I laid it out for him straight: I had just left my life in California and come to Brooklyn, to Yes House, to work. I would do anything to get involved.

He must have suspected I was serious after all those annoying voicemails, but now that I was here, a foot away from him, he had the proof. As I spoke, he nodded slowly, all the while looking at me. I could feel him reading me, maybe judging my character, hopefully sizing me up as a future employee.

He was perfectly attentive, but committed to nothing. Satisfied to have told him face to face everything I'd been thinking about since Burning Man, I left the conversation at that. Around 3am I left the club, body exhausted, covered in glitter, and crawled into the back of my van. As I lay in my bed and stared at the blue fabric with which I'd lined the ceiling, I reflected on my journey. It was then I realized that leaving everything behind and driving across the country was the easy part. Starting from scratch, building relationships, learning and proving myself at Yes House would be the real work. As was so frequently the case in my short but colorful life… nobody was going to hand me a thing.

The next day I awoke to the skull-splitting sound of a truck's horn. I pressed a pillow over my face in an attempt to block it out, but it felt like the blasts were inches away from my face as the fucker honked relentlessly. I threw on some pants and went outside, barefoot and shirtless. I saw that the hellish tuba blasts were, in fact, coming from an arm's length from my face, because a tractor trailer sat next to my van, unable to make it past on the narrow street. The driver was wearing a ripped tee shirt and a MAGA hat, and didn't look like he was about to give me a "top o' the morning!" Still mostly undressed, I jumped in the driver's seat, clenched my teeth, grunted, and drove around the block.

After parking again I checked my phone. I had received a text from an Australian babe I met at the Burn. The text read, "What you doing today? Wanna do me?"

I instantly forgot about the irate Trump trucker and began driving her way. *Maybe this city is going to work out after all.*

I arrived at her apartment and met the olive toned skin, model face, athletic beauty. She was painting the face of a dog while wearing only a silk robe, untied and open. We went to her room where I gave her a massage and then closed the blinds. A couple hours later I headed to Long Island City, Queens. The Aussie connected me with a couple who had a room to rent. Three subway trains or 45 minutes by car from Yes House was a bit far for my liking, but I had to start somewhere. The apartment was a spacious two bed, one bath apartment with a couple small doggos and various photos of their years at Burning Man. I paid $2000—first month's rent and a security deposit—leaving myself with a few hundred bucks to my name. I needed a job, and fast.

At 4pm I headed back to Yes House for another long night. It was like Groundhog Day: I watched Ketamine the Musical, danced at the late-night party, and bugged Juicy for a job. I could tell he felt the pressure. I must have been wearing him down with my perseverance. This time he said he's working on it.

The next day was pretty much the same. I was starting to get into a routine: wake up, eat breakfast, fight off a crippling panic attack brought on by my impending financial doom, then head to

Yes House. Instead of the show they had an early Sunday Pantless Dance Party, and I had just the outfit: a leopard-print leotard that couldn't be any tighter if it was painted on. In it I looked like I belonged in a Broadway production of Tarzan, or Lion King, maybe. I threw it on, put on pants for a bit of decency for the ride, and jumped on the 7 train.

I arrived at YES, stuffed my phone into the side of the leotard, and gave my pants to the little lady in coat check. Then I joined the party underway in the yard, dancing through the hundred moving and grooving butts. I was surrounded by panties, boxers, and a few Baywatch swimsuits in a sunlit, concrete patio. In the middle of it all was a big kiddy pool filled with water and a few people sipping margaritas. I climbed inside and made acquaintances.

My phone vibrated and I hunted around for it in my leotard. A text from Xavier read, "Nice outfit," followed by a winking emoji. A video arrived next. I couldn't believe what I was seeing! There I was, on the screen of my own phone in black and white, dancing in my leotard.

Turns out Juicy was in the office and saw me on one of the screens showing images from the security cameras all over the club. Feeling inspired, he zoomed the camera in on me, took a video, and sent it to all our mutual California friends.

Phone in hand, I jumped out of the pool, ran through the Front Room, cut through the kitchen and entered the empty Theater. Above the stage behind one of the go-go platforms I could see Juicy's head as he worked in his office. "You took a video of me!" I yelled from down below, dripping kiddie-pool water on the dance floor.

Juicy laughed, got up from his desk and peered over the edge at me. "Settle down Tarzan. It was priceless," he said. "Good news, though. I think I found you some work. Show up tomorrow at 9am." And just like that he went back to whatever he was doing like he didn't just change the course of my life forever. I, on the other hand, stood alone in a theater, transfixed by the moment, tiny leotard crammed between my buttcheeks, feet in tiny pools of water on the hardwood floor, a smile stamped on my face.

~~~

I was so worried about sleeping through my alarm I awoke three times in the night, each time fumbling for my phone to check the time. At 7am, when my alarm actually went off, I jumped out of bed like a kernel of corn popping on the stove. My eyes were barely open, but my body was moving like I was caffeinated from my nose to my toes.

Brushing my teeth and flashing monkey smiles at myself in the mirror, I thought of all my possible roles at Yes House. Barback? Juicy's personal assistant? Hype man? Oil massages during club hours? I didn't care one bit. I was down for it all.

Out the door by 7:30, I grabbed an everything bagel with tofu cream cheese at the corner bodega, inhaled it in a matter of seconds, and hopped on the 7 train. As I stood in the corner smushed between a fat bald guy and a loudly belching old lady, I began to sweat—in part due to the nervousness at the prospect of being late on my official first day of work, but also because I was stuck in the warm scent prison of baldy's pungent head cream and grandma's hardboiled egg burps.

To ensure I didn't miss my stop, I kept asking the gassy old lady what the next stop would be. She stopped responding after two stations.

I eventually transferred to the G train towards South Brooklyn. It was less crowded, thankfully, but had three homeless people sleeping on the benches. I experienced a nostalgic yearning for the fresh sporty scent of the scalp cream. Between the three sleepers the stench nearly defied description, a nuanced mixture of urine, feet, cigarette butts, and dried up malt liquor. I attempted to hold my breath for five stops but nearly joined the unconscious bums when I got a wicked head rush and almost passed out. Finally, after what felt like an hour, I arrived at Lorimer Street in Williamsburg, the L train, and entered air-conditioned serenity. Few people were heading into the wilds of Southeast Brooklyn at that hour. I sat on the blue-gray bench and enjoyed a few untainted breaths.

A woman's voice announced, "Next stop: Yefferson Street."

Yefferson Street! That's my stop! The doors were barely open enough to allow me through when I squeezed out and found myself on a mostly deserted platform. I checked the time. 8:30. *Yesss.* 30 minutes to spare.

I walked past Yes House to Zana and bought a pack of Camels. I slapped the top of the pack against my palm, peeled off the plastic, popped one in my mouth and lit up. I stood outside the store, smoking and watching the people go by. Hipsters, goths, suits, hippies, normies, and laborers heading towards the subway, and work, presumably. All neighbors, westward bound, leaving en masse... none of them looking up or making eye contact.

I finished my smoke and walked up Wycliff Avenue. At 8:45 I was at Yes House, next to Juicy at the bar in the Front Room. He was texting, elbows pressed into the wood, cigarette hanging from his lip. He finished sending his message and sent me to fill out some paperwork with his office manager, Cora. He told me to find Amar once I was done with the W2. "He'll find something for you to do," he said with a smirk.

Amar was out back, giving a crew of four laborers their tasks for the day. They were wearing paint-stained jeans and long sleeves, construction boots on their feet. I assumed I'd be joining them, and guessed that Hype Man was out of the question.

Amar turned to me. "Alright, let's get started," he said sharply. He walked out the exit door and onto Yefferson Street, leaving me to jog after him just to keep up. Twenty feet past the main entrance he stopped, bent down, and pulled up a metal storm door from the sidewalk, revealing a horror movie staircase, like a ladder, feet landing in black puddles on the steps. Amar flicked a switch and the fluorescent glare revealed a low-ceilinged tomb, a concrete clusterfuck of broken shelving, bins, crates, random construction materials, tools, hardware. On the floor were waist-high boxes full of crap you'd find in a junkyard one hundred years ago. Amar and I stood shoulder to shoulder; movement in any direction was impossible.

"So. I need this room completely organized, and I need a full inventory of everything. And pictures. I need pictures of everything," Amar said. He speaks slowly and evenly, in a hard to place accent, his rich voice never rising. Still, the man commands power and obedience.

"An inventory of everything? What about all that old silverware I see in the back?" I asked, nervously.

"Everything," he responded. "Take a lunch break later and let me know if you need anything," Amar said, a face as expressionless as stone, then walked out.

Damn. I took a deep breath and took stock of my reality. What a literal mess I had gotten myself into.

It took me two days in that moldy subterranean nightmare, but I did it. I even put together a presentation-grade inventory, Google Doc complete with photos. I was proud of my work—the basement was neater than Amy Winehouse's pill cabinet, and there were more than two hundred items in my inventory list. I couldn't wait to show Juicy and Amar. I found them at the bar in the Front Room. It was around 6pm on a Tuesday, one of the club's "dark days," and though all the lights were bright, the place was quiet as a library. I think we were the only three people in the venue.

Amar and Juicy were discussing some big Halloween party when I interrupted them by placing my laptop on the bar, the inventory on its screen. They paused long enough to give it a cursory look and mutter "thanks," before going back to their conversation. As they were talking, Juicy was responding to emails on his little gray MacBook, while Amar smoked and sat still as a meditator. Juicy seemed to always be working. He was a machine. From morning til night, if he wasn't in a meeting with someone, he was working on his phone or on the computer. Amar, on the other hand, worked hard for most of the day, but would relax afterward, sitting still and undistracted, just being. He appeared to be someone naturally at peace. I've often wondered if it's because he grew up in the desert—unlike Juicy, who grew up in New York City.

Despite the lack of praise, Amar must have been pleased with my efforts in the basement because he sent me to organize their offsite storage. This time, instead of one tiny room, I had a section of a warehouse to contend with. Two floors, 20 by 50 feet. One look and I suddenly missed the musty closeness of the Yes House basement.

At first glance I thought I had walked into the back closet of a Ripley's Believe It or Not museum. Dozens of couches (all different and in various states of decrepitude) stacked ceiling high; a multi-piece plywood castle facade bigger than my apartment; a Great White-sized fish tank… these were the items my eyes settled on first. I was instantly overwhelmed. "Why the fuck would they, or *anyone*, need *any* of this shit?" I said aloud, my voice taking on a strange quality in the weirdly soundproofed space.

"Because *they* are fucking nuts," said a man from somewhere, scaring the bejesus out of me, before bellowing laughter.

I poked my head out into the rest of the space to be confronted with the tattooed cupcake giant from the other night. He no longer looked like a violent pastry. In jeans and a black Napalm Death t-shirt, he looked more like the violent motorcycle gang leader.

"I'm Clay Stone," he said. "I do most of the fabrication for Yes House. This is my warehouse and shop." I shook his hand, fearing that I'd never get mine back. "Anyway, " said Clay, "good luck with this crap. They probably need it for that Palace of Gods party. Not only are they throwing the biggest Halloween party in Brooklyn at Yes House, but they are renting a massive hotel in Long Island City, plus the warehouse next to it, to throw a five thousand person, twenty-four hour event. Probably their biggest endeavour yet, those crazy fucks… Anyway, let me know if you need anything." He chuckled, waved a meaty hand, and went back to his work.

"Thanks…" I said, my words swallowed by the space as if it were a living thing.

I faced the colossal disaster of the storage room, sighed, mentally rolled up my sleeves, then got to it. I climbed and counted the couches, organized the castle, and sorted through hundreds of different light fixtures, whips, sex toys, stacks of two-by-fours, steeldeck staging, and disco balls. I noted and photographed. Another Google Doc was born and grew.

After three days of being up to my neck (sometimes higher) in this shit, and many smoke breaks with Clay, I was done. I once again presented my work to Juicy and Amar, head high and proud.

They gave it a couple of seconds of their time and another unenthusiastic "thanks."

After a full week of toiling away, the subject of my pay finally came up. The three of us were standing in the office, Amar towering over Juicy and me. In matters like this Juicy deferred to Amar. Amar thought about it, far too briefly, in my opinion. "Hundred bucks a day," he said. It didn't exactly sound like an offer, more like a non negotiable statement. I did the arithmetic. $12.50 an hour. The New York City minimum wage. This I knew from the Department of Labor poster in the kitchen.

After taxes, that was a whopping $70 a day, about $1400 a month. My rent was a grand, plus I had to eat and buy the occasional leotard. I would be slaving away just to be in debt to this city.

I didn't know what to say. I'd be busting my hump for peanuts (less, based on Zana's peanut prices.) On the other hand, I'd been dreaming about being involved with Yes House, and was grateful for the opportunity.

"Okay," I finally responded, then walked away with my head down.

I had to work my way up. *And soon.*

~~~

The October days dragged along. I spent them mostly solo, scraping gum off the floor, unclogging drains, patching and painting the walls. Occasionally I'd jump in to help others on their projects, but this never seemed to go well.

Amar had a regular crew of workers, his personal maintenance detail. Hardworking Spanish-speaking pros, handy, good at their jobs. One day he had me jump in with them to do some tiling out in the Patio. Me, a Gringo hippie who can't tell wet cement from peanut butter. So I'm watching these dudes, who are making it look smooth and easy the way professionals at everything seem to do, mixing in just the right amount of water and cement, gently setting it on the working surface with practiced flicks of the wrist. After I got the gist, I grabbed a trowel and started doing the same.

"No aqui! No aqui!" two of them yelled, which caused me to literally jump and land on one of the not-yet-set tiles they had just placed, moving it and leaving a smear of cement. One of the guys began screaming at me in Spanish. I didn't need to understand the individual vocabulary to get the point he was conveying. As punctuation, he threw his trowel which clattered across the Patio and continued with the onslaught, glaring, veins standing out on his forehead. Jeeze, you'd think I shat on an altar to the Virgin of Guadalupe or something.

I just stood there and took it, feeling dumb and embarrassed, with that stress-shame feeling setting in the muscles of my neck and shoulders. I couldn't walk away. To walk away was to quit, so I grabbed a broom and began sweeping. The guy settled eventually, his head veins stopped bulging, and I sensed forgiveness emanating from him. Nevertheless, I kept a wary eye on him, in case he decided to set the next tile on my face.

The only guy from that crew who was sympathetic towards me was Victor. He was Puerto Rican but grew up in NYC and spoke English. He was the designated driver of the company box truck, and after the tiling incident he began to take me on varying errands and runs to the storage warehouse. I guess he figured I'd be safer that way, and one of his guys wouldn't get deported after brutalizing me with a tape measure.

We were in the truck one day, sharing stories as guys working together have been doing since forever ago. Victor was wearing his usual outfit: black baggy jeans, Timberlands, a black tee, and a red snapback hat. Tattoos covered his body, flowing from neck to torso, limb to limb. There was cursive lettering on his neck and I occasionally glanced at it as he drove, trying to make out the words in Spanish. *Amor Mortal*, I silently lipped.

Victor told me he had been working for Amar since the owners of Yes House signed the lease for the building, about four years ago. Before that it was a defunct, one-story laundromat. Transforming the space was a massive project that took countless hours of back-breaking labor, most notably raising the roof to three times its previous height. This involved basically tearing the building apart, building up the walls, and installing a new roof. "Plus, to make everything more difficult, we were on a shoestring budget." Victor remembered how he and Lada would throw on yellow rubber gloves and go dumpster diving behind warehouses, looking for scrap material, things they could repurpose, anything they'd be able to use either structurally or superficially. He laughed, tickled by the memory. "You know those wooden benches out on the Patio? We heard a church was going out of business, or whatever, so we jumped in every vehicle we had, laborers and owners alike, and rolled up that same afternoon. They were giving away nearly everything and we took every single pew in that motherfucker. I'll bet Amar would've taken the crucifix, if they'd let him, that sick fuck. Back at YES we put some of the benches out back for seating and cut the rest up to use for the bar surfaces." Victor chuckled. "Another reason I'm going to hell…"

I wished my ride with Victor took longer, because when we got back to the club, Amar assigned me to Sable, the short, stocky, production manager.

She was clear with her directions. Grab carpets, chairs, and three blue lighting fixtures from the basement and the production truck parked outside the club and bring them to the Theater. "And quick!" she added. I ran around, gathering the requested items, then placed them gently in the center of the Theater. That done, I came back to her looking for further instructions. I showed her where I put the stuff and she went ballistic. She looked through the stuff I brought, her face reddening and body becoming visibly tense. Finally, she grabbed my arm and dragged me out of the Theater, through the Front Room, and out to the stained, concrete Patio.

Apparently she felt better about yelling at me outside. "This is all wrong!" she raged. "Where is the new curtain? The hand tools? These are blue lights—I asked for red! Red!"

"But, you sa—"

"Useless! This shows me exactly how unaccountable you are. You are unfit to work for me!" Her arms were rigid at her sides, hands balled into little fists. I thought if she clenched them any tighter, she'd puncture her palms with her fingernails. Around us the wind picked up, as if stirred by Sable's fury. It's like she was venting a lifetime of stress and frustration, and using me as the whipping boy! For the second time that day, I just stood there and took it. What was I supposed to do? Fight back with a superior at my "dream" job during my first week?

If this wasn't bad enough, I was being scolded like a small child for all to see, but the owners and staff walked by us without a second glance, like they didn't notice this public lynching. Once Sable wore herself out, she stormed off. I stood there, pinned to the stained tile by my tense fury. I did exactly as she asked! And quickly, goddammit!

I felt a palm on my shoulder. "Well she really gave it to ya, huh?" Juicy giggled. I turned to glare at him. The way they stung, I could tell my eyes were bloodshot. My jaw hurt from clenching my teeth. "Don't take it personally," he said. "She has been dealing with a world of shit. Pretty much from the beginning she has been single handedly handling the day to day production, the scheduling, stage managing all the shows, overseeing all the communication between producers and tech… God knows what else. She's been putting in between 60 and 80 hours a week, and that's conservative. Plus Amar has been throwing surprises at her so often her hair is starting to gray. Today, you just happened to be one of them."

With every word he said I felt tension leaving my shoulders. Hearing about Sable's too-full plate calmed me down. My face and fists slowly relaxed back to their natural state. There was something about the way Juicy spoke—sympathetically, lightheartedly—that inspired those qualities in the person listening.

Sympathy is not forgiveness, though. Okay, so she was drowning in work and her own stress. She was under a lot of pressure from every direction. Did that give her the right to indulge a white-hot wrath and publicly take down her subordinates (thirty minutes after meeting them, no less)? Nuh-uh. Toxic, I decided. Only a toxic person would act like that in a wondrous place like this.

Disgusted, I lit a cigarette and took a deep inhale. I held it, exhaled, shook my head and walked to the train.

This was my life. Wake up at 7am, take three trains, scrape gum off the floors and get yelled at by everybody, it seemed. All for a hundred dollars a day. Switching from my breezy California life to this was tough, to say the least.

Something kept me going, though. First off, I was on a mission. But more than that, there was something special here, something I didn't have back home: a family. And a family of circus freaks and sodomizing cupcakes is better than no family at all.

Not to say everybody in my new family was a performer. Take the crew who worked at the Front Room bar during the day. These five sat in the same seats every day, laptops and coffee cups scattered about the bar. Griz sat all the way to the left. A flamboyant bear with an immaculate beard and buzz cut, his laugh was so unique and raucous, you could be underwater in the hot tub, a pair of things pressing against your ears, and you'd know if something tickled him in the Theater. Griz booked DJ's and events. His phone was forever pressed to his ear and he spent all day talking to producers, artists, and agents.

Sola, Griz's emotionally unbalanced assistant, came as part of the Griz package and sat immediately to his right. Erratic and all over the map, the one unwavering thing you could count on from her was an at-least-once-daily crying jag.

Mack, the sweet as cherry pie graphic designer, sat in the middle. She made all the constantly changing bar and bottle service menus, as well as the wacky online event flyers. Mack was so petite you had to do a double take just to make sure a child hadn't snuck into the bar and started pantomiming a digital nomad. Incidentally, she and Clay Stone were an item.

After Mack came Kev, the twenty-something with the stylish brown hair and ambitious-yet-sparse mustache and beard. Laid-back and with a slight lisp, Kev was solid in every way: he never missed a deadline and could be counted on to have an assortment of powdered drugs on him. Like I said, a solid asset to the team.

Last on the right, small and fierce, was the genius marketing director and public relations executive, Julia. She had more influence on the owners than the rest of the staff combined. Rumor had it that ticket sales jumped 20 percent in her first month at the club due to her social media outreach and strategy of selling tickets on different platforms.

I'd occasionally hear Zoe talking about Julia taking Yes House to the next level. It's funny, one person sitting on the same stool everyday, tapping away on a keyboard, barely moving a muscle, can make such a difference. But the Bar Quintet, that's what they all did. Five days a week, sitting in their silently agreed upon wooden bar stools with plush red cushions and bronze tacks along the sides, hunched over their illuminated screens. They were always working, it seemed, except for the occasional gossip break. I would overhear how Kev had to drag his friend out of the club after he did too many drugs with the DJ; or how Sola had to watch her ex, who swore he was straight, make out with Tyson, the goliath ballerina door queen.

There was no shortage of parties, that's for sure. I could stop by any night and count on having an amazing time.

Wednesdays were vogue, reggaeton, or funk nights. These were usually smaller events and free. Limited to the Front Room, they were popular with the locals and always full of Brooklynites cutting loose on Hump Day.

Throwback Thursdays had an 80s or 90s theme, but sometimes were artist specific, like on a Bowie night. Ironically, these attracted a younger crowd, early to mid-twenties. Tecates and Long Island Ice Teas flowed, contributing to a wilder, more rambunctious vibe. Super popular, if you wanted to get into these events, you had to get in line which wound around the block.

Fridays and Saturdays were the all-star nights. Top billed DJs from Berlin and London, big performances, elaborate themes. Almost everybody came dressed up for Glitter Disco, Unicornitopia, Atlantis, Leather and Whips. Those who didn't have a costume had to purchase one from our costume truck parked outside the entrance. The crew in the truck would transform a mere attendee into a participant, complete with the persona and freedom that came with the dressing up. T-shirt and cargos? No worries, bro—here's your fishnet top and vinyl chaps! Lose that boring little black dress, honey, and become a fantasy. Forget your day-to-day life and its inherent "issues." Now you're a mermaid. Or a queen. Or a badass leather daddy who's not to be disobeyed.

Sundays were a bit of a wild card. It could be a Brazilian cultural event or a shirtless, sweaty gay night. Or something altogether different. Whatever the event, they always drew a crowd, but for the most part I'd be so partied out by then I would stay home and eat a pint of Van Leeuwen's vegan mint-chip ice cream on the couch. I had to have some boundaries, and going to the club four nights a week instead of five seemed like a good place to start.

After a couple of rest-and-ice-cream days, I was ready to go out again, but not to party all night long. Oliver recommended a happy medium: Filthy Circus, the Wednesday night theater show. "It's like all the shows," he told me, eyes twinkling, "an acrobat cabaret, crazy clown shit and whatnot, but this one' better—there's an extra raunchy twist to each act. Go see for yourself."

I walked the few hundred feet from Yefferson Street subway station, gave Crius a hug at the entrance, then went out to the Patio and sparked a ciggy. I took a couple of drags, enjoying the cool evening air and people watching. Lada, dressed as a pizza slice (complete with sewn-on mushrooms) stomped over in eight-inch black heels and gave me a big hug. I was so taken aback, I barely put my arm on her, just let her wrap around me. Frankly, I was surprised she even recognized me, for all the attention she paid me during work hours. After the half-assed hug she pulled away and smiled at me. Her breath was rich with the earthy, vegetal tang of agave, which explained her sudden bonhomie.

She had a lime-garnished drink in one hand and a Juul in the other. She was holding a plastic golden goose against her body, and through the opening in its back I saw a roll of pink raffle tickets. "I'm not supposed to do this," she said, smile widening, "but here you go." Placing the goose on the bar and switching her Juul to her tequila hand, she ripped a raffle ticket from the reel and handed it to me. She picked up her golden goose, did a passable curtsy, and skipped like a schoolgirl through the doors and into the Front Room, where I saw her lean provocatively on the bar and shake the ice in her otherwise empty glass at Oliver.

I threw out my cigarette on the black and white tiles and joined them. Lada bounded off as I arrived, heels clicking with every step, while Oliver looked at himself in the wall mirror behind the bar and fixed the top button of his Hawaiian shirt.

"How's it going? You alright?" I asked.

Oliver got the button right, gave his collar a tug, and turned to me. "Living the dream, mate," he replied, then turned back to the mirror and leaned in close to look at his eyes. "Just served Lada her ninth Patron soda of the night, so the show ought to be good. Enjoy."

I walked into the Theater and took my customary spot in the corner as the show began. Zoe, dressed as a 70's pornstar—Beatles wig, large mustache, a half opened plaid button-up, bell-bottom jeans—stood on the stage alone, lit up in front of the curtain. After waiting a showman's beat, she put the mic to her lips and introduced herself as Karl Karlson. I don't know how she did it, but Karl sounded like he had been drinking Jim Bean and smoking unfiltered Lucky Strikes since the day he was born. He regaled the audience with politically incorrect stories about his colorful exploits and thousands of exes in New York City, getting a few laughs. After a few minutes of warming up the Theater, Zoe passed the microphone to Lada.

A spotlight illuminated the pizza slice, standing on a small platform in the middle of the audience. Lada held the microphone in her right hand while her left stirred the raffle tickets inside the golden goose. She spoke slowly, her husky voice enticing. "Hello, sexy humans. Are you raffle buyers ready to find out what you could win?" The audience hooted and clapped, no doubt lubricated by Oliver's cocktails. "You're in for a treat. One lucky winner will get to watch the show from a warm, hand stirred, bubble bath!"

"Hand stirred bubbles-s-s," Whiskers's voice echoed through the speakers.

The spotlight Left Lada long enough to illuminate a vintage, claw footed bathtub to her right. "Where you and a friend can watch the show completely naked while we bring you all the free drinks you can gulp down!" said Lada, her voice rising to a carnival barker's call.

"No clothes-s-s..." Whiskers punctuated.

"In a city where no one can afford an apartment with a bathtub... your fantasies can all come true at Yes House!"

"Broke ass bitches-s-s..."

Lada dropped to her knees and shoved the microphone into the golden goose as she stirred the tickets with her hand. The papery shush-shush filled the Theater. Her hand stopped and came out of the goose holding one pink ticket, the spotlight making it glow. She lifted it to her face. "And now, the winner is... Five. Four... Oh, stop it—everyone has a five-four! Now... Five. Four. Seven. Six. Six. And... One!" Lada boomed.

A wave of sighs flowed from the audience. "Oh, c'mon!" cried a man wearing a Kelly green designer coat sitting a couple seats in front of me. He threw a bundle of pink raffle tickets in the air like a kid at Chuck E Cheese's who'd just been told he didn't have nearly enough for the life-sized panda bear of his dreams.

Six, six, one... Oh shit.

"I won!" It took me half a second to realize that the voice piercing through the din of the audience was my own. Cheers and whistles accompanied me as I walk-jumped towards the pizza slice on the center platform. My smile felt like it was radiating enough heat to warm my whole head of long hair. When I got to Lada my face was brighter than the spotlight shining on us—hers fell flat in disbelief.

Our eyes met briefly, then Lada addressed the audience. "Well everyone! Tonight's winner is our cute, harmless little production assistant! And it appears that Loki, here, needs a companion for the tub." She let the sentence dangle in the suddenly quiet air of the Theater. Her voice dropped to a more playful register. "Who would like to join him?" she asked, circling around me and the platform with slow, exaggerated steps, her mushrooms bouncing fetchingly.

A few hands went up, but with the spotlights on me I couldn't make out their owners. Lada looked at me and gave me a slight nod, her eyes black under her shapely brows. Squinting, I let my eyes rove through the crowd, recited a tiny prayer, and chose a hand. I heard a squeal of delight and a figure detached itself from the audience and joined me.

My smile cooled a few degrees. This was not going to be the porn-perfect tub fantasy I had envisioned. The girl next to me would diplomatically be described as "big" or "plus size." The truth of the matter is, she was nearly as wide as she was tall, with severe, traditionally masculine features. The pizza spoke up, bringing me back to the matter at hand. Lada was suddenly no-nonsense as she turned to us. "Alright, guys. Here at the Yes House we're all about consent and feeling good, so you have the option to go to the bathroom, take your clothes off, and come back in a towel, or… you can get naked right here and now for all to see." The crowd expressed its preference by cheering after choice number two.

I turned to my tub mate, tilted my head, raised my eyebrows, and pointed towards the ground. She nodded, a shy smile on her face. I faced Lada. "Here."

Lada pointed up at the tech booth. "Hit it, Whiskers!"

Immediately the hot white spotlights turned a deep, velvety red. The crowd ooohed and a couple of wolf whistles and one chicka-bow-wow rose out of the darkness. Ginuwine's "Pony" began to slither from the sound system, the drum machine high-hat stirring everyone in the Theater. People began to move in their seats and there were more catcalls. The whistling was pretty much nonstop now. It was clear what I had to do. I began to gyrate my hips, slow, as I peeled off my black shirt, in no kind of hurry. The crowd became more frenzied with every inch of skin I revealed. *Channing Tatum's got nothing on me,* I thought.

The big girl followed my lead without hesitation, ripping off her white shirt and throwing it into the crowd, revealing two plump, creamy white watermelons. It wasn't the prettiest sight, if you ask me, but the crowd absolutely worshiped her. Next came shoes, then socks, which are generally more challenging to take off sexily. I am glad I wore one of my newer pairs. The pants elicited the biggest cheers, yet. And as we stood there in our birthday suits, the audience was collectively losing their shit. We then both submerged in warm water and hand-frothed Dr. Bronner's (the original peppermint, which I think is the best) and the cheers began to subside.

As I luxuriated in the tub, comfortably pressed against that cushiony body, I realized it had taken me exactly two weeks to get completely naked in front of all my co-workers. How would HR feel about this? Was there even an HR?

Karl Karlson brought me a champagne flute filled with orange juice, the glass covered with condensation. Sipping the ice-cold beverage while ensconced between a stranger's warm thighs was bliss. That's right, I was the small spoon and I settled right in to enjoy the show. Lada was right—the bubbles were a nice touch.

The curtain opened on a woman wearing black panties and a black sports bra, inked up in demonic symbols. One by one she showed us several swords, their blades glinting in the stage lights, then proceeded to sink them down her throat until the hilt was an inch from her rose-red lips.

Karl Karlson, the emcee, followed, too-detailed stories of misadventures with transvestites in the 70's rolling off the tips of his highway patrol mustache. Later, a couple named Cross and Bones slammed each other onto a bed of nails.

The show was thoroughly entertaining. When it ended, Sparky, the short, bearded production assistant who, like myself, also started at the club a couple weeks ago, handed us towels. I said goodbye to my tub companion then dried off in the bathroom and got dressed.

It was 10:30. I had to be back at 9am the next day, so I sternly told myself to go home. And I was so, so close to doing just that. I put my hands on the release bar of the backstage exit door. Just a couple pounds of pressure and I'd be on Wycliff Avenue, a stone's throw from the L train. A sound caught my attention: the laughs of the performers, so joyous and inviting. My hands froze on the handle. *Ah, I don't want to miss all the post-show fun! A few more minutes won't hurt,* I thought. I made a promise to myself: *One lap around the club and then I'm out!*

I found Mrs. Miss and Dreams hanging out with Crius out front, Oliver and Dan Rockies shooting the shit with Romeo at the bar, Sable having a beer with the guys in the tech booth; and the owners laughing with Birdy, the manager, out in the Patio. With them was a regular named Dash. He was like a better looking Michael B. Jordan—similar physique and facial hair, but with a sharper jawline and better abs. Dash brought two things to the club, without fail: a smile and a bottomless bag of blow. Later, I found Dash and half the staff stuffed into the shipping container costume closet out back. Let's just say nobody was there looking for a wardrobe change. We came out chemically, visibly refreshed.

Dan Rockies was behind the bar, the man in the designer green coat in front of him, on the customer side. He looked all of 22. "I'm from Long Island," he said to Dan.

"Long Island, eh? Let me guess: vodka soda?" Dan broke into hysterical laughter as he reached for the liquor. I'm not even sure the guy responded, but Dan said over his shoulder, "Yeah I knew it. I fucking knew it all along!"

The young man didn't laugh back.

I checked the time. 2am! Christ. Three hours gone in a flash and I still couldn't leave this little adult playground. The early alarm didn't matter to me anymore. I couldn't come up with a single compelling reason to leave these people, this place... this family.

Out in the Patio I lit a cigarette and sucked until the tip flared a molten red.

"You ready?"

The voice out of nowhere startled me. I turned to find Amar looming behind me, eyes narrowed like he just saw me stick my hand in a tip bucket. How long had he been standing there?

"For work tomorrow? Yeah, I'll be ready. I was just heading home now," I fumbled.

Amar paused for a moment. "For Palace of Gods. We're putting on a big Halloween party at an offsite hotel and neighboring warehouse. Six thousand people. It's gonna be wild." As usual his words were measured and even, wild Halloween party or not. He drew slowly on a cigarette, the cherry briefly brightening his features in the after-hours gloom of the Patio.

"Sounds fun!" I said. "I get in for free, right?"

Amar chuckled, his belly quaking. "Oh, you'll be there," he said, "but you won't be partying. None of us will. We don't party for holidays, you see. We work. And I have just the job for you." His mouth became a smirk I didn't love and the bluish smoke he exhaled through his nostrils filled the space between us.

CHAPTER SEVEN

I open the Theater doors and come this close to getting trampled by a sexy stampede. I nearly pull my right hamstring as I leap to the side, barely avoiding injury as a fleet of shimmering heels clack and stomp past. With my shoulder pressed against the wall beside the entrance, I watch as at least two hundred people pour into the Theater, a mixture of curiosity and desire in their eyes.

The room radiates excitement. There are limitless possibilities here in the darkness. I see you at the bar, looking up, watching a beautiful black man's razor-defined abdominals glisten as the sweat trickles down his body. He's in the cage hanging four feet above the bar, gyrating, spinning, making eye contact with you every rotation. Somehow you look away and notice two tight waisted, busty dancers on the gogo platforms twenty feet above the crowd, grinding on the very railings preventing them from falling to their death.

The pulse of the bass pulls you. You hardly feel your feet touch the dancefloor as you climb the platform in the center of the dancefloor. Others are already there and you begin to move with them. You feel immersed in some sort of dark energy that intrigues your curiosity and moves your body for you. The feeling of doing something wrong which feels so right is at your fingertips.

You look around, but never see everything. The darkness is punctuated with beams of red light painting the crowd, freeze-framing only a slice of the picture. Flash—two genderless beings in black leather meet at the lips. Flash—a studded black paddle connects with the exposed ass of a person bent over a railing.

You're pulled in every direction towards the madness and suddenly your feet are carrying you off the platform and to the even darker edge of the room. *Fantasies will be fulfilled* flashes in a sultry red neon in your mind, though you're not sure if this was ever promised.

You get to table 105, but that's how I know it. To you it's just the booth closest to the stage. A man with a razor shaved head and sleek shoulder pads is playfully shocking a woman with the tips of his fingers. Some kind of device is wired to his hands and every caress sends jolts of electricity into her most sensitive skin. She is standing with her arms tied behind her head as he strokes her back and sides. Her shoulders tighten, the muscles flex taut, and her beautiful body tenses with every touch… but the closed eyes and gently open mouth are a vision of ecstasy.

Next to the electric pair is a dominatrix wearing a tight-fitted, latex nun outfit that ends where her buttcheeks begin. She's showing a sinful amount of skin in all the right places, which may add to her popularity: there is a line of people waiting for her to tie them up with special rope from Japan.

The swinging red light seems to show you where to go next. Now you're on the stage. Next to the DJ is a tall man wearing black leather gauntlets and matching pants. He's shirtless, and you trace his bulging veins from his forearms to his shoulders and chest. He's standing in front of a large wooden X, a flogger in each hand. There are leather restraints at each end of the X, empty for now. Of all the players in this strange game, this man is the most formidable. He radiates power and dominance; and from the way he surveys the Theater, he is obviously the head dominatrix in charge.

How could the darkness be so inviting? You think to yourself.

You don't have an answer. You just surrender to it. You close your eyes, reach to the sky, bite your lip, and get lost in the music.

Meanwhile, I'm still standing by the Theater door, taking it all in, and shaking my head (not unkindly). At this point in my life, it is so easy to spot the people who are obviously on copious amounts of Molly. They're the ones reaching for the stars, eyes closed, smiles transformed into something altogether different by their clenched jaws and grinding teeth. *Amateurs.*

I leave my post and slowly weave through the sweaty, pungent bodies on the dance floor, monitoring the crowd. A sight stops me dead in my tracks. A couple of my friends are dancing with a fit blonde woman wearing only a black thong and a tight black top that stops just below her nipples. She holds my gaze and smiles as her hips roll from side to side.

I begin to question just how important this job is to me. See, I've promised Juicy that I wouldn't so much as hold hands with anyone while I'm managing, let alone perform the kinds of things flashing through my mind now as I look at this goddess. But as all the blood drains from my brain and into my penis, taking all rational thought with it, my employment is becoming less and less of a priority. If someone offered me the choice to have sex with this stunning creature and get fired on the spot, I'd be blissfully unemployed right there on the dancefloor.

I start to walk towards her, the invisible lasso of her stare pulling me inexorably forward. Finally, I'm close enough. My smile wants to split my head in two. "I'm Lo-"

She never gets to hear the rest of my name because a beautiful tall man, no less stunning than she is, walks up and kisses her on the cheek about fourteen times. She closes her eyes tightly and I realize the smile for me paled in comparison to the one she has on now. I am desperately trying to not cry. He looks like he belongs in the pantheon of Norse demigods.

After kissing her, Sven, or whatever, finally notices me standing there and sticks out his hand. I shake it, mindful of not over squeezing angrily, and mumble through an introduction. I shake with the temptress next, letting my dreams fall aways with her hand, before turning around and walking away. There is no trace left of the excitement I felt just sixty seconds before. Ditty my hard-on.

Eyes closed, I let out a big exhale. Rational thinking returns. I look at the time. It's 10:38. I see Sabrina the bartender in position behind the Theater bar. *Perfect.* Her call time is 10:30. I'm not sure if she came in on time, but she's there now, efficiently taking care of customers, slinging drinks, and that's good enough.

Sabrina is a beautiful black woman covered in tats. She's got one of those "don't fuck with me" looks forever stamped on her features, due in no small part, I'm sure, to her double life. By day she's a clinical therapist; after the sun goes down she's a dominatrix-bartender.

None of our other women bartenders enjoy working the Theater bar for Love House. "Smells like pussy the whole shift," they complain. They're not wrong, either. The bouquet is entirely due to the communal Sybian, a vibrator in the shape of a saddle, which lives on the bar for the entire event. Sabrina, fortunately, is not like the other women bartenders: she loves that fucking thing. I mean, just look at her, a shaker full of mezcal margarita in her right hand, the sexy toy's intensity controller in her left!

I watch as she goes back and forth between her now-biggest fan and the customers at the bar. "Come for me baby. Yes. Come. Oh, yeahhh…" she almost screams to the brunette woman convulsing on the saddle, somehow maintaining a sexy voice while making herself heard over the dj and the crowd. Sabrina snaps back when she notices a guy grab the margarita and begin to walk away without paying. All the sexy come-for-me is gone in an instant as she reaches over the bar and grabs the guy by the shoulder, stopping him in his tracks. "Hello? And ahem, tip your bartender." After verifying that the payment went through after he dipped his credit card in the POS, Sabrina turns back to the moaning rider without missing a beat. "Yeah, you close? You like all these people watching you come? You dirty slut…"

It takes more than just a dominatrix barmaid to ensure that the Sybian situation runs smoothly. Today's Sybian monitor is Sandra, one of our sexy, jack-of-all-trades employees. As Sybian monitor, it is her responsibility to replace the plastic wrap on the saddle between riders, and to help the various cowgirls achieve climax by any means necessary—choking, slapping, nipple licking/nuzzling/biting, hair pulling, whispering sweet nothings, whatever.

Sandra and Sabrina are an especially effective team. Having serviced half the women in the club, they're now working on a dark haired beauty with café au lait skin. She could be Hispanic or West Indian, Brazilian, maybe. Her lips are slightly parted and her eyes roll wildly, like a frightened horse, as she shakes her lustrous black mane. Sabrina increases the Sybian's intensity then lets off, driving her wild, as Sandra pulls the woman's hair with one hand and pinches her left nipple in the other. The gorgeous rider's moans have blended with the music like strawberries in a smoothie. A small group of people have stopped dancing and are fixated on this unplanned performance.

A young blonde woman wearing a flattering little black dress walks right up to Sandra, as single-minded as a heat-seeking missile, hardly giving Sybian chick a second glance. "Who's the DJ?"

Sandra's deft fingers don't even break their rhythm. "I don't know, honey. I'm just here to make girls come," she says, with a touch of dismissive contempt in her voice.

God bless this woman.

10:45. My phone vibrates. I've received two texts. Sparky, the Onyx Room attendant, needs my help. This is potentially bad. But the host just confirmed that the parties who booked all three reserved tables for the night have just arrived.

The tables take priority. Collectively, someone dropped five thousand dollars on them. It's a bit tricky, though. I give the black haired beauty one last look (she's laugh-crying through her hair, which is now hanging in front of her face in wet strands) and pull myself away from Orgasm Village. In the kitchen I am delightfully pleased to see the servers grabbing menus, preparing to meet and seat the high-rolling table folks. I'm overjoyed. I've managed countless Love Houses, and nothing gets me more aroused than a team that's on the ball. Well, almost nothing.

I unlock the top shelf liquor cabinet, grab a bottle of Don Julio 1942 and hand it to Romeo. The fancy cactus juice is for Adam's table. "Only the cheap shit for that dude, huh?" Romeo chuckles.

Romeo and I share a knowing smile. We've known him for a while, and agree that Adam owns an oil refinery, or something. The guy always comes in with a group of super models, buys the most expensive bottle on the menu, then hands us twenty hundred-dollar bills and asks for ones (he loves to make it rain onto the crowd). Every time I see the dollars floating above the dancefloor I feel both excited and repulsed, but the crowd is usually into it. Last time it happened I watched a girl in a sexy elf costume pick up what must have been 500 bucks, crumple them into the shape of a basketball, and continue dancing with an extra spring in her step.

The second table is Dimitri's, a birthday celebration. Should be pretty chill. We'll give him a cupcake with a candle in the hot tub or something.

Table number three is the nightlife nightmare: The Bachelorettes. I've been here for fifty bachelorette parties, and I shit you not, not one of them went well. A sure recipe for disaster, it's like they're designed to turn into a flaming dumpster fire of a night. The expectations of the bride-to-be, the responsibility of her girlfriends to give her a one-of-a-kind night of debauchery that she'll remember for the rest of her life… something—sometimes everything—is bound to go wrong.

Every bachelorette party starts out well (at least from my experience and anecdotal evidence). The girls meet at one of their houses, generally the nicest one. Morgan, the one from Connecticut, who lives by herself in a two-bedroom in Chelsea? Yeah, hers. It's at Morgan's where they finish dusting their upper chests with glitter, pin on their wigs and/or extensions, take selfies, drink champagne and/or a case of White Claw, and psych each other up with talk of dick and how much of it the bride-to-be will have in her face throughout the night. Sometimes this spills over into the Uber XL Suburban, where the party shoots booze "sneakily" and belts out off-key Beyonce jams. So far, so good, and there is not a ten-second interval in which a shrill cackle doesn't pierce the air. The driver, grateful for not getting pulled over, deposits the tipsy queens—for this is how they now see themselves—in front of the club. Their shoulders are back, their chests are proud, and the clack of their spike heels is extra loud as they stomp to the front of the line. They're very happy to share with the plebes in line that they are, in fact, a bachelorette party, and have a table. Sometimes they just yell, "VIP's coming through!" Once they're inside, we greet them, seat them, and get them a bottle of their choosing. A lot of these girls have never been to Yes House. Their eyes light up when they realize how edgy they'll look once they tag the location on their socials. At the table, shots and squeals commence with no delay. The girls then alternate between dancing with the masses and taking selfies at their table. The second, third, and fourth rounds of shots are gobbled down within the first hour of their arrival, because apparently the way to have the best night of your life is to drink like a high-schooler whose parents went away for the weekend.

The bottle, once so full of joy and liquid promise, becomes an empty vessel. Noticing this, Romeo and I stop by the table with a menu. They take a look, confer quickly but noisily, and arrive at the unanimous choice: Patron Reposado. Like, of course. Romeo and I exchange a look, knowing that this will be the source of all the trouble later on. I nod and Romeo explains slowly and clearly, making sure to make eye contact with everyone but the bride: "That bottle is not included in the original quote of the reservation and will cost you 600 dollars, plus tax and tip. Are you okay with that?"

The girls share a sloppy and mischievous glance. The bride-to-be, as is her right, curse, and privilege, abstains from all decisions or matters of money. Her friends *know* what's best for her on this night. After a couple more seconds of deliberation, they all bob their sparkly faces so vigorously their fluorescent wigs nearly fall off.

Romeo and I deliver the bottle, there is much applause and whoo-hoos, and the party rages on.

This is when the emotional roller coaster begins its ratcheting climb. Here we go. One minute they are dancing and laughing, the next they are comforting the bride-to-be who's sobbing uncontrollably about the brown colored suits her fiancé chose for his groomsmen. Once that's settled, they are twerking on their table for all to see. Fast forward a few minutes and they are sitting at the table, arms crossed, complaining to the server. "You were gone for, like, two hours!" (He had checked on them 20 minutes before). Romeo apologizes and asks if there's anything they need. "Nothing," the pink-haired one replies, "Just making sure you didn't forget about us."

This cycle repeats itself many times for the next few hours until the second bottle is finished and the club is about to close.

Now it's time for the bill. I send Romeo to the table and say a prayer for him after he leaves. *Please God, don't let these bachelorettes tear Romeo to shreds. I can't afford to lose another server, especially one as good as Romeo…* He's hardly gone five seconds before I head to the table myself, worried for his safety.

I watch as Romeo holds out the bill in a black faux-leather holder to the rainbow-haired posse. The bachelorette's friends fight over it like it's a tossed bouquet. The one with pink hair gets hold of it first. She opens it wide for all but the future bride to see. It takes but a second for things to get ugly. They turn Super-Saiyan—colored wigs extending to great lengths. They turn on Romeo with eyes full of betrayal and vengeance and the yelling commences. Romeo, self-preservation instinct keen and undulled by tequila, begins to distance his face from the danger zone. "What do you mean this is the bill?" says the one with green hair. "How could you do this to her on her bachelorette night?" the blue haired one follows. "You are a cheating monster! You're ruining everything!" the pink haired one yells. Romeo is defenseless against the nine women who are fully convinced that he is trying to rip off the future bride, despite the bill actually being just two bottles, tax, tip, and total…

I let them go at him for a bit then squeeze in. "Alright, everyone!," I mostly-yell, and the girls pipe down. "Everything is going to be okay! I'm the manager and I'm here to help." Once I have their attention I slowly go over the bill with the bachelorettes. I pretend to sympathize with them, telling them I understand their frustration and that the bill is, in fact, confusing (blatant lying usually helps in these situations). Jesus shows up right on cue, just as we rehearsed. He sets a tray of shots on the small round table just as I finish explaining the baffling tab. This tray has a name: "The Diffuser."

After a few moments deciding whether to accept the peace offering (and Jesus and me praying they do), they begrudgingly take the shots. The pink-haired one pays the bill with a black metal credit card, they sulk as she signs the receipt, almost trying to rip the paper with her signature, then they all storm out—as upset as the last bachelorette party.

This scenario had repeated itself time and time again until we finally deemed bachelorette parties an occupational safety risk and implemented a solution. They have to pay a week before the event. Plus, if they want more alcohol the night of, they have to pay *before* receiving the bottle, which completely goes against the "fun now, consequences later" customer mindset we profit on. Normally, we avoid this at all costs because when people pre-pay they rarely end up ordering as many bottles as they would if they were to pay after. Makes sense, right? Once you've spent a cool thousand dollars, you'll think twice before ordering more booze. This takes some serious dough out of the club's and servers' pockets, but we had had enough. We'll take the pay cut and walk away without the bruises.

Let's hope tonight everyone is peaceable.

Back on the floor, Krystal and I weave through sweaty bodies, making it out the front door slightly damp. Outside, we find Lacera "consenting" all three parties and informing them of the perks of table service: the VIP bathroom, hot-tub bookings, front row seats to watch the Sybian, etc. I stand aside and give a nod to Fidel, the second head of security.

Fidel is an essential part of the team. At six-foot-four and three hundred pounds, he's a friendly giant who, without hesitation (or my consent), would carry me home if I twisted my ankle. He drives me home nearly every night, in fact, despite my house being a ten-minute walk from the club. He's hardworking but joyous, always saying, "good morning," every time I walk past him at some ungodly hour.

During his first month at YES his family's house in Queens burned down. Some of his family died in the fire. He had lost everything.

At the time no one really knew Fidel, him being new and all, but that didn't matter to us. We organized a GoFundMe campaign and a food drive. In three days we raised $3000 and brought in multiple bins of canned food. Hundreds of people donated, despite only a few actually knowing the guy. It brought a lot of hope to Fidel, and he's been a loyal member of the family ever since.

Fidel opens the Patio door for Krystal as she grabs Adam's hand and leads him inside. Lacera takes Dimitri, leaving me with the bachelorette party. I hold my hand high in the air like a tour guide outside the Met, and move through the club at a turtle's pace. I definitely do not want to lose one of these girls in this dungeon of sexual deviants. We eventually arrive at table 106, the booth next to the Theater bar and kitchen entrance. Romeo is there with a menu and a smile with too many teeth showing. I melt away. The bottle team has it from here.

My pocket vibrates. I take my phone out and see that the Onyx Room attendant has texted me again, this time with a triple question mark.

I quickly type out, "Sorry, got caught up. I'm on my way," and hit the blue arrow to send.

I take a quick peek to make sure that Daisy, the second bartender, is back on time and behind the Theater bar. She is the tall, lean blonde jumping up and down and punching the air like Rocky. It's her warmup and I've seen it before. She claims it "gets her in the zone," but I know it has more to do with the twenty or thirty em-gee's of Adderall she eats before every shift. I shake my head. Nobody would ever compare our crew to suit-and-tie nine-to-fivers, that's for damn sure. Grateful that Daisy in is place (albeit a bit jittery), I move towards the Onyx room.

The Patio is a kinky speakeasy full of laughter, smoke, and consensual booty smacks. Red light reflects black leather and white cigarettes. Almost all the people out there are gorgeous and wearing harnesses and matching collars, smiling into each other's eyes.

I spot Juicy speaking to two hotties, a burning cigarette between two fingers. You can almost see waves of charm flowing from him as he runs the fingers of his non-smoking hand through thick salt and pepper hair. I look away before we make eye contact. I'm not ready to speak to him, and won't be until I have an answer for him. The pressure of deciding has me feeling nauseous. You would think his proposal would be a simple one for me to make a decision about, Yes House being my family for over two years and all, but it isn't. After recent events, I'm not even sure what family is anymore...

"Come repent for your sins! Ha!" This snaps me out of my thoughts and I look around for the source of the hearty bellow. By the nook with the fake white marble angel statues is a short, stoutman looking like he just left a World of Warcraft fan club meeting—leather pants, a red tunic, epaulets, and a helmet

(Christ, is it really metal?). Two thick golden braids hang behind his ears. His bear paw of a hand grips the handle of a large wooden paddle. A small crowd of people with enticing smiles stands around him as he repeats his invitation in a deep, sonorous voice, adding another "Ha!"

I decide to check this guy out and make sure he's not some sort of creep. He's not one of our guys, and a random dude in a horned helmet wielding a large paddle could mean trouble. I come closer and see his free hand resting on the small of a large woman's porcelain white back. She's wearing a large, tightly laced corset and black leggings. She's bent over a stool, face pressed against the belly of one of the angels. With a whoosh the paddle lands on her colossal booty. The sound of impact is admittedly satisfying, and both the paddler and the… repenter, seem to be enjoying themselves. Neither is an amateur, that much is clear. Between each swing he raises the paddle high above his head with a roaring laugh before bringing it down on the now pink bottom. With every strike her head jerks against the angel's belly and ripples race up from her cheeks all the way to her neck.

I decide that the situation, for now, at least, looks kosher. I slip behind the group of spectators and head towards the Onyx Room. I almost make it there, too, but stop short when I see Carlos Surfista posted up on the wooden staircase leading to the hot tub. He's changed back into his normal pirate attire, but kept the silicone titties on. Now he looks like a Jack Sparrow who's about to get fucked by Tommy Lee. He's got a clipboard in one hand and the wine glass he brings from home in the other. He takes his drinking seriously, and it appears tonight he's drinking rosé.

"We ready, Carlos?" I call out to him. It's after 11 and the hot tub should be open.

"Yes matey, soon's we get some refreshments!" His cheeky smile extends to the twirled tips of his mustache. He knows I know what he wants: more rosé. Bottles of it. And rum, of course, but he knows I won't give him rum so the rosé will have to do.

"They're on their way," I assure him, unable to look up from his peachy double d's. "Start her up! These dirty scoundrels need a bath!" My pirate accent is embarrassing, but what am I gonna do. I take off an imaginary hat and bow to Carlos, then finally step into the Onyx Room.

Sparky, dressed as a naughty schoolgirl, is placing cushions on the floor for the "movie theater" experience. It's cozy in here—black folding chairs sit along three of the walls as the cushions from The Foreplay now cover every inch of the floor, a small sea of red fluffiness. Another one of Amar's vintage films is being projected onto a screen that takes up an entire wall. A pharaoh is pumping into Cleopatra in a grand stone room, in an Egyptian palace, presumably. Just missionary, nothing fancy, until the camera zooms out to reveal two giant servants lifting the pharaoh's ankles back and forth, effectively thrusting on his behalf.

Sparky is relieved to see me. He needs an empty bucket for trash, a walkie, a bathroom break, and, most importantly, alcohol. I respect his candor. I give him some drink tickets and my blessing, and tell him to go pee and grab the things while I watch the room.

Sparky departs fast enough to send a breeze up his plaid skirt, which flares up to reveal a white, hairy ass. Before the door closes I see a small line of people already waiting to come in. People are excitedly speculating, curious as to what's inside.

In the past this room has been home to dungeons, naked disco parties, peep shows, and other fun happenings. My personal favorite: naked disco. There was something special about a room of naked strangers dancing the night away. The vibe was joyous and pretty much platonic (except for Tyson getting a blowjob from Cora's boyfriend during a Whitney Houston track).

I walk outside to schmooze with the people in line, but my phone is vibrating off the hook with messages. The bottle service babes are messaging about bottles while security deals with "an awkward creeper, not predator." The second got my attention. A Consenticorn noticed the guy following groups of women and staring at them as they danced. The women just danced with their backs to him, hoping he would get the message. After a few minutes they moved to the other side of the dance floor. This didn't seem to stop him from getting close and standing there perfectly still and staring, too close for comfort, with a blank look on his face.

Fidel ended up walking him outside and having a chat. He explained how his behavior was making some people feel very uncomfortable. The man didn't see that he was doing anything wrong, but promised to try and be less creepy.

This gets kind of tricky. This is clearly someone we don't want in the club, especially on an explicitly-sexy night like this, but he didn't touch anyone, and according to Fidel he was dead sober, so we gave him a warning and set him loose. Except now he was definitely a person of interest to security, management, and the Consenticorns.

I look up from my phone to see two young men in front of me, holding each other's sweaty hand. They are both short, clearly gym rats by the look of their toned arms and eight-pack abs. I can see all this because they're wearing nothing but black speedos. It's cold out here, but their clenched jaws, dilated pupils, and thin layers of sweat glistening across their foreheads tell me they're chemically bundled against it.

"What's inside this time?" One of them asks.

I smile: half mystery, half mischief, full enticement. I search for a description worthy of their state. "I am delighted you asked, my beautiful friends! Behind this here door is an over-the-moon ride on a cloud of lush, red cushions… and a viewing experience that will leave you boys feeling positively… *tumescent*," I finish archly.

Their faces radiate light as if in a candle's glow. Over their shoulders I see Sparky returning, a drink with a lime garnish in his left hand. He thanks me with a kiss on the cheek, his bristly beard tickling my face. "The movie theater is open!" he announces, and throws open the door with a theatrical bow. I give them a wink, and the speedo boys slink inside. I decide to do a lap around the club.

I reflect, a bit sadly, that as keeper and "protector" of the space I see everything differently. Rarely am I wowed by an aerial performance or find myself blissfully lost on the dancefloor anymore. Now I just notice every detail of the operation—where the staff are positioned, whether each guest is enjoying themselves, is the bass too high and overdriving the speakers, and so on…

Outside the Onyx Room six naked people skip past me, on their way from the Patio shower to the hot tub. Droplets of water shine on their skin and they each have a clean white towel in their hands. Their private bits are visible to all, perhaps a bit affected by the brisk night air. They don't care and I love that they don't.

The guy at the spanking station is still slapping away, the sounds of the paddle-on-flesh and moans filling the Patio. His audience has grown. They look entertained. To the right, three black men with six-pack abs and white jockstraps are the first customers at the Patio bar, now open.

I walk out the exit door to find Fidel at his post. "Good morning," he says as I pass. I smile at him over my shoulder and head to the main entrance. Consenticorns dazzle patrons in groups of five with their illuminated horns and consent speeches. Tacks is fast-walking up and down the line, trying to scan everyone's tickets before they reach Crius at the door. How's that for sexy? A 60-year old man fiddling with a smartphone while breathing heavier than a 1960s Buick as you patiently hold your own iPhone to be scanned, fingers getting cold. Hot, right?

Crius is at the door checking IDs, using both a flashlight and black light on each one. I step past him and through the gold doors. Harlequin is collecting cash from three women wearing black corsets and black bunny masks with golden specks on the ears. After the money is in the drawer, she stamps the backs of their hands. They head straight to the bar, grabbing each other in their excitement, all bending over the bar to reveal bunny tail butt plugs.

Three bartenders are at their stations, all pumping out margaritas in less than twenty seconds—lime and sugar bottles in one hand, tequila in the other. A quick, vigorous shake is followed by a perfect pour. Bunny mask crew orders theirs. In between the bartenders is Armando emptying a garbage bag full of ice into the ice bins. He scans the shelves for bottles running low then runs out to the server station.

Once the bunnies get their drinks they bee-line it for the photobooth. More of a photo stage, really. Here Zester is sweating buckets as he jumps around his set of a well lit, black velvet couch. Currently, he's taking photos of a group of four in lingerie reenacting a scene from Amar's pharaoh film. I move through the server station into the kitchen, where bright-eyed bottle girls are gossiping about one of our "gay" bartenders actually being bisexual. Also in the kitchen are two barbacks, who have actual work to do, stacking clean glasses into black porter trays to be brought to the bars. Licky, the Nigerian dishwasher, passes the glasses after drying them. He is working through a mountain of glassware, putting load after load into the industrial machine belching out great clouds of steam that fill the kitchen.

I leave the humid kitchen by way of the narrow, white-tiled hallway, tracking black footprints in my wake, and emerge in the Theater. The bachelorette party at table 106 is going notably well: the women are dancing on top of the couch and the bride-to-be has a bottle of Grey Goose in her fist, which she's holding so far above her head it's nearly hitting the tech booth. A porter grabs several empty cups from the table then squeezes through the few hundred near-naked bodies grinding up on each other, stopping every few seconds to pick up an empty cup or can. He makes his way to the stage, where one of our giant security guards stands in front of a thin black curtain and between the staff-only areas—DJ booth, employee bathroom, backstage—and anyone not authorized to visit them. The security guard waves to the two bartenders for their attention, probably trying to get some water, with no luck. Heads cocked, they are too mesmerized by the shadowbox performance. Black against a white sheet, a silhouette neck of a woman kneeling before him. With his free hand he slaps the girl in the face. Her head snaps sideways upon impact, then returns to its original position, ready for another. I cringe a bit. This isn't my cup of tea. If the bartenders' wide eyes and smiles are any indication, I'd say it's theirs...

Nearly seven feet of bald security guard moves to let me behind the back curtain and into the DJ booth. The DJ bobs his head, headphones halfway on, while twisting knobs on the decks. Beside him is the DJ liaison, who doesn't look like she's *liaising* a damn thing but just standing there. *She's helping somehow,* I try to reassure myself.

Across the room I see the tech team in their booth, open mouthed, pressing lit-up colorful buttons. From here, it looks like they're all just playing a video game. I move backstage and find it super crowded and chaotic. Most performers are changing clothes, taking shots, and idly chatting; while two seem to be having an emotional moment in the corner, their sulky mouths and smeared eyeliner dead giveaways. To me it looks like an out-of-control mess, but Koochy has his clipboard in hand and seems confident that everything is going according to plan.

I once again reflect on how different my experience is from that of the people cutting it up and shaking it out on the floor—from *my* experience when I was one of them! Here and now I almost forget there is a wild party going on, right in front of my eyes to see, my nose to smell, my ears to hear, my hands to touch. I only see the pieces instead of the whole puzzle. After all these nights on the other side of the clipboard I just see information: this is going right, these numbers are on, those customers are satisfied, that barback needs to hustle more. Data, emotionless, neither fun nor boring. Amongst the hundreds of dancing bodies I notice the one staff member not in position. Over the roar of the crowd, the voices of my friends, and the stories the night is writing… I hear the digitized words of the security team in my earpiece.

Maybe I should enjoy myself more, I solemnly think, and immediately after, *But how?*

Crius's voice crackles in my ear. "Loki Loki, we got a problem,"

11:21pm. Shit hits the fan.

CHAPTER EIGHT

I had dreamt of the amazing world of New York City nightlife. My new reality was far less dreamy. The twice-daily, three-train commute, combined with back-breaking labor for peanuts, was starting to wear me down. When things looked bleakest, I tried self-talk. *You'll work your way up,* I encouraged, *Sure, you're doing all the shit work now, but imagine all the possibilities coming your way!*

Admittedly, these keep-it-positive efforts didn't usually work. On a day when I could really use some good news, though, Dan Rockies delivered and boosted my spirits.

"Yes!" I exclaimed. "When do I move in?"

"If you survive next week, it's yours November 1st," he replied.

Dan was referring to Palace of Gods, but I was too excited about his news to think about the epic party. He and Meloza were moving out of Strom's, and their room would be up for grabs next month. The apartment, only five blocks away from Yes House, was a four-bedroom duplex with a rooftop. *The* Yes House after-hours spot, legend had it that in the past year an estimated 200,000 cigarettes had been smoked on that roof between the hours of sunrise and noon.

All that was mostly in the past, though. Now the apartment was known as a quiet, mature household, where the occasional gathering was a low-key affair. Fine with me. I was perfectly happy to live a quiet home life a stone's throw from my job and seek entertainment elsewhere.

I gave Dan Rockies a hug, my cheek pressed against his chest as we squeezed each other tight, and he walked out of the gold double doors and out onto Yefferson Street. He would normally never be there at 10am on a Monday, but with Halloween weekend around the corner it was all-hands-on-deck from dawn till, well, dawn. Palace of Gods was more important than your family, pets, personal hygiene, physical and mental health. Say goodbye to your Netflix account, because for the next week you were going to be working. Period.

Starting early that morning, the maintenance team, barbacks, production staff, decor squad and I began to pack a few dusty box trucks with enough supplies to furnish and host a sexy party in Times Square. We emptied half the basement and most of the offsite storage. Condoms and dildoes of every shape and color; furniture and pillows; mannequins of every gender; rugs and steeldeck staging; tools and hardware; booze and mixers; and enough rolls of gaffer's tape to fill a bathtub. Also, our porcelain bathtub. We packed enough fake flowers to cover an entire fake spring meadow. And Christmas lights, because nothing says "sex party" like a million twinkling colorful lights.

The next morning, Safari Tahoe, a production manager, began to drive the truck of booze to the Paper Factory Hotel, where the event was to be held. He made it about fifteen feet before the truck broke down in the intersection directly in front of Yes House. Traffic was backed up for blocks. It was a nightmare. We spent most of the day unloading and loading everything from the broken one.

"Pick that up and put it over there! Stop slacking!" Sable yelled at me. It seemed to be the only phrase I heard that day.

After the fiftieth "Stop slacking!" I decided to fight back, however passive-aggressively, and take bathroom breaks in the restroom farthest from her, the one in the Theater. The walk gave me a total of sixty extra seconds away from Sable's active aggression. Perched on the stage were the head honchos finalizing event details. I listened to their muffled voices as I took my time in the tiny cell of a bathroom dimly lit by an illuminated fishbowl.

On the other side of the wooden door I heard Cora's voice. "Questions that still need to be answered: Do we have enough alcohol and mixers for six thousand people? How about enough water to prevent two thousand people on ecstasy from dehydrating and dying? Do we have sufficient staging for eight different music areas? Have all the sound systems been tested? What's our Port-a-Potty situation? Hundreds of packages are showing up here—do we have a system for logging them, checking them off, and ensuring they find their way to the right department? Lastly, it's not a question of *if* something goes shitways, but when, and how badly. What are our contingency plans for these situations?"

This was all above my production-assistant pay grade—I was a lowly pawn in the big game—but even hearing these conversations made me feel like I was more than my minuscule role. These people had real power, big decisions to make. Decisions that would affect literally thousands of people. It was so… enticing. I wanted to be a bigger part of it.

"Loki! Where are you?" Sable's voice echoed through the Theater.

Fuck me. I washed my hands and returned to the trucks.

After everything was finally reloaded into the new truck we were ready to start setting up the venue. Just one day into preparing for the biggest event any of us had ever dreamed of and we were already slumping around with droopy faces and glassy eyes. Sleep was a nostalgic commodity at this point.

Things were bleak enough for us grunts when Amar shared some unexpected news: the Fire Department wanted to cancel half the party. "Something to do with the warehouse not having the most up-to-date sprinkler system," he said (a month later we would find out there was no sprinkler system at all). If this happened, we'd have to refund more than three thousand tickets.

If the FDNY had their way, we'd be fucked. New Yorkers looked forward to Halloween the way Brazilians looked forward to Carnaval. Yes House could not be the ones to crush their spirits, we just couldn't…

The Chief of the FDNY wanted to discuss possible solutions for the sprinkler issue. Amar, who could negotiate with a bunch of nuns until they bought expired condoms, was our last hope, and would take the meeting.

We were anxiously awaiting the Chief's decision and hanging outside the club. It was a pleasant sunny day and I leaned my head against the truck, soaking up what was probably the last warmth of the year. I closed my eyes and rested my body against the cool steel. I was so exhausted it felt like a fancy Swedish mattress.

An hour later Amar arrived back at the club. Despite his best efforts, the Fire Chief's decision was firm: nix the warehouse. Our morales fell so hard you could almost hear a Wile E. Coyote slide whistle echo through the alleys of warehouses. We had been working so hard…

In classic Amar fashion, he was utterly unperturbed by this development, and immediately began dishing out instructions. I was to drive one of the 26' trucks to the Paper Factory Hotel for immediate unloading, and start setting up the space. I expressed my reluctance, telling him how little truck-driving experience I had (zero), to which he responded, "Get me a pack of Camel Blues on the way. Don't be late." He fished around for some keys in the pocket of his holey jeans and tossed them to me.

I pulled myself up into the cab, wiped my sweaty palms on my pants, put the key in the ignition, and started the truck. The motor rumbled to life. It sounded like a garbage disposal that someone put marbles into. I adjusted the side view mirrors, seeing what seemed like fifty yards of truck in them. I had never driven anything bigger than my van before. This truck was about ten times the size. I took several deep breaths, put the shifter in gear, eased off the brake, and rolled away from Yes House.

I continued my yogic breathing as I drove the beast through the congested streets and highways of Brooklyn and Queens. It was either that or have a panic attack.

I gripped the steering wheel hard enough to leave a permanent imprint. I was so stressed, my eyes hurt. I don't think I blinked once during the whole trip, I just kept checking my blind spots and praying. An accident now would spell doom for me, for Palace of Gods, for Yes House—maybe the planet.

Forty excruciating minutes later I turned off the engine. Inside the hotel's staff parking lot, I allowed myself to slump in my seat and close my eyes. I hadn't gotten Amar's cigarettes. Maybe he forgot.

Tuesday evening, and we were about to begin setting up. I looked up at the hotel, five stories tall and taking up an entire block, and walked in. The space was sleek and modern. It had stained concrete floors, multi-colored stained hardwood walls, leather couches, tropical plants, and several avant garde sculptures that were taller than me.

There was a London-style red phone booth next to the reception, and standing next to it were the two production managers I was to be working under for the next few days: Spunk and Safari Tahoe.

Spunk pressed his lean frame against the reception desk as he flirted with the receptionist. He had light brown hair in a bun and a mustache twisted up at the ends. He said something that got the receptionist to smile. She then whispered something in his ear which made him cackle so loudly I flinched and covered up like a boxer.

Safari Tahoe did not look like Spunk. His bushy beard and stout figure made him look like a pot farmer from Northern California. Tahoe was another Bay Area transplant. Nearly everything that came out of his mouth was a joke, which was refreshing after Sable's iron-fisted mouth.

First thing Tahoe made me do was unload fake flowers and place them all over the venue. Up and down the stairs I went, running. My quads burned and my ass quivered. I had never gone up and down so many stairs in my entire life.

With the help of a few other production assistants, the three of us unloaded an entire truck and began to transform the hotel into a Disney Mansion.

Our workday ended around midnight when Amar called, this time with good news.

With less than 72 hours before the event, Amar had secured another location. We wouldn't have to cancel the party, after all. Cheers erupted and fake flowers flew as we celebrated.

The mirth did not last, though: we quickly realized that we now had to move half of what we already unloaded to another venue. Shoulders and expressions slumped.

The tasks of installing hundreds of lights, multi-stage sound, a truckful of decor, and ten fully stocked bars in a different venue was daunting. Doing it in the next three days? Absolutely demoralizing. Not that I really had to think about that part of it, but how would the administrative team redirect thousands of ticket holders to a whole new venue? The owners were really out of their minds this time.

After Amar's call, the production team and I shared an Uber XL back to Bushwick and caught a few hours of shut-eye before returning bright and early Wednesday morning. We reloaded one of the trucks and set off for the new spot. Grand Prospect Hall was located in South Brooklyn, an inconvenient 45-minute, traffic congested drive from the Paper Factory Hotel. I didn't have to drive, thank God, and was able to catch a thirty minute nap on the way.

It was noon when we pulled into the parking lot next to the venue. The decor, maintenance, bar, sound and lighting teams were already there, standing beside their trucks. Like us, they were dressed in all black. Together we looked like a motley, somewhat out of shape team of commandos ready for a covert mission. We quietly took in the sight of the four-floor, white building. *This is no warehouse,* I thought. It looked more like a millionaire's 19th-century mansion on a faraway estate. We gawked and smoked another minute, then went in. A receptionist met us in the foyer and gave us a tour.

Our eyes lit up as they gazed upon a marble butterfly staircase that wrapped around a golden altar, something you'd expect to be set in Olympia leading to Zeus' throne room. Hallways went in every direction then split into smaller hallways, each leading to a high-ceilinged room bigger than my whole apartment. There was exquisite art everywhere—wood carved animals, ten-foot tall Neoclassical and American-Colonialism paintings with golden frames, bronze sculptures of giraffes and elephants, and marvelous antiques and treasures from faraway places and long-ago cultures. Some of the rooms had pristine hard-wood flooring, while others had Moroccan red and blue carpets. All were beautifully lit by delicate bronze light fixtures on the walls.

The place was stunning, inside and out, but the real jaw dropper was the ballroom. Every floor had a garland-wrapped mezzanine that looked down on it. Larger than half a football field, it had scratchless hardwood floors and a stage large enough for a

100-person orchestra. More than fifty-feet above, three UFO-sized chandeliers hung from the ceiling.

Some of us tittered with excitement while others were stunned mute by the opulence of the space, but we were all thinking the same thing: *We're going to destroy this place.*

Immediately after the tour, we went to work with our same speed and precision of our 10 o'clock flip at Yes House. Five sound guys hauled in massive speakers on dollies and dispersed them around the venue. Five lighting guys wheeled in giant metal crates of gear into the main ballroom and began to set it up. Ten production staff worked tirelessly to unload the trucks and distribute everything from couches and staging to extensions cords and dildos. Five maintenance guys rushed to set up electricity and wifi hotspots for the ten different bars scattered throughout the labyrinth. Five barbacks began building the actual bars.

The venue, while dazzling, was also ancient. Multiple issues presented themselves within the first hour of setup.

The one elevator was a manually operated, brass cage that accommodated one person and a suitcase (if the person was skinny). This meant a lot of dragging heavy, cumbersome shit up many flights of stairs.

Built at the end of the 19th century, the Hall simply wasn't designed for a party that required more electricity than a small midwestern city. It was easier to find a million dollar painting than a working outlet. The nearest Wifi was a Starbucks half a mile away. The massive building had no sound system, apart from one room on the first floor in which opera music quietly floated down from the ceiling. It was downright eerie. I asked several Hall staff about it. None of them knew what I was talking about. The fine hairs at the base of my neck still stand up when I think about it.

As we were setting up, an elderly man in a historically-cut suit emerged from somewhere. I swear, nobody saw him come in through any traditional door. What little hair he had left was white and slicked back, framing his wide forehead and big lizard eyes which stared out half-lidded from beneath his bristly white brows. Picture Mr. Burns from The Simpsons and add a decade (or three?). He introduced himself as Mr. Stern, the owner of the venue for the past forty years.

Mr. Stern not only didn't do us any favors, but he seemed to go out of his way to make our lives more difficult. On the day before our event, he refused to turn the lights on in the venue for us. He said it cost thirty bucks to run the lights during the day. Juicy, tamping down his frustration so hard his left eye began to twitch, reached into a pocket of his Diesel jeans, took out a wad of cash, peeled two twenties and offered it to him. Mr. Stern refused the money and Juicy flounced off. We continued to work in the semi-dark, with some people using headlamps.

Ten minutes later, all the lights turned on. Maybe the parsimonious old fuck had a change of heart, but more likely he just wanted to let everyone know who was the boss.

About an hour later I was hanging out in the ballroom with a group of production folks. We were chatting by the snacks-and-water table during our first break of the day when I felt a steely grip on my arm. I stopped mid-sentence to look down and see Mr. Stern latched onto me like a buzzard.

"How long has Grand Prospect Hall been here?" he asked. Before I could respond he proudly answered the question himself. "Eighty years. And how long have I been working here?" His reptilian eyes never left mine or blinked.

"I don't know," I said, knowing, but wanting to give him the pride and joy of the grand reveal.

"Forty years!" Mr. Stern said, triumphant, looking at us as if daring us to challenge him. His eyes grew wide and he grinned unkindly. Forget lizard—the man looked downright extraterrestrial. He just stood there. Unsure of what else to do, I congratulated him, and he walked off, still smiling like he won an argument.

The grueling setup continued as the hours to the event counted down. The day was a blur of thousands of stairs punctuated by the occasional inane "conversation" with Mr. Stern. While we were at the Hall, the other half of the team slaved away at Paper Factory Hotel. Like many of Amar's projects, what seemed impossible a couple of days ago was coming together. Now, on the night before the event, the stages and bars were nearly completed, the already-grand Hall was dressed to the nines, and all the ticket holders had been notified of the venue change. This party was going to happen, after all.

I got home around midnight and passed out the second my face hit the pillow. It was a beautiful rest until six in the morning came along. My phone alarm screamed in my ear and I screamed back. Eventually, I rolled out of bed with a grunt and put on my all-black outfit, brushed my teeth, applied too much Old Spice deodorant (Aqua Reef edition), and ran out the door.

By 6:55 I was stepping around dog shits and last night's vomit stains on Bushwick sidewalks as I walked wearily to the club from the train station. The day before, Amar told me to grab something important from Yes House at seven in the morning. I wasn't going to let him down.

I was through the front door at seven on the dot, already dialing Amar's number. He answered right away.

"Hey Amar, I'm at Yes House. What do you need?"

"Oh, shit. Now I can't remember." he said calmly in his raspy voice. There was silence on the line for three frustrating seconds. "Hmm… Oh, yeah! I need my makeup case. It's black, by the office door. Grab it. See you soon." He hung up without waiting for my response.

Outfuckingstanding. I'm here at seven goddamned a.m. on what may be the longest workday and biggest event of the year to get your motherfucking makeup case? Just beautiful. Really? I rolled my eyes and took two deep breaths. On my way to the office I walked by the cleaner, who was mopping music and blasting reggae from this phone. I found Amar's black makeup case, which weighed at least twenty pounds, and made my way towards the Patio exit.

I was a step away from the door when I heard a rustling sound behind me, by the Onyx Room. *Unusual,* I thought, as only the cleaner should have been there at that hour. I decided to investigate and followed the sound into coat check.

Juicy, eyes bloodshot, was throwing rubber-banded bundles of cash, each larger than my fist, from a large black garbage bag into a three-by-three-foot black safe. It looked like a scene from a movie—the police banging down the door of the gangster's house as he's desperately trying to hide all the cash before they break in. Juicy looked so stressed I thought he might have a heart attack right there.

"Oh, great, you're here!" said Juicy, his eyes not leaving the safe for even half a second to recognize me. "Help me move this thing!"

We lifted the heavy safe and awkwardly side-stepped it out onto the street. We half lifted, half swung the thing into the trunk of Juicy's blue Honda, and slammed the trunk lid closed. I ran back to grab Amar's makeup case, put it in the backseat begrudgingly, then jumped in the passenger seat. Juicy sat behind the wheel, smoking. I looked at his pale face and disheveled hair. He started the motor and we took off, slowly making our way through the Brooklyn morning traffic. My curiosity finally got the better of me and I asked him about the cash, jokingly alluding to a bank robbery.

He mumbled something about it taking a lot of starting cash in the registers to throw these big parties. It made sense, I guess, but it still felt like we were doing something criminal. The whole thing was surreal. After just three weeks in New York, here I was, helping my sleepless, twitchy boss stuff a safe full of cash into his car so that we could put on one of the biggest events in the city.

We stopped by the Paper Factory Hotel to drop off some cash and grab a couple of things for the other venue. We lugged the safe through the lavish lobby ("don't mind us, just a couple of guys with a safe full of money!") and into Juicy's personal hotel room on the first floor. We set it down on a shelf in the closet.

"Hey, buddy," someone said behind me. I immediately recognized the voice.

"Xavier!" I shouted as I spun around. I ran to him and we embraced tightly. A tingly warmth spread through my body. It was so good to see my old friend.

Juicy needed some backup he could trust, so he flew his brother out to help manage the event. As is frequently the case, it didn't take Xavier and me more than a couple minutes to go from hugs to drugs. As Juicy counted out stacks of bills for each register, Xavier reached into the hip pocket of his black jeans and pulled out a small orange bottle with a white child proof lid. He shook the bottle once, sending dozens of little blue pills clattering, and gave me a wink. "There are just two rules for managing

Palace of Gods. First rule: no drugs besides Adderall. Second rule: you must eat copious amounts of Adderall."

Xavier's face lit up with a mischievous grin, and without looking at it he began to shake the pill bottle, his methamphetamine maraca, rhythmically. The look on his face, his staring me dead in the eye... I couldn't contain myself any longer and started laughing my ass off. Soon he joined me. Even Juicy, serious and committed to his task of reorganizing the cash, a Camel already hanging out the corner of his mouth, left eye squinted, looked up at us as his hands continued their practiced task. There we were, three friends—brothers—in a small hotel room, neat bundles of cash all around, with enough FDA-approved speed to power a whole fleet of truck drivers for a month. My life officially peaked.

I wasn't one of the event managers, but I took Xavier's pill bottle, expertly circumvented the childproofing, and took out a few Addies. Throwing them in my back pocket I thought, *always better to have and not need, so they say...* My next thought, as I looked at the two brothers, was one of envy: *Man, I wish I was managing Palace of Gods. That would be a dream come true.*

Juicy was going to be running things at the Hotel, while Xavier and Oliver would be the managers at Grand Prospect Hall. Xavier and I hung around for a few hours to lend Juicy a hand with the cash and setup, then bounced to GPH. Just a couple of dudes with two suitcases: one filled with cash, the other with Amar's makeup.

The drive took us forty minutes, which was about 39.5 minutes longer than we would spend together during the entire event.

We walked through the ornate front doors of the Grand Prospect Hall at twelve o' clock on Friday afternoon. The party wasn't starting for nine hours, but everyone was running around like it was starting in ten minutes. Adjusting my rhythm and taking direction from the rest of the crew, I picked a direction at random and began running, too. The extra blood flow didn't hurt, and soon enough I found Safari Tahoe and Amar. Amar greeted me with a friendly, "Oh good. Gimme that, take this and put it upstairs," as he snatched his makeup suitcase from me hard enough to damage some connective tissue in my elbow with his free hand, while shoving a three-foot-tall speaker at me with his other. He released the massive black thing before I fully had it and I nearly shat myself scrambling for a grip. What Amar could easily hold with one hand I could barely handle with two, let alone lug up the stairs. To the observer I must have looked like a rock n'roll Sisyphus, in my leather pants, toiling to get the speaker up the stairs, only to stumble back down every few steps.

The running around, lifting, and desperate schlepping continued for hours. Time lost all cohesion. Some minutes felt like hours; certain hours felt like seconds. I wrung out my sweat soaked shirt enough times to fill a tin bucket outside a side door. Had I eaten? I couldn't remember.

"What time is it?" I asked Amar.

"8:30," he replied.

Fuck! Thirty minutes until doors. I swear, I felt a shot of adrenaline hit my system, like in one of those dumb Jason Staham movies. I ran around like a manic retriever, picking up tools and scraps, while placing finishing decor touches around the venue. I was both stressed and feeling amazing about it, somehow. I felt useful, needed. My people were counting on me. I loved it. I wanted more.

CHAPTER NINE

At 11:21pm I hear two security guards talking over each other on the walkie. In between bursts of white noise I make out some concerning words. "Out front… Shhhhh… Man on the ledge has… Shhhhh... Screaming. Big scene… Shhhhh… Need medic... Shhhhh…"

I'm instantly on the move. Slamming through the push bar of an emergency exit door I'm on Wycliff Avenue and running around the corner towards the front entrance of the club, knowing that cutting through the crowd inside would take extra seconds I may not have to spare. I run past two guys in flannel shirts, sloppily (probably drunkenly) slurping down hot dogs by the food truck on the corner. They look up as I pass, oblivious to the condiments dripping onto their white sneakers.

I get to the entrance and take in the scene. There's a big white dude on the sidewalk in front of the entrance. Young, at least six-and-a-half feet tall and massive, muscular in that big boned way of a heavyweight boxer. He's pounding his Pug sized fists on the faux-grass woven fence that separates the patio from the sidewalk and bellowing like a bereft hippo. His face is an angry blooming rose (if roses did drugs and sweated). The fence appears to be on the verge of structural jeopardy. Three of our most sizable security guards are standing around him, not getting too close, yet, just trying to talk him down. You can see in their stance, however, that they are ready to pounce.

The door staff have moved the people in line farther down the sidewalk, away from the scene. They are doing their best to appear and sound casual, not ignoring the situation by the fence, but trying to keep it as light as possible. Tacks says, "Looks like someone is having a bad day! The security team is on it. I guess he'll miss tonight's party. Nothing to worry about! We will all be inside having fun and being sexy in no time!" The people who have shown up to have fun and be sexy, however, are now witnessing a disturbing scene, and the look on their faces, eyes glued to the raging giant, reflect this.

"What happened here, Mrs. Miss?" I say to the towering queen.

She is standing mere feet away from the action and smoking a cigarette while repeatedly swiping her finger from the bottom of her iPhone screen. You look up "nonchalant millennial" in the dictionary and this is the image you'll find. She looks up, reluctant to be distracted from the real action. "Oh, he's just drunk and having a tantrum because we won't let him in. Too intoxicated." Having delivered this summation, she went back to her Instagram.

Fucking Mrs. Miss. Before Lacera, Mrs. Miss was our VIP host. After two years in that illustrious position, she had seen it all. Guests rolling too hard on Molly have thrown up on her white platforms. Belligerent bros have flung hateful homophobic slurs at her. She's seen overdosing girls frothing at the mouth, being carried out by EMTs. Mrs. Miss was the most dramatic character of them all, but it was going to take a lot more than a hostile drunk to unnerve this queen.

Unflappable drag queens notwithstanding, the situation had escalated beyond the point where my involvement would be beneficial to anyone. Security had it mostly under control, though buddy was still pounding on the fence like an enraged gorilla behind bars. Besides, if this was the screaming problem I heard about on the walkie… what and where was the medic situation?

I skirt the scene, slip through the front door and hook a right through the golden doors. Out on the Patio everyone's staring at the grassy fence, and with good reason: it's shaking because of causes unknown and there are screams coming from the other side. The sexy vibes have faded faster than an American Spirit exhale on a windy evening. This is a problem—vibe is everything.

I take a central position and preparatory breath, and yell, "Hello, sexy humans!" It worked and there are now a hundred pairs of eyes on me. "My name is Loki and I'm the manager tonight! All is well and you have nothing to worry about! The security team is handling a bit of a disagreement outside. It seems another one of those Bushwick crazies desperately wants to get inside and party with you beautiful motherfuckers, and who could blame him, but he won't be let in and is just letting out his frustration! Everything is under control!"

A wave of murmurs ripples across the crowd, followed by acceptance and subsequent relaxation of tension. Pack animals we certainly are, and the herd is settling. *We are safe. Something is amiss, but someone in a position of authority has assured us that we are not in immediate danger.* Conversations start back up and get louder. Drinks in hand are remembered and sipped. Cigarettes are bummed and lit. Having relaxed, they are once again in touch with the biological imperative to procreate, and the flirting has resumed. I comb my fingers through my hair then squeeze it into a ponytail, feeling my scalp stretched upward, as a sign of relief.

My work on the Patio is done, but there's no time to rest. I weave through the club, careful to not inadvertently touch various sex organs, often covered with the flimsiest outfits or just plain underwear. Ever have somebody unexpectedly brush against your back or front side when you're wearing nothing but a thong? I hear it can be jolting. I tap people on the shoulder, wait for them to make some space, and squeeze past while sucking in my stomach. A couple minutes of this and I'm on the ledge above the stage.

Another academically interesting but testicle-shriveling scene here. Two security guards stand over about 350 pounds of collapsed man, illuminating the space with the fluorescent beams of their flashlights. Crouching beside him is a girl of about 25. Tears are streaming down her face and her hands are shaking. Clearly she's with the inert behemoth, who, to be fair, is muttering contentedly. Sammy Saves, our house-EMT, is kneeling next to the man on the other side and hovering over him. Sammy has a biblical-grade beard and is calmer than the Dalai Lama after a Xanax—as befits a first responder who's chosen to work a nightclub.

There's a bizarre juxtaposition to the whole situation though: a tranquilized grizzly on the dance catwalk of a nightclub, as if tonight's performance will be this man just dead on the floor. How thrilling…

Generally in these situations we will carry the person to a back room for inspection and care, but since this guy is built like a sumo wrestler, we're staying right here.

I squat next to Sammy as he examines the man, feeling for a pulse and looking for any visible damage. The man is breathing evenly, even if a bit too slowly and deeply, and muttering soft gibberish. This is somewhat good news—according to science and all the hospital dramas, being somewhat conscious is better than dead. Sammy leans closer to the crying girl, the grizzly's friend, so she could hear him over the music. I know he's asking her important questions to help him determine what comes next. He moves his ear closer to her hot pinked mouth and nods along as he receives what I imagine is a confirmation to his professional guess: Ketamine. Big boy's in the depths of a K-hole.

Terrific. We have a 350-pound viking enjoying a street tranquilizer / anesthetic-induced siesta as a wild party rages around him. People on their way to the shadowbox are literally stepping over his inert legs like he's a puddle on the street. Fucking people. They won't stop partying until the music stops or someone turns the lights on. The place could be in flames and these degenerates would keep on dancing. Unless, that is, they blast themselves into an extreme disassociated state, like a K-hole… which brings me back to the matter at hand.

I scream down to the performer monitoring the entrance to the ledge stairway. "Pluto! Pluto! No more people coming up! Only down!"

"Roger that!" Pluto replies, flashing a confident smile and enthusiastic thumbs-up. His pink hair flips as he whip-turns his head to the crowd in front of him. "You heard the man, people—if you're waiting to go up, you're just going to have to be sexy with me down here for a while!"

I chuckle and relax slightly, seemingly for the first time tonight. The wall of stress I've been trying to scale feels a little less steep. I'm grateful for the performers for always making me smile, even if everything feels like it's spinning out around me.

It's nearly midnight when I feel good enough about the K-hole situation to step away. I leave it to the EMT and security to handle. I take a moment to jot down notes about each incident on my phone then continue on my rounds. I make my way to the DJ booth and tap Arc on the shoulder. "You all good?" I ask.

He does the classic DJ thing when somebody walks up to the deck: gives me a double take, lowers the headphones off his head to the base of his neck, and screams, "What?!" He doesn't stop moving his head to the beat.

I repeat the question, this time cupping my hand between my mouth and his ear.

"Rosé!" he screams. Putting the headphones back on his head, he turns his attention back to the decks. I've been dismissed.

"You got it," I say, unheard. I go past Pluto and up the stairs again. I compose a text to the barbacks about the DJ's rosé as I maneuver around the security guards who are now trying to lift the gargantuan Ketamine cowboy (kowboy?), mostly unsuccessfully. I hit send as I open the office door and walk in on Clea taking a selfie in Juicy's office chair. On the desk in front of her is an iMac and the dildo she picked up from earlier. She makes a couple more duck faces at her iPhone. As usual, she is utterly unaffected by my presence. I roll her office chair across the office like a nurse at a retiring home for their least favorite patient then turn towards the computer.

"How's the Shadowbox?" I ask as I wake the device with a couple taps of the spacebar.

"Well," she begins, after one last selfie, "there's a couple in there now having the most basic bitch, vanilla soft serve sex ever! To be fair, though, ever since that time I helped that one guy inject drugs into his penis in there, nothing seems to excite me anymore." Clear juts out her lower lip in mock sadness. Like Mrs. Miss, she didn't take her eyes off her phone to answer my question.

I have no comment to her lament, so I look at the three closed circuit monitors above the desk, hoping to see signs of a resolution to at least one problem. I find none. Not much has changed. Shirtless berserker guy outside is still banging on the fence and hollering—I have no audio, but I can see his mouth moving in what is surely not a rendition of "Bohemian Rhapsody." The security guards are standing around him like penguins in a blizzard, and people in line to get into the club are still warily observing from a safe distance. The security guards on the ledge have given up on lifting the ketamine napper and Sammy appears content to casually watch him sleep as he chats to his friend, who has stopped crying. Plus, people are no longer stepping over him like garbage put out too late and not picked up by the Department of Sanitation, so I guess there is some improvement, after all. The rest of the club is carrying on as if nothing is amiss, which is always better than the alternative.

How I envy them! The partiers, that is. Even now I hear their ecstatic moans and whooping over the music as I slump in front of the computer and try to relax by slowing my breathing down, my ex next to me, oblivious. I haven't been able to let loose for about a year now. Always working, always tired. I've never been good at keeping calm when shit goes sideways.

I finish typing notes into the DMR and leave the office and Clea behind. Between me and passed out big dude are five gym-sculpted guys dancing and groping each other. Looking beyond the stage I see hundreds of people dancing, moving, jumping, dry (and wet?) humping, doing shots, slamming beers, making out sloppily, spilling drinks and their dignity… A small parade of costumed performers is snaking towards the center dance platform. One at a time, they jump up and swiftly yet sweetly get everyone else off. I check my phone. 11:59. Right on schedule. It's time for the midnight moment.

Everyone takes their place. The stage manager and his assistant are at stage right, on the dance floor, holding a rigging rope that goes to the truss and back down to the apparatus dangling over the center of the room. They're using their strength and weight, leaning back, feet planted wide, veins like snakes popping on their forearms. The performers form a circle around the center platform with their arms extended outwards, long red and black fingernails touching at the tips. Nasty is peeking over the edge of the tech booth, eyes flicking back and forth between his lighting board and the center platform. Dancing slows as hundreds of people turn their dilated pupils towards the center of the room. Blue and red spotlights illuminate the platform as Sheba and Justice climb up.

The black and beautiful god and goddess are breathtaking in their tight leather outfits: form-hugging chest harnesses, crotch straps, and muzzles. They circle the platform like stalking felines, eyes afire, unblinking stares promising pain and pleasure in equal parts.

Sheba stops in the center of the platform, thrusts her shapely arm skyward, and whips her head back, flipping her hip-length, lustrous black hair over her shoulder. That's the cue—Koochy and his assistant start releasing the line, hand over hand, slowly, to control its descent. The audience now understands what Sheba is doing: reaching for the two loops of heavy-duty chains, their links glimmering in the orange spotlight as they get closer to her outstretched hand.

Cold hard metal meets the warmth of a calloused palm and Sheba clenches her fist. Justice reaches up for the second chain loop. Chains in hand, eyes locked, they continue gliding around the platform like two cage fighters. You can feel the animalistic ferocity grow in the space between them. Without breaking eye contact they leap, swiftly and fluidly gliding into the air. Koochy and his helper quickly take up the slack by reaching high on the line and pulling it down with all their strength, their butts coming down to the theater floor. They repeat this again and again. The result is two sexy, leather clad and muzzled performers soaring over the heads of the audience, who, understandably, is watching, mouths agape, wonder in their eyes.

As they move through the air with increasing speed, Sheba and Justice weave themselves in and out of the chains, undulating, snaking through the loops, contorting their bodies, alternating their grips on the links and finding seemingly impossible positions. Looking at them the average person might be surprised just how many visible muscles a human can have. Suddenly they collide, tangling into a seemingly inescapable knot of chains and limbs—two muzzled prisoners. With one push of a button in the tech booth, Nasty turns all the lights in the theater a sexy but unnerving red, keeping the intertwined acrobats lit up with a separate red spotlight. They somehow come apart and continue with their routine, releasing their grip on the chains, maneuvering into impossibly deep backbends, arms thrown overhead as the chains bite into the sweaty flesh of their torsos.

Despite the driving bass thump coming from the speakers, the crowd is still, absolutely unable to behold the spectacle and dance at the same time. I can't blame them—I'm watching from the ledge above the stage, rapt, and I've seen this performance rehearsed countless times. In the air above the theater the duo links hands and spins as one, gaining speed with every rotation. Justice straightens his body and fully extends his legs until he is perfectly parallel to the floor, the chain around his abdomen and hips. The core strength necessary to achieve this apparently easy shape must be incredible. In one impossibly smooth transition, Sheba pulls herself closer to Justice, swings her leg through chains and over his body, and straddles him. For twenty seconds they're in this pose, airborne lovers close to orgasm, a pair of mating birds of prey, before they disengage, flip backwards, hang upside down and "walk" on the sky while holding hands. A couple out for a stroll.

That's the final move. Koochy and the rigging tech do their thing and Justice and Sheba descend majestically. A few feet from the platform they link one leg at the knee, extend their arms, and let centrifugal force take them into a dizzying spin. As they pull closer to one another they slow and stop just as their bare toes touch the platform.

Sheba and Justice stand with their arms around each other's waist, the other out at their sides, holding the chains briefly before releasing them. They return to the ceiling from where they came, with considerably less effort from Koochy. The performers, now breathing heavily and visibly sweating, rip off their muzzles, smile for the first time during the entire performance, and take a bow. The crowd loses it. Ecstatic screams and whistles fill the theater.

The applause goes on long enough for Sheba and Justice to take more bows and dazzle us with their smiles, and still the crowd won't stop. For half a minute, at least, this goes on before tapering off.

I hear an excited voice in my ear. "Did you hear them clapping for us? The crowd loved us!"

Not understanding, at first, I turn to see the boring sex couple next to me, rosy cheeked from their vanilla exertions, smiles yay wide. Behind them Clea is rolling her eyes and making exaggerated and hilarious faces.

"Uhh…" *Imbeciles… Just be kind and help them keep having a magical night, Loki.* "Yeah! Oh, man, you guys were so fucking hot. The crowd ate it up with a spoon and wanted seconds! Did you hear them cheering?"

Gushing, the couple scampers past me, hand in hand. I can't help but smile and shake my head.

At 12:10 I am back on the floor, weaving through the crowd, always looking in every direction, checking my surroundings with every step. The kink team we hired is enjoying some action at the edge of the dancefloor. A muscular man wearing leather boy shorts puts the last knots in a shibari rope wound tightly around a blonde woman's breasts, the nipples purple and protruding. A few bystanders gawk while others participate in the other stations.

Ten feet beside the blonde in the net is a spanking station occupied by a female duo wearing latex Batman and Robin outfits. Robin has Batwoman bent over a padded bench and begging for mercy as she swings a paddle large enough to canoe across the Black Sea onto Bat's latex butt. The strike is direct and true, jolting a few audience members upon impact.

Beyond the superhero repentance is a wide, dark man tied up on a wooden cross. Behind him is a six-and-a-half-foot tall man swinging dual floggers like two windmills in a tornado upon one of the largest asses I have ever seen. I mean, it must be at least two of my torsos beside each other. A very unpleasant sight that's nearly impossible to get my eyes away from.

I finally find the strength and find the last kink station: a couple, both in all red, seated on a leather couch. In front of them is some sort of Professor X looking guy (without the wheelchair and crippling disability) wearing bionic gloves. You would think they were some cheap Toys R Us knockoff, but no, these are the real deal. He touches the skin of the man and a tiny blue lightning bolt is visible for a tenth of a second as an electric shock is sent through the couple.

Some of the participants are sexy-grimacing; others are hamming it up and moaning like they're on PornHub. A couple even have their eyes closed and are truly enjoying the moment. People are standing or dancing around the scene, drinks in hand, watching, smiling.

The air is thicker, hotter in my nostrils, and my steps become shorter as I continue to shoulder-sway my way into the packed Front Room. It's tighter in here than usual, even, and I'm not surprised. Love House is a no-phone event, so when Zester sets up his legendary "photo booth"—literally the only way to document your crazy night out with friends, lovers, and friends' lovers who you wish to befriend as lovers—it's a hit. I say "photo booth" because this isn't the curtained box in a suburban mall you and your first girlfriend kissed in. Nor is it the basic-ass situation from your buddy's wedding, the one with the oversized sunglasses and colorful wigs and signs you hold up that say, "Maid of Dishonor."

Zester's stage takes up nearly a quarter of the Front Room, and is American Horror Story meets victorian boudoir: a lone black leather settee in front of a velvet blood-red curtain. Zester wears black athletic shorts and a blank tank as if he's going for a summer run and has the manner of a mad genius at work in the lab. He makes his subjects feel like Victoria's Secret nymphs as he takes dozens of shots from various angles with his formidable SLR camera, the flash both rewarding and inspiring sultry pouts and medium-grade obscenity. Everybody wants to be immortalized at Yes House and the line winds messily around the room.

At the moment, the photo booth is causing a bottleneck between the Front Room and Theater as people clump there to gawk at Zester's current model. She's wearing an American Dental Association approved thong and a black bikini top. As she seamlessly transitions between titillating poses, giving the camera and growing crowd everything, her wild black curls bounce off her olive skin. It's clear that this isn't her first time in front of a lens.

Her outfit and moves, however, aren't what stops people dead in their tracks, sometimes bumping into the person in front of them and spilling their drinks. It's the *confidence* with which she is showing up in this magazine cover, Instagram world. To say she's big boned, or "plus size" would not do her body justice. She's straight up *large*. Rolls of fat are hanging over her thong, her stretch marks zig zag down her belly, sides and thighs. I imagine that any Western doctor would deem her at risk for obesity-related illnesses. In this moment, though, she's a superstar. She's truly stunning, and deserves the attention she commands, the hundreds of eyes staring at her. She is sexy and she knows it. If she is at all self-conscious about her body, or has a less than iron-clad self concept, she sure as hell is doing a good job of hiding it.

People are still catcalling and whistling for the large and in charge goddess as I slip past the narrow, black curtain and into the server nook between the Front Room and the kitchen. Here it is quieter and bright with fluorescent lights. I walk up to the POS tablet there and punch in my manager's password. "All right, hit me with some updates," I say to Romeo and Krystal without looking at them, as my fingers flit over the touch screen and I open up table tabs. I simultaneously check the reservations app on my phone, to ensure that everything matches—especially the bottles of top shelf booze sold. It's not that I don't trust my employees—Romeo and Krystal, especially, I would trust with my life—but everything needs to be on point these days. Any error and Juicy would have my ass on a spike.

Krystal is the first to speak up. She quickly brings me up to speed, her voice, as always, bright and animated (like her personality). Dimitri and his crew are friendly, fun, and low-maintenance. A server's dream. Adam's table is "fine." She rolls her eyes, a perfect, perfectly adorable valley girl, and crosses her arms. We've worked together long enough for me to know that this means the table is happy, but she's not thrilled. They're either rude, too drunk, too high, pains in the ass, or all of the above.

"Krystal…" I say, by way of my next questions.

"There's nothing *really* wrong, they just keep shoveling blow onto the table and snuffling it up for the whole club to see. I asked them to stop and they said yes, but they keep doing it."

Seems about right, I think to myself. I mean, I can't say I blame them. Still it's not ideal. "Okay, don't sweat it. I'll keep an eye on them," I tell her, then turn back to the POS. "How are the bachelorettes doing?"

There is no subtle evasion or arm crossing this time. Krystal's whole demeanor changes. Gone is the sweetness, as her brows come together and sparks fly from her blue eyes. *Uh oh,* I think, *here we go.*

"Well… First off," she starts (I can tell that this might be a sizable list of grievances), "They are all rolling so hard they can barely speak!" she slaps her palms against her bare legs.

"Fucking *rolling,* man!" Romeo adds for emphasis.

"They keep texting me, asking me to stop by," Krystal continues, gathering steam. "Then, when I do, they just ask me who the DJ is. They've done this three times—and it's been the same DJ the whole time!"

"Asking stupid questions!" Romeo chimes in.

"And they keep putting their hands on me! Everytime I'm at their table they won't stop petting my shoulders and touching my wig and telling me how soft my skin looks!"

"No consent!"

I pat Romeo's shoulder, telling him to simmer.

"Look," I tell them, gently but seriously, mentally counting the seconds I have before I have to run off. "You're both doing great. I love you guys. It's part of the job, so please put up with them a while longer. Now go check in with your tables and I'll see you soon." And back through the curtain I go.

It's 12:30 as I stop by the front entrance to check in with Harlequin. At this point her register should be loaded. "How's it going?" I ask her as I pop open the black drawer under the iPad.

"Well," she begins, and I know I am in for a story. How much of it will be about work, I don't know, but I'll settle for 50/50. I sigh inwardly and begin grabbing all the big bills out of the drawer as she continues. "My life is a total mess—surprise!—and I think no one will ever love me…" (Her tone does not match the dark sentiments she's sharing, so maybe that's good?) "… but I am working on a new dance piece which I hope to perform here! Oh, and there's this really cute girl here that I have a crush on, and I'm supposed to see her after I get off." She winks. The effect is mildly creepy. "Oh, and it's like at the stroke of midnight everybody coming through the door finally got hit with the Molly they took in the Uber, because let me tell you, these kiddies were grinding and chomping their teeth like a horse with a mouthful of peanut butter, and they couldn't count for *shit*—just stood in front of me pawing at their money... Haha! Oh! And..."

By now I had a fist-sized wad of cash, which I stuffed into a back pocket. "Gotta run!" I tell her, "You're the best!" and I'm out the door and on the street.

Things out here are back to normal. The fence pounder is nowhere to be seen. I nod at Crius, at his post by the Patio door, and he updates me. After an hour of hollering and abusing the fence, ape-man tired himself out, sobered up enough to see the futility of his position, or both, and just left. But not before vowing to write a formal complaint. I consider the absurdity of a sweaty shirtless man outside a nightclub promising a strongly-worded letter, and shake my head.

"Outstanding," I tell Crius and mean it, "I look forward to reading it. He seemed like a really talented writer." I walk up to Tacks, on the other side of the vestibule. "How we doing out here?" I ask. He seems frustrated, squinting at the ticket scanner in his hand in the classic Boomer-With-Technology manner. He is having trouble with the Eventbrite app. Until we hired an older person to manage the line/door, I never considered just how technology-based the process was.

"Good, good," Tacks lies, still scrunching up his eyes. As I watch, I swear I see a new wrinkle being born. "I just can't seem to unclick this ticket I accidentally checked in."

I take the scanner from him (he's all too relieved to pass it over), swipe my finger across the screen a couple of times, and presto—it's done. All good: the line is short and he isn't holding up many people. Most folks who are supposed to be here have already arrived. Classically fashionably late, even New Yorkers are excited to come early to a sexy party.

I return Tack's scanner and zip to the Patio door. Fidel holds it open just wide enough for me to slip through sideways, my hand over the knot of cash in my back pocket. "Good morning!" he wishes/observes.

Juicy is leaning on the outside bar, smoking what must be the thirtieth Camel Light of the night. Behind the bar is Shuk, Juicy's cousin, a fair skinned Moroccan-Israeli with short, dark curly hair and strong, attractive features. At the moment he's doing more flirting than actual bartending. A petite blonde in tiny swatches of red lace leaning across the bar, on her tiptoes, telling him—is he actually perspiring?—about her fetishes. Beside her and nearly twice her size is a lumberjack of a man waving a twenty, literally under Shuk's nose, agitated and thirsty. Shuk continues to ignore him.

"Shuk!" I whisper shout. I hear blondie finish a sentence with "...butt plug collection." Shuk moves little black straws and garnishes out of the way so he can lean farther across the bar.

I try again, a bit louder. "Shuk!" I'm an arm's length away and might as well be on the moon. The twinkle in his eye is brighter than the glitter on his face.

Finally I reach over, slap him on the shoulder and yell, "Shuk!" This breaks the spell and he spins around like a caught cookie thief.

"Yo! What's up papi?" He asks, all twinkly eyes and joy. I raise my eyebrows and tilt my head towards the guy with the 20-bill, who's now waving like he sees a plane from a deserted island. Shuk gives me a guilty grin, gives the girl a thousand-kilowatt smile and a don't-go-anywhere finger, and takes the guy's order.

I see Juicy looking at me with those hunter's eyes, inhaling smoke. "See? You're made for it. So what's it gonna be?" He asks, smoke coming off every word. It's the question of the night, and I promised him I'd have an answer, but I'm still unsure.

"I… I'll let you know soon," I spit out as I back away and into the crowd. I squeeze past the line to the Onyx Room and head up the rickety, wooden stairs to the hot tub. Beside the tub is Carlos Surfista, an empty rosé bottle in his hand hangs like an accusation between us.

"Ah, perfect timing! I was just going to text you. It would appear that our bathing beauties would love a couple more bottles of rosé." Carlos gives me an impish smile, his mustache curling (even more) at the thought of more alcohol.

It's all a game at this point. I know for a fact that he drinks every last drop of the rosé, sharing none, and gives the patrons champagne, which he doesn't like. He knows that I know, too, but keeps up his end of the rosé act.

"Oh, yeah? They need rosé, huh?" I point my chin towards the group in the tub. Carlos looks over, does an exaggerated double take, and jumps in place like a vaudevillian. In the hot tub two people are making out like it's a conjugal visit at a prison, while another pair is humping and bouncing, and the last couple is either performing oral sexy on one another or practicing holding their breath. My money is not on the latter.

Hot, yes, but we allow only kissing in the tub, for hygienic reasons, and Carlos knows this.

Surfista makes pistols from his thumbs and index fingers and holds them at his waist, pointing at the bathing beauties. "Hands up, everyone!" he announces in his theater stage voice, "Hands where I can see them!"

All handjobs and other jobs come to a halt as everyone in the tub raises their arms.

"Don't shoot! Don't shoot!" they respond, guilty smiles plastered on their hot, horny faces. They know the rules.

The hot tub party continues, a bit more P.G., which means we did our job. To be honest, though, they could've kept doing whatever they wanted and we wouldn't have stopped them. Six naked people in a hot tub at Yes House during Love House. What did we think was going to happen? They're not here to play Patty Cake and sing Kumba-fucking-ya.

I hear a commanding, sassy voice from below. "If you want in this spectacular room, you need to move your degenerate asses over and get into a single file, like, pronto! *Thank* you!" That would be Sparky. Ah, the benefits of being a drag queen. In this day and age if a sis hetero dude talked like that, he would be labeled a dick, or worse. I walk downstairs and see him now in faux fur, eyeliner as sharp as his tongue. The crowd has formed a neat single line (obviously).

I pass the newly-formed line, avoiding eye contact with everyone but still seeing the angry "he's cutting!" looks they're shooting my way. I don't always have the time to explain that I work here, so I keep walking confidently without looking back. Ninety percent of the time if you act like you own the place, no one will say a word.

"And remember folks, no penetration allowed!" Sparky says to the next group waiting to go into the Onyx Room with an exaggerated wink and open-mouthed smile.

I walk up to Sparky and bring my lips within an inch from his ear. "You need anything?" I ask. We're facing in opposite directions with my ear close enough to his mouth for his breath to tickle me. We've learned how to speak like Secret Service agents just so we can hear each other at the club.

"All good," Sparky replies. He reaches behind him and opens the door. I slither through and hear the door close behind me with a thud.

There are three fit, mostly naked men playing with each other in the corner of the room. The glow of the projector playing another of Amar's vintage pornos paints them in a light both subtle and bright. One of them, tan and clean shaven, is sitting with his back against a wall of red pillows. Sweat runs down from his veiny neck to his sculpted abdominal muscles. He is kissing a Middle Eastern looking man with a clean, short haircut and a five o'clock shadow. As I watch, the darker guy grabs the sweaty dude's hair, pulls his head back, and bites his neck. I hear a moan. A third man, a beautiful light skinned black guy in a black leather harness and booty shorts, puts the sitting guy's cock in his mouth. I smell sweat and testosterone.

There are about thirty other people in the room, enjoying the film as if there wasn't an orgy taking place a couple feet from them.

To my surprise, the threesome is the only raunchy thing happening in this room. I half expected a human centipede, and/or juices flowing like wine, but apart from the gays, everybody is keeping it pretty middle-school-dance. It's just a handful of couples sucking face (monogamously), and a few women dressed to the nines, sitting still, like they're watching a fucking Fellini flick. I make my exit.

I cut across the patio and into the club. I take a moment to feel fatigue set in and blanket my body, bringing with it various aches and soreness. This is how I know without looking at my phone it's around one-in-the-morning. My stomach churns. *Food. I need food.* I can't remember if I've eaten today.

I step past the curtain and into the kitchen. Score: My Mexican food from coat check! I rip off the plastic lid, throw it across the room, and attack the cold cheese and bean enchiladas, standing over the prep counter, hunched like some feral night creature. The rich red sauce dribbles down my chin as I rip the next bite after barely swallowing the previous. For a moment, I've literally bitten off more than I can chew. Twenty-four seconds later the meal is gone, eaten too fast to have been wholly nourishing. I mourn the enchiladas and push the plastic container away with one last look of longing. Wiping my chin with the back of one hand I retrieve the wad of cash from my back pocket with the other. I take a look around the deserted kitchen—you can't be too careful—and begin to count. Five hundred… One thousand… Two thousand… My mind keeps track of the numbers, almost on autopilot, even as it registers the burst of applause and cheers and notes. *The 1am performance in the Theater is halfway over.*

When I am done counting, I rubber band the whole wad, grab a stick of tiny Post-It notes and write the amount on the top one, stick it on the top bill and throw the bundle in the centuries-old, rusty kitchen safe. I chuck the empty container from my supper into the trash and leave the kitchen through the other set of black curtains, popping out by the Theater bar.

The performance has just ended and Vish, our young, take-no-shit, National Pole Dancing Champion from Harlem stomps off stage, eyebrows arched, not even a hint of a smile on his handsome features. The crowd claps loudly as he passes through the curtain and goes backstage.

Something went wrong. I want to go check on him, and start making my way along the bar, only to run full tilt into the bachelorettes and bride-to-be. At the moment she is on her Sybian throne, with the rest of the girls around her within reach (she's holding one's hand), clapping and squealing—the perfect cheerleading squad.

I peek over their shoulders just as she starts to come. Legs shaking, she grinds harder on the device. She throws her head back and the tiara flies off her head, lands on the floor, and is immediately stomped to pieces by one of the excited hopping bachelorettes. Not that she notices—her eyes have rolled so far back in her head it looks like she's having a seizure. I take a second to reflect on life, and how some of us look cute as we come… but most of us do not.

I side-step around the bachelorettes, dip under the bar, and pour my usual seltzer on the rocks with two limes. Drink in hand held shoulder-height, I head backstage.

As I place my hand on the silver door handle, muffled yells penetrate through the doors. *Here we go,* I think as I swing open the door and step into the bright, narrow room.

"I'm so fucking pissed!" This is from Vish, before the door has had a chance to shut behind me. He's breathing hard, either from his exertions on stage or how *fucking pissed* he is. A sheen of sweat shines on the brown skin over his toned body. He's pacing in the cramped space, visibly distressed but still frequently looking at his reflection in the mirror and pouting at himself. His short black hair is sparkling with sweat and I see it running down the shaved sides of his head. Finally he settles down and sits on one of the barstools in front of the mirror; giving his Furious Righteous Superstar another glance as he relaxes all the muscles of his face, lets his eyes droop, and goes for Dejected Diva. It's pretty good, I have to say. The other performers quiet down, lower their blush brushes and eyeliner pencils and come over to us.

"Everything went wrong. Literally fucking everything." Vish says.

"Fuck, what *happened*?" asks Dreams, genuine concern in her voice.

"Girl, where do I even *start!*" Vish stands. Tall, back erect, one hand on his hip, he cuts an impressive figure. He waves a finger in front of his face to complete the look. He tucks the index finger and holds up a thumb. "First of all, the DJ did *not* play my song, so I had to perform to some shitty house music. *House, bitch!*"

"Oh, no bitch!" (This is, of course, the only appropriate response at this juncture).

"Yes, bitch! Then, whoever the fuck was doing lights hit me with the goddamn orange spots, even though I specifically asked for blue!"

"No!" says Dreams, putting her palm on her upper chest.

"Not the orange!" Romeo adds, his voice coming from behind me. I turn to face him, shocked he's even back here, and shoot him a *shouldn't you be working* look.

"Yes! But none of that even comes close to Koochy's fuck up! That motherfucker didn't unlock the pole! It was locked in place and didn't rotate. I had to change my whole routine on the spot. Ugh!" Vish expels.

"That. Is. Fucked *up*!" says Dreams.

"Didn't rotate!" notes Romeo, inches from my ear.

"Girl, I know!" responds Vish.

"Oooh girl, Koochy is gonna be in *trouble*." It takes Dreams a full four seconds to say that last word. She purses her lips and nods a few times, as if to confirm it to herself.

"I can't even," Vish says, shaking his head and sending sweat flying. Some of it hits me but I try not to flinch. He's so upset he is struggling to put on his sweatpants and hoodie. "I just can't."

He finally gets dressed and storms out, slamming the door. We hear the push bar for the emergency exit door and a gust of cold air rushes in under the green room door. I consider going after him, but decide against it. He's a pro—pulled an amazing performance out of thin air, essentially, and wowed the crowd—and now just needs a minute. I'm not gonna further indulge his dramatics.

A bang on the other side of the green room door tells me someone kicked the backstage door open. Kooky blows into the changing room. "What a fucking performance!" He beams, utterly clueless. Looking around the room he says, "where is Vish, that fucking superstar?" The performers and I exchange a meaningful look.

Koochy begins to sense something is wrong, but he's definitely *not* a dramatic performer type. "Well, what the hell is wrong with you fart nuggets? Y'all look like Gaga *and* Beyoncé just died!

I decide this is the perfect time for me to see if I am needed elsewhere.

CHAPTER TEN

Palace of Gods had begun.

An hour after doors opened there were lavishly dressed guests wandering around, with staff running to and fro, desperately trying to complete last-minute tasks. There were still decorations to put up, and a few rooms were lit up hospital-bright. On the first floor, electronic music poured out from the various rooms into the hallways, bleeding together in a chaotic symphony. The security guards sauntered around like lost puppies (if puppies weighed 300 pounds and scowled).

I found Xavier, now in a black tuxedo and top hat, and Oliver, wearing a gold king's robe, by the long bar on the first floor, huddled over a POS screen, heads shaking. "Hey, we're open!" I said. "So exciting! How you guys doing? What can I do to help?" I was so amped my words shot out in one uninterrupted stream.

It took Xavier a few seconds to respond, his eyes not leaving the touch screen in front of him, head still shaking. "We're just dandy," he said, his tone indicating that they were anything but. He explained that none of the credit card readers were functional at any of the bars. "Looks like it's going to be cash-only tonight. Luckily, we have an ATM—one, for three thousand people, so we should be fine!" he pauses, before whispering, "we're so fucked…"

I didn't say anything, just watched Xavier and Oliver's faces, eyebrows knitted together. After a few seconds I tiptoed away from them and into the hallway, blending into the stream of costumed guests. I watched them as they took in the space, the decor, and the Grand Ballroom with looks of wonder on their faces. I was genuinely shocked. *Surely these people see this for the slapdash shitshow that it is,* I thought, but apparently that wasn't the case. They were in wide-eyed awe as they explored the various rooms and stages, navigating the labyrinthine layout. Phones were held at arm's length and angled down towards bright smiles as they took selfies at every turn, ignoring the people dashing from room to room with tools in hand.

As the night unfolded, I reflected on all the big events I had attended and enjoyed. Concerts, festivals, parties that appeared seamless and perfectly orchestrated. *Was it all a facade? Were they also barely held together with spit and baling wire, chaos behind the scenes?* I kept thinking this as more and more people arrived and colorful lights reflected off the made-up smiling faces of thousands of dressed up party-goers.

In fact, the only distraught faces I saw were those of Xavier and Oliver. The credit card readers not working at the bars was a complete nightmare for them. There were long lines at every bar. People would get to the bartender only to be told that they couldn't pay with card (despite the makeshift signs we put up), then start patting their pockets and asking their friends if they had any money. Many had to leave their long-awaited spot to wait in line at the sole ATM. It was a fiasco.

"How you doing?" I asked Oliver.

Oliver glared at me. "Fucking peachy, mate," he responded before slamming a shot of whiskey and storming off, disappearing into the sea of costumes.

The bar issue didn't seem to put much of a damper on anyone else's night, though. People were just as joyous at two in the morning as when they walked in.

Before I knew it it was five a.m., and the party was just about done. *Had we pulled it off? Had we successfully put on a six-thousand person event—with just a couple of days to prepare?*

We had, but as people were pouring out into the street and getting into Ubers, perhaps in search of an after-party, our job was far from over. In a classic Amar move, at 5:05 he told us that because GPH had another event, we were contractually obligated to clear the entire second floor by noon. As in, seven hours from now. "But don't worry," he added. "Paper Factory Hotel is going for another thirteen hours, so we'll have plenty of time to party."

The music ended and the lights came on. As people shuffled towards the exits, we began to break down the event. Xavier went to all the bar and door registers, took out all the cash and shoved it into a black duffle bag. This done, he left without looking back. I knew he had to go to PFH to help his brother. It was just Amar, the production team, and myself left to do the heavy lifting. We had been working for nearly twenty-two hours and didn't have much juice left. I kept taking Adderall, but they might as well have been Mentos, for all the boost they provided. There was an entire party after the amphetamine-fueled set up, and now the breakdown felt like a ketamine trip gone bad. We, the staff, looked at each other through red eyes, each of us wondering if we looked as bad as the person we were looking at. People stumbled on perfectly level surfaces. Our speech was slurred, and communication degenerated to grunts of assent or denial. It was an ugly scene.

Every step felt heavier than the last, as if I was on the last quarter-mile of a marathon. As we carried the steeldeck staging down the rickety metal staircase on the side of the building I was certain that one or more of us would die or be maimed during one of the fifty trips we took. Disassembling the cuddle puddle areas was torture—the sight of the pillows and cushions elicited a nearly-physical pain. I knew, though, that if I lay down even for a minute, nothing or no one would get me back up. Maybe ever.

By eleven a.m., when we walked out into the alien sunshine, we had been working for twenty-eight hours straight, and exhaustion had given way to pure delirium. I had never felt so fucked up: no Molly comedown, no cocaine binge crash had ever felt like this. When we arrived at Paper Factory Hotel, I swear we looked like Mr. Potato Head with his face on wrong. As bad as we felt, though, we didn't care: we had just pulled off one hell of a party.

In the lobby, after my eyes and brain adjusted to the dim lights, I caught sight of Mrs. Miss strutting and elbowing through a group of people as she headed towards the first-floor hotel rooms. Where I got the strength, I don't know, but I ran to catch up to her, careening off people and not caring. Her strut was faster than my shambling run, evidently, and I barely caught the room door before it flattened my nose into a pancake, pushed it, and walked in.

I barely registered the sound of the door closing behind me with a subdued click as I took in the sight. Remaining perfectly still, for fear that any movement would alter the beautiful scene, I seriously considered the possibility that I had passed out back at the Grand Prospect Hall and everything in front of me was a dream. *My* dream. Like, *the* dream of my life.

There were about forty people, Yes House staffers and club friends alike, crammed into the small hotel room. This was the biggest cuddle puddle I had ever seen, and that's saying a lot (remember, I am from the hippie nation of California). The psychedelic surf-rock of Khruangbin oozed and vibrated from a Bluetooth speaker, and every surface not occupied by bodies was covered in faux fur coats, boas, heels, boots, purses, bookbags, bottles of booze, and cans of beer. Safari Tahoe, beard wet and matted, chemical joy sparking from his dilated pupils, was up and gesticulating emphatically as he recounted every possible thing that went horribly wrong during the night—to applause and uproarious laughter from the cuddlers. Dan and Meloza half reenacted, half interpretive danced Safari's narratives. Spunk's piercing cackles cut through the din like a hot knife through butter, and Sable was actually smiling. Tyson was barely visible under four bodies lying across him. Dreams demanded more drugs—citing gayness and blackness as the reasons she deserved them—then received some. Kev kept passing baggies around that never had a chance to close. Love reigned over the room. Once I was convinced that this was, in fact, happening, I kicked off my boots and leaped into the pile.

We were all here, not on the dancefloors, not in line at the bars with the patrons, because this was the real party, and everybody in the room knew it.

It was such a joy to laugh at Mrs. Miss's stories, commiserate over mishaps and troubles, hug and kiss while inhaling nitrous oxide and scavenging through the many baggies that now littered the floor.

We were one beautiful, beautifully fucked up family.

I don't know how long I was in that room—one hour? Seven?—before I resolved to go home. Walking out I ran into Xavier in the lobby. As I was waiting for my Uber, we talked about the night, our individual and collective experience; how despite the hiccups and downright fiascoes, the two events were overall successful. Xavier told me that he had to put Juicy to bed, he was so exhausted, and that his final words were, "we're never doing a twenty-four hour party again."

And that was that. We somehow came out of it on top and mostly unscathed. Mostly. Because Xavier told me something else: Juicy was off the wagon.

~~~

Fast forward a few days. The stress of Palace of Gods is but a memory. Our toes are in the sand of a Puerto Rican beach, the name of which I can't pronounce without sounding like a frat boy in Tijuana. We hold condensation-coated glasses of margaritas (mine a virgin) as our pink sunburns transition into mellower shades. The Caribbean orange sun sinks below the unblemished line of the horizon. After the unprecedented (unexpected) success of Palace of Gods, the owners shut Yes House for two weeks and took the entire staff to P.R., all expenses paid.

Okay, here is what actually happened: the very next day we began a grueling breakdown, load-out, and drop-off that lasted three twelve-hour work days and left our bodies devastated. We finished on a Tuesday, just in time for our regularly programmed ten weekly events.

Winter's official arrival did not make things easier. Remember, this was my first *real* winter. The wind was a hundred daggers that assaulted my exposed skin every second. There was a strange and horrible mixture of cold and humidity that I had never experienced in the snowy mountains of Tahoe, or the high-altitude crispness of Denver. Even though it wasn't technically that cold—well above freezing—the humid air chilled me to the marrow. I was in pain, succumbing to this new, sneakier frigidness.

Neither my California body nor soul knew that the worst was still to come.

With the proper gear I would have been fine, but I was an amateur. I bought a bulky Northface jacket the subtle color of a traffic cone. I looked like a giant Cheesy Poof rolling down the street. Because I opted for the cuter, waist-length variety, my ass and legs remained exposed to the elements, and I still froze.

My freezing ass was one problem. My head wasn't exactly warming up to the fact that I was still toiling away for $12.50 an hour. Working maintenance under the slave driving Amar was a great foot in the door, but I couldn't last long at that rate. Hell, I wasn't sure I could keep doing it, for any amount of money. I was convinced that the work would kill or seriously injure me well before I received any pay raise. Besides, even with a raise, what would be the end goal? "Director of Maintenance?" Yeah, no. I needed another gig at the club.

One Friday afternoon I decided to spend my lunch break on the Patio. Clouds weighed low and heavy in the sky, giving the outdoor area and my mid-day mood a gloomy kiss. I had just reorganized the storage and basement areas for the fourth time. Between soggy bites of an overpriced eggplant sandwich from Zana, I stopped chewing to let my eyes wander and to seriously consider shooting myself in the temple. I finished eating, put most self-euthanization thoughts on hold, and went back inside.

Inside the Front Room was a lone Oliver, scheming up holiday cocktail specials. He was behind the bar, wearing blue jeans and a black hoodie. He comes off as reserved, a bit preppy, and unapproachable, but since we did a couple lines together in the costume closet about a week ago, I felt we were tighter than ever. I walked up to the bar and with no preamble said, "Hey, can I be a barback?" I heard the barbacks made a few hundred bucks a night in tips, and I wanted in.

He looked up at me, and with none of his usual sarcasm said, "Things aren't looking good, mate." I appreciated him being real with me. He wanted to help, but explained that the two main bars were well staffed, and with the outside bar closed for the winter, he had nothing for me at the moment.

"Thanks," I said, meaning it but exhaling defeat. I dragged my feet across the scuffed black and white tiles, and went back out to the Patio to smoke a cigarette. I flicked the lighter and held the flame half an inch away from the end of my unlit smoke for a second, then sucked on the filter tip and watched the fire bend towards the cigarette, took a long drag of tobacco (and rat poison, so they say), then exhaled for six seconds. Deep inhale, deep exhale. Meditation for Nogis (those not on the yogic path).

Juicy and Matteo, his well dressed accountant, were sitting on a rickety wooden bench beside the shower. Matteo had a gentle European accent and took the words *business casual* to heart. Today he was wearing a white button-down tucked into black slacks, a stylish belt with a not too showy belt buckle (matte black), and black leather shoes. His angular facial features and steady gaze below his short black hair conveyed a confidence born of intelligence and experience.

Without trying to eavesdrop I overheard them discussing Palace of Gods, insurance policies, and hiring a new bookkeeper.

When I looked back at my cigarette, it was nothing but a smoldering filter. I flicked it and it landed ten feet away on the Patio floor, and began to roll in a lazy arc. It didn't get far before winding up under a big-ass brown boot.

"What's up, man?" I asked Dan Rockies as he made his way towards the black exit door. Seeing me, he walked over. "How are you? Ready for your trip?" I said.

"Just about," he replied, a plume of breath joining the words as they escaped into the cold air. Even though he was wearing only blue jeans and one of those flannel shirts that are *almost* a jacket, but not quite, he seemed unaffected by the crisp gray day.

"If you're looking for the bossman, he's just over there," I said, indicating with my chin.

Dan looked in the direction of Juicy and the accountant, squinted briefly, then turned back to me. "All good," he said, with that perpetual twinkle in his eyes and an enigmatic half-smile playing on his lips, "I'll see him when I get back someday. Later, bud. You, I'll see at home." He pushed the black exit door and was gone. As the door swung shut, I briefly watched the wintry Bushwick street and bits of litter swirling around a concrete world.

I thought it odd that Dan didn't say goodbye to Juicy. When I first met them at the Burn a year ago there was nothing but warmth between them. They showed that easy physical affection that exists between certain men who are comfortable in their bodies and sexuality. Standing together, Dan would casually drape an arm over Juicy's shoulder, for example. Shit, I have seen him run up and plant a big wet kiss right on Juicy's cheek, the two laughing like schoolboys. Now, not even a goodbye as he leaves for I don't know how long? Maybe something had gone down. Maybe Dan was in a bad mood. Maybe I should mind my business and go back to work.

I took one more long look at Juicy and Matteo sitting there chatting, then headed back inside. I'm sure Amar had something fun for me to do.

A couple of hours later I clocked out, threw on my bright orange puffy coat, gloves, and scarf (I compensated for my ass and legs being cold with a lot of up-top warmth) then walked through the same door as Dan had. I paused on the sidewalk, tilted my head back and took a long breath of cold air. In through the nose, four, three, two, one... out through the nose, four, three, two, one. I took in the graffiti, the trash, the leaden sky, the dogshit and twinkling pieces of broken glass... and smiled as wide as the Kool-Aid Man. It was Friday and I had off the next day—my first day off in two weeks! I pumped my fist into the sky once, gave a modest who-hoo, and began to walk home. Oh, yeah: having moved to my new spot on Yefferson street, I was walking to and from work these days... and fucking loving it. This was a big, badly needed win for me during this cold and dark winter.

The New York City streets in February were much different than those sunlit playgrounds I walked when I arrived in October. People were bundled up, revealing a slim slice of face or a red button of a nose. Especially on these fashionably derelict blocks, everybody but me seemed to have gotten the memo about looking good while staying warm. Mine was the only bright poofy jacket for miles, it felt like, as everyone around me model-walked in their black or brown pea coats, thin yet somehow warm, hanging down (flatteringly) to the knees. Slim-cut pants that showed an inch of wool socks between lined leather boots. And it's like there was a collective agreement to not look or talk to anyone else. Everybody just kept their head down and shoulders up as they hurried from point A to point B in their snazzy coats, leaving a trail of even colder air behind them.

I got to my new home, opened the door, stamped my feet a couple of times on the welcome rug, and went up the dark wooden stairs. I hung up my bubble jacket on the coat rack. The house was quiet except for the occasional thud from upstairs. I went to investigate and found Dan Rockies in his room, packing stuff into large clear bins. His room was a mess: clothes, shoes, books, and bags were scattered all over the floor and bed. There was already a stack of full clear bins as high as the ceiling.

I asked him what was next, and he said he was going traveling for a year with his girlfriend, Meloza. "After that," he said, rolling a leather belt into a tight circle then packing it into a bin, "I'll figure it out."

"Are you going to miss Yes House?" I asked, thinking the answer surely had to be yes, no matter what was going on between him and Juicy. He stopped packing and looked into my eyes for a few seconds. His eyes left mine as he reminisced, watching, for a moment, a memory real.

"There are many things I will miss... and more that I will not," he said. He sat on the bed and looked blankly around his disheveled room. His hands were clenched into fists resting in his lap. After a few beats, he began to speak, as if making up a free form poem.

"Strange, now, looking back on the Yes House. A place that had been such a catalyst for so many things—all communal... but empty now. I don't know if there's a metaphor there, or what, but it seems ultimately fitting to consider the Yes House from here. No longer in my life, what kind of emptiness will it leave behind? Chiaroscuro. Maybe through the filter of nostalgia it's impossible to tell you accurately what went on in those early days. As I last saw it, today, it resembled its earlier self the way the adult resembles the child. Changed. Matured. There was something unique and fragile, tenuous, in those early days. Like at any given time someone with a badge would burst in and turn the lights on bright, push the needle off the record with a screech, and inform us that

everything we were up to was illegal. And maybe it was. But that was the real magic of the place: it felt like we were getting away with something. Like the rules of everything—good and bad—were suspended. It was where heavenly bodies descended from their celestial perches and hover above your upturned face, close enough to touch. Everything was allowed and nothing was taboo. All you had to do was ask, and it was given, the permission. Probably most important? It was a place where you gave yourself permission to dive in with an emphatic YES, the only permissible answer, knowing that your life was liable to be changed forever, for the better.

"The Yes House, long before it was what it is now, was a myth. It was somewhere in Bushwick. Maujer Street? Ten Eyck? I don't know, drive past the warehouses, we'll find it. Park out front, there is always space in this desolate wasteland. There's the bus always parked across the street. Just drive around. Between Morgan and Bushwick. Those warehouses. No, between Grand and Meserole. Yeah, you'll find it.

"Bushwick in those early days was something to behold. Once-vacant warehouses leased to commercial ventures at commercial prices, redesigned, coopted, switched-around, repurposed, up-cycled madness. Licenseless bars, metal fabricators, dollar-store variety plastic garbage importers; a fortune cookie factory. Sudden flashes of energy—the burst of youth sprung forth from the sewers out there. Ten people living in a warehouse. Silks hanging from the ceiling. A bar. A Christmas show. Two hot girls who owned the place. I heard it burnt down. The New York Times wrote about it. Nobody died. But it's gone now.

"The memories of those early days in Bushwick were of their Danger parties. I didn't know them to be them at the time, but Koochy was walking around on stilts. Lada *hanging upside down from silks next to a hot tub made from a cauldron. Chinese noodles from a cart. Indifferent servers and an excellent veggie burger at Northeast Kingdom. A lot of sunrises on rooftops. The Neverlands. Consider the Source playing a sunrise set on that one rooftop on Johnson.*

"It's hard to pinpoint any particular memory that sums up the experience of opening Yes House. *Juicy* was living in what is now the Onyx Room. The Patio shower was his actual shower. Before the shipping container was delivered, the whole lot was open. The container was a lounge area before it was the costume closet. The place was mad. We came in one morning to find Adriano, the Brazilian artist that was painting the bathrooms by hand, sleeping there. I remember going to Materials for the Arts and loading truck after truck with random supplies—instruments, luggage, fake plants, pebbles, fabric, everything. We did everything we could to get the place open. After we were granted a temporary occupancy permit, I remember Lada riding her bike to get the temporary liquor license every night, an hour before doors. The cops showed up once and told us it wasn't valid—it was, but they still killed the party.

"You know what's strange? Looking back, I don't remember the parties. I mean, I remember a lot of the parties, and some not at all. But the real gift? The memories I cherish and refuse to forget and want to keep forever even if they are tangential and somewhat meaningless in the grand scheme of things are of when the bar was shut and the doors were locked. When the money had been counted and we all smoked cigarettes inside and drank straight from the mouths of passed-around bottles. We did the drugs we found on the dancefloor or used our tip money to buy, and we sat there laughing until the cleaners showed up at nine the next morning. There was a party before, sure, but for me the real Yes House was after the last guest stumbled out onto the early morning street. The way that our lives braided together as only they can after creating a beautifully strange nexus for the outcasts, misfits, free spirits, and weirdos. Lifelong friendships were forged in those after-hours as the staff and the visitors who made it into our weird oblong circles bonded. You can feel the joy snowballing, even as we picked up people and things along the way. I met my wife there, and most of the guests at our wedding. How we danced, all of us, to Total Eclipse of the Heart, while Nasty projected a lightshow onto our warm skin. We'd walk to my house, sunglasses on to protect bloodshot eyes from the fiery orb that breaks night every day, and keep it going. We'd sleep through the *days and wake up and do it all again. The Yes House was the center of our universe as we traced ellipses around it. This story is not unique, but it is ours.*

"Now, though… Now it's changed…" Dan said. He looked down at his hands, now open in his lap. "And you know what they say, Lokes: shit rolls downhill."

I had never heard this bit of wisdom, but I kept my mouth shut.

"I dedicated my life to YES, man. Sixty-hour weeks? Try eighty, sometimes. A bartender called out? Let's get Dan in here. He's Johnny-on-the-spot. We're out of water? Throw Dan the keys to Amar's banged up truck and send him to Western Beef—never mind that he's the *bar manager*—so he can shlep forty cases of Poland Spring back to the club. Dude, I missed birthdays. Fuck me, I missed *funerals.* To say nothing of date nights with my wife. And you know what Juicy or Amar would say to me when I mentioned that I needed a day off, I needed to recoup? They'd say, 'stop complaining.'"

I noticed his hands were fists again.

"'Stop complaining,'" he laughed without any joy. "This thing, this miracle that breathed life into my days and nights became a grind. I began to feel like shit, to dread coming into work. You see these purple bags under my eyes? Them's Yes House baggage. The candle burned at both ends burns twice as fast, and this candle is done burning, my friend."

We sat in the blanketing silence following Dan's soliloquy. Having released his words, given them voice and color, he appeared at peace, and I felt it, too. It was impossible not to be moved by his recollections, but in many ways I just couldn't relate. *Being tired of Yes House?* Impossible. *Becoming disenchanted, burning out, and leaving my newfound family?* Inconceivable.

After a couple of minutes that felt like an hour, I gave him a hug. "Glitter only shines when it's in the light," he whispered in my ear before I headed down to my unpacked belongings.

I popped the tops off a couple of these containers, grabbed a towel and laid out some clothes for the night, then hit the shower. Until recently, I didn't have much extravagant club clothing, but then I discovered the Yes House lost-and-found corner, where the selection was out of this world.

Every week we would fill a couple bins with clothes, accessories, and other (sometimes absolutely bizarre) belongings that we found strewn about the premises like discarded toys in a sandbox. If after two weeks nobody claimed the stuff, it was up for grabs (not the valuable items, like phones, wallets, etc.—Juicy would diligently try to reunite them with their now-sober owners). Decorative necklaces, full-length furs, bags, purses, carry-on luggage, dazzling fuck-me heels… it was a gold mine. Oh yeah, and drugs. Once, I put on a visibly expensive fur coat, stuck my hand in a pocket, and pulled out a rock of Molly bigger than my fist. Don't ask me how I found out it was Molly.

Some of the things found a delighted new owner; all of it inspired humorous imagination.

Like pants. Sure, taking your pants off at a club with a hot tub and sex machines makes total sense. But leaving *without* those same pants, stepping out into the cold in your thong, feeling your testicles shrivel into angry jelly beans, and *not turning around to go look for your pants* was incomprehensible. At least to me.

Then you had the aforementioned bizarre shit. After one of our Jewish Purim parties were life sized wooden swords. Someone at a Love House event left behind a strap-on that strapped onto one's forehead. One of my favorite finds was a foam roller. I could be completely wrong, but I picture some exercise enthusiast who wanted to dance all night then roll out their muscles, right on the dancefloor (?), so they could keep going (or prevent next-day tightness). Roll on, my ingenious friend, and bravo.

After a quick rinse, I got dressed and threw on the latest new-to-me piece: a belted black blazer coat with silver studs and embroidery. I brushed my teeth while admiring myself in the mirror, slapped on some Old Spice, and left the house, leaving the orange poof behind. After a hard couple of weeks, I needed to cut loose. Turning right and stepping over a still-steaming pile of dog shit, I headed to Yes House.

After two weeks of back breaking labor, few people would choose to spend time at their place of employment, with their coworkers. But that's only because most people didn't work at Yes

House. From about a block away I saw the glow from the colorful bulbs of the enormous blue arrow and YES sign, lit up like a Coney Island roller coaster. My heart beat faster and I got a couple degrees warmer in my cinched blazer coat. I put some pep in my step and closed the distance between myself and the crowd already forming under the sign.

As I walked up to the venue I saw a line of about forty people who looked like they were answering a casting call for Fifth Element go-go dancers. As they waited, a YES clown walked up the line scanning their tickets. Five minutes later they were in front of Crius, our head of security, who scrutinized their IDs (and faces). Crius stands just shy of six feet and probably clocks in at a solid 250. He's originally from Nicaragua and still has a trace of Central America in his deep, jovial voice. He has short cropped salt and pepper hair, lovely dark skin, and the brilliant smile of an old-timey Coca Cola ad (if Coca Cola used brown people as models back then). It is with this smile that he greeted each guest. The Papa Bear saw me as I walked up.

"Loki!" he said, then wrapped his arms around me and hugged me so hard I couldn't breathe (somehow I was still able to smell his cologne). I patted him on the back, half in affection, half to tap-out, but I think only the affection part registered because he lifted me clean off the ground and squeezed even tighter. I felt my face turning an unnatural color for a breathing person and tried to make a sound. No sound came and I swear that had he not released me right then I would have passed out.

I was still gasping for air as I walked into the packed Front Room… and down the rabbit hole. Despite seeing this view everyday for the past month, I took time to appreciate it again. In the daytime, this space was just a brightly lit meeting room, essentially, but now it was a nightlife wonderland. Each of the twenty disco balls hanging from the ceilings shot off hundreds of beams of light as they slowly rotated, each with its own spotlight. The short hallway to the bathrooms was covered floor to ceiling with thousands of tiny mirrored squares, and was a favorite for "influencer" selfies. The disco didn't stop when you were waiting to pee. Presently there were three girls, independently making duck faces at their iPhone cameras as they sucked in their bellies. The two doors led to gender-neutral bathrooms, one labeled *urinals* and the other *stalls*.

I walked up to the bar to get a seltzer. "What's up with that sign?" I asked Oliver, pointing at a professionally burn-engraved wooden rectangle that said, *No blowjobs on the dancefloor* in ornate cursive. He didn't even look up, just threw a few cubes of ice into a rocks glass, pumped some seltzer into it, garnished it with a lime, and slid it to me across the bar. "Just blow him in the bathroom," he said, then pivoted to the next customer.

I grabbed my drink and waded my way through the human sea to the back of the room. The seven-foot-tall polar bear stood guard next to the theater entrance. He (or she) was on his (or her) hind legs, wearing a sparkly black fedora, fake Ray Bans, and holding an empty cocktail glass with a little umbrella in it. Next to the big white party animal was an infinity mirror—a double-sided mirror in front of another mirror that gave the illusion of an infinite tunnel of reflections heading off to eternity. It was lit with bright bulbs and at the moment two youngish women appeared in it, seemingly locked between dimensions and hopelessly lost forever. Above the enormous wooden theater doors, currently closed, were the two exercise-ball-sized eyes, complete with mechanically blinking (but out of synch) eyelids.

The color scheme was mostly black and white, giving the space a harlequin chess board dichotomy, and white mannequin torsos with animal heads looked impassively down from their perch above the black curtains that led to the kitchen.

I moseyed about, enjoying the view and my drink for a minute or so, then turned around and headed towards the gold colored doors to the Patio. As I began to push through the crowd the large wooden doors opened and people from the Front Room began to pour into the Theater. I almost turned back to join them but then saw Juicy outside, and decided to join him for a quick smoke.

Even when I wasn't exhaling smoke, small clouds left my mouth as we stood in silence, just us two, breathing and smoking. The music from inside was muted and there was a stillness to the empty Patio that was pleasant, even as my bare hand shivered while I smoked.

There was a bar out here, unstocked for the winter, the front decorated with squares of fake grass. The wall behind it had similar patches stapled to it. Some of the staples had popped out, and in places the grass hung in sad tufts, with exposed rotting wood behind it. On the other side of the patio were the two long church pews that looked about a century old, and they very well might have been. Behind them was a wall entirely made of white doors that would never open again.

Towards the back of the space, behind the pews, was the shipping container with a plain white door (a door that did open). On it was a black and gold sticker, the kind you can get at any hardware store. *69.* There was a brass handle with a keypad. This was a staff-only area, the costume closet, but that didn't stop at least a hundred guests giving the handle an experimental jerk every night. The container was filled, more or less in an organized fashion, with shelves holding bins of varying sizes. Each bin had a piece of masking tape with enigmatic classifying words: Boring Panties, On Your Knees, Dinosaur, Space Cadet... like that. I knew that these were wardrobe themes.

A wooden staircase next to the shipping container led up to the bamboo-enclosed hot tub area on top of the metal costume closet. The hot tub, a favorite among the more exhibitionist partiers, had a strict nude-only dress code and was open only on Friday and Saturday nights during the warmer months. Carlos Surfista always ran the show up there, with the help of a sexy assistant—a flirty French maid or a pretty pirate wench. The two directed small groups as they disrobed, showered, and got in the hot tub, where they could frolic for about twenty minutes before being kicked out so the next group could enjoy the bizarrely fun experience of being in a hot tub while at a club.

Behind the staircase to the hot tub area were two doors: the coat check and liquor room combined on the left, Onyx Room on the right.

"Well I'm cold," Juicy said and shrugged his shoulders up to his ears, "come find me at the table with Sauce." He flicked his cigarette and scurried away, leaving me to freeze and smoke alone.

Sauce! I thought, as I heard a blast of music and watched Juicy disappear into the warmth. I hadn't seen Sauce since the Burn.

I took a last drag of the smoke, flicked it as hard as I could for distance, then ran inside. I just slipped through the Theater doors as they were closing and joined Sauce and Juicy at their private table.

Sauce was wearing a rich red button down, mostly unbuttoned, and black slacks. His bulging muscles stretched the expensive looking shirt. The pair of black and gold Ray Bans perched in his thick black curls complemented the gold Rolex on the dark skin of his left wrist. Sauce was a doctor, head of the emergency room at a big hospital, and his duds always reflected his economic stratum. But all the Rolexes and Porsches didn't change one important fact: Sauce was a Burner. Shortly after I hugged him hello and sat down he pulled out about half an ounce of magic mushrooms. He opened the Ziploc bag, threw a few dried stems and a couple of caps into his mouth, and passed it along. I didn't hesitate. I accepted my boarding pass and boarded the flight.

It didn't take long until my head started tingling and every physical sensation was heightened. The cushioned horseshoe shaped booth we were in got softer and… spongier. I felt like I was sinking into thick moss. We watched, pleasantly stupefied, as Marseille began a straps routine on stage. A short white girl, Marseille was pretty much the leanest, fittest, strongest human I had ever seen. Absolutely world-class, I heard she performed with Cirque du Soleil, and charged a steep minimum of $1200 for appearances. We got her for 250 bucks because she was a homie. We were in for a treat.

Now she was twenty feet in the air, wearing a white leotard and holding onto the straps with just one hand. She moved her muscled body sinuously, as if lacking the same rigid bone structure as the rest of us mere mortals. The blue and purple spotlights created a hint of shadow under every defined muscle they hit, as she twirled and spun with apparent ease, rolled and flipped in the air; smooth and hard as stone yet beautiful as a sunlit cloud.

Lit up like a European statue, Marseille went for her grand finale. While spinning, she inserted one foot into the loop of a strap, then put her other foot in the second strap. Holding on to the straps overhead she extended her legs and slowly lowered herself into a full split. Once her legs were perfectly parallel to the ground, one in front and one behind, she released the straps. Arms straight out, palms up, she rotated above the crowd, supporting herself with the superhuman strength of her toes. With her steady, fierce gaze focused a million miles away she looked like an avenging demigod.

The crowd lost their shit. People shot up and out of their seats, whistling and clapping, cheering. We lost our shit, too, but, unable to pull away from our now-velcroed booth, applauded from a seated position. As the standing ovation wound down, two production staffers worked the rope that lowered Marseille to the stage. She stepped out of the straps like a ballerina, lightly yet deliberately, held them out to her side with an outstretched right arm, gave a deep bow, and walked offstage. The straps, swaying back and forth, looking forlorn to my enhanced imagination, then retracted, as if by magic.

The rest of the show was a blur of colors, clowns, fire and laughter. Before we had a chance to process what we had witnessed, the party began. Colored spotlights and laser beams cut through the darkness with razor sharp precision as Sander Kleinenberg, a renowned DJ from Amsterdam, spun Happy House music that raised heart rates and the corners of our mouths. The crowd pulsed and bopped, and glitter covered go-go dancers dressed in all silver go-goed under white spotlights.

Five of Sauce's friends joined us at the table and I immediately felt like I was on a yacht in the Aegean Sea. Three girls and two guys, they were prep school-white, beautiful, and immaculately dressed. They had dentist-enhanced dazzling white smiles and muscles that were toned with the help of personal trainers and nutritionists. Their clothes fit like they were sewn for them. They even *smelled* rich. Or maybe to me anything that wasn't Old Spice smelled fancy. And, like most uber-successful folks I had met... they had a taste for partying. And by "taste" I mean, "ravenous appetite." Within seconds of arriving they ordered two bottles for the table, Patron Reposado and Grey Goose. The waitress had barely cracked the seal before they were pouring double shots for everyone. Then they got up on the seats in their designer white sneakers and Gucci heels, respectfully, and started to dance.

Sauce stuck his right hand deep into the hip pocket of his fashionable slacks and pulled out a couple small baggies of blow. He flicked one in my direction and I snatched it out of the air as it was spinning end over end in slow motion and leaving a colorful trail. "A sign-on bonus," he winked. I was raised better than to reject a thoughtful present, so I thanked him and tucked the marching powder into my own pocket. Fully equipped, and fully tripping on mushrooms, I decided it was time to stretch my legs. As I walked off, taking a couple of steps to find an equilibrium, Juicy and Sauce were clinking two shots of tequila together.

The walk from the Theater and through the Front Room was fun, if a bit anxiety-inducing because of the tightness. The cool air and cigarette smoke of the Patio felt like a gentle hand on my warm face. I saw Klea and Fox walking into the costume closet. "Wait!" I blurted, skipping across the black and white tiles, "I'm coming too!" Fox heard me and turned around, waving a hurry-up. I got there just in time to squeeze in and close the door behind me.

We made a motley foursome, that's for sure: Klea, a lean redhead go-go clown extraordinaire; Fox from the door, short and tattooed like a sailor, with bleached blond Eminem hair, pants bulging with what can only be packs of cigarettes; and Spunk, lying on the dirty carpet scrolling his phone.

"Hey, I'm Loki," I said to the group. We'd seen each other around, working or dancing (I was definitely checking out Klea at the Palace of Gods cuddle puddle), but hadn't introduced ourselves properly.

"Why are you guys crashing my party?" Asked Spunk.

Klea, rummaging through the bins, said, "I'm looking for a little flair." Inspecting feather boas and sparkly tiaras but ultimately rejecting them, she exaggerated a frown and rubbed her fists under her cheekbones. "But none of this will do!" She was the most adorable crying clown in the world.

"I'm escaping the annoying people," said Fox, dragging the final word.

"Well, I came to do drugs," I said, pulling out my white baggie and giving it a few shakes at eye level.

I was suddenly the center of attention, Spunk's phone and costume bins instantly forgotten.

"What's *that*, Lo-ki?" the three asked simultaneously.

"Blow," I said confidently, suddenly realizing that I had no idea. I assumed it was cocaine because that was Sauces's drug of choice.

Frankly, I don't think they cared what was in the bag, because even as I was answering they had all stood up and produced rings of house keys, as if by magic. We took turns dipping our keys into the bag, carefully transporting small mounds of white powder to our nostrils, then explosively sniffing while holding the non-active nostril shut with the fingers not holding the keys. The smell of magic marker soaked in gasoline filled my sinuses. Okay, it was blow.

We repeated the process and shared our How I Ended Up in a New York Shipping Container story. Spunk's took the cake. He used to have a corporate job in Sydney. "I showed up to work every day in a suit, briefcase in hand. I would go to my cubicle, put my briefcase on my desk, and open it. Inside the briefcase was a solitary banana. I would sit down, eat said banana, and pretend to make phone calls for the rest of the day. After a couple years of this I decided I should do something with my life. So now I just hide in a dirty costume closet and scroll my phone."

After many stories, snorts, and laughs, the coke bag went the way of all coke bags everywhere: torn in two and licked clean. I wasn't worried. Finding coke at Yes House was like finding dog shit on a Buswhick street. There was an abundance of both. We left our smelly drug den and filed out to the Patio, avoiding the curious stares of patrons. Back in the Theater, Juicy, Sauce, and his band of sexies were still at it, with no sign of letting up.

I plopped down next to Juicy and put my arm around him. He was talking to Sauce, and again I heard him slur, "I need a fucking bookkeeper... but life is perfect."

Bookkeeper, I thought as he sucked the last drop of tequila from an upturned shot glass and slowly turned his head to look at me. Though his eyes were open and unblinking, he did not see me.

He was blacked out.

It took him a full five seconds to recognize who I was. If you've ever dealt with someone who is chemically disassociated, you know how eerie it could be. Finally he smiled and grabbed the back of my head, roughly but affectionately pulling it to his until our foreheads touched. We stayed like this for a magical beat, then he released and got up to dance with the others. If you didn't know him, if you saw him dancing and smiling and cracking jokes, you might think he's drunk or high on something, but you'd probably not realize that the man before you was on full autopilot, the conscious essence of him... gone. The staff, though, the people who had been witness to this numberless times, knew the drill.

I saw Crius and waved him over. He moved through the crowd like a gentle, smiling, but inexorable force; a wrecking ball in velvet.

"What do we do?" I asked, leaning close to him to be heard over the party.

Apparently there was a protocol in place. Generally, nobody was too worried about Juicy while he was on the premises—he was, for all intents and purposes, home, surrounded by people who cared about him (and others whose literal job it was to keep him safe). The bigger concern was getting him to his house at the end of the night. Operation Keep-Juicy-Safe looked like this: One of our most senior and loyal security guards, Yonathan (think Arabic Arnold Schwarzenegger, circa T2), would follow him around the club at a non-intrusive distance and ensure that he always had eyes on him. If Juicy got to the point of losing control of his gross motor skills, Yonathan swooped in, hoisted Juicy up into his massive arms, and carried him home the way a husband crosses the threshold of a hotel room with his new bride. Fortunately, Juicy lived just a couple of blocks away.

"During the first year of operation, this was the routine," said Crius. Juicy managed the club all day and night, got absolutely obliterated well into the morning, then was carried home. Lather, rinse, repeat. Everybody looked past this. More than that, they really loved him. Even Yonathan. The truth is, Juicy worked harder than any one person at the club (sometimes two people). One. Two, sober or blotto, he was a sweetheart to all of us. And three, he was the unanimously but tacitly recognized leader of this thing, this family. Our beautiful dysfunctional family.

I walked home late that night, the word circulating in my magically induced brain. *Bookkeeper…*

~~~

Monday morning I got to work and went up to the office, looking for Cora. I found Juicy, instead. He was sitting at his desk, a lit cigarette in his left hand, his right on a white mouse. On the large iMac screen in front of him I saw an endless stack of unread emails. "Hey, man," I said, somewhat cautiously. "How are you doing?"

"Good," he said, and clicked on another email to open it.

I decided to push on. "How do you feel about the weekend?"

He took a drag on his cigarette and stubbed it out in a plain black ashtray next to a little tray of paperclips and rubber bands and such. He let his back settle into the tattered fake black leather of his office chair, tilted his head back and let out a smoky sigh. He swiveled in his chair to face me. I lowered myself into Cora's chair (in marginally better shape than his) and just looked at him, willing him to share, to see that I was there to hold space for him.

"Damn Sauce," he said. "Those first shots hit me like a freight train, and the last few did wonders to smooth out the ride…" He looked down at his hands. I said nothing. He met my eyes and must have seen something there that allowed his shoulders to slump with resigned vulnerability.

"Ah, shit," he said. "I shouldn't have kept drinking, Sauce plus supermodels or not. Blacking out at your own club… that's not a cute look, is it?"

I wished that I could do something to take away his shame, and the pain beneath it, but from my own experience I knew that he had to get there on his own. For now it was time to just listen.

"Maybe I should get some help or check out a meeting or something…" he whispered.

"You know," I began, when I saw that he was done, for now, "I used to black out, too. All the time, in fact."

Allowing myself to lay it all before him, to access my own vulnerability and trust, I shared my story. The drinking, the losing myself, my old cellmate Ray Pork. How I had resolved to begin a cleaner life (at least as far as booze went.) Juicy's face was utterly unmoved, the face of a statue. I didn't detect any softness or compassion. It was a bit intimidating, if we're being honest, but I told myself that my story had nothing to do with him—and his reaction had nothing to do with me. After I finished we just sat there, letting the heaviness of our individual and shared experiences fill the air. Finally, to my surprise, he thanked me for telling him; said that hearing my story gave him hope and that he was happy for its happy ending. He asked me for advice. I told him that for now he needed an accountability buddy more than any words or 12-Step truisms. I offered to be one, and he nodded, sealing the deal. I would help him stop drinking.

"How's everything else going?" I asked.

"Really good, man," he said. "Apart from the drinking, everything is fine. I'm enjoying myself. The club is doing well. We still need a bookkeeper, but I'm sure we'll find someone."

Bookkeeper! Tell him. Say it now. This is what you've been waiting for! I yelled inside my own head. I took a breath and just went for it.

"I can do it!" I blurted out, louder than strictly necessary. "I can be your bookkeeper!" He nearly flinched.

"Sorry, I mean… I can do it," I went on, calmer. "Okay, I've never done it before, but I used to do calculus in my head in high school. I know I can do this." That's it. It was out.

His response was swift and final. "No," he said, then turned back to his Gmail. "You have no experience. Besides, you don't want to be in front of a computer all day."

The mouse click was like a door slamming in my face.

I let myself out of the office, the weight of rejection mingling with the prospect of busting my hump all day for Amar and bringing me down.

I forced the heaviness to the back of my mind and got to work, but the feeling stayed in my stomach all day. *He didn't even give me a chance*, I thought. Then, *Given the chance, I could prove him wrong. Yeah…* What if I… gave *myself* the chance? So that's what I set out to do.

After a long day of scraping the Patio tiles clean and picking up cigarettes (how many of them were mine?) I nearly ran home. I plopped down on the couch, opened my laptop and began Googling bookkeeper courses. Endless options populated my screen: community college classes, Quickbooks courses, dozens of online courses that all promised to turn me into a Certified Bookkeeper.

Indecision, paralysis by analysis. I had no clue. Hell, I didn't even know the word "bookkeeper" had two k's until Google, ever helpful, asked, "Did you mean, 'bookkeeper?'"

When in doubt, do what has worked in the past. *What do we want?* "Cheap and fast!" I said to the empty living room, repeating an often-used motto of mine. *When do we want it?!* "Now!" I started clicking.

Community college classes required enrollment and attendance, so I tossed that out straight away. Quickbooks courses seemed good, as I'd need to be intimately familiar with that software if I were to take on the role at Yes House, but my gut told me that there was more to it than that. Many of the online offerings required a months-long commitment and cost a pretty penny—some upwards of five hundred bucks. Not a king's ransom to most adults, certainly, but I had just sold my van just to be able to pay this month's rent and security deposit on my new pad, so I wasn't exactly flush.

Then I found it. A pay-as-you go online course in which you could pick and choose your own bookkeeping knowledge adventure, and not have to shell out a bunch of dough right off the bat. I instantly pulled out my debit card and signed up. Fundamentals of Bookkeeping for fifty bucks? Yep, *uh-huh*.

Still holding on to the debit card, I went on Seamless and ordered a Chana Saag from a nearby Indian restaurant—surpassing my daily spending limit by about sixty dollars—then got to work. I was determined to get through the thirty-hour Fundamentals class as quickly as I could.

Eight hours later it was three in the morning and my eyelids felt leaden. I was taking unintentional micro naps. It was time for bed, but I was completely tapped, lacking the strength to take myself to my room.

I shut my laptop and was asleep before my head hit the couch cushion.

This became my new daily routine: wake up at 7:30, work at Yes House from 9-6, then rush home to continue the course.

"One oat capp, please," I said to a barista at Wycliff Starr three times a day. Before, during, and after work I walked the block from YES to the tiny coffee shop. The baristas were tattooed and pierced, unsmiling to a one, and about as welcoming as a broken bottle. They seemed either too cool for school or not cool enough, a group of nerdy outcasts rebelling against the in-crowd one aggressively mediocre coffee at a time. Despite this and the always-weepy music they played (I mean, fuck, Elliot Smith before 9 am? Just off yourself, already) the ritual (and that sweet, sweet bean juice) gave me a badly needed boost during those cold, impoverished days.

Come Thursday I had some serious FOMO. The Throwback Thursday party at YES was my *jam*... but the end was in sight and I felt the strength of a marathon runner who has seen the finish line.

At home, I ordered another meal (Vietnamese, this time), opened my laptop, and got to work. I listened to the excruciatingly boring tutorials, completed the stupefyingly lifeless readings, and took dry-ass quizzes.

Then, at one in the morning, I was done.

I sat back and stared at the *Congratulations—you passed Bookkeeping Fundamentals!* banner on my MacBook screen. I exhaled through my lips and felt a weight evaporate from my chest and shoulders. I was free! No more seventeen-hour workdays. I could go back to sleeping more than a couple of hours a night. More than the relief and freedom, though, I felt the pride that comes from having established a worthy and quantifiable goal and crushing it. I had done it. This would show Juicy how committed, how serious I was.

The next morning I ran as fast as my cappuccino would allow from Wycliff Starr straight to Juicy's office. I burst through the door, shoulders erect, head held high, beaming. *The look on his face!* I thought.

The only face I saw, though, was Cora's, bob-framed and placid. "I'm not sure where he is, or when he'll be back. I think he has a bunch of meetings in the city today," she said. Despite my best efforts, the frustration on my face must have shone through.

"Ah, that's fine, I'll catch him tomorrow, or something," I said through tight lips. "Do you mind if I print something?"

With the official-looking Bookkeeping Fundamentals certificate folded in my back pocket giving me extra strength, I spent the day on various Amar projects. More gum scraping (Christ, people really loved to chew/spit gum while dancing) was followed by touch-up painting in the Theater, a trip to Oriental Lumber, a hardware store around the block, and unclogging the dishwasher drain.

Thoroughly exhausted, I decided to check the office one last time before going home to sleep for about fifteen hours. No dice. I let out a sigh and stepped out onto the catwalk above the stage, shoulders slumped. Suddenly I heard a sound that lifted me right up: thundering footsteps coming up the wooden stairs.

I knew it was Juicy because he never walked leisurely, instead opting for a half jog at all times. In the next second he appeared, a green backpack slung over one shoulder and a bright green and blue embroidered Moroccan scarf around his neck. He was clearly in a rush, but what else was new? These days, unless you caught him in the early morning, effectively trapping him in his office, you grabbed Juicy's attention however and whenever you could get it.

"Juicy!" I said, like a kid who's been waiting for his favorite parent to walk through the door. He closed the distance between us in a couple of steps.

"What's up?" he asked, already eyeing an evasive maneuver around me and into the office.

I blocked his path with my whole body and held both palms in front of me. "Please, wait just a second." I looked into his eyes with the same intensity he looked into mine when I first asked for work. I pulled out the certificate and unfolded it so enthusiastically I ripped it a bit. I held it out to him. "Like I said, I was a math whiz in school, and I just completed this bookkeeping course. Juicy, trust me: I can fucking do this!"

That's all I had. I shot my shot. My heart was beating twice a second and the hairs that had escaped my ponytail were sticking to the nervous sweat on my forehead. Juicy stopped. *Really* stopped, and looked at me. I didn't blink. The three seconds of silence bungeed into the chasm of eternity. Finally, he nodded. "Alright. Let me talk to Matteo and get back to you."

He slapped my shoulder as he stepped past me and into his office.

CHAPTER ELEVEN

"You're such a good girl, I bet you've never even been to an orgy," Amar says with a cheeky smile.

"I am, and I haven't," says Sally, "but that doesn't stop me from being the best bottle service girl at every Yes House event and the last one standing in the costume closet." Laughter erupts at her reply. Sally is Oliver's girlfriend and the picture of the gorgeous blonde cheerleader dating the quarterback in the Valley. From Connecticut, she certainly has her Barbie moments, but is sharp as a tack with a lightning-quick wit.

Juicy, Amar, Oliver, Sally and Strom are in a smoking circle in the Patio. I am standing a few feet from them, facing away. Normally I'd join the group, but things have been kind of tense between Sally and me since our argument last week. Things have been weird with Juicy, too, since he popped The Question. I didn't even know how to act around him. I certainly didn't have an answer for him. The fact that not so long ago the answer would have been obvious, was fucking with me, too.

I sneak away before they notice me. I pop into the costume closet and find Zoe, the co-founder, rolling on the floor, barely able to breathe, with tears streaming down her flushed cheeks. Towering above her is Mrs. Miss in a full-body purple dinosaur costume, head and all, talking through giant T-Rex teeth.

"And then, at Bonnaroo... oh, this is baaaaaad," The Missus chuckles and both the dinosaur head and tail shake. "Remember I told you about Danny, the allegedly straight cook from the staff cafeteria? Not so straight, anymore, let me tell *you*! Anyway, after we did it in the pantry tent, I was ravenous. So I put on my shorts and walked to the cafeteria, as one postcoital queen does. I'm in the full cafeteria, standing in front of the buffet with forty other people, happily heaping instant mashed potatoes onto my plate, when I realize that I am still wearing a condom—a condom that, as my dick gets softer, is starting to slide off. And off it goes, down the left pant leg of my loose shorts, and plops onto the floor. Thank god it was loud in there, because I bet it made an actual plop. I'm mortified, looking down at the rubber, then my mashed potatoes, then the people in line to my right, waiting for me to move. So I do the only sensible thing: I squat down, ladylike, with knees closed, pick up the condom, put it on my plate, and nonchalantly pile ravioli on top of it. Head held high, not looking back, I sit down to eat."

Zoe is laughing so hard I can see her abs through the leotard. I don't think I have ever seen her like this. I try to conjure up a smile, but don't have it in me. I've heard this story a hundred times. It's 1:18 am and my legs are weak, my eyelids weighted. I feel myself becoming less patient and more irritable.

I stay another minute, hoping that Zoe and Mrs. Miss's joy gives me some energy and lightness. It doesn't. I breathe in and accept my exhaustion, then leave the shipping container as the Missus says, "...but now it was covered with pasta sauce!"

Out in the Patio someone has stuffed a large, black dildo into the hand of one of the angel statues, instantly transforming the area into a Sacrilegious Selfie Zone. We don't allow photos at Love House, but I'm tired, and this is harmless enough, so I look the other way. People have really stepped up their smoking out here. "Now that I am drunk and on drugs I want to smoke fewer cigarettes!" Said no one, ever. The fake life size hippo head mounted on the wall looks like it's poking out of a misty swamp. It's also weeping audibly... Wait a minute. Fake hippos don't weep, to say nothing of sob lugubriously. I decide to investigate.

I follow the pitiful cries through the exit door, to the other side of the fence. There, in the torn blue entrance vestibule I find our crier.

"She... She... She dunnit luv me anymore!" whines Tristan, one of our coat check people, and the only non-Latino in that department. Today is his day off, so what he's doing in the vestibule, perched on a barstool and holding on to it for dear life, is not immediately clear. However, this is the fourth time this month, so we're all getting used to it. Crius hands him a tissue, which Tristan balls up in his fist.

His eyes are bloodshot and leaking liberally. There is a six-inch rope of snot hanging from his right nostril that I am trying not to stare at in disgusted fascination. He looks up at me and the snot settles onto his lips and chin, unnoticed by him. He turns his blotchy cry-swollen face to mine, clearly looking for—needing—my sympathy. Whether it's the tiredness or my own precarious grasp on my emotions, I don't know, but I just can't seem to muster any for the crumpled, young, scrawny man in front me.

"Here we go again…" Crius whispers in my ear.

I shake my head. *Fuck, Tristan, this shit has got to stop,* I think, as the line outside moves and people enter the vestibule from the sidewalk. Two beautiful women in red lingerie and black silk robes come in, all fuck-me smiles and bedroom eyes—expressions that change sharply to disgust in the blink of one teary eye. I cringe. No sympathy from them, either. Maybe it's not just me.

I grab Tristan's bony shoulder and give him a light shake. Bringing my face close to his I smell what is certainly vodka, and not the stuff we serve our VIP's, either. "Tristan," I say quietly, my mouth an inch from his ear, "I love you, man, but you have to stop coming here wasted on your days off and crying about how your girl left you." I look around, offering a fake-ass smile to a guy in leather pants and nipple clamps. I feel myself getting frustrated, know that it won't help, but still lean in again and say, "When was that, anyway? Six months, now? You need to cowboy up, dude. If any of the owners see you here like this, they'd shitcan you faster than you can say, 'Do you have your ticket, please?'" Tristan releases a wretched sob that earns him a concerned glance from a woman in a pink bob wig and more black eyeliner than Courtney Love. "Get a hold of yourself, man," I say through tight teeth. "Where are you staying now? Let's get you in an Uber."

He slowly lifts his head, causing a fresh trail of tears to slip down his cheeks. The miraculous snot string has traveled all the way down to his belt. He sniff-snorts violently. "I'm kinda between homes at the moment," he says, then hangs his head.

"God*dammit*," I whisper.

"What do you want to do?" Crius asks, from behind my left shoulder.

I rub my forehead, willing my over-tired brain to spark an idea. What to do, what to do? *Throw him on the roof? Stuff him in a corner somewhere for the next few hours?*

"I got an idea," I say to Crius. "Help me out."

We put Tristan's arms over our shoulders and gently lift him off the barstool and into a standing position. Tristan begins to resist, bucking and trying to pull his arms back. Crius and I tighten our grip. I am aware that we are officially causing a scene. The phones will come out any second. We have to move. "Tristan, stop it. Everything is okay. We're taking you to bed. Safe and warm. You're okay."

Tristan lets out a sad but adorable sigh of resignation, then goes boneless. We walk-drag the whole soggy mess onto the sidewalk and towards the Patio door, which Fidel holds open. "Good morning," he says with a smile.

At this point in the night, hardly anybody notices two men dragging a third through the Patio crowd. We barely draw a glance. Everyone around is too busy flirting, getting spanked, or both at the same time.

In the costume closet there is still a whiff of sweat and perfume. The coast is clear: Zoe and the dinosaur must have just left.

"Hold him for a sec," I tell Crius as I pass him my half of Tristan. I immediately realize that he probably didn't need my help with him in the first place. I look at his face. Yep, he's still smiling, eyes easy and mildly entertained, and I love him more for it.

"Ummm..." I think out loud as I look at the costume bins. *Space Cadet, Get on Your Knees, Basic Bitch Underwear, Cupcakes*—Bingo! I take this last bin from the shelf and empty it onto the stained carpet. I kick the foamy cupcake costumes around a bit then admire my resourcefulness: at my feet is a makeshift mattress. A colorful inch-thick child's drawing of a mattress.

"Alright, buddy," I say to Tristan, who more than ever resembles a hanging trench coat, "welcome to your new room. Get comfy, we'll come back to check on you soon." At my cue, Crius slowly lowers his body onto the cupcakes, where he immediately curls into a ball, sighs contentedly, murmurs something that sounds like, "Good night, Rebecca," and passes out.

Crius and I step out to the Patio, closing the door to Tristan's new bedroom behind us.

"Zoe going to be okay with that situation?" Crius asks. "How about Clea, aka the costume manager and your ex-girlfriend?" He laughs.

I look at all the laughing faces, the lights, the smoke. I hear a dozen conversations and twice as many voices. I'm so tired, and cold in a way that has nothing to do with the November air pinching my face.

"What do you think?" I say. "Of course they won't be *okay* with it."

I continue, stoically. "Zoe will berate me while smiling and drilling into my soul with those witchy eyes... And Clea? Clea will just kill me." We both scan the crowd, instinctually looking for even the subtlest signs of trouble.

"But that's it, tonight was the last straw," I say. "Tristan is done."

"You're gonna fire him?" I hear in his voice that Crius's smile is gone. I can feel him looking at me.

"Do I have a choice? Did you see the way people looked at him?" I am starting to get angry, and know that Tristan is just a part of it. "What are we about here?" I stick out a fist and pop the thumb. "Fun." I continue counting with my fingers. "Freedom. Sex. Escape. Joy." I hold my open hand in front of Crius. "Oh, yeah, did I mention 'sex'?" Crius looks away.

"Is there anything less sexy and fun and free than a heartbroken, snot nosed drunk with no place to go except his place of work?" I add.

Silence from the big Nicaraguan. The questions were rhetorical. He knows as well as I do. He sighs.

"Yeah, but he's been here longer than you, one, and two, he's *homeless,* Loki,"

"Not tonight, he isn't," I say, and disappear into the crowd.

CHAPTER TWELVE

It was Friday and I would be meeting Juicy at five p.m. My occupational fate would finally be decided. At 4:50 I was elbow-deep in a clogged dishwasher drain, Amar standing above me. It was so backed up with black sludge that only a human hand, with its strength and tactile dexterity, could clear it out. This was according to Amar, obviously. I kept reaching into what may have been the actual anus of our entire universe and coming out with fistfuls of amorphous, gelatinous gunk. Whether it was the sight or smell of the globs that was worse, all depends on which sense you more closely identify with. On the whole, it was (and remains to this day) one of the most repugnant tasks I have ever performed. Eventually, though, water was once again draining freely, and I was off the clock. I was nearly late to the meeting with Juicy because no matter how much I scrubbed my right hand and arm with disinfectant and antibacterial soap, I could still smell that putrid effluvium.

I met Juicy and Matteo in the Front Room. We sat on the black couches in the corner nook, and I gave myself a surreptitious sniff. I looked at Matteo's crisp white button-down, Juicy's designer black hoodie, and my gray long-sleeve tee shirt, now liberally splattered with drying goop. I looked at the white mannequins with animal heads staring down at me (judgingly, I am pretty sure). This was not your average Accounting Department interview.

With little preamble, Matteo began quizzing me on the fundamentals of bookkeeping. More than that, I felt him boring into my very center with his piercing green eyes, assessing my character and integrity. I was used to this type of eye-fucking from Juicy's baby blues, but the two of them were nearly too much to bear. I was this close to confessing to crimes I hadn't even committed. Staying calm took real effort. My head was buzzing with excitement and with every correctly answered question I felt myself getting closer and closer to this unexpected dream. I momentarily reflected that from the start this whole Yes House thing was like a certain style of poker playing: all in, all the time.

As I calmly held their stares, I told them about my calculus background and that I could be trusted. My trump card? "Come hell or high water, I can commit to this role for two years." Matteo was impressed. There were people who worked at YES and couldn't commit to one gender for a month. Juicy was inscrutable.

Matteo cupped his hand around Juicy's ear and whispered something. Juicy nodded while looking at the ground. I felt like I was witnessing a tête-à-tête between a mob boss and his consiglieri. Finally the two looked at me, and Juicy smiled.

"We'll have you on trial, but you start Monday," he said. I jumped high enough to be eye-level with the bull-headed mannequin, some six feet above me.

"Yes!" I grabbed Juicy's hand and pumped it. "Thank you, Matteo," I said to the accountant, "you're the fucking man!" And I meant it. I picked up my coat, already thinking of celebrating in a few hours.

"Oh, Loki?" Juicy said, and I swear I thought he'd say something like, 'Nah, we're just fucking with you—you're deffo not qualified for this!'

"Yeah?" I replied, using the last of my self control to stay cool.

"Get yourself a different shirt before Monday."

~~~

Some six hours later, I had eaten enough molly to end a war between two of the smaller Baltic nations. And why not? I was in full on celebration mode. No more scraping gum! No more near-fatal avalanches in the storage unit! No more clogged drains! No more smelling like a vomit-glazed cat turd after work! I'd be learning! Working closely with Juicy and Matteo! "I'm going to be the fucking bookkeeper!" I said through grinding teeth.

I enhanced each exclamation point with a deep drag of my cigarette. I was highschool high and didn't care. I had always had quite a double edged relationship with molly. Somedays I felt my best and most open when I took Molly, leading to some of the best nights of my life, like when I met Rico and Xavier in San Francisco. Other days it was the sole reason I cringed and regretted certain moments of my life.

For the last couple of hours I had danced and jumped and frolicked around the club with a newfound pep in my step. Jaw muscles bulging, sweat pouring down my chest, wearing a smile that was becoming legitimately painful, I rejoiced. Now I was smoking on the Patio as if I heard that cigarettes would be banned forever starting tomorrow morning.

I saw Lada sitting on a bench with her boyfriend, who looked like an improbable combination of a Norse god and Indian guru; like someone who was both vegetarian *and* would take a bite out of your face then fuck your skull. He and Lada were involved in what looked like a close discussion, and while normally I'd not risk either of their wraths, tonight I was invincible.

I knew that Lada wasn't very affectionate or super into being touched, but tonight I was sure that I had enough love for both of us. I walked over and plopped right onto her lap and put my arm around her neck. Her tree trunk legs didn't even budge under my small ass. I looked at her with the eyes of a saint in a Renaissance painting and continued chewing my own face like a horse with a mouthful of peanut butter. I looked at the vegan demigod and said, "hiya, big fella!"

"Um, hey, Loki, how's it going?" Lada asked, visibly uncomfortable.

"Outfrickingstanding!" I responded. "And I've come to bring you some spectacular news. Guess who's the new Yes House bookkeeper. I'll give you a hint: it's me!"

I don't recall the last time I felt this proud to share an accomplishment with somebody. Maybe grade school, bringing home a math test with a big fat "A" in red at the top of the sheet and handing it to my mom. Now I smiled and continued to sit on Lada's lap, waiting for the three of us to start celebrating together.

Her black eyebrows met in the center of her brow and she bored into me with flashing black eyes. "Says who?"

My heart thumped faster and harder as drug-fueled anxiety replaced drug-induced jubilation. Her lap, already a cold, hard place, felt even less friendly under my clenched sphincter. Thor-Ananda looked at me as if I had just farted out of my mouth.

"Juh-Juicy," I said, barely refraining from raising the last vowel to a question. Lada continued to stare at me. "And Matteo?" I added, crumbling before her very eyes and unable this time to refrain from the upspeak. Despite the cold evening, I felt sweat forming on my forehead. This was definitely not how I had conceptualized the interaction.

Lada finally released me from her retinal kung fu grip, and looked off towards coat check. I took the opportunity to remove my arm from her shoulders and slither off her legs. I imagined she was thinking about how this young cheek chewing drug addict was going to be handling her business's money.

She finally said, "Okay," and gave me a look that said it definitely wasn't.

Thoroughly dismissed and deflated, I got the hell out of there.

Out of the two types of nights that came from Molly, this one surely felt like it was going to be the latter.

~~~

On Tuesday morning, the day after I started in my new role, I was sitting in the Theater and eavesdropping on the weekly partners' meeting happening in the Front Room.

Halfway through, Juicy announced that he hired me to be the new bookkeeper, which resulted in immediate and vocal dissent. Amar was the only one amused, but to be fair, Amar could be amused at the sight of two cows fucking in a pasture. Amusement, however, does not mean approval.

"Ha!" he said, then, quickly, "No fucking way." At that point, I'm pretty sure he saw me as just another Burner, to be trusted only with the most menial and unfavorable assignments. Zoe hardly knew me, and most of that knowledge was also from

Burning Man, where I spent an absurd amount of time exquisitely high on molly. Ditto Lada, but she also recounted our lap conversation over the weekend. "No," I heard them both say.

Three hard no's; three partners against one. Things were not looking good. I briefly considered going to the large black toolbox in the corner of the Theater right then and there, picking out a newish razorblade, and getting a head start on some gum scraping.

But Juicy wasn't convinced. His voice reached me, semi-hiding in a booth to the right of the Theater doors. "We're trying him out, and that's that." There was no response from the others

To this day I still don't know what he saw in me in those early days. Was it my confidence that won him over? My single minded drive to prove myself? His intuition? Maybe it had less to do with me than the fact that he had been desperately looking for a bookkeeper for months, the only one of the partners burdened with the task.

Whatever the reason for his going to bat for me, gratitude and relief washed over me in warm waves. *We're trying him out.* He was giving me a chance. He trusted me. Those words echoed in my head for the rest of the day. I made a solemn promise to myself (and later, Juicy) that I would do my absolute best and work as hard as I could.

~~~

I traded in my worn work gloves for special blue-light blocking glasses—untrained laborer to qualified specialist in just a week—and spent the last of my van money on a sexy new laptop. I wasn't sweating it, though, because now I was making the big bucks. That's right, fifteen buckaroos an hour, to be exact. Which was a twenty per-cent raise from my drain-cleaning rate.

I became one of the professional commuting masses, taking the L train to Union Square on Mondays, Tuesdays, and every other Wednesday. The other half of the week I was at YES. On those city days I dressed up as much as my wardrobe would allow, then sat on the train looking and feeling good with my cappuccino between my legs, singing in my head: "His palms are sweaty; knees weak, arms are heavy…" Head held high I walked south from Union Square to Bleecker and Broadway, where Matteo had his office.

Wasting no time, Matteo and I dove into accounting software and various payroll systems. Within two weeks I was fully responsible for running three weekly payrolls, paying out a hundred thousand dollars to more than a hundred people. I was in the big leagues and the pressure was on. Plus, I knew that I was on probation. One extra zero on somebody's check and my ass would be back on that dancefloor (or kitchen, or toilet), on my knees. Mistakes were literally not a luxury I could afford.

Payroll for Yes House wasn't exactly a straightforward process. This wasn't a Denny's. The door staff got paid different hourly rates for different events. The bar and bottle-service had separate tip pools, from which barbacks were paid out. In addition to all the full-timers in various departments, each week we had DJs, performers, temporary staff—each with their own rates, wages, and pay scales verbally discussed with owners. Monday mornings I would find as many as fifty invoices in my Gmail, most of them from the staff and talent who worked the previous week, but sometimes for events that happened weeks or months ago. I frequently felt like I had bitten off way more than I could chew, and I started stress-eating. I never got tested, but I am pretty sure that I nearly gave myself diabetes with the amount of chocolate I shoveled into my mouth while trying to keep my shit together in front of the computer.

In addition to the payroll, I was responsible for paying the bills—most of which were for amounts that exceeded my yearly rent. And guess what: forget a bill and you're fucked. Overlook a balance-due from a cleaning supplies company and next week you don't have any cups, to say nothing of garbage bags, mop heads or urinal cakes. Neglect to pay a liquor bill in a timely fashion and you're put on a State Liquor Authority Freeze List, which means you cannot buy booze from *any* vendor in the state. And I don't have to tell you that booze is the lifeblood of a night club. All this to say, one mistake from The Bookkeeper, a.k.a me, a.k.a. the guy who just a couple weeks ago was vacuuming the Theater curtains, threw a wrench into this intricate (and lucrative) machine.

Then there was the cash. A *lot* of cash. Before, the most money I had counted was a few hundred bucks after getting paid for some gig. Now I felt like a character in a Scorcese movie. I walked around the club (while it was closed, obviously) with two paper Trader Joe's bags, stopping by each of the hidden safes to fill them with green stacks, casually nodding hi to performers rehearsing in the Theater. *Oh, these? No, not groceries, just enough money to buy a BMW. No big deal.*

Despite all the stress, I felt incredibly proud and gratified as a result of my new position. Juicy entrusted me with this all-important part of the business and I was honored to serve him and the greater Yes House good. When he offhandedly told me that there were a total of three people he trusted to count the cash (himself being one; me, the second), I felt my heart turn into the anime-eyed smiley emoji and my face lit up. I now had a sense of purpose. I mattered to the team and I mattered to Juicy. I wanted nothing more than to make him proud of me (and to prove the other three partners wrong), and I committed to doing just that.

For the next couple months, *Make Juicy Proud* became a mantra, a meditation, an affirmation. I'm not a religious man, but by some grace of god it worked. I didn't fuck anything up. Nobody got under- or overpaid. No bills were overdue. The lights stayed on and the booze trucks kept rolling in—thick guys in black sweatshirts, watchman's hats, and weightlifters' belts pushing hand truck after hand truck of clinking boxes to the liquor room. I was doing so well, it seemed, that Matteo even delegated more duties to me.

In late January, after two years of Yes House being open, Matteo and I created the first Profit and Loss (P&L) reports for the business, which painted a bleak picture. Yes House was going broke. Despite the sold out parties and money bags; despite an endless line of ballers and shot callers dropping thousands of dollars a night; despite the ten-deep lines at every bar… at the rate we were going, the bank accounts would be more tapped than a four a.m. keg at a house party.

Everything was going so well—the club was enjoying success that could only be described as meteoric... So what was the problem?

After analyzing and crunching the numbers, the truth was self-evident. We were spending way too much money. Like a kid with her first paycheck... Yes House was living far beyond its means.

In the first year, everybody was playing it lean and conservative. The partners kept hiring to a minimum, bought only materials and supplies that were absolutely, verifiably necessary, and, when needed (often), did most of the work themselves. While stressful and incredibly taxing, Juicy, Lada, Zoe, and Amar's efforts paid off: at the end of 2016, the bank accounts were looking very good, indeed.

So, during the second year, with a collective sigh of relief, everybody allowed themselves (and the financial belts that they had tightened) to relax. Staff doubled and worked as much overtime as they pleased. Any tool, prop, equipment that was even peripherally needed went on the company Amex. Zoe and Lada approved any great—and, let's face it, not so great—creative project, price be damned. Five hundred bucks to make ten cupcake outfits for the whole cast, because, um, cupcakes are awesome! Sure. Pay a cool grand to an A-class performer to add some star power to this week's Filthy Circus? We'd be crazy not to!

Fast forward to the partners' collective grimace as they reviewed the financial reports we the bean counters had prepared for them, then fast forward another few seconds to the unanimously agreed upon course of action: to save the club there will be budget cuts.

There is absolutely nobody better at belt-tightening and frugal resourcefulness than Amar—the man practically built Yes House out of garbage! Okay, that's not *wholly* true, but what he did do was show up at clubs, bars, and restaurants (and churches and house fires) that were going out of business and offer them pennies on the dollar for everything from furniture to industrial kitchen equipment; soundboards to tiles. Our bomb-ass speaker system came from Roseland Ballroom, a once-renowned 3,000-person concert hall. Nobody doubted for a second that Amar was the man to captain this party cruise out of the storm, but all of us to a man, woman, and everything in between, trembled at the thought of his iron-fisted rule. In the faces of the entire staff was a bleak look: "Wild circus party's over, everybody out of the pool."

Amar's edicts came swiftly. First, he derailed the overtime gravy train. All OT had to be personally pre-approved by Amar or Juicy (which never was). If you worked ten minutes past your weekly forty without permission, there'd be hell to pay.

Second, Amar had to okay every single purchase. Whether it was a buck or a grand, if Yes House was paying for it, the green light had to come from him. In an unprecedented (and potentially dangerous) display, I watched him take a pair of steel dressmakers' shears to Zoe and Lada's credit cards.

Third, Amar had Matteo and me calculate budgets to a penny, and he enacted and enforced them. "Sensible" spending? Not anymore, it wasn't; there was no such thing. Costume department wants ten yards of sparkly fabric for the disco party on the weekend? Nuh-uh. You wanna sparkle? Get some old fabric you already have, throw glitter all over it and hope it sticks long enough to last through the performance. Those new state of the art spotlights the Lighting guys ordered? Send them back. Shakespeare used torches and lanterns for the original Macbeth, and it's still on Broadway half a millennium later.

"But Amar, we already agreed to that hot-shit DJ's rate and rider!" says the talent booker, lower lip a-tremble.

"Well, you better start making some phone calls, because I'm not paying him five thousand bucks or buying him a case of Veuve—I don't care what the fuck he gets in Ibi*tha.*"

Say what you will, but Amar's tactics (and general scariness) were effective. Spending grounded to a halt. People were afraid their requests would be denied, sure, but that was just one part of it. The other? People were afraid *of Amar.* It was hilarious (I write, from an island ten thousand miles away from the man) to see so many [nominal] adults afraid of one man. The funny thing is, at a party we would mooch off him shamelessly, asking for cig after cig of his smokes—which he would share, gracious as ever. But asking him for five bucks during business hours to buy screws to secure a wall that could come down on the entire back row of the audience, we'd be shaking in our boots.

The fourth and final step Amar took to reverse YES's financial trajectory was to trim the personnel fat. He fired two maintenance guys, halving that department and keeping just Victor and one other guy. Victor wasn't thrilled, because he just saw his workload double (not because he felt any real camaraderie with the other two). I, on the other hand, was pretty happy because one of them once threatened to staple-gun my dick to my asshole, and I inferred that his companion would assist in the undertaking.

The last two Production hires got the ax, too: Sparky and some woman I hadn't talked to much. Despite not being close to either of them, I felt a pang. Sparky started about the same time as I did. If I hadn't landed the bookkeeping gig, my head would be rolling off the chopping block along with his. The thought wasn't a pleasant one.

The day he got canned, I called Sparky to try and cheer him up a bit.

"You're still part of the family, you know, it's nothing personal," I told him. "Besides, I'll bet they'd hire you to perform now and then!" He was quiet so long that I had to look at my phone screen to see if he'd hung up.

"I'll be around," he said, all quiet and mysterious like Liam Neeson in literally every role he's ever been cast in, before hanging up.

Like me, Sparky gave Yes House his all… but I managed to hang on, and he was out in the cold.

I thought back to that seemingly long-ago night at Burning Man; to Amar and me talking in that sauna of a trailer. He told me then that Yes House was a family, a community, a magical place to call home… but it was a business. Now I saw that it wasn't always going to be hugs and cuddle puddles and a sense of accomplishment and communal blow. Sometimes it was going to be difficult decisions and kicking people out of the tribe *for the greater good.*

I thought of Dan Rockies. He wasn't thrown out in the cold, but that's where he ended up, all the same. Maybe it wasn't his grumpiness or plain old burnout that got him there. Maybe this sparkly wonderland had a shadow side. At this point, I had to face it: working at YES crushed Dan's spirit and defeated him, long before I arrived. He kept going back to the very place that was killing his light, like an addict or the abused half of a romantic relationship. For two long years Yes House was his life. For a while he didn't know how to live any other way. For the first time I asked myself if I was heading down the same tortuous path.

Glitter only shines when it's in the light… Dan's words echoed in my head.

I sent a prayer to Dan and Meloza, in some faraway land now, milking cows and gazing at stars or some shit. Whatever it was, I'll bet they weren't licking torn-apart baggies at five in the morning. We hadn't spoken since their departure, but that morning at home Strom told me they were well and happy to be gone, happy to have found peace on the road. This brought me joy. There was little peace to be enjoyed at Yes House, only sweet (and sometimes not so sweet) chaos. *I hope I get to see you shining again, my friend.*

The dumb marimba jingle coming from my iPhone pulled me out of my reveries. Amar. I hit the green button.

"Splitty!" He liked to call me, "what you doing, jerking off?" he asked, in that strange and fascinating accent.

We had been working together long enough for me to know when he was in a playful mood, but this didn't stop me thinking, *Oh, lord, please don't let him fire me.*

"What's up?" I responded, heart beating faster.

"I need you tonight for an activation," he said, and I could hear the twinkle in his eye. "First, The Foreplay—ha!—then to work in the Shadowbox for Love House. A hundred and fifty bucks, each. Can you do it?"

Can I do it? I used to come home with a hundred dollars after eight hours of back-breaking/disgusting labor, and now you want to give me thrice that to hang around hot-ass women in lingerie?

"Uh…" I made myself count to three as I fake-considered it. "Sure, I think I can shift some things around." I sent up a prayer to whichever deity or ambivalent concentrated energy beam was running the show.

"Good," Amar said. I heard him dragging a smoke. "Come over as soon as you can."

"Sure, I'll just be—" I began, then thought better of it and looked at my phone. He was gone. "Okie dokie, boss," I said to the plants. "Why, thank you! I really enjoy talking to you, too!"

I walked into the club an hour before doors to find Destiny, the veteran register girl, at the bar in the Front Room, throating a shot of tequila.

"I said, 'god*damn*,'" she said, then put the shot glass down with a clack next to three bowls of strawberries. She picked up a berry by its little green leaves and bit off most of it. No lemon for Destiny, I guess. She was a wild one, on and off the clock, and she made sure everybody knew it. When there wasn't much action at the door, she would climb onto the bar and twerk, or get into a lengthy monologue about how good she was at fellatio, and which of us boys at YES she'd love to blow. Frankly, it was almost too much for my twenty-three-year-old brain (and cock and pants) to handle.

"A bit of the pre-shift pre-game, hey?" I asked, only slightly judgy. She giggled. Destiny wouldn't allow herself to feel judged if she was standing naked as the day she was born in front of a priest, a rabbi, and an imam.

"Just taking the edge off, honeytush," she said, "I had a tough day babysitting." She slid the shot glass closer to the garnishes. "Hit me again, barkeep," she said to Oliver behind the bar. Oliver grabbed a bottle of tequila and filled the glass.

Amar was putting the finishing touches around the room. He placed tiny LED candles everywhere, then fiddled with the projector until it started beaming vintage porn onto the wall. A very white dude with a very pink cock and a Burt Reynolds 'stache was plowing a woman from behind, her very clearly augmented tits nearly slapping her face as they swung. They were on the home stretch, judging by the sweat, pace, and crescendo of grunts and theatrical whimpers. Amar disappeared behind the black curtain leading to the kitchen, then came back carrying a fondue pot. This he set on the bar next to the strawberries. "For the chocolate," he said, though nobody asked. He acknowledged my presence with his usual fake-surprise/real-delight raised eyebrows.

"Splitty!" he said, then slapped my back in what was meant to be a gesture of camaraderie but felt like a minor automobile collision. "Walk with me."

I followed him five steps before coming to a halt. We stopped by a long table in the middle of the room. Black tablecloth, ornate plateware, shiny silverware, crystal goblets. "You'll be working here with Sandra, *attending* to the dinner guests." *So far, so good,* I thought, but then Amar smiled, and my worries stirred awake.

He launched into his vision. "You and Sandra will be on all fours on the table. You'll be in full body fishnets, with a fishnet sheath connecting your heads."

My mouth must have opened of its own free will because suddenly my tongue was cold and dry. *What had I gotten myself into?*

The brilliant pervert pointed at a black plastic bag on the bar and continued. "That one's yours. I already cut a hole in the fishnets. Well just yours, not Sandra's. You know, for your cock."

"My… cock," I said, understanding eluding me.

"Your cock," Amar went on, patiently, as if it was my stupidity that got in the way of my sharing his glee, "you know, your little soldier." He handed me a small blue pill. "You should take this now because it takes an hour to kick in."

"Kick in? What the fuck are you talking about?" I felt like Alice in Wonderland, if the Mad Hatter was throwing an orgy.

"Calm down, it's just Viagra," he said.

"What? Why? Amar, why am I wearing a full body fishnet at an appetizer table? Why do I need to have an erection beside the food?!" I was starting to lose my cool.

"Because, *Splitty*, we're going to tie a salt shaker to your penis with this, " he answered, producing a red ribbon from somewhere and dangling it next to my face. "And I don't know what you're packing, but I know I couldn't tie condiments to *my* cock if my boy's sleeping. You get me?"

Something in my face must have told him I did, because he continued. "It'll be cute, like a bow on a present!"

"Amar," I started, then realized that apart from his name, I was utterly speechless.

"During the meal, people can salt their steak by shaking your *meat!*" He laughed heartily, and it was then I knew that the man was actually insane. "Trust me," he said, "People are going to *love* it!"

I felt that mouth-breathing dryness again. Satisfied that I was properly apprised of my role and the logistics inherent to it, Amar walked away. *What in the actual fuck?* I stood there staring at the little blue rhombus in the middle of my open palm. I had never been hard in front of a group of perfect strangers. I had never taken anything for my erection before. I had never taken Viagra *in order to have a meal-long erection so that strangers could use my dick as a veiny salt shaker!*

Thinking of my little soldier at that moment, I realized that he had shriveled to the size of an infant's pinky; and my body had absorbed at least one of my testicles.

You know what they say, though: When the going gets tough, the tough pop a Viagra and slip into fishnets with a dick-sized hole cut out of them. With the same resolve I relied upon to get me through my nights of bookkeeping training, I closed my fist, picked up my "costume," and went backstage. Once there I poured myself a cup of water, took a deep breath and swallowed the pill. *Here we go.*

Backstage was a beautiful disaster of fit, beautiful performers, outfits, wigs, and makeup. Anita Ward's "Ring My Bell" was blasting out of a Bluetooth speaker. Sandra was sitting tall on a stool in nothing but a black g-string, applying makeup. I gave her a nod and immediately looked at my feet for fear of staring at her perfect breasts. I felt so out of place. I made my way to a corner and began to desperately try and untangle the fishnets and figure out what went into which hole. I made eye contact with Zoe in the mirror. She was sitting on the other side of the long thin room, getting her curly blonde wig just right. She must have seen the plea in my eyes because she put down her hairbrush and came over to me.

I let her in on Amar's plan. While I was happy that she was entertained enough to laugh for a solid ten seconds, it did nothing to help my mood or the tangled black nylon mess in my hands. After regaining her composure and wiping away a tear (hers—I wasn't quite crying, yet.) She said, "First, give me that." With a couple of quick moves from her nimble fingers she untangled the body stocking and draped it over a chair to her right.

"All righty, then. Now drop the drawers," She said.

I stripped unsexily, aware that my ass was white enough to leave a bright after-image on the eyes of onlookers. I'm pretty sure I had never felt more self-conscious in my life. I looked around, sure that everyone was staring at my pale ass and terrified penis, but everybody in that long narrow room was completely comfortable and used to being casually naked at work. Zoe waited, a smirk playing on her lips.

"Relax," she soothed. "They've seen far more scandalous things than your circumcised schwantz."

My ass cheeks may have been white as a Vermont snowfall, but I felt the cheeks on my face glow red.

Zoe helped me into the tight… garment? Full-body underwear? I don't know. But with skilled hands she got me into the fishnet from the toes up, inch by inch to ensure we didn't rip it.

Lada walked into the dressing room and came over to us. She and Zoe exchanged a look as I struggled to get my arms into the sleeves and they both laughed. I withered further.

"You forget sometimes that not everybody has done sex work or performed in an underground circus, huh?" Lada said to Zoe. As Zoe helped with the sleeves, as patient as a kindergartner's mother before school, I looked at Lada in the mirror. Her face, an unblemished, beautiful white with an attractive flush around the cheeks, was lit up by the bright dressing room bulbs. *She's beautiful,* I thought. I had never looked at her this way before, but at that moment I wanted her. A cheesy porn set-up briefly played in my mind: the young, naive stud knocking on his hot older boss's door. I felt movement in the area of the hole in the fishnet and quickly banished the fantasy.

"You're all set," Zoe said, and walked off with Lada.

"Showtime in ten!" Koochy yelled from the other side of the door. I looked over at Sandra, five feet away. With the body stocking over her thong she was absolutely stunning, a supermodel caught in a black net. I realized I was staring and couldn't take my eyes off her. Maybe staying hard wouldn't be so difficult, after all.

I looked at myself in the dressing room mirror and thought, *Maybe Amar was onto something.* I looked every bit the part of a sex party regular. With a bit more confidence I looked at Sandra and said, "No going back now. I guess I'll see you in a few." This earned me a very cute smile. I left the room, walked across the Theater and popped into one of the Front Room bathrooms to the left of the bar. Holding onto the sink with both hands I leaned in until I was six inches away from my reflection in the mirror. "You got this, man," I said to the scared dude looking at me. "It's just nerves. Breathe and stroke your cock a little, it'll help." Wise advice. I looked down and observed that I was softer than a soggy banana. Flaccid potassium, one could say. Outside the bathroom I heard Oliver, Juicy, Amar, and Destiny.

I pulled my junk through the hole Amar cut out and gave it a few strokes. "Buddy," I said lovingly but with urgency, "we have a job to do." I dug into my memory banks for images of sex with ex-girlfriends. Nothing. I thought of Miss Jacobsen, the hot guidance counselor at my high school who unknowingly helped me come countless times, but nothing stirred. I even pictured fucking Lada ("Do it harder or you're *fired!*"). No dice. Squishy and slinky as ever.

"Come on, come *on!*" I was shaking both heads with frustration, yet unable to suppress a smile at the utter absurdity of the situation. A young, recently appointed bookkeeper is jerking off (futilely, for now) in the bathroom at work, in order to cultivate an erection with enough structural integrity to support a salt shaker, while wearing a full body crotchless stocking. Christ on a crutch, I didn't know whether to laugh or cry or pack my shit and leave New York.

I took a deep breath, spat in my hand, and kept trying, this time imagining Sandra as I last saw her. The little soldier stirred awake and took a sip of coffee. Blood filled the necessary vessels and my drummer boy became a general.

The Viagra didn't make me physically or mentally horny, but once I was hard I stayed that way. The body was ready, and this was good… but the will was not strong. Shaft in hand I found my eyes in the mirror. "Just do it, Loki," I urged, "go out there." Before I could think twice, I threw the bathroom door open (nearly clipping my peen) and walked out into the Front Room. I scurried to the table, erection swinging like it was directing a plane on the runway. I jumped onto the black clothed table and assumed the position.

"Yes!" I heard Amar yell. "Our star is here. And just in the nick of time!" He walked over to the table and gave me an appraising glance. "Hey, not bad," he said, looking at my penis. Amar doesn't have an ounce of gay in him, but in that moment I was sure he'd give me an experimental tug. He refrained, trusting, I suppose, in my load-bearing ability. "Koochy!" he yelled, "The saltshaker—and move your ass, we're about to open!"

Koochy joined us and Amar handed him the red ribbon, which he accepted with a marked overabundance of enthusiasm. He looked at me, lecherous as a predator, and I almost wished my erection away. Koochy was wearing black pleather booty shorts and reindeer antlers. His not insubstantial paunch hung over the waistline. He was sweating, which added a whole other unwanted element. He shifted his eyes between my cock and my face. We had exchanged a few words in passing, here and again, but this was to be our first coworking experience. Another day at the office—just a clown tying a salt shaker onto the accountant's cock.

I heard clacking heels before I saw Lada. "Whoa, the bookkeeper," she said. "Who would have known?" She took a sip from what I imagined was a tequila soda and looked me up and down, lingering on the down. She raised her eyebrows and lowered the corners of her mouth, nodding a couple of times. "Not bad!"

"Right?" Zoe chimed in. Where did she come from? This was turning into a company meeting. "Hell, I would tie the salt shaker on myself, but I wouldn't put it past this opportunistic go-getter to sue me for sexual harassment," she said, winking.

Between Koochy's sweaty, silent appreciation and the two girls, my confidence grew and my ego got a tire-pumping. I blushed, thinking, *All right, ladies, don't stop now, keep telling me how hung I am.*

It took Koochy three tries—and would've likely taken more if Amar didn't tell him to stop fucking around ("Save it for when you two are dating, hotpants, doors are in five")—but he finally tied the red ribbon under the head of my cock, with the salt shaker hanging upside down a couple of inches below. *It looks like a Christmas present under the tree,* I thought, optimistically.

"Wow, it looks like a bald purple dog with a red collar and a cowbell," said Koochy. I frowned. Koochy shot me a smile. Despite the comment, we looked at each other and nodded, tacitly ushering in a new era in our professional relationship. Sandra walked over, hot enough to shimmer like an Arizona highway at noon.

"You ready?" she said.

I looked downstairs. "Oh yeah," I told her.

She climbed onto the table with me. The fishnet hood that would link our heads was around her neck. We got on all fours and came closer, like two dogs greeting. Foreheads nearly touching she pulled the fabric up and over her head and onto mine until both of our heads were in the black diaphanous tube.

The gilded doors opened and people began to walk in. Sandra and I were the first thing they saw. If Amar wanted shock and awe, he got it. Nobody is ready for this spectacle at seven o'clock—practically late afternoon for NYC standards. Nobody expects this kind of greeting right out of the gate, even at a sexy party.

There was finger food and fruit all over the room, and for the first thirty minutes it was no different from an after work event, with people snacking and mingling. Except everybody was in leather and latex, some with studded collars, crotchless undies, and chaps; and in the center of the room there was a living two-person art exhibit in fishnets, with tits, an erection, and a salt shaker. At first nobody came too close to Sandra and me. Eventually the room filled up, people got hungry, and the steaks came out. Sandra and I were doing a sexy snake routine on the table the whole time. I swung my dick back and forth, scattering salt crystals on the black tablecloth, and Sandra urged people over like a man selling frozen Snickers bars on Brighton Beach. "Get your salt here! Add some flavor to your meat!" At first the guests giggled like children and found something to do on the other side of the room, but then a bold few came over, held their plates under me and gave my cock a shake, sprinkling salt on the steaming, bloody steaks. They thanked me, I said, "No, no, thank *you*," and they walked off. It was entertaining for all parties involved, and they got a little more sodium in their diet.

More and more people began to find their steaks underseasoned. (Fun fact: Amar made sure that the cooks didn't add any salt or pepper while cooking the prime cuts of meat.) As they came by I found that I was starting to relax and enjoy myself. Go figure: the more strangers shake your cock, the better you feel. I certainly didn't mind—and it sure was better than the other "activation" Amar thought up, that sick fuck. On the other side of the room was a blonde giant, certainly Scandinavian, wearing a diaper and eating a chocolate cake that was smashed onto/into a woman's bare ass. Amar had forbidden him from using his hands. It's safe to say that contextually Sandra and I were the more traditionally sexy activation, though I did spy a couple of guests having a bite of cake.

The more I relaxed into the playful possibilities of my role, the more I felt like a star. I began to attract repeat customers. My banter got cheekier ("You again? Careful, you'll give yourself high blood pressure.") Even some staff came by for a second shake. Nasty, who could barely accept a hug from a man without going rigid as a board, indulged in a record three saltings, each one more assertive yet casual than the last. "Pardon the reach!", he'd say, grabbing my shaft unceremoniously, or, "Pass the salt, Lokes…"

After about an hour I began to become more aware of the salt shaker's weight. When a beautiful tall blonde in white thigh-high boots and pasties to match came by, I was dismayed to see that she didn't use her entire fist to get her salt, but just the thumb and forefinger. She couldn't see my sheepish smile behind my sexy executioner's hood. I started cycling through sexy thoughts again, but I realized that it would take more than jerk-off fantasies this time. Desperate times call for desperate measures, they say.

"Hey, uh, Sandra…" It was weird to talk to someone whose head was attached to my own. I took a breath and just went for it. "Can you, uh, maybe help me out?"

Sandra instantly clocked what was going on and swung into action. She reached the short distance to my cock, took it into her hand, and stroked it, efficiently but gently enough to not mess up the bow. Some salt inevitably escaped the shaker. She continued for about thirty seconds, which gave me the opportunity to reflect on just how wondrous my life was. I had my own fluffer! And a damn good one, too. The little soldier woke up from his siesta, stretched and yawned, then picked up his salt shaker. He'd be hard at work for another thirty minutes.

By 9:45 the event in the Front Room was dying down, and the show in the Theater had ended. It was time for the flip. Amar came over to our table and tossed a black pair of undies to me. They were of the banana hammock variety.

"Good job, Splitty," he said, "you can put that thing away, now. Be in the office in ten minutes." He walked off.

Sandra rolled the fishnet cowl off my head, leaned in, gave me a peck on the cheek, and scampered away.

I sat on the edge of the table with my feet dangling for a few seconds, then carefully untied the red bow. I looked at the salt shaker, now nearly empty, in my palm, and shook my head. I jumped off the table and stowed my boner in the black Calvins. I did myself the favor of not smelling them before stuffing myself in. It was like trying to put a water bottle into a small Ziploc bag.

I walked through the kitchen and left the salt shaker on a counter next to a box of disposable gloves and a stack of neatly folded white rags with a solitary blue stripe on them. I briefly wondered if I had just violated a health code, decided that if I had, Amar was to blame, then walked through the hallway, past the mop buckets and hanging chef's whites, and into the Theater.

I squeezed through the crowd on my way backstage. Having achieved minor celebrity status, more people wanted to touch me, it seemed. I wasn't mad about it. I made it past the black curtains and heard a commotion behind the dressing room door. I pulled the door open and walked into a storm. Clothes and costumes were strewn about the place. A black leather purse narrowly missed my head as it flew past. I backed up against the closed door and made myself small.

"Where is my fucking *phone!*" Lada cried, tears welling up in her eyes. The rosy cheeks I found so lovely before were brighter, accentuating her dark eyes and making her look more hysterical. My boner shriveled, and brought my mood down with it.

"I do so much for this place and for everyone and yet no one seems to give a single fuck about *me!*" Lada wailed. Apart from the muted bass thump coming from the party on the other side of the mirror, the dressing room was silent. Around Lada and her tearful rage was an energetic black hole that no one dared approach, even with words. The several performers present pointedly avoided looking at her, not even braving a glance at her reflection in the mirror—perhaps for fear of finding those desperate, mournful eyes outlined in black connecting with their own and somehow pulling them, wig and all, into the tempest of her raw pain. They changed costumes as if they were tiptoeing away from a sleeping lover; touched up their makeup with extra careful dabs and brushes. I felt both sad and angry at them. *Look at her! See her! She's your friend and she's a coworker, and goddammit, she's a fucking* person *who's struggling!*

I pushed away from the door and walked up to her, earning alarmed looks from the others. "Do you want my phone?" I asked. "I don't have it, uh, on me…" I looked down at my outfit, suddenly grateful for my flaccidity (I have found that raging hard-ons never make crying girls feel better). "I mean, I don't have it on me, but I can get it and you-"

"No!" Lada snapped at me. Maybe I was wrong in my judgment of the save-yourself performers. Lada turned on me as if I were the one who stole her phone and stuffed it in my underwear. "I need to call my *boyfriend* and don't know his number!" She had a good set of pipes on her, I'll give her that, and her usual kind of cute husky hoarseness now had the snap of a riding crop. I backed away.

I've seen her stressed before, but this was my first time seeing her have an Engineering Disasters-grade meltdown. Tears were now rolling down her flushed cheeks liberally and her makeup was shot to shit. She had goosebumps on her arms and little dark hairs stood straight out of them. She looked like a cornered animal, ready to pounce. Along with empathy, I felt surprise and dismay. This was an owner, creative director, and head performer?

I looked around at the others. The newer performers were palpably freaked out and pale beneath their makeup, but the more seasoned in the troupe were unfazed, ignoring Lada like a barber shop TV. Don't get me wrong, they gave her a wide berth, but aside from that? Just your average day at the office.

I left them to their coiffing and pouting, and Lada to her breakdown, and climbed up the ladder to the office. I was pleasantly surprised to see Clea waiting for me in one of the office chairs, long legs crossed, phone in hand, duck-mouthing as she used the selfie camera to check herself out. She was wearing a white corset and white thong, and I wondered if her ass cheeks were sticking to the fake leather under her. Her chili red fingernails matched the phone case. Even though we only hung out that one time, doing bumps in the costume container, I really liked her.

Clea had worked the Shadowbox more than anyone else; she'd be the one training me on how to host and manage the folks that came to get freaky here. She was no-nonsense right out of the gate, even sharp tongued, which would've been more impactful had her eyes left her phone.

"First and foremost," she said (to a FaceTime caller, for all the attention I got) "you let everyone know: Consent is mandatory! Yes means yes and maybe means no. No also means no, but that's fucking obvious.

"Second, we provide condoms, lube, and cleaning supplies. And do you know *why* we provide them, Salty?"

"Sure," I said, eager to be the good boy student, "So that—"

"So that we're not held responsible for the next chlamydia outbreak in Brooklyn, or vaginal or anal fissures, or babies, for fuck's sake, pardon the irony." She looked at me for the first time. "So you tell these people—especially the drunk or high ones—to use the gear, clean the gear, lube the gear. Got it?"

I nodded and she went back to her phone.

"Third, let everyone know that when you flash a light at them, that's their cue to wrap it up. When there's a line out there yay long, I don't need some coked up stud jackrabbiting the night away, waiting to shoot his shot. You getting all this? We clear?"

"Crystal," I replied.

"Thank god for small favors. Lastly—and this is of paramount importance, you little pervert—When you're hosting, *you keep it in your pants*. Or panties, or whatever the fuck you're into, you deviant. No sex for you in the Shadowbox." She offered me a lovely little glare. "Because Loki..." I felt an impish smile creeping up. "Yes House cannot legally pay you for sex." Disappointment pulled the corners of my mouth back down.

"However, your shift ends at three a.m., and the Box stays open until four..."

I may have gulped audibly, I don't recall.

"Do you, uh, smell what I'm stepping in here?"

"I read you loud and clear, bawss," I replied and saluted. She was damn cute being all bossy like that. Looking hot, too, in her Penthouse getup. And... was she flirting with me? I decided to go for it. After all, you miss one hundred percent of the shots you don't take.

"Maybe, uh, you and I can put on a bit of a show later?" I said, then quickly added, "After I punch out, of course."

"We will see," she said, giving away nothing. Her face remained stern, but I could tell she was thinking about it. She swiveled towards the desk, lifted the silver and white Mac keyboard and took a small baggie from its hiding place under it. "Also, I found this in my wallet." She held the baggie out to me. There was a pinkish crystally powder filling the last couple of millimeters. "It's molly," she said, "which I don't really fuck with these days. You want it?"

"Sure, why not," I responded. An interesting and beautiful night was about to get even more so. She put the bag on the desk, stood up, adjusted her corset and squeezed her tits together, then walked out the door without so much as a word or a look back.

I picked up the MDMA and rolled the top of the baggie between my right thumb and forefinger, opening it (like a pro), then tilted my head back and poured the contents onto my tongue. The taste was absolutely vile, the way it should be, almost intolerably bitter. Then, like a good little druggie, I ripped the bag open along the seams and licked it clean, wincing all the while and even shuddering out an *ughhhhhh* to the empty room.

It was 10:45. The shadowbox was about to open. I went to the ledge at the back of the office and peeked through a gap between two black curtains. Below me the Theater was starting to fill up and there was some action on the dancefloor. I figured about a hundred more people and the place would be packed.

I turned around and looked at what would be my "work area" for the next few hours. For maybe the first time I really took in the details and quickly realized that, aside from the actual fuckbox, this was quite possibly the least sexy space in the whole club.

Past the office ledge was a go-go platform, shielded on three sides by drop cloths and the side facing the office was open for ease of entry. For shadowbox events there was a candy-apple-orange cushion on the floor. On the way to the platform, past the two black safes was a table laden with sex toys and rubbers, like a torture tray in a cheesy horror movie, but with LED tealights. A large, powerful red spotlight hung above it, lighting the shadowbox and half the office with an otherworldly red glow. Whatever and whoever was happening in there, the shadows on the white cloths were perfectly defined and visible to everyone below. This area, while a bit dungeon-ey and grungy, was not the worst part of the space.

To get to the shadowbox you half walked past, half stepped over one wooden support beam with rigging attached to it, and two scoffed up desks littered with paperwork and other office detritus, as well as two giant Mac desktops. The wall behind the desks was a mess of tacked-on receipts, Post-it notes, memos, keys hanging from thumbtacks, postcards, and promotional material. Not exactly a sex club vibe, though for some reason there was confetti all over the floor. "I TOOK $$ FROM SAFE. AMAR 10/05," said a pink sticky. The newly-minted bookkeeper in me cringed. The real panty droppers, though, were the three monitors mounted above Juicy's desk, brightly but monochromatically displaying the live feed from thirty-six security cameras.

I did the only thing I could to sexy the place up a bit (organized the mess of paperwork on the desks into neat piles and checked my reflection in a dark computer monitor) then opened for business. I found Clea on the other side of the office door after I flung it open, drink in hand. There was a lime perched on the rim of the glass and a lipstick stained straw sticking out between the ice cubes. I noticed the lipstick was a different shade from the one she was wearing, but asked no questions. A line of would-be shadow porn stars was already forming behind her. She walked past me and sat in the chair she had vacated earlier.

"I'll host the first few," she said, but made no move to do any kind of hosting until she checked her social media, then her reflection, then social media again.

I was sitting in the other office chair beside her (at my bookkeeping desk, incidentally) ready to watch and learn. Finally she got up and pulled a couple of short, fit, smooth-chested guys from the front of the line and brought them to the adult Toys-R-Us table, where she gave them the spiel. "Enjoy," she said after laying down the rules, then smiled. "Make it look good."

My first shadowbox! I sat back to watch the show. The two danced around and giggled for a bit, then got down to the business at hand. And mouth. After about ten minutes of exaggerated fellatio and unnecessary noises, the boys thanked us and left, radiant in their newfound stardom. *That was pretty cool*, I thought, but I was kind of disappointed. They didn't even sodomize each other. Ah, well.

After they left, high-fiving the people in line (gross) and other folks dancing on the catwalk, Clea wiped down the mostly-unaffected cushion, then grabbed the next group. Right then the molly slapped me like I was Chris Rock at the Oscars. My body began to tingle pleasantly. It was potent stuff, that's for sure.

Clea brought in two guys and two girls and closed the office door. All of them were dressed in Adult Halloween Chic. The girls were prettier than the guys, but not by much. She didn't tell them what to do or not do, just gave them all warm hugs. Smiling, the four undressed without wasting any time on making it look pretty, then walked single file onto the platform. I felt my eyes go wide as I looked at Clea, not because of shock, or anything, it's just that I was suddenly higher than a cosmonaut. Plus I was curious about the newcomers, who by then had gotten into position: the girls on their hands and knees, facing each other (lips connected, in fact), with the guys on their knees behind them. *Kind of like the Tower*

Bridge, I thought then giggled. Gentlemen, start your engines.

Clea told me that this crew came to every Love House party and by now were Shadowbox royalty. I just nodded—possibly in Extreme Slow Motion—and felt the chair begin to assimilate me into itself. I watched Clea's mouth, the orgy, and the three security camera monitors. I thought about how each was an art form unto itself, then about how good it felt to have profound thoughts like that.

The four in the Box were in full synchronized pump mode (you don't want bloody noses or split lips at these things, I surmised), and I was really happy for them, watching from my bookkeeper's desk, dopey smile on my face made dopier by the fact that my mouth was fully open.

I came back, kind of, when I heard Clea say, "You good here? I'm popping out for a bit."

My "Mrrrmmmmm" must have been a satisfactory reply because suddenly it was just me and the Tower Bridge—looking more like a rope ladder in a hurricane by now—behind me.

The molly coursing through my veins told me that we were ready to stretch our legs a bit. Standing up from my chair I was filled with a radiant gratitude for my feet and legs and gravity. I went to the office door, feeling like a Slinky the whole time, and stepped out onto the catwalk. The narrow ledge was full of people dancing, vogueing, throwing their arms in the air, and otherwise hamming it up for the crowd below.

I could tell the ones who were in line for the fuckbox by the way they eyefucked me the second I opened the door. I smiled politely, closed the door behind me, and rested my elbows on the railing, ignoring their stares. The Theater below was a sea of sexy maniacs, appearing and disappearing with every flash of the colorful lights, rearranging itself into waves of heads, arms, torsos, and legs. My dilated pupils allowed this all to flow in, uncensored and undiluted. A torrent of visual ecstasy. I was grateful for the support of the railing under my forearms. The music was perfect, and rolled over me in a way I had never experienced before. Each beat melted a layer of resistance off of me, exposing beneath pure openness, vulnerability, acceptance, gratitude. My skin, reborn, sprouted new nerve endings and tingled with indescribable pleasure, accentuated by little peaks that correlated perfectly with the bass beat. As everyone around and below me danced, I stood stock still, yet felt every cell of my body boogieing. With some very pleasant effort I lifted my right arm off the railing and ran my fingers through my hair. It was orgasmic.

I was aware of someone next to me, moving and gyrating. When I looked to my right I saw that it was Vish, our very own Prince of the Pole. He was incorporating the railing into a dance routine that was probably outlawed in many states. We made eye contact and he moaned "Zaaad" at me. It was some hip, queer way of saying "dad," and it was the word of the week for all the performers, but that's as far as my understanding of it went.

I laughed heartily and felt it down to the tips of my toes, then cupped my hand to his ear and asked how it was going. He put his shiny lips *onto* my ear (they were warm and velvety) and launched into an impassioned monologue about how horny he was. He was in a monogamous relationship for the first time in the wanton sexual walkabout that was his life, and didn't know how to cope. A talented multitasker, he continued humping the railing in rhythm to the music.

"I could fuck a jelly *doughnut* right now!"

The laughter bubbled out of me like boiling joy. "Why don't you just fuck your boyfriend?" I yell-laughed over the music.

"He's out of town! I'm dying!" Vish yell-kissed into my ear, stretching the last word for a full three seconds.

I tried to compose my melting face into an expression of compassionate understanding but couldn't stop laughing. Pouring his heart out about his troubles while grinding the railing hard enough to take the chrome off... I just couldn't. Vish was a sport about it. I thanked him for sharing, gave him a very tight hug (hugging while on molly, not sure if you know, is legit better than sex on nothing), told him to stay strong, then went back to work.

The Tower Bridge had disassembled. The four squeezed past me, looking no more jazzed than coworkers leaving a successful meeting. I collected the bunched up condoms with a paper towel then gave the shadowbox a quick wipe down with rubbing alcohol. I sat down, closed my eyes and did box breathing until entire galaxies swam behind my closed eyelids, then went to grab the next people for the Box.

Carlos Surfista stood at the front of the line with two stunning women and a shirtless stud.

"Young bookkeeper," he said in his sonorous thespian's voice and pointedly looked at my outfit. "Seems the management has a plan for you other than counting beans, my boy." He twirled the right side point of his black mustache. I laughed. Was this man a figment of my imagination?

"Well, anyway, I was on my way to get more rose juice when I discovered these sexy scoundrels disobeying a house rule regarding the you-know-what on the dancefloor, if you get my meaning. Hmm?" He raised his eyebrows. "Licking the old lollipop in the wrong part of the candy store, as it were." With every word I felt as if I were being drawn into a pornographic fairy tale. "Punitive measures had to be taken directly, you see, my hung little fishy. That's why I brought them right to the front of the line here."

In my current state, playing along was the only available option. I bowed deeply. "Your commitment to your duties is exceeded only by your integrity, sir. I shall see to it that the culprits are made to pay for their transgressions—and that our benevolent overlords hear of your selflessness in leaving your hot tub post to police the dancefloor. How kind of you to skip your duties to find hot couples for the Shadowbox Carlos."

"Much obliged, young Bookkeeper," he took off his trilby, releasing a tangled mess of greasy black hair, returned my bow, and backed away. Halfway to the other side of the ledge he straightened up, turned, and bounded for the stairs.

I walked the threesome through the office and laid out the rules and regulations by the toys table. I assumed one of the girls was with the guy and the second one was a unicorn, but who could tell? The possibilities were endless, all of them hot. I could feel the horniness radiating off of them as they looked at me like I was a slice of lemon meringue pie.

"Well, you're all set. Have fun. Any questions?" I asked.

The blonde looked at me with soft blue eyes. You didn't have to be Esther Perel to see what she was thinking. We enjoyed the eye contact for a couple of seconds, then she said, "Perhaps you'd like to join us?"

She was perfect. Yoga- or pilates-fit with a movie star face and a smile that would stop the Brooklyn Queens Expressway. Her outfit consisted of a red thong and matching pasties, which certainly wasn't hurting the presentation any.

I gave a brief thought to my finances, confirmed that I had enough to pay one more month of rent, and decided that whatever this girl was offering, it was worth getting fired for. I smiled at my new friend and she took my hand. I will save you all the titillating details, but suffice it to say, the four of us bounced around that shadowbox like popcorn on a stovetop.

I was glowing before, but when we were finished I was absolutely incandescent. I was also sweating like a fat guy on a stationary bike. My fellow orgiasts got dressed (if you can call it that) and left the office. On her way out, the blonde gave me a lingering open-mouthed kiss, leaving a taste of cinnamon on my lips. Yum. I closed the door behind them and sprawled sideways on an office chair. My limbs dangled off the edges and I looked at the black ceiling. The smile on my face felt like it was staple gunned to my skull, and I must have looked like the happiest corpse in the world.

I'm not sure how long I lay there, because at some point my Self dissolved into a million little particles to be blown about the club by the ventilation system, but at some point Clea came back to man the box. I slithered off the chair and onto the floor, yawned deliciously, and stood up by dragging myself up one of the wooden beams. I needed water and electrolytes. It was time to go down to the Theater.

As I got to the bar Armando and Jesus, the barbacks in their tight black tee shirts, started laughing and making a big show of applauding and nodding their heads. "Muy *bien*, Loki! Muy, pero *muy,* bien!" they yelled.

Uh oh. I thought. *If they know…*

I ignored the barbacks, leaned against the long, wooden Theater bar, and tried to make eye contact with Sabrina, who was slinging drinks tonight. She was busy with other customers, but I was in no hurry. To my right, a few people down, I saw Juicy. He threw back a shot then slapped the empty plastic rocks glass on the bar. In that moment I tasted the raw booze sliding down his throat and grimaced (he did not). *Some accountability-buddy I am,* I thought. I sensed pure disapproval boring into the back of my skull and turned around, in case an attack of some sort was coming. I was pretty on the money. Lada was plowing through the crowd like a T-34 tank, muscular shoulders up and ready to displace anyone unlucky enough to be in her way. Her black eyes had found her target: yours truly. The party parted before her like the proverbial Red Sea.

Uh oh, I thought again, and tightened up as she walked right up to me.

She held her face an inch from mine, eyebrows arched, electricity coming off her like a Marvel villain. I realized I was holding my breath. My pleasure- and drug-addled mind was only able to produce the following plea, *Please don't kill me please don't kill me please don't kill me.*

"You're lucky you're the bookkeeper!" Lada somehow yelled and hissed at the same time. I froze like a field mouse before a viper... Then she gave me a smile that had my mind producing more oxytocin than it had at any point in this molly trip. Gorgeous, beneficent, forgiving. She would not kill me, probably. She may not even fire me. I started to breathe again.

"Um, what do you mean?" I asked, stupidly.

Lada shook her head, then grabbed my hair in an iron fist. I nearly yelped. She just held it for a moment (did my cock move? you bet it did) then gave it a non-flirty yank and stormed off.

It took a moment, but I got there in the end. My hair! Of course! It was long and full and there wasn't another person in the club with a 'do like mine. Anyone who saw the long-haired fuckboy cavorting in the Shadowbox knew without a shadow of a doubt that there was more to the studious bookkeeper than meets the eye.

I thought about the situation as I went back to the office with a cold bottle of water in hand. It was three a.m. and apart from a few committed dancers on the catwalk, the place was emptying out—time to close the Box. In the deserted office I started putting away the sex toys and condoms while fantasizing about the walk home and sliding into my bed. I was spent, still pretty high, and glad I still had a job.

That's when Clea burst through the door like she was on the SWAT team. I didn't even have time to react before she marched over to me, slapped a foot-long veiny black dildo out of my hand, and pushed me into an office chair which rolled back until it connected with the wooden beam—*Christ, were people just gonna assault me for the rest of the night, or what?* She threw one long leg over me and straddled my lap.

"Now listen up," she said and patted my cheek with a warm hand. I'll bet this girl had a dom streak in her a mile wide. "It's your lucky night. Tonight, now, this one time only, I'm gonna let you fuck me. Got it?"

This place is fucking nuts, I thought. "That's amazing!—But I'm wiped, I actually just had sex... And that molly you—"

"Do I look like I care about how wiped or high you are?" She snapped. She didn't, in fact, but I sensed that no response was required from me. Her forwardness was super hot and I genuinely *was* flattered. And she was technically my boss tonight. Besides, my hands were pretty much tied (or would be?)

"Now get in the fucking box," she said, and stood up.

Clea and I had never touched before. It was electric. We fucked, sweating buckets, as our shadows humping for all of Yes House and our colleagues to see. At one point I turned to see Vish's head poking through the curtains. He closed his eyes and bit his lower lip. I would bet my bottom dollar that on the other side of that curtain he was running his hands all over his beautiful body and dry-humping something, the poor guy. I gave him a wink, and continued.

The sex was incredible and I experienced a much deeper connection than during the orgy earlier. Our bodies synched in a fluid dance that crescendoed and fell, and we tumbled through space, end over end, losing ourselves in one another.

Thirty magical minutes later, we were putting on our clothes and saying goodbye.

~~~

The rest of the winter went like that: work, party, sleep, repeat. There wasn't much else to do, anyway. It was so damn cold. I became a much more formidable bookkeeper and had countless wonderful nights at the club.

New York City got spring's first warm kiss in early April, and both the people and the flowers eagerly turned their faces up to the sun's caress and bloomed. People opened their doors and coats and took to the streets. As a Californian, especially, it was wild to see the change.

I couldn't stop smiling at strangers on the street, and they smiled back. I think we were just so goddamn happy to see people walking around again that we forgot that smiling in NYC wasn't *cool.* Suddenly I couldn't find a seat at my favorite cafe because the population of my neighborhood seemed to quadruple overnight. I wasn't mad about it. The howls of winter winds on dark, desolate streets were replaced with warm laughter and groovy music pouring out of the open windows and doors of bars, restaurants, and cafes. People walked down the street with a little extra pep in their step, and sometimes a look that said, "It's spring and I'm feeling the biological imperative to reproduce." Also known as, "I'm a get laid to-night!"

Change was in the air at Yes House, too. The family had shifted; some didn't make it through the winter. It felt sudden, the absence of familiar faces. The owners had fired Griz, the event booker, and his assistant Sola, supposedly for unsatisfactory work. Sable, my old archnemesis, quit, saying she had had enough of the scene. *Hallelujah,* I thought.

Safari Tahoe and Koochy took over Sable's duties. Julia's boyfriend, a short and frail looking music nerd named Smooch, replaced Griz and Sola. Throw in all the new DJs, bartenders, security guards, and performers… and the place just didn't feel the same.

My life wasn't much different, apart from my no longer splitting time between the club and Mateo's office in the city. I preferred it this way, anyway. Yes House was far more entertaining. During the day, the office, in the upper corner of the Theater, provided an ideal visual and auditory vantage point. Anytime I needed a tiny break I just looked up from my laptop and over the edge (or up towards the ceiling) to see performers doing their thing. Familiar faces and ones I had never seen, they trained, practiced choreography, performed incredible acrobatic feats—all of it sexy. Once, I was counting a couple stacks of cash when Clea glided by on a heart-shaped lyra (a steel aerial hoop). She came within inches of my face and we looked at each other briefly and touched our fingertips before gravity took her away from me, once again.

On Wednesdays, Lada taught a lunchtime Silks class for the employees. On this particular Wednesday, I scarfed down my veggie sandwich, threw on some gold leggings and joined them in the Theater. It was humbling, to put it lightly, but I felt great after the midday movement and no-mind time.

After I changed back into my non-circus clothes and sat at my desk, I found it hard to concentrate on work. I had Quickbooks open on my laptop, but couldn't figure out where in the Expenses section I was supposed to put "Dildoes, Vibrators, and Miscellaneous Butt Paraphernalia." Down in the Theater, Lada elegantly rolled down the silks while a group of drag queens practiced a dance routine. Conversations drifted up to me like warmed carbon dioxide, which, I suppose, is all conversation is, in the cosmic scheme. Dreams bemoaned her short hair; it was difficult keeping her wigs on during aerial performances. Clea, long haired but troubled nonetheless, responded by sharing her latest K-hole experience at The Box, which left her crawling down the stairs and through the venue to escape. Mrs. Miss described a Grindr hookup: a man with his leg in a cast who, upon ejaculation, immediately pulled out a half-eaten bodega sandwich and started munching.

Eavesdropping without meaning to, I smiled. Life at the circus was grand, distracting though it was to my duties.

Unlike myself, the owners were apparently unaffected by this wacky work environment. Zoe was in one of the leather booths at the back of the Theater under the tech booth, having a meeting with the producers of Glitterbox, a massive London/Ibiza based queer party collective. I watched as her curly red hair bounced with every animated body movement. I was impressed. It was her sixth meeting of the day. Six months ago she was goofing off with the performers for most of the day. Now she was an owner, a planner, a negotiator.

Lada was on the stage, working on a new act for her and Mrs. Miss. The stage looked like the scene of an arts and crafts store explosion. Hand tools, paint cans, oozing bottles of glitter, pizza costumes, piles of fabrics, mannequins, googly eyes, and hot glue guns were scattered about. Safari Tahoe and Spunk surveyed the scene from the tech booth, shaking their heads. They knew they would have to clean up the creative's mess.

Amar popped into the office and stood in front of the bulletin board, squinting against the smoke rising from the Camel in his mouth.

"Hey Amar, how's it going?" I asked.

He nodded while taking a drag. "Good. What's up with you?"

"I'm good, man. Just tried the silks and got my ass kicked." Amar gave no indication of having heard me, as per usual, but don't let his manner fool you: nothing gets past him. "Hey, you want to grab a quick bite somewhere? I'm starving."

"Can't today," he said, reading something on the board. "I'm fasting. Haven't eaten in ten days. Next week, though, I'm down." He took a last drag off his cigarette, threw it on the floor, ground it out with the sole of one of his enormous Blundstones, and walked out.

Christ, is there not one *normal person in this whole place?*

Five o'clock rolled around and Juicy pushed himself away from the desk at which he sat for about fifty hours a week. As usual, he spent the day answering emails and taking calls from lawyers, booking agents, insurance agents, financial advisors, the Fire Marshal, the NYPD, the liquor distributor, and about a million other people a club owner has to communicate with on a weekly basis. As is frequently the case, he realized that he had neglected to eat anything all day.

"Wanna grab some Italian food?" he asked.

"Hell, yes!" I told him, and shut my laptop.

We went down the block to Pizza Works, a spacious pizza and pasta joint with a real wood-fired oven. The design was funky yet simple, and the two young Italians who owned it made sure that they served some of the best food in the borough—from Neapolitan pizza that took your breath away to handmade ravioli that melted in your mouth. Not too expensive, either. It didn't hurt that half the time our meals were comped due to the fact that the owners partied at Yes House on a weekly basis.

Over little gem salads, pasta (gnocchi for me; meat ragu tagliatelle for Juicy), and a funghi pizza with the airiest, crustiest crust this side of the Mediterranean Sea, we chatted about life, Juicy's brother on the west coast, and the club. Sex gossip, more specifically.

"I fucked Lada in the cage after hours one time," he said.

"Nice!" I said, and meant it. I was surprised, them being business partners and all.

"Well," I offered, not to be outdone, "Clea and I fucked in the Shadowbox last weekend."

Juicy's hand, holding a folded slice, paused halfway to his mouth and he raised his eyebrows. "While you were running it?" He asked in an even tone.

"No! Of course not!" I said too loudly, and forced a chuckle that couldn't have fooled anyone. "It was after three," I assured him, wondering if he was playing it dumb about the foursome *before* three.

Juicy just nodded, and whatever thoughts he had on the topic remained his own. "Are you going to see her again?" He asked.

"Actually, yeah." I said as I poured some chili oil on a piece of crust and tossed it into my mouth. "We're supposed to get dinner later. It's going to be our, um, first date, I guess."

"Ha!" Juicy slapped the table happily. "Fuck first, date later. Love it."

A bearded waiter walked by with a carafe of water, filled our glasses, and asked if everything was okay with an adorable accent. We thanked him and he walked off.

"So how's the club doing?" I asked.

"Everything's good!" Juicy said then sat back in his chair and interlaced his fingers behind his head—a picture of a man who had just eaten for the first time in twelve hours. "We're back in the black, thank god. I just need to find a manager for Sunday, then everything will be gravy."

"What's Sunday?"

"Sunday is Daybreaker, a dance party that starts at eight in the morning. These happy hippies go to bed early on a Saturday night—sober, to boot!—just so they can be bright eyed and bushy tailed to dance their hearts out Sunday morning. It's actually really cool. You gotta try it sometime." Having caught the waiter's eye, Juicy scribbled an imaginary signature in the air. He drained the last of his water. "I'd do it, but I'm out of town that day, going upstate with my mom. And the manager Birdy is managing the Saturday event, which will let out at six in the morning. He'll unlikely be ready or willing to start work again at eight."

"Will the bar be open?" I asked. A glimmer of an idea began sparking.

"No way, *José*. They're strictly no-alcohol parties. These adorable freaks survive on kombucha and get drunk off good vibes. That's what they say, anyway. I wonder how many of them are blowing rails in the bath—"

"What about the door?" I interrupted him.

"Nope, not on us. Daybreaker does all their tickets online and has a team of volunteers here on the day to keep entry smooth. We ain't gotta do shit."

"So, essentially," I half-thought aloud, "you just need someone to unlock the doors and look... managerial?"

"Essentially," he said. "I mean, there'll be a couple of tech guys, a security guard, and one performer, but they'll all be doing their thing and don't need supervision, or nothing like that."

"I'll do it," I said to him.

Juicy gave me that look he likes, his eyes assessing, judging, running the risk/reward ratio all at once. I'd seen him do it a thousand times by that point, but would like to think that there was a very specific *one* reserved for me. After a couple of seconds he looked off and slowly nodded his head as if finishing an inward dialogue. I held my breath.

"All right, you're on," he finally said.

I managed to look more or less blasé and simply said, "Cool." Inside my head, though, was a ninety-person orchestra playing the climactic part of the William Tell Overture.

I brought all that excitement to my date with Clea. At one point she literally grabbed my lips between her finger and thumb to make me shut up about it. She looked cute, her curly red hair resting over a white tank top and matching her red jeans. We were at Bunker, a warehouse converted into a Vietnamese restaurant. She had a veggie pho with extra noodles, and I got my usual shrimp banh mi. Halfway through her soup she complained I didn't order any appetizers, but I was so full from earlier I wasn't even going to finish my sandwich.

We got to chatting and it turned out we were both from the Bay Area, and had a similar dorky sense of humor. After I paid for the meal she leaned in and said, "I'm a liar."

"Oh yeah?" I asked. "How so?"

"We're gonna fuck a second time."

On that note, I called us an Uber.

CHAPTER THIRTEEN

Coming out of the kitchen hallway into the Theater I hook a hard left and climb the black steel ladder on the wall. Just in the nick of time, too—a torrent of puke from a shirtless fat guy narrowly misses my right Blundstone as I step on the first rung. Hand over hand I climb above the party and into the tech booth. Less of a booth, really, more of a roofless balcony bunker.

Like a lot of spaces where highly specialized weirdos work, it's an anxiety-inducing control center of wires, gadgets, LED lights, screens, and expensive looking equipment that the average person couldn't identify.

The very cramped area is dominated by a plywood-top desk that could've come from a church basement AA meeting in a shitty neighborhood. On the desk are two laptops, four black microphone receivers that look like old school cable boxes, an enormous sound board with dials, sliders, and knobs; a video projector the size of an Italian car from the fifties; another, smaller board with a monitor (lighting); a half-drunk glass of amber colored booze on the rocks sitting in a small puddle of its own condensation (whisky, my nose tells me); and a spoon the size of my pinky. Snaking between, around, through, over, and under all of this are about a thousand wires, cables, and cords.

Leche, wearing a black T-shirt and ripped blue Levi's, is leaning back in a wobbly wooden chair with his legs crossed and feet on the table. The picture of leisure, he's single handedly controlling the club's sound with his iPad. Inches away, knobs and sliders move on the big soundboard, apparently of their own accord. It's cool and spooky.

Next to him is Barney, the VJ (visual projection artist). He's tall, buzz-bald, in his mid-40s, and has a Steve

Jobs-meets-Professor Xavier look about him with his frameless glasses in front of his eyes that telegram intelligence and competence. As always, he's wearing a flannel shirt and Dickies jeans. He lives in Connecticut but still drives over a few nights a week to work here. The glow of one of the laptop screens is reflected in the oval lenses of his glasses as his fingers fly over the keyboard and trackpad. As a result, trippy sexy human shapes are projected onto the curtains behind the stage; they melt and morph into one another in time to the music.

Lada, in a black unitard and shiny black heels, is leaning with both elbows on the back of a lopsided office chair, legs straight, ass sticking out like a strip club sign silhouette. In the chair is Nasty. He is wearing trashed black jeans, a too-long leather belt, and a plain black t-shirt. At the moment he's using the bottom of his shirt, already stretched out, to polish the lenses of his glasses. In the gloom it's hard to say if they're cleaner for his efforts. He and Lada are having a conversation I can't hear over the music, her head behind his left ear. He's not quite crying, but visibly distraught. He puts his glasses back on, then hits a button on the lighting board in rhythm with the beat, activating a strobe and adding some excitement to the party below.

"How you doing?" I ask Barney, giving his right shoulder a squeeze and startling him out of his flow. Like any artist in the throes of creating, when he's video mapping, time stops and it's just him and the computer.

"All good! How about you?" he asks as he smiles at me, but I know that he doesn't actually care—not when all he wants is to return to his lasers, or whatever they are at the molecular level.

"Good good, just checking in," I say. He turns back to his computer, and his face reforms itself into the classic slack jawed look of the professional screen gazer. As far as he's concerned, I've poofed! out of existence. I keep standing behind him, watching the party from above. A bit closer now, I listen in on Lada and Nasty.

"I don't know…," says Nasty. "And half the time, everything is fine! Like, we've been together for a minute and love and trust each other. We're all snuggly and I-love-*you*-more!

then—wham!—out of the blue, a kick in the dick." He shakes his head as he watches the party, then hits the strobe again.

"What happened this time?" Asks Lada.

"Literally fucking nothing," he says, and throws up his non-strobe hand, palm up. The international sign for 's/he's fucking nuts.'

"One day she loves me and I'm her teddy bear, the next I'm a piece of shit and she wants to kick me to the curb. I go out of my way to check in—constantly!—to see how I can make her happy. I bring her pizza and write cutesy little notes on the box. I read that stupid book on attachment styles, and even listen to Esther Perel's podcast! But god forbid I take some space to take care of me, or do my own thing for a day… and just like that I'm a selfish prick. And she's so insecure! I can't hang out with any of my female friends without her thinking I'm fucking them. And you know me, I'm not like that—I don't cheat. I mean, I made out with that one fire dancer chick at Burning Man, but what's one sloppy kiss? At *Burning Man,* for Christ's sake! Ugh. I'm generally pretty even keeled, but this thing's got me *down*. For the first time I think I understand these poor depressed fucks, dragging their feet everywhere they go, with their chin on their chests. I find myself struggling to get out of bed some days, and it's not because of some… some…" he hit a button on the board and the lights changed to a velvety red, then found the right word. "Some chemical *imbalance*!" He stabbed the strobe button harder than strictly necessary.

"That sounds shitty," Lada comforted. "Seems like she's dealing with some unresolved stuff and it's showing up in your relationship."

Nasty grabs the rocks glass in front of him and throws back a hefty swallow. "'Unresolved *stuff*'?!" He grimaces. "She's batshit-fucking-crazy!"

"Well, yes," Lada concedes, "that is the less clinical term."

The two say nothing for a minute. Nasty activates some spotlights and changes the main lighting to blue, adding an icy sci-fi vibe to the dancefloor.

"What about you?" Nasty asks. "Any crazy bitches ruining your life?"

Lada takes a tall thin glass off the shelf behind her, puts the straw in her mouth and takes a sip. The clear liquid drops an inch. "Just one," she says.

"Oh, yeah? Is he as bad as mine is?" Nasty asks.

Lada nods . "She makes yours look like the picture of perfect mental health."

"Ooh!" Nasty is intrigued. "Anyone we know?"

"Yupp," Lada says. "You're looking at her."

"Ha," nasty says without actually laughing, but some of the tension has left the conversation. "C'mon, you're not that bad."

Lada brings a bedazzled Juul to her lips and takes a long hit. As the thick fruity cloud dissipates, she says, "You've seen me lose my shit how many times? Act like a complete fucking lunatic. You think I don't know how crazy and manic and unstable I look? But that's not who I *am*. That's just how my emotions are manifesting themselves in that moment. Anyway, all that was just a roundabout way to say, 'hang in there, buddy—you're better than you feel."

Nasty nodded for a few seconds. "Thanks for that, Thich Nhat Hahn, but I still *feel* like shit." He smiles for a moment and his eyes lose some of that despairing shine.

"It gets better," Lada says. "Then worse. Then better again." She gives Nasty a kiss on one stubbled cheek and stands up to her full height. "I gotta go. Love you."

She sucks up the last of her drink and puts the glass back on the shelf. "Hi, Loki, bye, Loki," she says and gives me a little smile. She steps out of the tech booth and onto the ladder, then carefully maneuvers her high heels down the rungs. I watch the top of her head disappear, then her hands. When I turn back, Nasty's watching the party and changing the lights with his left hand. In his right is the whiskey. He brings it to his mouth and doesn't stop until the only thing hitting his lips is ice. Washing down Lada's dose of wisdom, I imagine.

Her words echo in my head as I let my eyes survey the party. The guy on the ledge is still napping blissfully as Security and the EMT keep watch. People keep dancing, grooving around or over the blockage, black latex flashing and colorful fingernails reaching for the ceiling. Below me and to the right, Juicy and Amar are chatting by the Theater bar.

My emotions are not reality, or whatever she said. From Lada, of all people! The girl has more ups and downs than the Venezuelan stock market. Her outbursts were legendary, and if you worked at YES for more than a couple of weeks, you'd likely as not wind up on the receiving end of one—or collateral damage, at the very least, an innocent bystander unlucky to be in the blast zone. Of course she, herself, knew this, but I had never heard her talk about this side of her so frankly, with so much awareness. It gave me hope. For her, for me, for Nasty… for all of us stumbling through life, trying to do our best with the hands (and hearts and minds) we were dealt.

I snap out of my philosophizing and look at the time. 1:53 a.m.

"Smell you later," I yell over the music, but neither Barney nor Nasty acknowledges me. I climb down the ladder and into the lingering cheesy fug, then take a big step around the barback mopping up the pile of puke.

Walking into the kitchen hallway I hear Juicy and Amar talking. I round the corner and see them between the industrial dishwasher and the prep counter with their backs to me. I don't want to interrupt, but I can't get past them without doing just that. I hang back for a second, leaning with my shoulder against the white-tiled wall.

"So what do you think?" Asks Amar.

"What do I think? Are you kidding me? That sounds fucking incredible," Juicy says.

I tell myself I'm not eavesdropping on purpose (again), that I am waiting for a break in conversation to walk through, but I make no move to leave, either.

"It would definitely be a wealthier, more vanilla crowd than Bushwick," Amar says. "But we can make a lot more money. A *lot*. We're talking about Williamsburg here. I mean, a bit of a sellout move, for sure, and the scene is way less diverse and artsy… but can you imagine? After a couple of years we'd have enough dough to take Yes House to the next level." From my place next to the laundry bin overflowing with bar towels, I see Amar's smile.

A lot more money… a sellout move, I repeat in my head.
I quietly turn around and go back the way I came.

CHAPTER FOURTEEN

Daybreaker went off without a hitch. Hundreds of juice-cleanse ravers showed up at the crack of dawn with a smile and a clean conscience. Well-rested and pure of body and mind, they rocked up with a joyful eagerness to dance their yoga-toned tushies off. Kombucha flowed like wine; alkaline water like, well, regular water.

The mood was diurnal and bright. For my part, the whole thing took very little effort. Mostly I walked around or just stood there, smiling. Everybody smiled back. There was none of the night-life darkness. The only questions I had ("Where is that other case of guava juice?" and "Do we have any tree tea oil?") were answered by the one security guard there. Sure beats, "Fuckfuckfuck where's that EMT?!"

Juicy showed up at noon, after everybody left. He went out back to the Patio, took off his shirt and shoes and sat on a bench. The spring sun kissed his olive-ish skin as he tilted his head back and closed his eyes, happy as a photosynthesizing plant. I sat next to him.

"How'd it go?" he asked, eyes still closed.

"Yeah, good. Pretty easy. No alcohol or money or anything. You know."

"Want to do it again?"

"Shit, yeah!" I said, grinning big.

And that's how I became a manager.

~~~

The day before my next "first" shift I had my official Manager Training. I showed up thirty minutes early in the nicest black jacket I owned. I was buzzing with excitement and two cappuccinos coursing through my veins (probably 1.5 too many). Juicy rolled in ten minutes late in a form fitting tee shirt, ripped jeans, and scuffed up sneakers. He put his small uncovered paper cup of steaming espresso on the bar, lit a cigarette, and yawned.

We spent the afternoon doing an in-depth manager walk-through. I followed Juicy around like a puppy, pen and notepad in hand, asking a million questions and scribbling his responses in a chaotic shorthand that looked like Arabic. *Front Room: two disco ball switches, three light switches behind bar, two light switches in kitchen. Garbage bins by front door—new liners. Water station, full, clean. Theater doors open. Door cash to black safe...*

Juicy was adamant about making sure the "vibe" was just right, and spent a lot of time talking about things like lights, temperature, and even smell.

"If you come in and there's a funk in here from the night before, or from all these performers rehearsing and sweating and shit, air the place out, light some incense, I don't care what you do. You walk into a place, you don't want b.o. to be the first thing you notice."

No b.o. I dutifully wrote in my pad.

"And that's basically all you need to know," Juicy said.

"Sounds good," is what I said to him. In my head, however, I heard myself shouting, *Waahooooooooo* while doing mental backflips. How was this real? Was this man for-real giving me the opportunity to not only be involved with this community I followed out of the desert, but to actually *manage* it? And not just any old crew in any old place, but a group of some of the most special humans I had ever met, in Yes fucking House! By then I would have done anything for my new family and home, and here I was getting paid to watch over them a couple of nights a week. I felt like I won the karmic lottery. Though I suppose that's the wrong analogy, because that's direct cause and effect. Whatever it was, I've seldom felt so fortunate and grateful.

"One more thing," Juicy said. "In the beginning it's best to walk lightly as you earn everyone's trust. What I'm saying is, don't go around barking at people, laying down the law. If you see something off or someone fucking up, big or small, you just let me know and I'll handle it."

"Understood. You got it." I would have agreed to cut off the last joint of my left pinky right then, if that's what he needed.

I went straight home and studied my notes until I could recite them.

The next day I put in my eight of bookkeeping, then shadowed Birdy during the evening theater show. Birdy was small statured and slight of build. He wore his jet black hair short and combed to the side, and with his pale skin and fine features reminded me of a nocturnal Elijah Wood. He was Peruvian, but his eyes, like many South Americans', had a decidedly Asian tilt to them. Birdy had an interesting sense of fashion that defied category but worked, somehow. Think Michael Jackson (the motorcycle jacket MJ, not the flowy white shirt one) toned down a bit. He was the serious, cool-as-ice Batman to my keen young Robin (if Robin was a longhaired west coast hippie with a taste for molly and Batman wore black leather gloves with the knuckles cut out).

In the kitchen we read every single expiry date, from the milk in the fridge to the boxes of salt on the stainless steel shelf above the industrial stove top. In the office we went through hundreds of credit card receipts from every single bartender, then sat and watched all six monitors showing the feed from the security cameras, scrutinizing every area of the club like hawks. I'm not sure what we were looking for, but Birdy's face told me whatever it was, it was serious.

If someone came in a minute late—barback, actor, sword swallower—he had a talk with them. He was non confrontational and calm about it, easy with his words and body language, but never turned a blind eye to anything.

This was a bit too by the book for me, but I was serious about this shot that Juicy was giving me, and I committed myself to Birdy's lofty standards. For now. As Picasso said: Learn the rules like a pro so you can break them like an artist (although he probably said it in Spanish). With time and practice I knew that I would develop my own managing style, but this was the time to prove to Yes House—the owners, producers, and staff, but also to all the employees I knew only as names on the weekly payroll—that I was dedicated, willing, and able to take the helm… and would take no shit.

The first evening event I managed solo was called Haiku Brothel. It was outside-produced, which means that someone unaffiliated with Yes House contracted us for the space and staffing. My call time was six, and I arrived a few minutes before then. Doors would open at seven and there was a small crew finishing with the set up. The decorators had transformed the Theater into a classy speakeasy. The lighting was as velvety as the maroon curtains, and there were small, black-clothed round tables on the dancefloor. In the center of each one a thin candle burned, beads of wax running onto gold rimmed saucers with tiny flowers on them. There were old-looking tchotchkes, too: a crystal perfume bottle with a little hose and pump bulb on one, an art deco steel ashtray with a push button on another, a little burnished figurine of an equestrian on a prancing horse on a third, etc. Very classy. There were leather chairs and settees on the stage. Between them was a subtly colorful rug, on which was a small drum set, a cello on a stand, and a hollow body guitar leaning against a tweed-covered Fender amp. In front of the instruments was a mic stand. At that moment a gorgeous woman in flapper girl get-up, complete with elbow length gloves, a bowl hat with feather, and a cigarette holder as long as her forearm, stood in front of it, reciting haikus for a last mic check. When Whiskers in the booth was satisfied with the levels, the pretty poetess turned off the mic and walked off stage. A stagehand pulled the curtains closed. Everything was ready.

The guests began to arrive shortly after seven. Most dressed according to the theme. Bejeweled headbands sparkled, feather boas adorned shapely throats, and tasseled pencil dresses titillated with their climbing slits. The women looked nice, too. From behind the curtain the cellist was playing a serene melody that I felt in my solar plexus. People took their seats quietly and conversed in hushed tones. All very urbane. It was easy to forget that in this very spot unspeakable debauchery took place a couple of times a week.

When every seat was taken, the lights dimmed and the curtains opened. There were fifteen women on the stage, some sitting on the furniture, others kneeling beside it. For the most part they were dressed similarly to the woman I saw earlier—Roaring Twenties cool girl—but a few wore kimonos, and a couple wore corsets, garters, thigh-highs, and heels. One wore a very sparkly, too-teal dress that fit the scene about as well as a disco ball at the Kremlin.

After giving the audience a chance to take in this eclectic tableau, the one in green stood up. I knew that her name was Karen, and that she was the head honcho. Maybe that's why she opted for that horrible dress? Picture the Little Mermaid, as reenvisioned by Donatella Versace.

Karen walked up to the microphone stand like she was on a Fashion Week runway and took the mic with her left hand. What I at first took for feedback was Karen's actual voice.

"Good evening!" she whine-screeched, "I am KAREN!"

Some people in the audience frowned, and I saw a few instinctively raise their shoulders towards their ear canals. I, myself, considered if it was too late to sneak behind the bar and grab some earplugs that I knew the bartenders kept in a clear plastic box on top of the little Red Bull fridge.

After giving us enough time to be impressed, Karen continued the assault. "And *here* are my *fourteen haiku whores*!"

I was clenching my jaw so hard I began to question the integrity of my molars. Also, *she did just say, 'haiku whores,' yeah?*

One by one, the whores rose, came forward, introduced themselves with two lines of rhyme, then went back to their seats or knees. Each had a voice sultrier, lovelier than the last. Unlike some people.

Alas, the intros ended and we braced ourselves as Karen took the mic. Whiskers must have turned her down, because while it was still almost intolerable, it was better than before. She explained that during the entire performance the audience was free to walk around and mingle with the haiku whores who would be working the room. She also informed us that if one wished, one could pick a poet and pay her for a private "recital" (Karen's voice provided the quotations, not me) in the Onyx Room. Now I understood the nature of their hyphenated job title.

Our ears took a collective sigh as Karen handed the mic to a PW, a compact brunette in a scarlet kimono with koi on it, then exited stage left. Kimono inserted it in the black ring of the mic holder then followed her like a chastised geisha. The band struck up a jaunty French jazz number and the guests got out of their seats and began to mingle. The performers circulated, some accepting drinks from patrons.

The jazz trio played all night, sticking to upbeat standards, which they performed with style and skill. They took short breaks to allow for five-minute haiku readings and drank like fish. The vibe was playful and sexy, with a sprinkle of bohemian. When not on stage, the beautiful bards sashayed around the Theater and flirted with the guests and each other. Occasionally, one would lead a customer by the hand through the Front Room and out back to the Onyx, a smile of nervous anticipation on the latter.

I did my rounds, peeking in on backstage, the office, the Patio, out front on Yefferson Street. I stopped by the Onyx Room to see what kind of private poetic services were on offer. Quietly cracking the door, I looked in. Red pillows covered the floor and a matching dim light illuminated the cozy space. A sweet woodsy perfume drifted out. Opium den meets bordello. Two women sat cross-legged on the pillows, and a man was reclined in a corner, nearly supine. The PW's kneeled next to him, and with their lips inches from their john's ears, spoke softly. Whether it was actual poetry or phone sex, I could not hear, but the guests all seemed to be into it. The man more visibly than the women, with the little tent he was pitching. I left quietly, thinking that to call them "whores" was both demeaning *and* false advertising, but what do I know.

It wasn't a big event and staffing was appropriately thin. Daisy, the tall blonde, was tending bar, Crius was security, Whiskers was running sound, and Macaw controlled the lights. Nasty didn't work Tuesdays, so Macaw was filling in. In a nightclub (or speakeasy) he stood out like a klansman at a BLM march. A vegan Phishhead, Macaw wore baggy tie-dye tee shirts and red corduroy pants, while in our business all production staff went for black and tight. In a sea of chic bitchface, he smiled openly and looked at life through rose-colored glasses. Literally. His were heart-shaped. And despite being a filler-inner, he was damn good at his job. With the support of this ace crew, my job was little more than smiling, walking around, and writing reports.

I ended up working every theater show for the rest of the week. Each one a different show with a different crowd.

Wednesday I managed an in-house production: Beginner Burlesque. About a hundred people came to watch a dozen non-professional grade bump-and-grinders strut their stuff. Burlesque isn't stripping, *per se*, but it's not *not* stripping, you know?—and the audience was encouraged to tip the performers. The raunchier and wilder the acts, the louder the cheers and whistles. Dollar bills rained onto the stage (or were shoved, slowly or unceremoniously, into various garments and skin folds). One woman really brought the house down. She came out in a Trump mask, blue suit, and red tie, then stripped (non-amateurishly, I might add) to reveal a pair of enormous breasts and a strap-on the size of a Subway five-dollar-foot-long. Then, with what must have taken enormous core and waist control, she swung all three violently, eliciting a roar from the crowd that rattled the bottles of booze on the shelves behind the bar.

Sparky was the showrunner. I was surprised, but happy to see that he had gotten his foot back in the door with this production. He emceed the event in full drag—big blonde wig, heavy-handed makeup, spaghetti-strapped black cocktail dress that accentuated his broad shoulders, and black high heels. His legs were muscular, bare, and very hairy. He announced performers and talked them off stage, and ran little fun activities between acts. One such activation was Blow the Churro. Before you start thinking of that one time you were drunk in Tijuana, I just want to say that I'm talking about the Mexican fried dough tubelets.

Sparky invited audience members who were confident in their fellatio skills to come on stage and prove themselves in a friendly little competition. Before he was fully done with the last word, squeals of delight and pick-me's filled the room as women and gay dudes nearly knocked over their seats jumping out of them. Sparky pulled six guests onto the stage, then selected six performers to line up in front of them. With great ceremony he took an oil-spotted paper bag that a stagehand passed him behind the curtain, and removed from it six golden brown sugary treats, each about ten inches long, as wide as a broom handle. Letting the bag fall to the floor, he splayed them in front of his face like a card hand, to the audience's delight. Going down the line of performers he handed each a churro, which they held with one of their hands in front of their crotch. Trump held hers right next to her veiny strapon.

"Are you ready to play, Blow the Churro?" he bellowed like a wrestling announcer, to shouts of assent from the three men and three women on stage. "Ready, set… BLOW!"

Without hesitation, the self-proclaimed bj kings and queens dropped to their knees and began to stuff their faces with churro. It was a sight to behold. I've seen my share of deepthroating and sword swallowing, but this was something else altogether. I swear the winner's churro didn't have one granule of sugar left.

Thursday was The Get Down, and if you were a white girl with dreadlocks living in the Tri-State Area, you did not miss this monthly event. Our very own Fox greeted every patron at the door with a warm hug and a piece of fair-trade dark chocolate. The DJ's spun tribal house as shirtless drummers unaffiliated with any tribes slapped tribal drums. The kombucha was free, wrist tattoos suggested that one *breathe* or *be here now*, painters created real-time psychedelic art, and twenty-somethings pontificated about such heady topics as ethical non-monogamy, the abolition of borders, and the barter system, as they escaped from their tech jobs to makeout with hippie strangers. The smiles were as wide and the b.o. was a living, breathing entity that you could almost pet and try—futilely—to pacify. From the lingering funk I guessed that most of these environmentally-minded folks conserved water by showering once every lunar cycle.

On Friday, Rollerskate transformed Yes House into a roller disco. Afros, bell bottoms, knee-high white socks, spliffs the size of my finger, and Diana Ross pumping out of the speakers. Colorful roller skates carved up the dance floor, toned bare legs flashed, and velvet pant legs swished the '70s back to life. Smiles lit up the room and headbands soaked up sweat. Nobody quite as carefree as a roller skater. The only pinch point was in the Onyx Room, where wheel-less people waited in a long line to receive their skates—the line was made slower by the fact that the skate-dispensing team, a shirtless man with cornrows and an extra-large woman in a tank top named Dro and Poss, were higher than Snoop Dogg and Willie Nelson at a Damian Marley concert. Apart from that? The event went off smoother than Travolta in a white suit.

By Saturday I was beat. My legs were Jello and someone pulled the drainplug from my soul bathtub. Did staying after my shift and partying until sunrise help either situation? It did not. Still, something kept me going. I felt... *fulfilled.* Not too long ago, I was a fanboy in the desert, hanging on their every word, and now I was *overseeing* this community. I mean, sure, Juicy was there most of the time when I worked, and the staff still went to him with any questions or concerns, but I was *The Manager*. The word floated in my head, accompanied by waves of pride and ego. I'd be lying if I said that it wasn't already going to my head. It felt so good, though, so gratifying. I realized that this is what kept me lit up and gave me the strength to power through the exhaustion, the overwork, the too much *YES*.

If the entire week was a build up, Saturday night was the climax. Blunderworld: a hallucinatory rabbit hole of a circus variety show. It sold out every week and was produced by the one and only Grandma.

Grandma was, of course, a man.

Clea talked about him incessantly. "He is one of the absolute greats," she said. "He works with the legendary Susanne Bartsch! You know, the *Queen of Nightlife*? She does Bartschland Follies at the McKittrick on Fridays? When we're lucky, me and my clown troupe occasionally get to perform. Grandma, though? He's got an open-ended residency. He's gonna be a Hall of Famer, for sure."

Before Saturday, I knew Grandma only by reputation and his somehow shrill *and* deep voice on the phone. He called me every Wednesday, a couple hours before I submitted the weekly payroll, to make sure he and his performers were getting paid. I almost never got their invoices on time (common performer habit, I found), and was the one to break the news to Grandma that they'd be paid the following week. He quickly identified me as both the bad guy *and* the messenger, and devoted several minutes a week to verbally killing both.

"Well let me tell you what, Mr. Monopoly Man!" He'd project admirably, as if he was on stage. He's the only person I know whose voice was not made less substantial by the telephone. "We do *not* bust our butts on stage to not get paid in a timely manner! This ain't the fucking sixties, my green little intern! Now we have *di-rect de-posit*, you get me? I flash a titty tonight, my money better be waiting for me in my checking account, pretty as you please and eager for me to spend it on poppers and Prep! And now—let me just make sure I'm understanding you—you're saying my hardworking boys and girls have to wait an extra week? Because you *didn't receive their lousy invoices* 'on time?' This is egregious, absurd, and out-fucking-rageous! Get your tightfisted master on the horn right now, you pathetic, insubstantial—"

I usually never got a word in, and why would I even try? I was clearly outgunned. I would hand the phone to Juicy before things got too ugly. After a few minutes of a seemingly much calmer exchange, Juicy would return the phone and give me a nod. When I put the earpiece to my head a different Grandma was on the line.

"Thanks," he'd say, his voice down in pitch and decibels. "Anyway, sorry about that. Talk to you next week. Have a great day!"

Now on stage with a microphone, lit up by a spotlight, I was seeing him in all his glory. He was well over six feet, thin and long limbed with a small gut. He wore sparkly red clown shoes, high waisted polka dotted white pants, sequined blue shirt, and an elaborate blue ascot. Over the ascot he had on a red and white polka dot bandana that had two little disco balls hanging from it. White grease paint covered his face, and he had purposefully smeared red lipstick on and around his mouth. Glitter and asymmetrical purple eyeshadow circled his eyes. To top it all off, he wore a purple-fro wig with an extra-large shiny blue bow-tie tied around his head.

Grandma stomped around, his enormous shoes slapping the stage, as he laid down the rules. "First off, don't flash us, we'll flash you—there's no need for flash photography because we have more spotlights than American Idol, dumbass! See?" With this, Nasty in the tech booth hit all the spots and Grandma ripped off his shirt. The crowd exploded in laughter and whistles. He had a dad-bod thing happening, and there was something both unattractive *and* appealing about it. "That's right, boys and girls, feast your eyes. I got a hot-dog body with the world's smallest nipples here, folks! But you're getting more than your money's worth!" The crowd was eating it up with both hands. And it was true: Grandma's nipples were minuscule, sticking out of areolas no bigger than pennies.

"Second, no drinks on stage!" he yelled before punting someone's cocktail. The front row covered their heads and ducked as the plastic glass went flying, showering the first five rows with booze, ice, straw, and lime.

"Lastly," Grandma lowered his voice, "If you needed an excuse to see a doctor, come find me in the bathroom during intermission." Grandma winked then let out a mad scientist cackle. "Let the show begin!" The audience clapped and the lights dimmed to black.

After a few seconds of darkness and soft rustling on stage, blue and white lights illuminated the red curtains as they parted, revealing a man standing on stage holding two enormous fans made of peacock feathers. Only his face showed between them, war-painted blue and pink. He gently shook his wondrous wings twice and the colorful feathers undulated around him, cueing the music, which poured out of the speakers. Accompanied by triumphant strings, the man began to sing a beautiful aria. I don't speak Italian, but his words moved me like a gentle hand on my chest. Even without a microphone, his clear, deep voice penetrated the air in the theater, traveling to every corner and sweeping over the audience, wide eyed and still. Still covering himself, he began to move, slowly, at first, with exaggerated steps, then leaped and pirouetted, occasionally moving the fans to accentuate a held note. Landing from an especially athletic jump in which his legs scissored apart nearly to horizontal, he opened his wings fully, arms outstretched triumphantly. Beneath the feathers was the body of a Greek god, naked but for a pair of white bikini bottoms. Not one of these gym boys with the defined abdominals and obliques, he had the thick, muscular trunk of someone who eats with his bare hands and drinks liters of wine from an ornate chalice. He was large. His thick legs looked capable of tearing a pair of pants with just one flex of his quadriceps, and his gravity defying Olympian's buttocks jutted out like boulders. I had never seen such a glorious butt on a man. He held his final note, belting it out loud enough to vibrate my soul, as he shook the peacock feathers. After giving the audience one last second to marvel at him, he tucked his chin, wrapped his wings around himself, and the curtains closed in front of him. The audience clapped and cheered with abandon, and in that moment I realized that the audiences at Yes House shows were both incredibly discerning *and* supportive and generous with their praise.

Grandma walked on stage with the exaggerated strides of a marshland bird, head turned towards the crowd, a goofy smile on his painted face.

He put the mic too close to his mouth and exhaled through his nostrils. "That bootie. You *guys*, I know!" He then arched his back and made a show of looking behind him and down at the conspicuous absence of a "bootie," and sighed dejectedly, letting his shoulders (and the place where his tailbone ended) slump back down. "Ah, well," he said, "I got other talents. And speaking of furries, this next act is for all you animal lovers!" He bounded offstage, every movement a precise part of his act. I understood why he was considered a master of his craft.

All but one spotlight went out, its white hot circle on the curtains as they parted. Dreams stood on stage in a black and white cow onesie, complete with a large pink udder with six long teats. Some kind of rubber or latex, but I couldn't tell without personally milking. For hooves, Dreams had six-inch black stilettos. The hip-hoppy bass drum and snare of Doja Cat's "MOOO!" began to pump out of the speakers, and instantly heads began to nod to the infectious beat. Dreams strutted around the stage, pausing to lip synch along to the moos in the song and fondle her teats. She stopped, slowly undid her zipper from throat to crotch, and bent over, hands on her straight legs. Her white butt had one black spot on it and a little rope of a tail. She began to slither out of her costume in one of the most absurd strip teases I had ever seen. The udder hit the floor with a slap, and the rest of the outfit settled around Dreams's pretty ankles. Her second outfit kept with the sexy bovine theme: a white and black spotted thong with a matching crop top cropped high enough to nearly reveal her own mammaries. She straightened up, stepped out of the cow hide, and continued to move around the stage flashing her gams, hips swaying like a bucket of milk. She stopped on one side of the stage to retrieve a chair and a full gallon of milk from behind the curtain, then returned to the middle and sat in the chair. Whole milk, I noted. Good for her. She sat in the chair, lifted the milk up to her mouth by the jug handle and ripped the plastic seal off with her teeth. She spat the cap, still attached to the broken red ring to the side. Just then the song went "moo!" again and Dreams lifted the gallon over her head with both hands and upended it while looking up. As the full-fat, creamy white liquid ran down her face, hair, throat, chest, and crotch, she moaned orgasmically and convincingly. Evidently, the audience that night was especially passionate about dairy, because I don't think I had ever heard cheering like this. When the plastic jug was empty, she lowered her arms and let it fall to the stage. As the curtains began to close, she used her fingers to wipe milk from her eyes, and just before she disappeared she sucked them dry.

Grandma came out, mic in hand. He didn't have to say anything, I realized—just watching his face was entertaining enough.

"Well," he said, then paused. His timing and delivery were flawless. "All that calcium sure is good for *bones!*" Everybody laughed, myself included. He had us eating out of his hand.

The next act was called Sparrow and comprised of two beautiful women in shiny latex suspended from straps, acting out a choreographed fight scene. They were dressed as Frost and Scorpion from Mortal Kombat and performed with upbeat music that incorporated punch and battlecry sounds, occasionally adding "Finish Him" over the beat. They floated back and forth, sometimes battling mere inches over our heads, with such ease and grace, demonstrating their extraordinary athleticism.

Several acts followed, all unique, interesting, and entertaining, but none compared to the grand finale.

"And now," Grandma said, "Coming to you from across the pond, all the way from London Town, an act you will never forget." He paused. "I am *egg*cited to present to you… Mause!"

Aggressive drum n' bass began to pound from the speakers as the curtains opened on a short blonde wearing only a white apron, moving around a makeshift kitchen. The crowd, those incorrigible sexist horndogs, clapped and cheered immediately. Me, too. The underdressed chef appeared to be in her mid-twenties and looked every bit the English lass with her pale skin and freckles. She hopped between two tables covered with pots, pans, various cooking utensils, a black funnel, a large mason jar filled with peeled boiled eggs, a gallon of milk—two percent this time (*Another lactose act?* I thought), a stick of butter, a stack of big plastic cups, and a brown carton of white eggs. As she whirled around, smacking the pots, pans, even the tables themselves with a wooden spoon, she emitted what sounded like "mer-mer-mer-mer-mer" in a high-pitched cartoonish voice. Not words, exactly, they sounded like something that would come out of a Sesame Street character or a Japanese porn star.

The crowd and I were understandably confused, but after a night of some avant garde shit, we just sat there, waiting for something sexy and/or disturbing to happen.

Mause kept merring merrily, seemingly oblivious of the audience, as she made her way to the side of the stage with jerky jester steps and disappeared behind the curtain for a moment. Reemerging with a stool with one threaded post and four rubber tipped steel legs, she came back to her kitchen, faced away from the audience and slowly bent over to set it down between the tables, giving us a brief view of her lovely white backside topped with the white bow of her apron strings. "Mer!" she remarked, satisfied, then grabbed the plastic cups off the table, shuffled to the edge of the stage and gave them out to five amused people in the front row. Another "mer!" indicated a task completed, and back to the kitchen she went.

She returned with the egg jar and sat on the stool, about ten feet from the expectant faces in the front row. She used her bare feet to push off the stage and spin around once. "Meeeeeer!" she wailed, making it sound like a playground "weeeeeee!" This not being my first Yes House rodeo, I started putting two and two together. Judging by the fidgeting in the front row, I wasn't the only one. For the first time she gave the theater her full face, smiling shyly but with a devilish twinkle in her bright eyes, and spread her legs wide. Her little white toes and unpainted nails seemed to glow on the black stage. The apron hung between her thighs and I wondered if they were as soft as they looked or if there was a leanness beneath the milky skin. She slowly pulled the apron to the side and let it drop over her right leg, revealing a large hairy bush a shade darker than her golden locks. Mause then unscrewed the lid and removed an egg from the mason jar. She held it over her head between her thumb and middle finger.

I think by then it was clear that Mause wasn't there for a live taping of a cooking show. *Oh, shit,* I thought, and looked at the cup holders. Four of them looked like they were rethinking their seat selections, while the fifth, a striking brunette in a little black dress just smiled—all twinkle, zero shyness.

Mause brought the egg to her mouth and gave it a lick, then another. Then, in one efficient movement she stuffed it into her pussy and held up both empty hands for the audience to see. I half expected to see her bush moving as it chewed, and wondered if the eggs were pre-lubed, or her pussy, or both. Mause stretched her arms up and away from her and extended both legs. She squeezed her fists tight and scrunched up her face until her cute features bunched together, then yelled "mer!" and launched the egg out of her vagina.

The shot went wild, hitting a woman sitting in the third row on a bare shoulder. The innocent bystander was visibly disgusted. The rest of the audience both gasped and cheered. Mause was undeterred. "Mer mer mer!" she jabbered excitedly as she blindly reached into the jar and reloaded. Four cup holders stuck their cups out at arm's length while turning their heads as far around as anatomically possible. The sexy brunette held the cup between her breasts with both hands and opened her mouth wide.

Mause adjusted her aim by rotating a few degrees on the stool, and I pictured a tank turret ratcheting into place.

The second egg flew and time slowed. It was a scene from every sports movie ever: the digital clock shows four red zeros, the buzzer or whistle sounds, the ball or puck spins, tumbling end over end as players, coaches, and fans watch, mouths agape. The egg traced a beautiful arc through the air, wetly catching the light, as it headed towards a man with a cup. The guy, a skinny yupster in an expensive looking leather jacket, screwed his eyes shut, his chin nearly touching his spine.

The egg-in-Dixie-cup *slap* was unmistakable…

…And the crowd went wild! Ecstatic cheers and whistles of approval filled the space and people jumped out of their seats. After a few moments everybody settled but was still talking excitedly. There was a last-act feel to the accurate egg launch and subsequent standing ovation, but the aggressive electronic music kept going, and Mause was up again, moving erratically around the stage and merr-ing. The audience quieted.

After a stop by the tables, Mause came back to the stool with the black funnel in one hand and the milk in the other. These she put on the floor.

She climbed onto the stool and balanced on her hands and knees, bare ass stuck out towards the audience. Her pink anus was mostly obscured by another blonde puff of hair that connected to her bush. It was a sexy pose and she struck it well, arching her back, crossing her ankles, and looking over her shoulder at us. With no warning whatsoever, she picked up the funnel and crammed it into her asshole. I have about as much ability to read minds as the next guy, but in that moment the collective thought in the Theater was, "What in the actual fuck."

She opened the milk and brought it over her shoulder. Keeping her back arched so the funnel faced up and holding the gallon behind her must have taken a lot of strength and flexibility, but she made it look easy. She began to empty the jug into the funnel at an alarming rate, the milk pouring out like it does in those cereal commercials where it hits the corn flakes and that one raspberry and goes all over the place. Even as the last of the milk dripped out of the container, the funnel never filled up. I know I wasn't alone in thinking, "How fast can one human ass absorb a gallon of liquid, and where is it going?" Was this basic colorectal capacity or a magic trick?

Mause tossed the empty milk jug over her shoulder (a bald guy with big hoop earrings caught it like a bride's bouquet) then took the funnel out of herself. Still balancing on the stool, she *carefully* lowered one foot to the ground and kicked off like she was on a skateboard, sending herself into a spin, then brought the knee back onto the stool. Her apron flapped in the breeze. There wasn't one set of eyes in the place that wasn't glued to the spectacle.

I was behind the Theater bar at this point, elbows on a rubber pad that said Patron. There was a familiar voice in my ear. "Duck," said Grandma who had materialized next to me. How a guy six and a half feet tall wearing clown shoes snuck up on me, I don't know, but I didn't hesitate. We both crouched down until the top of the bar was at nose level.

As with every unfortunate twist in the performance, a "mer!" preceded this one. A geyser of milk erupted out of Mause. It was like watching a small carousel to which someone rigged a firehose. She must have had exquisite sphincter control, because for about ten seconds she discharged ass milk in an impressive radius. She got the curtains, stage, liquor bottles behind me, and about twenty audience members. People screamed and chairs fell over as they desperately tried to flee. I couldn't help picture it all as a commercial commissioned by the Dairy Farmers of America gone horribly wrong. Got milk, indeed.

Finished with her milk enema, Mause nimbly jumped off the stool (I'd be feeling pretty sprightly and light, myself). She patted down the front of her apron, curtsied, and bowed. The curtains closed.

"Well, *that* was egg-citing." Grandma's voice came through the speakers, causing me to snap my head to my right. I was alone behind the bar. Unbelievable. He walked onstage wiping his eyes with a red and white polka dotted handkerchief.

"Oh, Mause. Maybe she has a hollow leg?" he laughed. "I suppose a chocolate milk joke would be in poor taste?" he lifted his eyebrows high in mock innocence.

A few people laughed, but for the most part the audience was shocked into quiet existential navel gazing.

"Well, folks, that's our show. I hope you enjoyed your visit to Blunderworld, a place absolutely *filled* with magical characters—and orifices!" The curtains opened on cue to reveal the full cast standing on the milk splattered stage. From the back came clapping, whistles, and whoo's. I looked over to see Sparky, Carlos Surfista, Clea, Zester, Julia, Smooch, Juicy, and Zoe cheering from the safety of the catwalk behind the tech booth. The rest of the audience hesitated for a beat, but joined in. In no time at all everybody except the front rows was up and clapping and whistling.

That was my cue. I ducked out through the kitchen to begin my flip duties. I grabbed the cash from the bar and front door registers, then made my way to the office, skirting mingling audience members being ushered out of the Theater and into the Front Room. Members of the Production crew were already moving purposefully around the Theater, unholstering drills and other tools from their work belts faster than gunslingers.

Birdy was in the office, putting a radio earpiece into his right ear, the clear curly cord dangling in front of his chest. He was wearing skinny black jeans and our new staff shirt: a black tee with a geometric diamond in the middle made from an iridescent reflective latex. In the diamond were three gleaming letters, YES, made from the same spot-lit-disco-ball material. Over the shirt he wore his usual collarless, form fitting motorcycle jacket.

"Big Birdy!" I said, genuinely pleased to see him. "How's it going?"

Walking up to him I put out my fist. He looked up, his unique eyes small behind the lenses of his black thick rimmed glasses, then touched his fist to mine, firmly but gently. In many ways, that's how I'd describe Birdy: firm but gentle.

"Good man, good," he replied, attaching the alligator clip to his shirt collar. "Nothing to report."

I swear, when he's dead and buried his tombstone will read, "Here lies Birdy: Nothing to report."

I stepped over the giant beam and squeezed past him to get to the far desk. I put all the cash I pulled through the electronic money counter and for a few minutes a satisfying whirr and whisper of the bills filled the office. I banded all the stacks, stuck on colorful Post-Its with the amount and source, and put them in the big black safe. I typed up the Manager Reports and hit *send*. I was done for the night. Leaning back in the reclining office chair I interlaced my fingers on the back of my head and sighed. I was free to go home and *sleep*.

Just the thought was sweeter than ten MDMA orgies.

"What are you up to tonight?" Birdy asked. With his walkie, handful of square drink tickets, and black tote bag of cash, he was armed and ready for the floor.

"Nothing, man, I'm going home." I replied, the sentence like wildflower honey on my lips.

"Want to stay and shadow me for the night shift?"

My imagination tingled, and curiosity pushed out all thoughts of sleep.

"Are we looking for another manager, or do you just need a hand, or…?" I asked, curbing my enthusiasm.

Birdy looked down at the stack of drink tickets in his hand and snapped through them with his thumb, reminding me of the money counter. Finally he said, "I haven't told too many people about it, but I'm opening a restaurant in the West Village, and won't be around as much here. I'd rather have someone trained up to take over a couple of my shifts sooner rather than later."

Despite the more than twelve hours of work I was suddenly wide awake (but felt like I was dreaming). This was it! Birdy was straight up offering me a night manager position at Yes House.

A minute ago I was so tired I would have turned down a double-team blowjob from the Brazilian Beach Volleyball team (women's); now my heart was pumping like I just came from one.

"Yeah, that makes sense," I said, after pretending to look thoughtful for a moment. "And sure, I'll hang out."

Birdy smiled and put out his fist. I bumped it. "My man," he said. He opened a desk drawer and took out a stack of drink tickets. Tonight's color was hot pink. "Here," he said and handed them to me. "You're gonna need these."

I took the drink tickets, already looking forward to handing them out to the people in the coolest outfits, put my own ear piece back in, then followed Birdy out the office door.

Walking through the Theater then the Front Room, I thought, *I am a manager at the coolest place on Earth during a peak weekend shift.* My ego swelled like a busted knee, and I let it.

When we got to the Patio, Birdy stopped and turned to me.

"Tonight will be a little different," he said. "I'm going to shadow you, rather than the other way around. I want to see you take charge a bit."

A little knot of anxiety instantly coagulated behind my breastbone. "But I've only done super chill shifts, and only a few of them—"

"That's fine," he said, squaring his shoulders to mine and moving a bit closer to me. He always made you feel more comfortable in any situation, I realized, and that made him a great manager. I promised myself to remember that little lesson. "Don't worry about it," he continued. "This isn't a test. You're gonna do fine, and learn more in the process. Trust me and just do your thing. It's just like the shifts you've worked, but longer, louder, with more people drunker and way higher on more drugs." He gave me an easy smile, reminding me that there is always room for some lightness, and I believed him. I was gonna do fine.

"Besides," he said, "I'm right behind you if you need help."

I nodded and looked uneasily at all the people around me. The Patio was becoming crowded with smiling smokers. He must have sensed my reluctance, because Birdy put his hand on my shoulder. I turned back to him.

"I've seen the way you work, Loki. You got this."

If a buttoned up guy like Birdy believed in me, who was I to argue?

"Thanks, man," I said and took a breath. I smiled. "Let's do this."

Birdy clapped me on the arm with the hand that was on my shoulder, firmly but gently, and smiled back.

"A couple of things before we roll out," he said. "Keep an extra eye out for drug shit."

I laughed. That was like standing on Wall Street and saying, 'Keep an extra eye out for stock brokers.'

"Look," he said, patiently, "It's a dance club, people are gonna get high. That's just the way it is. But I'm told that there's been dealing happening, and that's a no-no. If you see something that looks like a sale, let security know and they'll handle it."

"Okay, I will," I said.

"Also, watch the staff. Two main things I'm looking for: are they where they're supposed to be at the time they're supposed to be there; and, are they on their phones. I swear, that phone shit is getting worse. Or maybe I'm just getting old. Either way, it looks bad, one, and two, if you're texting or scrolling, you're not working. Simple."

"Got it."

"Especially Destiny," Birdy said. "Check up on her."

Especially Destiny? Door boss, booty shaking, costume closet baggy-buddy Destiny? Destiny was the best, though, I thought. She worked every Friday Saturday night, came in a bodacious look, and was always spot-on with the cash.

"Will do," I replied.

"All right, let's do this," Birdy said. "I'll follow you." He held the door open for me, and I walked into the Front Room, already bumping.

We did a couple laps around the club, occasionally taking position somewhere out of the way to watch the staff work. I gave them nods of approval accompanied by thumbs ups. They nodded back and gave me smirks that told me they took me about as seriously as a sneeze in summer. To their credit, nobody outright laughed at me, the gum scraper turned accountant turned Shadow Box puppet turned manager. They knew I was shadow-managing tonight only because Birdy was close enough for me to hear walkie chatter from *his* earpiece.

About a half hour in Birdy let my leash play out a bit. I walked into the costume closet, alone, only to find Mrs. Miss (on the clock), Dash, and a couple other regulars doing blow. Mrs. Miss, caught white-handed, held the bag and a tiny silver spoon. The cocaine on her nostrils was only a shade whiter than her face makeup.

"Hello, Mr. Manager," said her mouth. Her all-knowing posture, one raised eyebrow, and expectant smile, however, challenged, 'The fuck *you* gonna do?'

Mrs. Miss was elaborately made up. Lashes as long as my finger, coiffed up platinum wig, a tasteful lilac lipstick. Her dress hugged her big frame like a glove, and in her heels she must have been close to seven feet tall.

"Um," she said, drawing the word out. "Do you want a bump or are you one of those boys that gets high on just watching?"

I nearly accepted her offer out of habit, but even though Birdy wasn't here, it was entirely possible that he had bugged the costume closet. "I'm good," I said lightly and winked. "Keep up the good work." I was determined to be the *cool* manager. But maybe I overdid it with the wink. I promised myself I'd be cooler next time. Mrs. Miss rolled her pretty eyes and sighed. I turned around and walked out. As the door was closing behind me I heard a very unladylike snort. I took a step and nearly bumped into Birdy's sharp nose.

"Christ! You scared the shit—"

"Who was in there?" Birdy asked, his serene eyes belying his intentions.

"Uh, just some people doing blow," I confessed.

Birdy stepped towards the door and reached for the handle.

Ah shit. If I don't stop him, it's gonna look like I just tattled on my homies, I thought.

"With Amar!" I blurted out.

Birdy paused with his hand on the handle, then stepped away from the door. He nodded a couple of times, as if in answer to an internal conversation. We both knew that owners were above the law, of course.

"Cool," he said, then disappeared into the crowd like a crow in the night.

I exhaled in relief, then briefly wondered why I had just lied. What would Birdy have done to Mrs. Miss anyways? It's not like we worked at a bank. I thought about it as I weaved through the hundreds of party goers in their flapper dresses, fedoras and pinstriped suits with wide lapels. I saw Sandra, my salt-shaking partner, in the Front Room. Tonight she was a cigarette girl, and if I didn't already smoke, she'd make me want to start. She was wearing a spaghetti strapped sequined black dress that barely covered the southern hemisphere of her tush, and several strings of pearls around her throat. A black Bandeau with a feather in it encircled her head at a jaunty angle. Suspended from a strap around her neck was a brown leather tray. Balanced on her belly and hips, it contained hundreds of loose cigarettes. She was perfect for tonight's event, Prohibition Disco.

Destiny was working the door, and there was nothing Prohibition Era about her. More like Marilyn Monroe Goes to Tomorrowland. All in white with the iconic blonde wig, a painted on beauty mark, and crimson lips, she also had LED's all over the place, flashing every color of the rainbow. I walked over to her.

At that moment, she wasn't *working the door*, she wasn't working anything, unless you counted her fingers. There was a bit of a lull at the entrance, and she was so engrossed in whatever was happening on the screen of her phone, fingers flying over the keyboard, that she didn't even notice me standing a foot away. The occasional person with a ticket walked past us, having been checked in digitally outside. Still, customers or not... not a good look.

Birdy's admonishment echoed in my head. *Especially Destiny.* I almost felt his presence behind me and turned to look, half expecting him to materialize out of smoke, or something, but I didn't see him. I was sure he was lurking somewhere, though.

I quickly visualized how I wanted the interaction to go, told myself, *You're the cool manager—cool but firm,* and cleared my throat.

Nothing.

Tap tap tap went her fingers as her eyes reflected the glow from the five inch screen. This, with the blinking LEDs and the whole Marilyn get up, made her look like some kind of sex cyborg.

"Hey," I said, wincing at my own voice, which, seemingly on its own, had dropped down an octave. She looked up from her phone and at me like I was a smear of dog scat on her high heels. I nearly ran away right then. *Cool but firm,* I thought again, and consciously returned to a more natural speaking tone.

"So, ah, they got me managing these days, you know." I said, all cool like.

She was back at it with the phone shit, typing even faster, somehow. To make up for lost time, I suppose. "Oh, nice," she said, a response I would've received, I'm pretty sure, had I said that her wig is on fire and her ears were catching.

"Yeah," I agreed. It *was* nice! "Thing is, it's now my job to enforce certain rules. Like the one about no phone while working the register."

She either didn't get the dropped hint or chose to ignore it. I felt like I was talking to a sitcom teenager.

There was the three second delay. If you have ever tried to have a conversation with somebody on their phone, you know exactly the one I mean.

"But nobody's even buying tickets," she finally said, with an unattractive whiney note in her voice. "Everybody coming in has already been scanned."

She wasn't wrong. All the people coming in now already had stamps. The *Glitter Bitch* diamond in black ink on the inside of their wrist, courtesy of Fox. Still, Destiny was either missing the point or choosing to ignore it.

"Just put it away, please," I said, as lightly as I could, earning myself a not-subtle eye roll. Destiny threw the phone into a handbag on the chair beside her. To complete the mini fit, she crossed her arms and looked up and away, like she was suddenly very interested in the HVAC ducts.

Anger surged inside of me. *You little brat*, I almost said, but bit my tongue. "Thank you," I said to her, pretending that her theatrics were lost on me. I turned around and sure enough, there was Birdy, giving me a meaningful nod. Juicy was next to him, but he wasn't looking at me. The only thing Juicy had eyes for at that moment (soft, alcohol heavy eyes), was the cute blonde he was chatting up. I gave Birdy a quick thumbs up, but inside I felt kind of shitty. I had been managing for exactly one hour, and already friendships were beginning to change.

I put those thoughts away and cooled my emotions with some even breaths. Move a muscle, change a thought, they say, and I started walking, at first without a clear destination. My feet took me to the Theater. Minutes after Production had finished transforming the space for Full On Party Mode, it was packed. The collective heat rising from the sweaty, bobbing bodies raised the temperature of the room significantly. I felt like a cookie in an oven heating up.

I still felt uneasy and tried to surrender to the bass, even if only for a second, and let my shoulders and hips move in rhythm with the undulating crowd I was cutting through, but I felt apart, groove-less, out of step. I stopped trying and stood still in the middle of the dance floor, just letting myself be jostled. I felt the friction of sweaty skin against my skin, smelled the heady mixture of corporeal and purchased scents, sensed the music and pounding feet through my feet. On my personal island of stillness in a stormy sea I suddenly felt at peace.

As I was being knocked around like a pinball I saw a tall white guy wearing sunglasses, a couple yards and several people away. He had unevenly cut hair and a thin mustache. In the red and blue flashes of light I saw that the exposed skin of his long, skinny limbs was covered in tattoos.

We made eye contact and he danced over to me. Somehow I knew he'd be European even before he put his lips to my ear and said, loudly enough to be heard over the music, "Hello. Do you want some blow?" I want to say with authority that he was German, but the truth is, he could've been Austrian. Or Swiss. Anyway, whether because of my long hair or the dark, he clearly hadn't seen the earpiece I was wearing.

I can't go ten minutes without somebody offering me drugs, I mused, then realized this was one of my explicit assignments for the night. I was going in for the bust.

"Yeah, let's go out back," I said, then started walking towards the Front Room. I felt like a DEA agent. It was exciting. I looked back and encouraged him to follow by tilting my head towards the exit. He was several steps behind me as I cut through the packed rooms slowly enough for him to keep up. I was trying to draw him towards the Patio exit door, where I knew Crius was posted up.

Once on the Patio, I used the toe of my boot to push the exit door open and yelled, "Crius!"

The bulky head of security was through the door in two seconds flat, the softness never leaving his eyes.

"This guy just tried to sell me coke on the dance floor," I blurted out, excited.

Seeing Crius's black shirt and crew cut, my new friend tried to melt back into the crowd. He was too slow.

"Hey, hey," Crius said, friendly as can be. "There's no problem here. Let's just have a little chat outside and see if we can't figure this out." He put his giant brown hand on the guy's scrawny back, in a gesture of camaraderie to anyone watching.

The tatted dealer started shaking his head, eyes wide, innocent as a Sunday School teacher, but allowed himself to be led outside and through the Patio door. I brought up the rear, feeling like a key player in an international sting operation.

There were about fifty people in line on the sidewalk, their curiosity instantly piqued. I don't blame them: I see a guy being led out of a club by security, I gawk, too. The nabbed dealer, sunglasses still on, kept looking over at them. I wondered if he was embarrassed. It was like he was being disciplined in front of the whole class. A very attractive, extravagantly dressed class.

Crius was still cool as can be. Nothing in his voice or body language suggested antagonism. His question, on the other hand, cut through the shit like an ax through brie.

"You selling drugs on my dance floor?" He wasn't *not* smiling.

"What? No!" (Said no innocent person with that much surprise, ever).

"I'm not sure what it's like where you're from," Crius said, "But dealing, here? Nuh-uh."

The guy's face turned pink. For the first time I noticed how young he was. He had to be at least twenty-one to get in, but I'm not sure if he'd celebrated many birthdays after that. He took off his sunglasses and I was surprised to see red, watery eyes.

"Why did you throw me out?" He said to me, "It's… it's because you hate Germans, yes?"

Crius and I shared a quick look. "We *like* Germans," I responded, silently congratulating myself on my correct ethnic profiling.

"We got no problems with Germans." Added Crius.

"It's because I'm gay, then, huh? You have problems with gay people." He was warming up to the victim act and his voice was rising and getting more shrill, but still quiet enough to not cause a full out scene.

Now Crius and I looked confused as ever. "Nope, wrong again," Crius said.

"Actually, we're known all over the world as one of the most queer-positive clubs on the planet," I added, helpfully and not without pride.

"So why, then?" he whined, "Why did you take me out here in front of these people? I bought my ticket, just like them. I was just dancing when he told me to follow him." He indicated at me with an accusatory and smooth chin.

"The reason you're out here and not 'just dancing' inside is because you tried to sell me cocaine on the dance floor. You remember that?" I calmly replied, looking him in the eyes.

"What? I don't have cocaine. I wish I had cocaine!"

Nice try, buddy, I thought, but something in the back of my mind began to tickle for attention. I ignored it.

"Blow. You asked me if I wanted some blow. You know, 'blow, charlie, coke, co-*caine*?' An illegal drug?"

The boy's face softened in realization… and relief. His shoulders slumped.

"I didn't try to sell you cocaine," he said, then leaned a little bit closer to Crius and me. "I was asking if you wanted a…" he shot a glance at the people in line, then finally whispered, "a blowjob."

His last word hung in the air like cigarette smoke on a rainy night. I looked at Crius. He was covering his mouth with his boulder of a fist, trying not to burst out laughing. He looked at me, hoping I would know what to say. I looked at the "dealer." Nothing in his red eyes told me he was bullshitting, and I suddenly understood his very real distress.

Crius also understood, I'm sure, but the big man came from a different time and a different place. He was smiling ear to ear. I wished he wouldn't. The situation had a certain absurdist comedic aspect, to be sure, but I just wanted to set the boy at ease.

"Well, uh," Crius started, then stifled a chuckle by coughing into his fist, "I, uh, I think we're done here, and I'm needed inside, anyway, because they just called me on the radio…" I looked at him, barely suppressing my own smile. He knew we were both wearing earpieces. He knew that I knew that there was no such call. "So, well, as *manager*, I'm gonna let you handle this, Loki." And with that he was gone, leaving me with the German. Whether he was telling the truth or deserved to be on a world class theater stage, I didn't know. I suppose it didn't matter.

I was still at a loss for words, so I opted for friendliness.

"What's your name, man?" I asked.

"Johann," said the guy who nearly got kicked out of one of the most queer-positive clubs on the planet for offering me a blowjob (or cocaine).

"I'm Loki," I offered him a smile. "Wanna go back inside?"

Johann smiled back and I saw the tension leave his face and body. He put his shades back on. For the second time that night I told him to follow me. Walking up to the side door I nodded at the security guard, who held it open and said, "good morning." We walked through the Front Room, then the Theater. I took him up the stairs at stage right, then across the catwalk, pausing so he could see the party from above. I unlocked the office and he followed me inside. I closed and locked the door behind us.

CHAPTER FIFTEEN

I look at my phone. 2:02 a.m. Sometimes we don't close the entrance until 3:30, but most people coming in after two are heavily intoxicated, and if the vibe inside is more intimate (i.e. Love House parties when people are dancing in their underwear and/or giving bj's on the dancefloor), we veer on the side of caution and keep them out by sealing it up early. "Close the doors," I announce to security on the sidewalk, and they immediately lock up the vestibule and pull in the stanchions. With that done, they each tell me their clicker counts, then move inside. One guy stays on the sidewalk by the exit door, just in case.

In the vestibule, Tacks breaks down the entrance station and brings in the folding table, stamps, bracelets, and other door-related bits and bobs. Harlequin maintains her post at the register until I grab the cash and iPad and throw both into a black tote bag.

Holding the bag tight to my chest I move through the party and up to the office. The ledge is clear but for a few people dancing. The k-hole behemoth had come to and was escorted to the kitchen, where the EMT was giving him a once over. I hadn't heard any updates on the radio, so assumed all was fine. My only hope was that he wouldn't blow himself into another drug nap immediately, but from experience I knew that this was a very real possibility.

In the office, I dump bundles of cash out on the table and run them through the money counter twice. I record the numbers, band the stacks, then drop them in the safe. I wake the sleeping iMac by tapping the spacebar, open an app, and enter the door sales. I compare the door entry numbers to the clicker count. 452 in the iPad, 461 on the clicker. A perfectly acceptable deviation.

Considering that owners and staff frequently walk friends and VIPs through... impressive, even.

Finished with my administrative duties, I lock up and go down to the Theater, where the party is still going. I lean against the wall by the tech booth and watch people dancing, talking, making out sloppily. There is some sort of threesome happening in one of the booths, all hands and mouths; licking, sucking, and prodding. Looks mostly cozy, but at this point what I am most envious of is the booth, itself, and the fact that two of the people are sitting down. I'm ready for it to end. The party, I mean. The oral triangle can go on until it has reached its logical conclusion.

I look over at Daisy by the bar, blonde and tall and J.Crew catalog perfect. Smiling and bobbing like a carefree bunny, she grabs a bottle of Patron, pulls the cork out with a couple of wiggles, and pours a liberal "shot" into a plastic rocks glass. She holds it in front of her face for a moment, perhaps pausing for a silent toast, then down the hatch. She squinches up her face, then goes back to smiling like she just got a bit of good news.

She looks over at me and I slice my hand across my throat. She's done. Cut. She gives me a dorky grin and two thumbs up, then begins breaking down her bar station.

It's her final shift, and we have a little something planned for her.

I text Koochy and Juicy. "Everyone ready?"

"Yes!" Juicy responds, after two seconds of triple-dot-typing.

Koochy: "Sí. Dos minutos."

It's 2:20. I walk up to the corner of the Theater bar, a few feet from the Sybian. Sabrina is doing more domming than bartending, but the bar is slow.

I keep an eye on Daisy, making sure she doesn't leave before her surprise. I watch as she moves bottles back to the shelf, turning so fast her shoulder length hair whips around. I'm reminded of a mouse navigating a maze after getting a dose of amphetamines.

I feel sadness wash over me as I realize yet another member of our family is leaving. A montage of our time working together flashes past my mind's eye. Laughing—so much laughing—and getting shit done. I smile, feeling the warmth of pride, like a graduate's parent. Daisy has been here for three years. Always on, always positive. Picking up shifts, covering for everybody, her lightness and joy never wavering. She was a rare breed of professional in NYC nightlife, a world she was leaving to move back to Oregon and become a nurse. On to bigger and better things, I suppose.

I catch movement out of the corner of my right eye. Juicy, Oliver, three barbacks, and Romeo, sneak out of the narrow corridor between the kitchen and the Theater. They are each holding a bottle of champagne by their legs—Veuve Clicquot, judging from the orange bands on the necks. Romeo is smiling so wide his teeth are lighting the way like a flashlight in the dark room. They're in position. I look at Koochy on the stage, giving me a thumbs up. *It's time.*

I walk behind the bar, grab Daisy's hand and tell her to follow me. She looks confused for a second, then looks up to see Oliver and the others, smiling. Her eyebrows go from knitted to up, and she smiles sadly. She understands what's happening.

I lead her through the sea of sweat and leather to the platform in the center of the dancefloor. Standing on the platform are Dreams and Sheba. They reach out their hands and Daisy lets go of mine to grab theirs. They gracefully pull her onto the platform and walk her to the center. It feels momentous. Lit up by three concentrated spotlights, all three of them are trying not to cry. A hundred upturned faces in the crowd reflect their glow. We start clapping—just the staff, at first, then the party people join in, even though they don't know what's happening.

Dreams and Sheba raise their arms. This is the cue, and what looks like a four-foot-wide half-full-moon begins to lower towards them from the rigging point in the ceiling. The two performers gently pull Daisy out of the way as The Bubble Chair stops a couple of inches above the platform, then help her into the cushioned seat in the hard plastic structure. There is a hand strap inside for safety, and Daisy is wide eyed as they put her hand through it with the solemn care of someone slipping a wedding ring on their fiancee's finger.

With Daisy safely inside, Dreams gives the bubble chair a soft push and it starts to spin slowly. Sheba waves to Koochy at the side of the stage, who begins to pull a rope. Daisy rises above the crowd like a goddess ascending to the heavens in a giant egg. Her smiling face glows with different colors as she rotates in slow motion. It's magical. I'm no longer in a Bushwick warehouse. This could be a Katy Perry Halftime Show, or a Broadway production of a hit musical.

It's a mesmerizing spectacle, and the audience doesn't have to know Daisy, or what a uniquely beautiful person she is, to clap and cheer. When her tears begin to flow, running past a sweet smile, it only makes the moment more magical. I look over at Juicy and Oliver, champagne bottles forgotten in their hands, and know that I'm not the only one holding mine back.

She soars and spins like this until the last notes of the song fade away, then Koochy begins to lower the Bubble Chair. Juicy, Oliver, Romeo, and I jump up on the center platform and reach up to grab it with the hands not holding the Veuve and guide it down. With her makeup streaked and blue eyes crystalline with tears Daisy looks like a heartbroken princess. She takes Oliver's proffered hand and steps out of her floating throne, arms wide for a group hug.

As sweet and heartfelt the moment is, teary hugs are not part of the program. This is Yes House, not Full House, after all. Beat-heavy dance music breaks the silence and before Daisy knows what's happening, we step away from her, shake our bottles of champagne, and, pretty much simultaneously, pop the corks. Four foamy geysers find their target, and in seconds, Daisy goes from bittersweet beauty queen to girl-gone-wild in Cabo. Laughing, she attempts to shield her face from the bubbly, but it's no use. When the bottles are empty, she's drenched. Her hair, now a wet, sticky, dirty blonde, is plastered to her face, and her sequined crop-top sticks to her.

Daisy is laughing and crying, unheard over the music and screaming crowd, some of whom, rightfully clueless, are chanting "happy birthday!"

I step forward and take Daisy into my arms. "I love you. You're family," I say into her ear.

"Thank you, Loki. Thank you. I love you, too," Daisy whispers back, sniffling.

As I tightly squeeze her shaking, champagne covered body, I feel other arms around us.

I guess we're a little Full House, after all. She squeezes back. I close my eyes, and everything and one that isn't on that lit up platform with us disappears.

We stay like this long enough for me to remember what I was so badly missing on the left coast, and what I drove three thousand miles to find in New York.

Family.

Before we release each other, before the moment is gone forever, I reflect on Juicy's question: "Do you want to run Yes House as General Manager?"

I know he needs a commitment from me, and at this moment I am ready to give it to him—my "yes" to Yes.

CHAPTER SIXTEEN

By four a.m. things were winding down. There were about a hundred people left in the club, floating from Theater to Front Room to Patio, depending on where they liked the music, whether they wanted a smoke, and which bartender they thought they had enough of a connection with to get a heavy handed pour. Birdy graciously cut me early; as manager, he still had a bunch of closing duties. My legs felt like Jello and my brain felt like pudding. I was very happy to leave. I grabbed my things from the office and walked directly to Clea's, covering the fifteen blocks in about five minutes, suddenly enjoying a second wind.

She answered the door wearing an oversized Looney Tunes t-shirt that went down to her knees. Her hair was a wet mop after a shower, the skin of her face shiny and scrubbed clean of makeup. Her go-go shift had finished about an hour ago. Her eyes were sleepy and sweet, and I wondered if she had already fallen asleep before I came. I couldn't help but smile at her. There's something about a girl you're falling in love with opening the door for you in the middle of the night. She gave me a soft kiss, open mouthed enough for me to taste the Dr. Bronner's mint toothpaste on her breath, then took me by the hand and led me to her room, barely slowing down enough for me to kick off my boots.

There were piles on the floor: some were wigs, others costumes, and the third category seemed to be regular clothes. There were also miscellaneous combinations. There appeared to be a system, but these colorful columns were tall enough for us to have to walk around on our way to bed. A laptop was open on top of a red and black plaid comforter, playing Ru Paul's Drag Race.

I quickly stripped down, jumped into bed, and assumed the big spoon position. Holding each other we shared details of our night. That's one way to say it. More accurate would be, I babbled excitedly like a coked up parakeet. I told her about the thrill of managing a night event; Mrs. Miss in the costume closet; Birdy shadowing me, and how I felt his eagle eyes on my back all night. I even told her about the German blowjob dealer (leaving out a... small detail).

Clea rejoiced with me and laughed along during the funny bits, but when I finished my story ("Walking over here, I swear the night air never tasted so good!") she was quiet.

"I hate that you manage now," she finally said, almost under her breath. I couldn't see her face.

"What? Why?" I asked, my lips behind her left ear.

Clea moved her head away from my mouth. "Thing is," she said, then took a big inhale, "I loved being the clown and the bookkeeper. It was fucking adorable. And now," she rolled over onto her left side and faced me. "Now you're my *boss*, and it's not fair," she finished, little girl petulance in her voice.

I put my left hand on the side of her neck, under the ear. "Look, I don't necessarily think that our open relationship is *fair*... but I go along with it because it's what you want." I was trying to keep my voice as placating as possible. "And right now managing YES is what I want. Besides," I said and smiled, "clown and club manager is still cute. A bit porny, but cute." A hesitant smile began to form on Clea's face. "And you don't have to worry about the whole 'boss' thing. I know better than to tell you what to do, believe me. Well, with a couple of exceptions." I waggled my eyebrows and she giggled, wiggling into me. I squeezed her tight and kissed her cheek.

"I love you," I said.

"Love you, too," she whispered.

And on that sweet note, we drifted off.

~~~

My phone's alarm jolted me out of dead sleep. It consisted of several notes, none of them sweet. I pawed at the evil device on the nightstand and managed to hit the stop or snooze button. My eyes felt like they were sewed shut as I rolled onto my back. I forced them open and stared at the ceiling, breathing deeply.

After a couple of minutes I rolled out of bed. Standing, swaying gently, I vigorously ran my fingers through my hair—half to comb it into submission, half to wake my scalp and brain beneath it. I slid into my pants and threw my shirt on. I looked down at Clea, sleeping peacefully on her back, face framed perfectly by her hair turned to one side, her features smooth and angelic.

Okay, that's a lie. She looked like she had recently been thrown through the windshield of a car during a head on collision. Her limbs tangled in unnatural angles, hair a matted mess, some of it sticking to her sweaty forehead, which was wrinkled as if she were working on a trigonometry problem. Her mouth was open unattractively, and there was a not-tiny trail of drool steadily making its way towards the ocean. And to me this scene was more beautiful than a sunrise over the mountains. I smiled, thinking, *This is how you know when you love somebody,* kissed her on the cheek, chugged a glass of water in the kitchen, then ran out the door.

An hour later I was in a church basement in Williamsburg, Juicy sitting next to me on a scuffed up plastic chair. The gray walls were bare and the ceiling was low. I felt like I was in a correctional facility or, at best, an outpatient clinic. I suppose it was both, in a manner of speaking. We sat in a big circle, about thirty of us. Almost everybody had an unlidded white styrofoam cup in their hands. Nobody was smiling. You could almost smell the despair, like a smoke layer hanging just below the ceiling. Or maybe it was just the smell of burnt coffee coming from the stainless steel industrial coffee maker on a folding table in the back of the room. At the appropriate time, we all stood up and joined hands.

Mostly in unison: "For thine is the kingdom, the power, and the glory forever. Amen."

The meeting had adjourned. We looked at each other and gave each other a nod before walking out.

"What do you think?" I asked Juicy. We had walked a few blocks to one of Amar's cafes, and were now sitting in a dark red leather booth. I was hunched over a white mug of black coffee, breathing in the aromatic steam. Juicy leaned back, holding his mug at his chest by the hefty handle.

"I don't know, man. I've been to AA meetings before. I just can't get into it." He looked out the big window, whether at Metropolitan Avenue or something within himself, I had no way of knowing.

"It's not for everyone," I conceded, then brought the thick rim of the mug to my lips for a satisfying sip. The coffee was just right, strong but not bitter. Fresh. Then again, after the sludge at the meeting, old motor oil would be an improvement. Despite being tired, I tried to inject a perky note into my voice. "We'll just find something else that will help you."

"I really fucking hope we do. I gotta stop drinking. I mean, last night... ugh." I almost saw Juicy's shame and regret pressing down on him and causing him to slouch lower in his seat.

I just nodded, saying nothing. If he wanted to tell me more, he would. I've seen enough to guess, though. Maybe he finally hit that rock bottom addicts talk about; or it was about Palace of Gods, one of the biggest events of his career, coming up again. Each in his own thoughts, we finished our mugs of coffee. A smooth faced waiter with a solitary paper clip tattooed on the inside of his right wrist refilled them, and we drank in silence. Juicy paid the bill, left a hundred percent tip, and we walked to the L train.

For a while we continued to go to meetings once a week, but that fizzled out once Palace of Gods was around the corner. This year we were committed to learning from last year's mistakes and smoothing out all the wrinkles (and patching up entire holes). With Murphy's Law in mind and contingency plans in place, we were going to make the event perfect.

In addition to Palace of Gods taking up so much time and effort, Yes House was busier than ever. Attendance was at full capacity—even on Wednesdays and Thursdays, not just the weekends—and we were having private corporate events every week. Just that week Montenegro, the Italian liquor company, bought the whole place out on a Wednesday night, for a cool $100k. Before that we were hosting HBO, who were filming scenes for their show, High Maintenance. The list went on. There was so much to do, even one free hour was hard to come by. Especially when that hour would be spent drinking shit coffee and praying for a higher power to drag you out of the bottle you were drowning in.

On the day of the event, we met at The Grand Prospect Hall at noon. One of the things that would make this year's event so much better and easier is that it would be entirely at this venue. The downside? Dealing with the intolerably tight-assed and crotchety Mr. Stern.

I was to be Juicy's right hand man for the set up and first few hours of the event. To my dismay, I would not be one of the managers at Palace of Gods. As a consolation prize, Juicy would have me manage the after party at Yes House from six a.m. to noon the next day.

We got to work setting up the bars and VIP areas, ensuring that every register and POS system was on line. After that I followed Juicy around as he speed-walked miles around the enormous hall, attending to little and big things that required his attention (and some that didn't). I did as I was told, from training bartenders to fetching him an endless amount of Americano's (black, not too much water).

Whether I was doing something vital to the operation or just being a coffee bitch, I didn't care. I loved being at his side, watching him run the show. I admired him and the way hundreds of people jumped at any opportunity to do his bidding. Our brotherhood meant everything to me, plus this was the kind of power I wanted to possess.

By around eight, we had set up everything that could be set up, and prepped for anything that could be anticipated. The rest would be up to quick thinking, creative problem solving, and whichever god or gods looked after the Throwers of Parties. We took sink showers, changed our shirts and grabbed a couple slices of pizza and a few minutes of seated calm before the storm.

Right as we were about to open the doors, a familiar hunched shape approached me in the low light. Skeletal, in a too big suit that's been out of fashion for two decades or more, Mr. Stern's paleness was accentuated by his red tie. His eyes were big and expressive, but so heavy lidded as to look reptilian. He looked exactly the same, and I wondered if he had been wearing this very outfit every day since the last Palace of Gods. Then I wondered if he slept standing up in a coffin. *Here we go*, I thought, steeling myself for what was certain to be an unpleasant exchange.

"Loki, yes? That's your name?"

"That's right, Mr. Stern!" I replied, laying the enthusiasm on thick as scallion cream cheese on an everything bagel.

"It is good to see you again," he said, voice mellow and accented, then opened his arms wide and smiled expectantly. I couldn't fucking believe it, and looked around to see if anybody else was seeing this.

"Uh, you, too, Mr. Stern." I put my arms around him, nearly reaching my own shoulders. I felt every bone in his frail back. It wasn't a bullshit hug, either; the old man was surprisingly strong. After a solid four seconds, he broke the clinch and walked away, followed by two giants in suits and sunglasses, indistinguishable from one another.

The clock struck nine. The City had opened. The Gods had arrived.

I stuck around, helping out and watching the magic until one, then went home, reluctantly, to get some rest before my six a.m. call time. I was experiencing so much FOMO, I couldn't sleep, but at 05:30 I got up. As the day's first navy light came through my windows, I got dressed and walked to Yes House.

~~~

The following week all the reviews were in. Palace of Gods and Yes House were praised as *the* event, and the organizers, of the year. We weren't just a nightclub anymore, but epic producers, too.

If it wasn't before, the word was out now: Yes House wasn't just on the map, it was *the* place to be. The scales had really tipped, and after Palace of Gods there was a line around the block filled with people who wanted to see for themselves the magic inside our little Bushwick club. In addition to our regular programming, we were getting more private bookings than ever, having Zoe and Juicy spending a dozen hours each day on the phone with such companies.

Very quickly it became clear that we were understaffed to accommodate our rise in popularity, so we went on a hiring spree. From hip twenty-something marketing wizards to door clowns; security guards to production grunts, we needed everybody.

All the extra hands on deck helped a lot, but they changed the dynamic. Walking through the venue at any given time and recognizing fewer than half the people working made everything feel less closely-knit. Less like a family.

Most of us accepted the change—change is, after all, the only constant—but some did not. Spunk and Safari Tahoe put in their resignation shortly after Palace of Gods. Kev, the marketing assistant, he of the perpetual open baggie at the ready, left. "No more Yes," declared Destiny. "I'm out."

I wasn't that close with the other people who left, but Destiny and I had forged a bond during all those early morning after parties. Despite the occasional manager-employee friction, I was sad to see her go.

To replace Destiny, we hired Harlequin. A short girl with a sweet smile, she was friendly and perfectly adequate at working the door. Destiny, she wasn't, but we quickly accepted her into the family.

Other changes included the redecorations. Zoe and Lada completely redid the Front Room as a disco hall for the Gods: the walls were layered with faux diamonds that shined brighter than stars. Mirrors were strategically placed around the room, making the fifty new disco balls they hung up seemingly never end. After that room they gutted the Patio. They filled the walls with fluorescent mannequin limbs and scuffed, vintage ballerina shoes. The rickety church pews stayed, of course, but the space was transformed.

We worked, we partied, we adapted to the "new normal." Birdy started managing two nights a week to my three or four. Juicy found a new bookkeeper so I could dedicate myself fully to my new duties. In addition to my time on the floor, I was scheduling staff and running the weekly manager meetings. The new (and sudden) normal felt strange, but I was thrilled to have the extra responsibility at a place that was quickly becoming so much more than a dance club.

~~~

Saturday evening. A month after Palace of Gods, winter had arrived, kicked off its shoes and made itself at home in New York City. I held my faux fur coat tight at my throat as I marched to work, still the frigid breeze found its way in and found my skin, not yet adjusted to the cold. It wasn't yet five but the sun was setting behind the four-story row houses on my Bushwick street.

I walked into Yes House, instantly grateful for the rush of warm air, and happily took off my coat and hung it on one of the high chairs by the bar.

Pushing the big Theater door open I had to stop in order to take in the scene (something that, by then, didn't happen that often).

Taking up most of the dance floor was a wrestling ring. Not a theater prop, mind you, but a *legit looking wrestling ring*, with spring loaded floor, padded corners, and stretchy ropes. A production crew of a couple dozen people stood around, dressed in all black, waiting for orders. I didn't recognize any of them. In the ring were two mammoth drag queens, four normal sized wrestlers in sparkly tights, and a man in a hot dog outfit who appeared to be choreographing a fight scene.

On the Theater stage was a table covered with a black tablecloth. On the table were two microphones, and behind these sat Spunk and Safari Tahoe. There were two identical glasses of ice and Coke next to the mics. This was the duo's last night working, but that didn't explain their outfits. Spunk was wearing a navy suit, white shirt, and black tie. Safari had on a beige suit, sky blue shirt, and maroon tie. In front of the table were ten white letters, cut out of cardboard. Together they said, *NIGHTLIVES*. The i's were lightning bolts. I figured these two must know what's going on. I skirted the ring and hopped up on stage.

"Um, what the fuck is going on?" I asked, smiling. I mean, how could you not?

"Oh, this?" Safari gestured at the ring expansively. "This is the drag event we were talking about at the Managers' Meeting."

"A drag… wrestling event… with a hot dog man." I didn't write it here, but there was definitely a question mark in my voice.

"And commentators!" added Spunk and hooked a thumb at Safari. "Me and him." He grabbed a microphone and brought it his mustache. The mic was live and a less than professional *hrmph* sound came from the sound system. Dropping his voice, he said, "Coming to you live from the greatest club on Yefferson Street—maybe in all of Bushwick—to announce tonight's event are… Nightlives!"

Spunk put his hands around his mouth and sighed loudly, mimicking the roar of an arena crowd. Safari *whooo'd* too loudly. Nobody in the Theater paid them any mind.

"Cheers!" Safari said to Spunk, and picked up the glass closest to him. The other commentator picked up his drink and the two slapped them together hard enough to spill some on the black tablecloth. From the smell, and their behavior, I now knew it wasn't just soda pop. They threw their drinks back and grimaced. I mock frowned and peeled back the black cloth by their legs, revealing a shiny ice bucket with a bottle of Jack sticking out of it at an angle. It didn't escape my attention that the bottle was more empty than full.

I shook my head and gave them an "oh, *you*" smirk. "Happy last shift, boys," I said, then ran up the stairs at stage left and went to the office to prepare for the night.

At six the doors opened, and thirty minutes later the place was full of people who looked like they were at a monster truck rally in the deep south. Cutoff t-shirts, denim vests, snapback trucker caps, and chain wallets. I had a bizarre thought: *Were these people the real McCoy, or did they just get all this shit at L-Train Vintage up the block*? The only thing missing was cans of PBR (Pabst didn't give us a good deal. You know who does, though, time after time? Good old Tecate).

A bell rang, a real ten-pound fight bell, by the sound of it, and the crowd quieted.

After a minute of inebriated banter, Spunk and Safari Tahoe got to the business at hand.

"And now, to start things off," said Spunk.

"The one, the only," picked up Safari.

In not-quite unison: "Mrs. Miss!"

The biggest French maid I had ever seen emerged from backstage amidst cheers, and crossed the room in about three steps, black stilettos landing as if on a tightrope. She walked right up to the bar, looked (down) into some dude's face, and said, in a deep voice, "Be a dear and help me up, would you, love?" The man had shaggy blonde hair and was wearing a sleeveless denim vest with a giant Lynyrd Skynyrd patch on the back. He appeared to have developed a bad case of animé eyes. Wordlessly he held a hand out, and Mrs. Miss climbed onto the Theater bar. She really was magnificent in her black thigh-highs, garters, and corset. Tonight she wore a coal black bob wig and lots of black mascara and eyeliner.

When the applause died down, "Don't Cha" by The Pussycat Dolls began to play and the Missus started lip synching as she danced from one end of the bar to the other. The crowd lost their shit, cheering ecstatically. "Don't you wish your girlfriend was raw like me—"

There was a commotion in the audience as a man came from backstage at a run and expertly hurdled the rope and jumped into the ring. The music cut out.

"What is this gay shit?! Homo propaganda? Not in my country!" he shouted. The crowd gasped. The newcomer wore forest camo cargo pants tucked into shiny black boots and an olive drab tee shirt tight over his muscular arms and torso. On his head was an American flag bandana.

"Wuh-oh, what is *this*?" shouted Spunk, in what may be the worst-acted surprise I have ever seen.

"That's right, I said it, and I'll say it again, too!" the trolling commando continued. "Someone get this tranny outta here! It's Adam and Eve, not Adam and *Steve!*"

The boos were deafening. This guy was perfect.

"Wanna say that again, soldier boy?" a voice boomed from the other side of the Theater.

Heads turned as a dark skinned man charged through the audience and jumped between the ropes and into the ring. He was shirtless with a rainbow headband between his thick eyebrows and hairline. He, too, wore army boots and camo, but was from a different army altogether, with his green dappled booty shorts. If the other guy was G.I. Joe, this one was G.A.Y. José.

"Oh, great," the appropriately clothed army guy said. "Just what we needed, another homo—"

A convincing kick to the mouth from booty shorts interrupted him. He fell back, rolling around in agony, holding his face. The crowd approved.

The gay rights warrior sashayed around the ring once, arms overhead, amping the crowd up, then ran to a corner and climbed the ropes. He/she/they jumped and soared through the air before landing ass first on the fallen homophobe, still writhing on the mat. The crowd oooh'ed appreciatively. The shirtless man positioned himself over his opponent, rolled him onto his belly and put him in a very suggestive armlock, facedown on the mat, his pelvis pressed against his butt. "No!" G.I. Joe pleaded, agony on his face, "You'll make me gay!"

The crowd roared with laughter. The bottom tapped the winner's wrist repeatedly and was released. He crawled around the ring on his hands and knees while rainbow bandana stood up and walked around the ring, fists held high.

Spunk's voice came over the speakers. "Well, that's one for Adam and Steve, I guess!"

The crowd went wild, jumping up and down and spilling their Tecates.

I swear, if I had a nickel for every time I thought, *Okay, now I've seen everything*, while at work… I'd have a whole bunch of nickels. A crowd of "rednecks" cheering for a queer wrestler in a dance club in the heart of Brooklyn. I mean, come on.

The lights dimmed and in the half dark Theater an ominous church bell rang out. A ghostly bell played from the speakers, one I immediately recognized from when I was a boy and used to watch the WWF. I hadn't heard the Undertaker's theme song in nearly two decades. What had these weirdos come up with this time? A white spotlight came on just in time to answer my question. From stage left emerged four people, solemn pallbearers with severe looks on their faces and shadows cast by the spotlight above. How they managed these expressions while wearing full body ketchup and mustard bottle costumes, I don't know. Above their heads they carried the hot dog choreographer, obviously. He was inert, the oval of his wiener face bathed in white light as if he were ascending to that great Oscar Meyer factory in the sky.

Okay, that's it, I thought, not unkindly. It was far too early in the night for lunchroom burials. Besides, I had work to do. I went back to the office.

I plopped into a reclining chair, reclined, and let my eyes wander and my thoughts bounce around my head unwatched. I looked at the six monitors in the corner, each showing a different part of the club. Besides the condiment crew launching the hot dog into two super-sized drag queens, nothing interesting shown there.

Amar's sticky notes were everywhere, as secure as an encrypted computer file because nobody could read them. I took out my phone and responded to time sensitive texts from owners, staff, and event producers, then looked at my personal messages. A bunch of my friends wanted me to put them on the list for the night's event, and while I would normally comp most or all of them, tonight was super sold out—there were no more tickets *and* the event producer gave us a massive guest list. Julia, our marketing director (that I haven't mentioned for two hundred pages), had even sent an email to all the managers: "Glitterbox comp list = closed!" The party was named for the producers throwing it. From London and Ibiza, Glitterbox were world renowned for their queer disco parties.

I scrolled through messages from friends and opened the one from Strom. Not just a friend, he was also my roommate, part of the YES inner circle, and veteran Chewbacca camper.

"I gotchu," I keyed and hit the blue arrow. Despite Julia's warning, I put Strom's full name into the guestlist, then started typing up reports.

The wrestling—and I use that term loosely—wrapped up a little before ten and security started kicking everybody out. I was helping usher people towards the exits, explaining that the next event was full and would be starting soon, when I hit a wall... of ketchup and mustard bottles.

"Why can't we stay?" whined their leader, the wiener. "They usually let performers stay for the next event."

Ignoring the absurdity of arguing with giant barbecue items calling themselves "performers," I gave them a kinder version of Julia's email and smoothed things over by promising all five free entry to next weekend's party, and free drinks, to sweeten the deal. After a brief and comic powwow, they agreed and left. I can't say I relished the thought of seeing them in a week's time.

At ten the front door closed behind me as I stepped onto the sidewalk. The door staff were in position. Mrs. Miss was no longer a French maid but was in a sequined nebula purple dress with a slit for her long right leg, and behind Fox and Crius was a sparkly line of people that went clear past the halal cart and around the corner.

"Jesus," I said. "You guys ready for this mayhem?"

"Sweetie," Mrs. Miss said, playfully condescending (aka the cornerstone of her entire persona), "This is nothing."

"Let's do this," Fox said, genuinely excited, and flicked his cigarette butt between two parked cars.

"That's the spirit," I said, and meant it. "Alright, you already know the drill for tonight. If they don't have a ticket or aren't on the guest list, they do not go in. I don't care which DJ is their boy- or girl- or theyfriend, how attractive or spectacular they are, or if they're fucking an owner. They could tell you they're fucking *all* the owners and every silent investor involved *at the same time*, but without a ticket or name on a list they can tell their story while walking. Anybody who's getting in has already been confirmed. Cool?"

All three nodded, and I went back inside.

Within minutes of doors opening, the venue was transformed into a sparkling wonderland. Apparently the name of the event wasn't lost on the guests. I felt like I stood in the aftermath of a disco ball factory explosion. I didn't know what a "glitterbox" was, exactly, but an hour later, Yes House was one. A hot, sweaty, glitterbox.

My phone vibrated against my left thigh. I took it out to see a text from Strom on the lock screen.

"We're at the front."

We?

Strom was standing next to Crius on the sidewalk, with none other than Dan Rockies at his side.

"Dan!" I shouted as soon as I saw him, then ran up to him and wrapped my arms around his waist and hefted him up. He laughed and grabbed my face in both hands then planted a kiss right on my forehead.

I walked them through the exit door and we hung out on the Patio for a good ten minutes, chatting. He and Meloza had just moved back to New York a couple of days ago. Dan was glowing like a guy after a spa treatment and his smile was so radiant that you couldn't help but smile, yourself. This was not the same Dan bitterly packing boxes and waxing philosophic about the end of an era.

He reached into a pocket of his black admiral's coat (complete with gold stitching) and pulled out a red pack of Marlboros. He flicked open the top, pulled out three cigs and held them out to Strom and me.

"You want?" he asked. We both grabbed one and put it between our lips, and Dan lit us up with a red Bic before sparking his own.

"So first, Meloza and I bumped around South America for a bit. I had to decompress and face myself. It got dark. I realized that I had to do 'the work' and all that blah blah blah." Dan momentarily stared off into the distance, the darkness and all those *blahs*, then pulled himself out and back to us.

"Then we hopped across the pond to Italy, and man oh man, *that's* where I came *alive*. We spent months in the rural parts of the country, vineyards and sheep far as the eye could see. We settled in a small town and lived amongst the locals. Two days in and I'm wearing overalls, pruning grapevines, making pasta by hand, and stuffing sausages at the butcher's house. This was my life for months and I fucking loved it."

Strom and I listened to his tales of bucolic Mediterranean life, ribbons of smoke drifting around us. Dan has always been a charismatic storyteller, and we happily let ourselves be swept away to a faraway land and a simpler life. A life all too easy to romanticize from where we sat in Bushwick's urban grime.

We smoked the cowboy killers down to the flecked orange filters and flicked them away, Dan's story on pause. We went inside, Dan following behind me. Every time I turned back, I saw him, his eyes darting around as if he'd never been to YES, looking at people he no longer knew or recognized.

We cut through the kitchen to get to the Theater bar. Lada, Sheba, and Sandra were performing on the platform in the middle of the dancefloor, surrounded by the crowd, most of whom were jacked gay guys.

Three golden spotlights illuminated the women, wearing nothing but black g-strings you could floss with. They were on their knees, embracing and slowly swaying like serpents under the spell of a snake charmer's flute, running their hands over their bodies and staring lustfully into each other's eyes. Three sirens in a sailor's lore.

"Yasss, honey!" The gays yelled shrilly.

I saw Koochy weaving through the crowd towards the platform. He unobtrusively put three carafes of gold glitter at the girls' feet then melted back into the queer sea.

Lada picked up a carafe and held it high. The warm yellow light hit the glitter and it lit up like golden coins in a treasure chest.

Sheba raised her enraptured face to the ceiling, arched her back and thrust her plump breasts forward as Lada slowly upended the carafe. The glitter poured out in a shimmery rivulet of reflected light, a thousand tiny suns. As it hit Sheba's chest and cleavage, her mouth fell open and her eyes closed in an expression of sexual ecstasy. The glitter ran between her breasts and past her belly button, some of it sticking to the front of her thong. Sheba squeezed her tits and ran her hands down her ribs as a sparkling shower hit the platform. She opened her eyes and offered the audience a simmering look that must have stirred even the gayest penis in the room.

Lada kept pouring as Sandra pressed herself into Sheba and stuck her ass out. She aimed the glitter waterfall directly onto their united bosoms, then onto Sandra's back, where it cascaded down her butt. For a moment she looked like a pornographic fairy peeing liquid gold. When Lada's carafe was empty, she set it down and insinuated herself between the other two performers. Sandra and Sheba gave a final shimmy before each picking up a carafe of their own.

Lada interlaced her fingers behind her head and tilted her face up to the beam of light coming from the ceiling, ready to receive her own golden shower. As her playmates began to pour the glitter onto her lean body, Lada closed her eyes and let her lower lip fall slightly to reveal a flash of teeth. She ran her hands up and down the front of her body, massaging her small breasts and squeezing her nipples between thumb and forefinger. Whenever her hands moved against the sparkling avalanche, the glitter sprayed away from her body and fell to the floor like sparks. Sheba and Sandra poured the last of the glitter onto Lada's head, and she began to whip her long black hair left to right, sending stardust into the crowd.

It was hot. It was beautiful. It was art.

The girls set the empty carafes down, and wrapped their arms around Lada. All three hung their heads and errant bits of glitter caught the light as they fell. All was still. The lights turned off.

The crowd began to clap and cheer in the dark theater, then purple and blue spotlights began to carve up the room.

"Oh, Lada," said Dan affectionately. "I'm happy to see at least one thing is still the same around here."

Strom and I chuckled as we clapped. I put my hands on their shoulders.

"Well, boys," I said, "some of us have work to do."

"Oh?" Dan said, innocence and surprise in his raised eyebrows, "Is there some gum on the dancefloor that Amar needs you to scrape, or..?"

"Nope," I said, deadpan, "I heard your mom's in the Shadow Box."

Storm held his hand to his mouth like a teenager witnessing a schoolyard diss battle. We all laughed. I slapped a few drink tickets into their palms and continued my rounds.

My patrol eventually took me backstage, where I found all the performers, including the three glitter goddesses. They were busy wiping the stuff off their skin with baby wipes and shaking it out of their hair like persistent golden dandruff.

"That was amazing!" Lada gushed, scratching her tilted head like she had lice. "But next time I'm taping my asshole and pussy shut—that shit gets in every nook and cranny."

Everyone in the narrow space laughed. I was getting a post-performance contact high just being there. I told the girls that theirs was one of the most beautiful performances I had ever seen. They thanked me and I left the heat and body smells of the green room.

A few hours later I saw Strom out in the Patio. Smiling, I walked over. It was always a joy to see him here since over the years, despite living a stone's throw away, he had stopped coming to Yes House for the most part.

As I got closer my smile died, though. He was smoking a cigarette and looking at the floor, eyes distant. When exhaling smoke he didn't move the cigarette farther than a couple of inches from his face.

"Strom, what's up, man? Where's Dan?" I asked.

He looked up and flipped his longish blonde hair off his forehead. His expressive eyebrows added a layer of gloom to his face.

"He left hours ago. I'm about to take off, too," he said.

"Places to be, people to see, I get it," I said, trying to keep it light, but suddenly there was a heaviness between us. "Did you guys have a good time? What did you think of the performances—next level, right?!"

"Yeah, they were fun, but…" he looked away, took a last drag on his cigarette, and tamped it out in a nearby ashtray. He turned back to me. "To be honest, I just couldn't get into it tonight. And I don't think it's just me. That's why Dan bounced after being here for all of thirty minutes. You wanna know something?" he asked, without wanting to know if I did, "I didn't see one person I know. None of the regulars, none of the homies. I think I saw Oliver once and I saw Lada, but apart from that, I didn't recognize a single bartender or performer. It's just weird, man. Anyway," he said and held out his hand, "I'm out. Thanks for the VIP treatment. See you at home." I gave his hand a quick shake and he disappeared into a crowd of twenty-somethings.

His words settled on my shoulders like a heavy pack as I looked around. The sexy clean shaven guy tending bar? We hired him three weeks ago. The barback in the tight black YES shirt that just brought him a plastic tub of ice? I didn't even know his name. I looked at the crowd. Beautiful, sexy, dressed the part... and most of them I had never seen before. Where were Dash and Sauce tonight, I wondered. How about Nasty and Mrs. Miss, those lovable degenerates? I looked at the walls around me and the corrugated plastic ceiling above; the statues and the ornate but empty picture frames. An unwelcome realization began to form, one that I had been blocking from my consciousness.

Of course Strom and Dan couldn't get into it.

Everything was different.

Ornate but empty.

CHAPTER SEVENTEEN

I pop into the kitchen wearing a smile that hasn't slipped since Daisy's flight. Licky the dishwasher is at the deep double sink, a metal pot scrubber in one hand and gooseneck nozzle in the other. The bald Nigerian has been with us for ages, solid as a rock, always behind the scenes yet an important part of the family. I admire him at his station for a moment. As I watch he loads a bunch of plastic glasses onto a blue dishwasher rack. Walking past I pat him on the back and he turns around and looks at me questioningly. I give him a thumbs up and he gives me a smile that I have never seen on someone who was born in the Global North. "Hey boss!" he says, his bristly mustache stretching to his dimples, then turns around and loads the tray of glasses into the industrial dishwasher. He pulls the lever that brings the metal enclosure down, and the machine automatically comes to life.

I look at my phone. Two-thirty a.m., which means I can get a jump on some closing duties. I send the barbacks a text telling them to break down the Theater bar, then head out back. At the Patio bar Shuk is still chatting to the same girl, except now he's more on her side of the bar than his and their noses are an inch apart. It took me two tries but I finally got his attention.

"You're out," I tell him. I've never seen anyone break down a bar that fast. Last I saw of him he was out the door and ducking into an Uber with butt plug girl like they were fleeing from a heist.

Sparky is sitting on a stool in front of the door to the Onyx Room. He greets me by fluttering his long fake eyelashes. I tell him that he can start slowly kicking people out of the room.

"Um," he says with a mischievous smile, "We may want to give them a few more minutes." Still smiling he reaches behind him and cracks the door, then inclines his head subtly: *have a look-see.* I look at him, then at the narrow opening spilling out dim red light and sex smell, before opening the door a few more inches and poking my head in.

"Oh, damn," I whisper involuntarily before pulling my head out and closing the door. I look at Sparky, who's wearing a what-did-I-tell-you smile. "How the fuck..?"

"I don't know, but they've been at it for almost a whole hour," he says.

"That's, ah," I muse, half to myself, still seeing the tangle of limbs and cocks in my mind, then give up and just repeat, "How the fuck?"

"Yoga, probably," says Sparky while holding his chin, as if he's been meditating on this for, well, an hour.

"Damn. Alright, give 'em fifteen more minutes then break it down."

"Roger that," Sparky says.

As I am walking up the wooden stairs to the hot tub I am still trying to make sense of what I just saw. *How many people were in that pile, and how did they manage to fit the*—I stop and promise myself that I'd give it more thought later, but for now I have a job to do.

The hot tub area looks like a bachelorette party just rolled through. I count seven empty rosé and prosecco bottles rolling around on the AstroTurf, along with countless clear plastic cups. Under a pair of lacy lilac panties is a Mason jar stuffed with five-dollar bills. Random shoes stand or lie about: one black pump, a sparkly loafer-type-thingy, a pair of sensible flats and, inexplicably a lonely and well-worn brown Birkenstock, looking like a hippie in the middle of the New York Stock Exchange trading floor.

"—and when she did that, this young first mate fell in love for the very first time in his life. Oh, ahoy, matey!" The pirate beamed when he noticed me standing there. Surfista was sitting on the edge of the tub, black boots dangling in the air. In the steaming lit up water was a group of four interchangeable blondes. One took a healthy belt from the mouth of a bottle of rosé, smiled loopily at me, and lowered the bottle until it was half in the hot water. I walked up to them.

"Carlos," I took off an imaginary hat and bowed. "How fare thee?"

Surfista reached into the tub and snatched the bottle of rosé from Blonde Number One, who briefly reached after it before Blonde Number Two pulled her arm back into the water. He took a sip and grimaced, then looked down at B1, disapproval (and rosé) dripping from his long black mustache. B1 looked back sweetly. He turned back to me and spoke into the bottleneck like a mic.

"Judging by the maidens faire in my midst, I'd say I fare well! And you, my young managerial sire, how goes your evenin'?" He holds the microphone under my mouth. I gently push it away.

"Off the record," I say, and look pointedly at the blondes. I see only three heads above the water. "Probably not as good as yours." I pull out of the game and say, "You're gonna close it up soon, yeah?"

"Aye, this is the last group."

"And you'll clean up after."

"Yes, cap'n, after we're done swabbing this deck there'll be nary a trace of us." Giggles from the tub. I don't think the blondes heard "deck."

I nod and go to leave.

"Oh, young Loki!"

"Yo." I turn back, hand on the rail.

"It would appear that our stores of rosé and bubbly have been mysteriously but thoroughly depleted." Surfista smiles at me with arched eyebrows. I make him work for it, saying nothing. "Seeing as how my trevails of the evening have been long and arduous, might you provide me with several beverage vouchers so that I—and the maidens fair, of course—may slake our thirst?" At this point one of the maidens finished the warm rosé and burped unmaidenly. The pirate casually plucked the bottle from her hand and tossed it onto the fake lawn. "I'll clean that up," he said quickly, his pirate shtick slipping momentarily. "Now, back to the matter at hand and the beverages you will graciously gift to us." He counted himself and the four women by pointing an index finger, eenie-meenie style. I wouldn't be surprised if he'd forgotten how many they were. "I reckon fifteen will be satisfactory." He grinned oilily at me, his yellow teeth flashing.

I smile lightly but stare at him stonily, half fed-up with his constant wheedling. I take a pack of drink tickets from my back pocket and count off five. I walk up to the hot tub and hold them out. When Surfista reaches for them I pull my hand back. "Don't forget to clean up," I say, then extend my hand again. He takes the tickets and I turn around and go downstairs, not waiting to see the look of disappointment that is surely on his face.

There are some twenty people still hanging out on the Patio—a quarter of how many there were an hour ago. I'm not surprised. Love House at three in the morning is usually like this. By now most people have either gotten their fill of sexy partying or took the sexy party (or parties) home with them. The folks still here are either happy to dance by themselves or too intoxicated to connect with someone—or both. Ideally a combo of both.

My phone vibrates and I dig into the pocket of my gold pants to pull it out. A message from Krystal, the bottle service girl: "We're ready to close out." I go inside and print out all the checks, then post up in the kitchen at the counter to go over them. I make sure everything's squared away and all bottles ordered are on the bill. Juicy always told me about how servers can sell bottles for cash that goes right into their pocket. I wouldn't ever expect that from Krystal and Romeo, but I still always check.

Everything looks good, gratuity has been added, and every table has met (and overshot) their minimum. As expected, the baller's table ordered a second bottle of Don Julio 1942, doubling their sales. *Perfect.*

After I sign off on the tabs, I watch the servers put checks on little golden saucers and run them to the tables, where the clients look them over. Credit cards, some of them metal, are collected and run at the POS between the kitchen and Front Room.

After they get the last signed receipt, I cut the servers for the night. Unlike the door staff (pretty much all staff), who will undoubtedly stay and party all night after their shift is done, Krystal and Romeo leave immediately. I know Krystal is running to meet a French guy she recently started dating; and Romeo will wake up early to work on his comedy show, "Call Center Series."

I'm on autopilot as I float through the club, cutting staff and collecting cash from the registers. Except for the dull yet nearly unbearable throbbing in my legs and the sweat pouring down from my hairline, I'm hardly aware that I'm awake and moving.

At four-twenty the music finally stops. Thank Christ. In the Theater Nasty turns up the lights as the crowd cheers and begs for one more song. I'm leaning on the bar and the DJ makes eye contact with me. I shake my head: not tonight. She must have noticed the kill-me-now look on my face because she briefly frowns and puts her fists under her eyes in a mock cry, then laughs. She blows kisses to the audience and takes her praise, then starts packing up her gear.

I use the last of my fading strength to put on a smile and jump up on stage. I grab a mic and shout, "Thank you, New York City, for being so goddamn beautiful, sexy, and fucking fabulous!" The cheering gets louder. There is something about cursing into a microphone that really gets people going. I continue stroking them. "Tonight you helped us put on the best party in the city. Give yourselves a round of applause!" The crowd is all too happy to oblige. "Now get to bed safe—yours or someone else's! We fucking love you. See you back soon!"

The house lights are turned on and suddenly the spell is broken. The shadows that moments ago painted faces with a mysterious sex appeal are gone, dispelled by the unforgiving light. It's not pretty, and my least favorite moment of the night, regardless of whether it's business or pleasure. The grinding teeth and dilated pupils, no longer under the velvety cover of dark togetherness, are grotesque. Sweaty bodies and disheveled hair; filthy clothes and missing accessories. Somehow the room even smells worse with the lights on. The people look at each other and see the reflected darkness staring back at them. Time, suspended for the last several hours, is relevant again as hands search in pockets and bags for phones. The light hurts their eyes; the reality it illuminates is even more painful. The crowd disperses like startled raccoons, and in minutes the club is empty of customers.

Security sweeps the place for stragglers. I put all the cash in the safe, bundled and uncounted, then sit down at the computer to type up the night's reports. My eyes sting as I fight to keep them open and my fingers take too long to obey the commands from my brain. From my solitary perch in the office I hear the staff still partying in the Theater booths: laughter, anecdotes from the night, and snorts fill the room. I am filled with an acute longing for the nights before I started managing.

An hour later the reports are done and submitted. The staff left in search of more drugs and an after party a couple of blocks away. I do a final loop around the club, checking for passed out partiers in the nooks and crannies and giving each door a push or pull to make sure it's locked. Besides Tristan laid out like a corpse in the costume container, the coast is clear.

Or, so I thought. I'm surprised to see Juicy leaning on the bar in the Front Room, smoking a cigarette. He is absorbed in his phone.

"Hey, you're still here." I say, not wanting to startle him. We're the only people left in the club. The bright lights don't seem to bother him. He takes a drag of his cigarette and blows smoke at the glowing screen of his iPhone. For a few seconds he doesn't acknowledge me, then thumbs the button that puts the screen to sleep and looks up at me, a tired smile on his face.

"You ready to run this place, or what?" he asks.

I take a breath and nod slowly as I exhale. "Let's talk."

CHAPTER EIGHTEEN

April came and brought with it more winter. The temperatures were above freezing, but barely. The same trees that were budding this time last year remained bare, and no flowers bloomed in Bushwick's few green spaces. When they had to be outside, New York City's residents tucked their chins and scrunched their shoulders against the relentless, joy-sapping wind, ignoring anything and one that wasn't a part of getting from point A to B. The smell of b.o. and urine hung in the fetid air of the underground subway platforms; street people, pitiable in their filth and/or insanity, fought over precious benches on which to bed down. Commuters waiting for the L stared unblinkingly at a point somewhere between the third rail and eternity. You could almost see it on their faces, the question: "I am paying two thousand dollars a month to live in a shoebox—in *this* shithole, no less… why?"

I liked my shoebox, and rent was relatively cheap. I didn't have to commute, and my bubble jacket kept me warm on my walk to work. Still, those were tough, depressing times. Clea and I were doing shittier and shittier as a couple, arguing nearly every day. She was distant and too independent; I was needy and too sensitive. I hated that we were in an open relationship but embraced the promiscuity available to me; she hated how much of a slut I had become. It finally came to a head, and after a long conversation we decided to give monogamy a shot. Frankly, I was surprised that she agreed. Shit, based on how much I enjoyed the extra-relational action I was getting, I'm surprised I was advocating for it, in the first place. Looking back, I should've known it could never work.

It was beautiful for three months, but then I fucked it all up. I reverted to Molly Loki, which, as we know, was not always the best Loki (for obvious reasons). One (off-duty) night at Yes House I ate a fistful of molly and had sex with some random chick.

I called Clea thirty minutes after I buckled my belt.

"Hey, how's it going?" I asked, too lightly. To my ears my voice dripped with guilt.

"Hey!" Clea said brightly, happy to hear from me. "I'm good, just made some potstickers. I'm gonna nosh on a few and leave the rest on the stove for you. I'm going to bed soon. Join me after you've eaten. If you don't want the 'stickers, put them in the fridge before coming to bed. But cover them or they'll dry up, 'kay?"

I closed my eyes. *Fuck.*

"Listen, Clea…" I took a deep breath and let the words tumble out before I lost my nerve. "I fucked up. I hooked up with someone."

She sounded cute and tired before, but all that was gone instantly. "Like hooked *up*, hooked up?" She snapped.

The second it took me to respond must have told her all she needed to know. "Yeah," I said, drawing the word out.

"No. Fuck *that*," she spat. I heard a plate shatter, then nothing. I looked at my phone, seeing nothing but the colorful app icons on my home screen. She was gone, and just like that, we were done.

The next day I felt terrible, and while it slowly got better, I was torn up about what I had done for many weeks. A painful sadness interwoven with thick threads of guilt churned in my gut. Every time I thought about that night and the last words she said, I felt a stabbing sensation behind my solar plexus. My thoughts were overrun with regret and hypotheticals: what if I didn't eat the molly? What if I didn't cheat? I spent countless hours missing her, longing for her touch and wishing I didn't throw away her love. You know what they say, though: shit in one hand, wish in the other, see which one fills up faster.

Despite the regret and sadness, however, a part of me knew that this was the right thing. The breakup, I mean. Of course it was fucked up of me to precipitate it with one dumb, selfish act, but in my heart I knew that we didn't belong together. The truth is, I suspected we both knew that we shouldn't have stuck it out as long as we did. With some space, time, and perspective I saw that our relationship was rooted in lust and unhealthy attachment, not compatibility.

Eventually after enough awkward shifts together we met in Falafel House. At first it was weird and I felt the hostility coming off her in waves, mixing with the smell of deep fried chickpeas, but then our conversation began to flow. I apologized, and she expressed how much I had hurt her. She didn't forgive me, and I didn't expect her to. We finished our sandwiches and hugged. It was sad but peaceful. It seemed that she felt better after expressing herself. Everything was going to be okay...

...Not.

The very next night, during my managing shift, she spent the whole night hanging onto some guy right in front of me, then left with him. I am certain that she waited to make sure I would see them. Maybe I deserved that, I don't know, but it hurt me bad. Then she fucked Dash the following week and called me in the middle of the night to tell me. We hadn't spoken on the phone since the breakup. She specifically called just to tell me, just to dig her fake nails into my skin then pour salt into the furrows. To this day I feel a stinging echo of that phone call.

I was livid. My anger was a perpetual tempest inside my body and mind, without an outlet, really. Dash should've known better, and been a better friend, but I wasn't even that mad at him. What would have been the point? He wasn't the one I had been in a once-loving relationship with. But just the thought of Clea painted my thoughts redder than her lipstick.

Being at Yes House started making me anxious. At any moment I could have walked around a corner to see her hooking up with someone—likely a corner she knew I'd walk around, a *someone* I was sure to know. Managing the club always came with a healthy measure of stress, but now, coupled with the anger and fear, it was a nightmare I couldn't seem to wake from.

I nearly quit; it was *this* close. I couldn't bear it any longer. Juicy barely talked me out of it. "How do you think you'll feel years from now, as you reflect on your time in New York City, if today you quit the job of a lifetime over some angry girl?" he asked. I felt like he didn't quite understand. I didn't have his ability to compartmentalize life so neatly, apparently. But he was right. In the end I didn't quit, but the following months were a motherfucker.

During the spring and summer I really grew in my role as manager, but stopped enjoying my job. At work all I could think about was Clea.

Finally, in autumn, nearly six months after our split, I sought professional help. Sauce was a consummate degenerate who did more mushrooms than all the attendees of all three Woodstocks put together, and either because or in spite of that was one of the wisest people I knew. I hoped he could draw on his mystical knowledge and help me.

One lazy afternoon I took the J train over to the financial district. Sauce lived across the street from the New York Stock Exchange in a one bedroom apartment on the 57th floor. We sat on his deck, larger than the base floor of my four-bedroom apartment, complete with views of southern Manhattan and the Statue of Liberty. I poured my heart out to him. Hell hath no fury like a woman scorned, and I told him how my scorned ex-girlfriend had turned into a blood sucking monster and was making my life hell. It took Sauce no time at all to hit on the heart of the matter.

Sauce put a nitrous balloon to his lips and sucked it down. "Dude," he said, blinking slowly, voice like a slow trombone, "Clea is not your issue. Clea is Clea's issue. Clea isn't *making* your life hell or heaven, not when you were together and not now. Nobody injects feelings into you—you do that all on your own. Sure, her fucking some dude and rubbing it in your face will affect you, you're not, like, the Dalai fucking Lama. Actually, I wonder if the Dalai Lama saw his chick hooking up with one of his monk buddies, would he be totally zen about it? Wait, are monks like priests, though? Not the kiddie shit, I mean not being able to—"

"Sauce," I gently guided him back to the conversation.

"Sorry, yeah, okay, where was I? Clea not being your problem, right. You know who is your problem?"

"Uh, the Macy's Thanksgiving Day Parade of dudes who wanna stick their dicks in her?" I ventured.

"No, not them, either," he said, sagely. "Loki is your problem. He's the only problem you have ever had, and will ever have."

I asked him to explain.

"I will answer your question with a quote from Buddha," he said, warming to the Yoda shtick, and I groaned. I'm just glad he didn't put on an inappropriate accent (never a guarantee, with Sauce). "'Holding on to anger is like drinking poison and expecting the other person to die.'"

I admit that as I reflected on what he was saying, I saw more and more truth in it. Of course he (and Buddha) was right! Clea wasn't suffering from my anger, I was. And since I was manufacturing the emotion... I was the agent of my own pain. Wow.

As an important part of my healing, Sauce had me write Clea a letter—not an email or text, but an actual letter, with a pen on a piece of looseleaf paper. He told me that in this letter I am to apologize for all the wrongs I did to her, then forgive her for anything she may have done that caused me to respond with hurt and anger.

"Make it detailed and sincere," he told me. "And even though you will never give her this letter, visualize her reading your words and feeling validated and peaceful."

Later—a rare no-work night—I did as he said. After putting the pen down and rereading the letter, I felt a peace I hadn't felt in months settle over me like a cool sheet on a hot summer night. I went to bed at nine p.m. and woke up twelve restful hours later feeling refreshed and lighter than ever. I know it sounds impossibly cheesy, but much of the anger I had been holding on to for six months had turned into love and forgiveness overnight. I couldn't believe it, but when I thought of Clea in the morning I found no rancor or hurt in my heart. Sauce was right.

After the letter, things smoothed out. Clea and I worked together often and the air between us didn't feel so loaded with animosity. I sensed that she was less angry with me; she didn't shove her hookups in my face like a wet spot on the rug. We still barely spoke, and I never created the opportunity to share with her the results of my illuminating chat with Sauce.

By early October, I wasn't the only one in our friend group dealing with a breakup. Xavier's girlfriend of five years left him in the most painful yet banal way: by dumping him then immediately dating one of his "best" friends.

Gutted by the breakup and unable to navigate the aftermath alone, he left the west coast and moved back to NYC. His brother set him up in his spare bedroom. Juicy, the younger sibling—but the stronger of will and spirit—was deeply concerned about Xavier, who was shattered, nearly immobilized by sorrow and anger.

I would stop by Juicy's Bushwick loft and sit next to Xavier on the couch. On the glass coffee table in front of our knees was an ashtray overflowing with Camel butts, a box of Kleenex, a can of Coke, and a takeaway container of Chinese noodles, congealed into an unappetizing little swamp. Xavier, in a stained black hoodie and baggy gray sweatpants, chain smoked and stared at nothing with bloodshot eyes. The couch and floor around him were littered with crumpled tissues.

"How you feeling, bud?" I asked Xavier, like I was talking to a Make-A-Wish kid. As if his state wasn't immediately clear.

No answer. I looked at the little tub of noodles, like yellow worms in mud, and felt my nose crinkle involuntarily.

"You hungry? Come on, let's go grab some lunch. Anything you want, my treat. Wanna hit Pizza Works?" I asked, referring to the pizza spot up the block. This time there was a response, a barely perceptible shake of the head. Nothing more. The silence was like a vacuum, greedily snatching any words I offered up. Xavier cried. Occasionally an ambulance or cop car sped by outside, sirens wailing. Every now and again he sniffed or blew his nose. Apart from that, the quiet was absolute. I said nothing and just sat with him, sometimes putting my arm around his shoulders and rocking gently.

Xavier spent every day on that couch, broken and silent, and that October I spent a lot of time next to him.

The loft was on the ground floor, spacious with high ceilings and large barred windows that looked out onto a quiet street of shuttered warehouses, a hipster real estate office, and a basement thrift shop where a Nirvana tee could set you back sixty bucks.

There wasn't a tree or bush in sight. With its exposed brick walls and cement pillars, Juicy's apartment matched the neighborhood's bare, industrial vibe, but tasteful touches gave the place color, texture, and a cozy feel. Thick slats of wood that appeared to have been scavenged from a sunken pirate ship served as shelves; African and Latin American hand drums stood and hung from hooks; and hand woven Middle-Eastern tapestries adorned the open-plan space. One of the most remarkable things about the lofts in this building was that the bathrooms weren't in the apartments, but down the hall. I was nearly offended by how absurd this was: Surely the owner of one of the most successful clubs in the city *would have his own shitter*!

My phone vibrated and I took it out of my pocket. Most people would glance over—not to be nosy, but just because suddenly there was a tiny glowing tablet in their periphery (okay, some people are nosy)—but Xavier didn't even move or blink.

"Come to YES," read a message from Juicy.

"Palace of Gods stuff?" I typed back.

"Yes, + more," his blue bubble appeared instantaneously.

I turned to Xavier and gave him a light squeeze with my left arm.

"I'll be back soon, homie," I said. "Have to pop over to YES and rap with your brother about a couple of things." He just sat there, the corners of his mouth sagging. If you told me that he had been lobotomized, I would have believed you. I got up and walked to the hallway.

I opened the heavy black door and looked at Xavier. His once-olive skin was gray and sagging from his face, as if even the muscles responsible for holding it to his skull had given up. He continued staring straight ahead. As I watched, a solitary tear slid down his right cheek. I felt my eyes well up. I walked out into the hallway and pulled the door shut behind me, giving it an extra tug to make sure the lock's tongue had engaged.

In the Front Room all the lights were on. A high school gym with disco balls. I didn't see anybody but Juicy, who was sitting on a black couch in the nook. He was wearing ripped black jeans, black Nikes, and a tight-fitting Radiohead t-shirt, also black. His thick salt and pepper hair was getting long, and he had a week's worth of beard to match. He didn't look up from his phone as the door closed behind me.

I sat heavily on the couch next to him and immediately thought about his brother, not even three blocks away.

"Lo-kee, what up?" Juicy said. I saw that he was reading an email. After another several seconds he looked up for the first time and gave me a smile that made me feel loved. "How are you? How's my bro?"

"Yeah, not great," I said. "Pretty shit, actually."

"Ah, fuck. That poor guy." He shook his head, and for a moment there was real pain in his striking blue eyes. He took a long breath with his mouth in a tight line. By the time the last of it left his nostrils, he was all business. He leaned back, crossed his left ankle over his right knee, and extended his right arm along the top of the couch. He lit a cigarette and turned towards me.

"Anyway. Fox is gonna be here in a couple of minutes and I gotta bring you up to speed real quick," Juicy said.

"Sure, what's up?" I asked.

"We're going to let Fox go."

"For real?" I was surprised. Fox had been working here for one or two years now and always loved being here.

"Yeah," Juicy said as he squinted his eyes against the smoke trailing up from the cig in the corner of his mouth. "The thing is, I've never really liked him. He's got a shitty attitude, and I guess I tolerated it for so long because he's good at working the line, but lately he's been fucking up. I've gotten complaints from both guests and staff about him being unprofessional or straight up rude. Anywho, I'm over it. He's done."

I didn't know what to say. Just two days before the three of us were shooting the shit out back like everything was peachy. "Shit, okay." I finally said. "When?"

"Today. In a couple of minutes." Juicy picked up his phone from where it was lying facedown on the couch between us. Under the time, his lock screen was stacked with notifications. He put it back down. "I want you to do it."

"Me? Why?" I had only ever fired one person, a dishwasher I barely knew (not Licky). I wasn't ready to give the ax to someone

I've been working closely with for a year plus, someone who had become a friend.

"Because you're a manager and I am asking you to, one. Two, because between my catatonic brother at home and Palace of Gods coming up, I'm stretched thinner than the front of Vish's g-string. And three, because the one I did this morning was *rough*."

We sat in silence for a few moments, me feeling dumb for asking and Juicy smoking. He finished the cigarette and tossed it into a small coffee cup at his feet. It made an insignificant hiss.

"Who'd you fire this morning?" I asked.

Juicy sighed. "Mrs. Miss," he said.

"No! Mrs. Miss!? Why would you do that, she's a fucking legend!" I blurted out and immediately realized I was talking to the boss. "Sorry. I mean, you must've had your reasons, but..."

Juicy blew a flake of ash off his jeans then settled back into the couch. He gave no indications of having noticed my little outburst. "Look," he said calmly in his let-me-give-you-a-bit-of-knowledge voice. "Mrs. Miss *is* a legend, and rightly so: she's one of the most gifted and committed performers I have ever worked with. But she's a lot, man. You gotta understand these people, with their big personalities and charisma... and ego! Christ, the ego on some of them. You have to handle them, and placate and stroke. Which is fine, they are stars, after all. And *I* can handle it. But when the complaints from staff and customers just keep coming in, I just can't have it. Somebody walks in here and my main priority—and yours, incidentally—is them having a good time and feeling great. If one of my employees is rude, or berates them, or otherwise makes them feel less than welcome, that's a problem. I don't care if it's Mrs. Miss, Fox, or the guy replacing the toilet paper roll. And it's not like I haven't given her a million second chances." Juicy picked up his phone, indicating that the passing of the wisdom was done, for now. Anytime he shared with me like this, I was grateful and paid attention.

He fired off a quick response and put the phone back on the couch. "She can still perform and stuff," he said matter of factly, "but I need to limit her interactions with the customers, so no more Door or VIP hosting for her."

"Damn," I said, and tilted my head back until it rested on fake leather. I couldn't imagine Mrs. Miss's larger than life personality not being a part of the entrance experience.

I heard the bang and creak of the front door and looked up to see Fox walking in and squinting against the lights. His black jeans and rasta-colored poncho-hoodie juxtapositioned the disco room.

Fox saw us in the corner and shot a little chin nod and patently false smile our way. Being invited to meet an owner and manager in the middle of the day? I'd not be able to muster a genuine smile, either. Juicy waved, with a face on like he was about to tell him that we got better dental insurance, and my stomach did a little barrel roll. In the time it took Fox to cross the room, I whispered to Juicy out of the left corner of my mouth, "I don't think I can do it—what the fuck do I even say?!"

Juicy gave me an assuring look and responded calmly (not at all *sotto voce*), "Don't sweat it, I'll take care of it." To Fox he said, "My man, thanks for coming in." He stood up and shook hands with the tatted up about-to-not-be door guy.

"Join us," Juicy said, then sat on the shorter leg of the L-shaped couch, leaving an empty spot next to me. The message was subtle but clear, at least to me: "This is not a tribunal." My respect for him bumped up another point.

"What's up, Loki," said Fox and put out his fist as he sat down to my left. I bumped it, feeling like I just sunk a knife right between his shoulder blades, and gave him a meek "yo."

Whether he sensed something in the air between us, an energetic portent hanging around like a whiff of subtle but distasteful perfume, I don't know, but his raspy voice betrayed a quiet dread as he asked, "So, uh, what's up?"

Juicy cut to the chase. "Listen, there's no easy way to say or hear this, but we called you in today because we're letting you go." He paused, giving Fox a moment to internalize what he said. I saw Fox's lips part but no words came out. Juicy continued, like a judge delivering a sentence. "We've been getting complaints. If it was the occasional too-drunk person or some vindictive asshole trying to cause trouble for you, I would be on your side, but it keeps happening, and it's not just the guests. Other staff and some of the security guys have told me about your attitude when you're working the door. Again, I get it. It's not easy being patient all night with people that are annoying, or fucked up, or entitled, or outright unreasonable—or all four at once! The job is not for everybody, but what I expect from the people I hire to do it is *radical* kindness, no matter what. You understand what I'm saying?"

I looked at the condemned man closely, fascinated by the dejection on his face. His mouth, still open, moved a couple of times, as if he were rehearsing what he was about to say without making a sound. He cleared his throat.

"I... but I thought I was doing great out there, keeping the vibe positive, you know?" He reached for the corner of his pancho and wiped his left eye, smearing his eyeliner and leaving a small black streak of it reaching for his temple. This made him both more clownish and pitiable.

"I mean, right? Nobody's even said anything to me! But," he sniffed loudly and I thought, *Please please please don't let me see another grown man cry today.* "But now," he said, swallowing snot and opening his watery eyes wider, "Now that I know there is a problem—was a problem!—I can do better, right? If you give me another chance? I can be kinder. I *will* be! I promise. I will be the kindest, no matter what they say or do out there, I'll just be super nice to everybody." His final words came as a whisper.

My prayer was ignored: big fat tears began to slide down his stubble cheeks and fall on the poncho. "Please! Just one more chance." Seeing nothing give in Juicy's face he looked to me, red eyes pleading. I understood the despair in them. It wasn't just a job he was losing: he was being kicked out of a family.

I was so caught up in the drama of the moment, I began to open my mouth, about to give him another chance without even being aware of it. But Juicy spoke first, softly but with finality.

"I'm sorry, but we've made our decision."

Fox bowed his head and strands of greasy hair fell in front of his face. His shoulders and back moved as his breath hitched between barely audible sobs. I wanted to put my arm around him. I wanted to put my hands over my eyes, like a kid willing something to cease to be happening. I did neither. After ten seconds that felt like ten minutes, a punctuational sniffle sounded from under the hair. To his credit, Fox stood up and looked at Juicy, offering his right hand, not bothering to clean his face. Juicy stood up, too. "Thanks, anyway," Fox said as they shook, then he turned to me. "See you around, Loki." I gave his hand a shake as I patted his left shoulder. He walked out the front door, slowly but with his chin up. When the golden doors closed behind him with a percussive finality, I lowered my face into my palms then ran my fingers through my hair. I felt nauseated.

"Well that sucked," Juicy said as he looked at his phone. "Let's get a coffee."

~~~

Out on the sidewalk, in the bright midday sunshine, Juicy lit a cigarette. We walked past a no-name ATM plastered with stickers then hung a right. I picked up my pace to keep up with Juicy. We passed a dive bar and two sets of tagged up steel shutters. The asian man selling bracelets on the corner smiled and said hello to us, the way he did every day. After passing a chain pizza shop and a Korean joint, we walked into Wycliff Starr. Juicy ordered coffee for both of us without asking (short Americano for him, oat cap for me), tipped fifty per-cent, then dove right into Palace of Gods as a surly looking blonde with a septum ring made our drinks.

"Right. Let's review." There were a couple of tourists, likely French, sitting down, and another two people waiting for their drinks, but Juicy spoke and looked at me as if it was just us in the office. "This year we got two nights at Grand Prospect Hall, Friday and Saturday. There will be six thousand tickets available for each night." He waited for me to nod before continuing. "We are partnering with Hero again for the main stage, they really crushed it last year. The other rooms will be for Burning Man crews. Eight of them, to be exact: Mayan Warrior, Comfort and Joy, Distrikt, Disco Knights, Glamcocks, Kostume Kult, Pink Mammoth, and Tierra Bomba."

I kept nodding, but I was only half listening. I couldn't stop thinking about Fox, practically on his knees. *Just one more chance, please!* How long would that image of him live in my head? How frequently would he visit my thoughts, looking at me accusingly through lachrymose eyes? Even now the Fox in my head said to me, *Why didn't you go to bat for me, Loki? I thought we were friends.*

Friends. How many more of them would I have to fire?

"Loki" ("*Low-KEY*") "You with me?" Juicy was looking at me.

"Yep, got it, seven camps," I quickly responded. Juicy looked at me for another second.

"Eight," he said.

"Right, that's what I meant."

"Short black ami and oat cap!" The barista called out as she put our lidless white coffee cups on the counter. She really was quite pretty, grumpiness and all. She had the kind of white skin that made all her tattoos pop, and her perpetual pout went well with her overapplied blue eyeliner. Shit, if I listened to Elliot Smith and Thom Yorke all day long, I'd probably be pouty and wearing too much eyeliner, too.

Juicy got our drinks and gave her his baristas-and-waiters smile, the one accompanied by a slow blink. I led the way out and held the door for him. Outside, he put our coffees on a small black table and lit a cigarette. I picked mine up and took a sip, letting my top lip linger in the fragrant foam. Delightful. Maybe she put so much love into the coffee that there was none left for the customers. Fine by me.

"Anyway," Juicy said after he took his own sip. "There will be a stage manager in each room, but it will be up to you to make sure they have the support they need and things are running smoothly."

"Copy that," I said. "Where will you be?"

"Bottle service, obviously," he said, smiling. "We already got five ten-thousand dollar reservations, one for the owner of the Empire State Building. My job will be to make sure that everything is perfect, and we are giving these ballers whatever their rich little hearts desire."

"So you're saying that I'll be in charge of…"

"Pretty much everything else," Juicy laughed. "I mean, the main focus will be the bars. They are the priority. By now I don't have to explain to you that the bars are where we make our money. But you will be the manager of managers. Which means that if something goes wrong, anytime, anywhere in that venue—from dancefloor to urinal—and a manager can't make it right, you need to step up. Amar and I will for sure be busier than a guy with two dicks at an orgy, so you're gonna need to know that venue inside and out. You with me?"

The more he talked the giddier I got. As I envisioned the event, and my role in it, my excitement began to edge out any remaining misgivings about Fox. Palace of Gods. Twelve thousand people in two days. Manager of Managers, number three guy. My dream come true. I smiled.

"How will I learn everything about Grand Prospect Hall?" I asked, trying to seem calm despite my elevated heart rate.

"Walkthroughs," Juicy said. "Enough of them for you to know that place better than the back of your dick."

Based on the size of GPH, and how well I knew the back of my dick, I was skeptical, but over the course of the next three weeks I familiarized myself with every nook and cranny of the Hall. Juicy and I met at the South Slope venue every afternoon, and as we explored the rooms, the floors, the outside areas and staircases—even the crawl spaces, phone flashlights lit up—the mastermind shared his plan with me. We spent a full day with each department (coat check, bottle service, security, lights, sound, production, bar, performers…) going over every detail of the two-night schedule and the layout, down to the location of every trash can. Juicy wanted perfection, and he was going to get it.

He was not only determined to throw *the* Halloween party of the century, Juicy was committed to making Palace of Gods the most environmentally-friendly event of its kind and magnitude, ever.

Long disgusted by the systemic pollution and waste perpetrated by the nightlife industry, he implemented a system created by the company called Cup Zero. There would be no single-use plastic cups at Palace of Gods. Instead, he partnered with the company and they provided us with 30,000 reusable cups. A customer would get their drink, pay a buck for the deposit, then get the dollar back upon returning the cup to the cup stations throughout the venue. A simple concept—incentivize recycling and keep tons of plastic out of the landfill (and, to be fair, make more money in the process)—but one that would be difficult to execute at this scale.

The reusable cups were just one of a thousand details; one of countless things that *should* go right, but could go wrong. During these three weeks of preparations and layers of contingency planning, I tried to take everything in stride and trust that all our hard work would pay off.

~~~

Friday morning arrived in a blink. I woke up on the first day of the event like a kid on Christmas… but also like one who had *the* final exam of the school year, and was starting to doubt all the cramming he did the night before. I popped out of bed like a jack-in-the-box, threw on a black shirt and black jeans, packed my costume, brushed my teeth, and was out the door, sans Amar's makeup kit, this time.

I arrived at the Hall at 10 a.m. to find the production team in their perennial all-black, racing around the place, their utility belts and hammer handles slapping their thighs. I spotted Nasty, our event's lighting director, and asked him how it was going.

Nasty looked even more disheveled than usual. He was out of breath and perspiring. There was a rank odor of nervous sweat, black coffee and cigarettes about him.

"Now we're more or less back on track, but before? We were proper fucked. All those lights I ordered? The dumdums at the lighting shop sent the wrong ones. We finally got what I ordered, but not until yesterday evening, so most of us worked through the night," he said.

"Fuck." I imagined climbing around, mounting spotlights all night. "You're a legend," I told him without exaggeration. "Thanks, man. I hope you get a nap in before doors open."

Nasty actually threw his head back and laughed. "Loki, you were here last year, so let me ask you: what do you think is the likelihood of that happening?"

"Zero percent," I admitted, "but you one of a kind, baby."

We shared a smile and a Top Gun style high five, then got back to work.

Juicy showed up around noon, with Xavier in tow. I had just finished triple checking the twenty POS computers, making sure that each had the right software and all the connections were secure. The number one rule in nightlife: every bartender must be able to sell booze from opening to last call. Just one POS that loses the wi-fi signal, for example, results in thousands of dollars of missed sales. I did all I could. The rest was up to god and the internet, which, these days, seemed to be synonyms.

Juicy was smiling, his arm loosely draped around his brother's slouching shoulders. I couldn't recall the last time I saw Xavier outside the loft, dressed in clothes that don't telegram, "I have given up." I greeted them both and gave Xavier a long hug. Juicy explained that Xavier would be a kind of managerial runner, jumping in when needed to help me, Juicy or Amar when we needed. This struck me as a terrible idea, at first—zero being the optimal number of crying middle aged men at a party—but then I thought about how being useful and busy would help Xavier take his mind off his ex and warmed to it.

Staff kept showing up all day, 150 of them, in total, and jumping in to help us get to the preparation finish line. The day flew by without us noticing when the sun finally hid over the horizon and night settled over the city, and suddenly it was seven p.m.—two hours before doors. Xavier and I ran around dispersing gym bags full of cash at select registers. After dropping one by the POS in the main room I looked up to see that everybody was trotting or full on galloping to their destinations—it didn't matter if they had been here for twenty hours, delirious with exhaustion, wondering where they'd get the energy for that last bit of setting up. There was an air of excited urgency and we were all breathing it. With all of us in black, it looked like some kind of commando academy before a raid on a villain's secret mountain lair.

One hour before doors, the rest of the staff arrived. Not production or any other behind-the-scenes operatives vital to any operation like this, these boys and girls were all flash and colorful tail feathers. The public, painted and glittering face of YES. The performers, the prancers; the dancers and divas. The door people and fabulous bartenders. A shimmering carnival of skin and textures and outlandish props. Intricate headdresses of sequins and chains. Golden shoulder pads that matched shining codpieces. Bronzed muscles constricted by belts and straps. Black leather pilots and latex dom daddies. Virginal gossamer-thin white dresses and braids, a belied innocence. Leotards bulging in all the right ways. Faux fur over shaven smooth skin. More sixpacks than a beer wholesaler. Steam punks and ancient warriors; earthbound demigods shoving fluorescent foam plugs into their ear canals as the last tests of the sound systems vibrated the marrow in everyone's bones. The DJs, too lazy to dress up, in street clothes under ethnic robes and sunglasses, maybe a hat they got in Tulum. The Palace of Gods, so long in the planning, was beginning to hum with light and life.

Sweat beaded on my forehead and ran into my eyes, as if the thoughts behind them were creating enough friction to raise my temperature. *Are all the DJs here? Is the security team in their places and on the right walkie channels? Are doors and coat checks ready for the stampede that will barrel in?* I knew that no amount of obsessive thought or triple-checking would result in a feeling of total preparedness. When doors opened, I would have to let go and trust in my team, in all the work we put in; and, more importantly, that *when* things went off the rails, I would handle it with grace and professionalism.

It was time to meet and onboard the thirty bartenders that we hired for the event. I'd not met most of them, and our communication was limited to a few emails. It was time to show them their stations and share pertinent details about the venue.

The Oak Room Lounge was pretty much what you'd expect from the name: dark, cozy, and appointed like a mid-century men's club. Plush red chairs clustered around small round tables. A moose head was mounted on the wall, the eyes looking glassy and sad. You could almost smell the cigars and bourbon. I walked in to find a couple of hundred people mingling. It looked like a costume party.

"Hey, everybody!" I shouted, and conversations stopped as people turned to look at me. "Where are my bartenders?" Hands shot up in the corner of the room and I began to weave through the crowd as I made my way to them.

Named for the long oak bar, the Lounge was a hive of activity. Six bottle service women, every single one of them a bona fide ten, waited for instructions. Sally, Oliver's girlfriend, was one of them. They answered only to Juicy, who had yet to arrive. They were all in heels, stockings, and dresses that highlighted their amazing… genes. They were so attractive that collectively they changed the temperature of the air around them, causing it to shimmer like turbojet exhaust. Also in the room awaiting orders, somewhat less attractive than the bottle girls, were ten security leads in black polo shirts. Under each would be a squad of ten guards. Two makeup artists were all set up in a corner, lit up mirrors, director's chairs, and all. Across from them were two tables full of ink and needles. It was set up as a tattoo station that would be available for guests all night. Two door people man the staff-only entrance that goes right to the street.

When I was in the corner with the huddled bartenders I saw that we would need a quieter space. "All right, people, phones down, heads up!" I announced. "We're moving. Everybody on me." I turned and walked out of the crowded room without looking back to see if they were behind me. At this point, if they couldn't follow a simple directive like that, they'd help me weed out the non-hackers. After all, I had a list of people I could call who would give their left nut (or ovary) for a chance to get gussied up and sling drinks at Palace of Gods.

We filed into the Speakeasy, the room next to the Oak Room Lounge. Sparsely decorated with muted maroon wallpaper and a softly glowing chandelier, I was happy to see that apart from one guy from Production gaffer-taping a cable behind the thirty-foot bar, we had the dimly lit space to ourselves. Compared to the rest of the rooms, it was boring—no art, no stage, no freaky shit—but from last year I knew that because of its location, the room and bar would be packed all night.

I faced the bar, wearing the outfit Lada and I patched together a few days ago. An eclectic look, we'll call it Golden Eagle Shamanic Pirate, it consisted of an open, sleeveless golden silk robe, black feathered shoulder pads (hot glued onto the robe), black pleather pants tucked into mid-calf boots, and a clipped-on golden mohawk. And glitter, obviously. All the golden glitter I could rub, paint, or throw on myself.

The bartenders arranged themselves with their backs against the bar, with those tall enough resting their elbows on the clean-for-now surface. Within seconds they started chatting the way groups of one or more people have been doing for about two hundred thousand years. I surveyed my troops, impressed but not surprised with the thought and attention they put into their outfits. They wouldn't be caught dead working a Yes House Halloween party in anything less than dazzling. There was a tatted sailor boy in dress whites and a sexy steampunk chick in a bronzed tophat. There were at least ten leather doms and subs (two with red ball gags around their throat) in various states of undress; some kind of fearsome Orc-like creature with exposed buttocks; a motley collection of angels and demons; and one Catholic priest in a black belly shirt—to name a few. In addition to unique costumes, they had another thing in common: they all looked as nervous and disoriented as a litter of puppies dropped into the middle of a lion cage at the zoo.

"Look at this crew!" I said loudly, and they obeyed by giving each other a once over. "We don't have much time, so I will make this quick. I need ten minutes of your undivided attention, so listen up." Hearing the stern urgency in my voice, they piped down immediately. I briefly allowed myself to feel like a general about to lead his warriors into battle. A bare-bellied general with tight pleather pants, that was. As one they looked at me expectantly and I am not ashamed to admit that I felt drunk with authority. With the minutes ticking down, I was in no mood for bullshit, either. *Let me catch just one of these fucks looking at their phone and I'll smash it to smithereens right here, in front of all of them,* I thought.

After thanking them for being on time and looking fabulous, I welcomed them to the team. "Even if this is your only shift," I said, heart swelling, "tonight you are part of the Yes House family." I paused until the weees and whoops died down. "And do you know what this family is here to do this weekend?" Again I waited a beat, this time to hype them up, before continuing, louder, "We are here to put on the biggest and best Halloween event in New York City!"

The bartenders cheered and high-fived each other like high school jocks before a championship game.

I ran the group through the particulars of the POS they would be using, familiarized them with the menu, and made sure they could speak (yell) more or less intelligently about the ingredients of all the cocktails. Based on their experience, seniority, and existing relationship with YES, I assigned ten of them the role of cash handler. Not to put too fine a point on it, but with an event of this magnitude, we simply couldn't trust everyone to work a register. There was no end to tricks and scams available to an unscrupulous bartender, but limiting most of them to card-only interactions greatly mitigated our risk.

I wrapped up just as the soundcheck began. Eight rooms, eight different sound systems, and dozens of speakers came alive. Zero to a hundred decibels at the speed of sound. My heart, head, and balls echoed the pounding bass as eight different sound engineers hit buttons on eight different mixers. Even though my calves ached from a day of running and my undernourished, overworked body was on the brink of collapse, that sound signaled my brain to dump dopamine faster than a drug runner spotted by the Coast Guard between Havana and Key West. The bartenders and I exchanged a knowing smile as the smarter/more-experienced of the group put in earplugs. I woke my phone up and checked the call sheet for the night, then told the five bartenders assigned to the Speakeasy to start setting up. To the rest I gave the follow-me wave accompanied by a turning of my head, and we left at a very brisk walk, with the shorter-legged of the bunch jogging to keep up.

The room next door was a cavernous rave cave with thick black drapes over the windows to ensure the lighting techs had total control over the darkness. There was a DJ booth along one garden-themed wall, also decorated with fake fronds and vines. Behind the booth was an enormous wooden triangle with eight wooden "rays" shooting out of its center. To anybody in the electronic dance music scene, this was the unmistakable symbol of Mayan Warrior, an international collective of artists and musicians. Initially a project that united likeminded creators from Mexico City and northern California, these Burning Man veterans were known for hosting the sickest parties on the *playa* (the name for the dry lakebed on which the festival is held every year) and building what may be the best art bus at the event. Rumors had it that with its lights, sound system, and art installations, the bus was worth five million dollars. Their room at Palace of Gods was guaranteed to be nothing short of epic.

There was already a haze of manufactured smoke hanging in the gloom, and the sound and light techs were putting both systems to the test. As a progressive house track dropped, a dozen green lasers shot out of unseen projectors and a Tron-like grid began to descend like a dystopian brain scan. The bartenders stood and stared like somebody dosed their Red Bulls with LSD until I grabbed three by the wrists and led them to the bar. I indicated to the rest that we were moving out, and led the way past an even darker corner of the room lined with hundreds of cushions and pillows. I could almost see the future of this area: heaping bumps of ketamine and bobbing heads in laps.

Next stop on the bartender delivery tour was the Glamcocks room. Glamcocks, true to their name, threw the wildest, gayest parties during the ten days when Black Rock City was an actual American city. I'd heard tales of forty-person ass-to-mouth choo-choo trains and glory holes that operated twenty-four hours a day for the duration of the Burn. They'd have to keep it just a bit tamer at Palace of Gods, but only because they were in one of the smaller rooms—and a glory hole required at least one extra wall in which to put it. The room was sparkly and rich with tinsel and dashes of color every shade of the rainbow. Predictably, delightfully, the Cocks hired DJs who spun disco, funk, and happy house, which always kept the vibe fun, playful, and light. Empty now, the room would be awash with beautiful hairless men and their more hirsute bear counterparts in no time. Having no bar here, we moved on to the next room.

A narrow hallway led to a long rectangular room with high ceilings. Dozens of towering potted plants and small trees created a dark jungle that required one to avoid giant leaves that caressed (or slapped) the face. This would be the home of Tierra Bomba, another popular Burning Man camp. Proud of their Latin American roots, these cats, for better or worse, drew the basicest basic bitches of them all. The boys and girls who will gravitate to this room will have flowing kimonos and expensive leather boots. From under the wide flat brims of their thick felt hats they will tell you about the frog poison they ingested in Tulum under the benevolent gaze of a shaman from Connecticut with a million followers (on Insta), and how after vomiting and shitting themselves dry they had a vision, and were now absolutely sure they should invest a portion of their trust fund into a retreat center in Costa Rica. A lot of the women here will be dancing while doing esoteric breathing exercises, in order to "awaken the snake," while longhaired manchildren, tantra masters to a one, will appeal to their divine feminine with bumps of kitty. The DJs in this room would spin tracks that had flutes or pan pipes—ocarinas, at the least—with a syncopated deep heartbeat thump for bass and Spanish language vocals that spoke of jaguar visions and eagle hearts.

I was pleased to see that this room and everybody in it were ready to go. The DJs were milling about near the stage, never too far from the ice buckets of top shelf booze and natural fruit juices their riders stipulated. And walnuts. Why all these DJs wanted walnuts was a mystery, but maybe it was a trade secret. The sound system here was maybe the thumpiest of all the rooms, and even now Nicola Cruz's "Colibria" was lulling me into an ayahuasca trance. I pointed to two of my 22 remaining bartenders. "Sasha, Alex, this is you." They peeled off and the rest of us left.

There is an ad that runs on certain NYC-only television channels, by now a cult hit. After a Vivaldi-scored montage showcasing Grand Prospect Hall's opulence there is a tight shot of Mr. Stern and his wife, standing on a step of a grand staircase like dignitaries from some Mediterranean nation. "Grand Prospect Hall!" Mr. Stern's buxom, sparkly-dressed, unattractive wife says in poorly modulated, heavily accented English, before her husband nearly yells, for some reason, "Where all your dreams come true!"

I passed this staircase now, looking as grand as ever, to get back to the Oak Room Lounge, where I dropped off none other than Dan Rockies and another bartender. I was excited as it was his first time back with the gang. Dan may not have liked what Yes House had become... but he liked the grandioseness of Palace of Gods (plus the fat paycheck that came with it).

I paused to catch my breath and snuck a look at the couple of bartenders still with me. *Are these people aware that in thirty minutes we will open the doors to the biggest event in Yes House history?* I banished the thought and any possible anxiety that might result from it, and stepped into the last room on the first floor.

With its chandeliers and dark rugs, the spacious Oak Room felt more like a banquet hall than a dancehall. There was a large stage in the middle and a two-POS bar at one end. If during the party you wanted to escape the boom boom vibe, this is where you came to chill and enjoy live performances by acrobats, magicians, and a five-piece New Orleans jazz band. Em-ceeing all night would be none other than Grandma, and Kate Cummings would raise the temperature of the room with her songs and moves.

I saw Mr. Stern in the corner. He was wearing a black tuxedo, spit shined black shoes that went out of style right around the time we invaded Vietnam, and a red tie. Completely ignoring the other chaos around him, he was hovering over Leche as he was setting up the final speaker, a literal inch from the tech's shoulder. From past experience, I knew he was making sure Leche didn't scratch his precious floors. You just had to laugh, but I bit my tongue to avoid doing so. I had to admit that the pain in the ass old man was starting to grow on me.

I left two of my crew here, then out the door and up the central staircase we went. I am pretty sure that I would have nightmares for the rest of my life in which I shlepped stuff and people up these stairs as Mr. and Mrs. Stern followed, yelling at me about my dreams coming true. I was sweating like a Catholic priest at an all-boys track meet, and the running in pleather pants helped not at all. As I topped the last stair I fanned myself by flapping my silk robe, winglike, an anxious golden waterfowl seeking a mate, but the sweat continued to flow.

A couple of sharp rights took us to the Spa-ship room, where my heart rate instantly began to drop. I smelled lavender and palo santo, and the continuous hum of tibetan singing bowls eased my frazzled nerves. The small room was white and dimly lit in a gentle blue. Without any dance space, nearly the entire floor was covered with white pillows, cushions, and beanbags. Spa-ship was a group of burners who were all about recovery and their camp on the *playa* was a perennial sanctuary. Tonight, in this cozy cocoon, there would be massage, reiki, and sound healing. Probably some low-key slow petting, too. This wouldn't be a room with a fifty-deep line for shots, so I just left one bartender at the small bar, a pixie of a human being named Courtney who would fit right in.

The nearly hundred-meter tall Grand Ballroom seemed to be both in the eye of the last-minute-prep tornado, and the calm before the event storm. It was beautifully eerie. Nearly empty, dark, and silent after the sound and equipment check, there was an expectant hush in the largest space in the building. Beams of lights from rotating projectors painted colorful circles on the empty dance floor, and lasers carved through the remaining smoke machine haze. The silence was a wall I walked into, face first. A part of me needed this moment to settle, regroup, ground, but at this point the only things keeping me going were nervous adrenaline and coffee, and if I stopped for too long I would collapse in a sweaty, golden heap and sleep for two days. My body and mind were tapped, but my heart jack hammered in my chest like I just blew a line as long as the fifty-foot Ballroom bar—and I was planning to keep it that way by inviting my friend, Adderall, to the party once doors opened.

I started moving again before my feet grew roots. The core of the whole event, this room would see the most action. Six bartenders would be busy all night, I was sure of it. I picked them out and sent them on their way to start setting up their stations. I crossed the Ballroom, my hair and robe billowing out behind me, and went into the Skylight Room, as long as the Ballroom but half as wide and a third as tall. Two large skylights gave it its unimaginative name, but with the sound overflow from the main stage and its hallway-like feel, this was more of an in-between transitory space, a wide traffic lane. Zester's photo booth was off to one side, set up and ready to go. For Palace of Gods he chose a divinely shimmering silver polyester backdrop. Skylight was the perfect room for the booth, as there would be a hundred-person line all night. Planning, creating, and showing off your costume all night was just half of the whole point. Everybody knows that until you've posted photos on social media *and* received enough validation in the form of views, likes, and comments like, "Erma*gawd* you're such a fucking *bae*!" to quiet the desperate child inside… it doesn't even count. And Zester's photos were as postable as they come.

Just because this wasn't a party area, per se, didn't mean it wasn't a buying booze and drinking area, as we learned last year. Skylight would have the third busiest bar of the event, and this time we were ready and able. Last Halloween there was a short bar with two bartenders, a guy and a girl we hired for the event, sight unseen. After the fourth straight hour of ten-deep queues of goblins and sexy nurses giving them the dick eye, their bladders filled to bursting, their eyes as bloodshot as those of a marine in Fallujah, they nearly quit. I have no idea how Oliver got them to stay. Well, that's not true, I have an *idea*. I'll give you a hint: it starts with the letter M and rhymes with "honey."

This year we had an all-star crew from Macao, a legendary New York City bar known for their mixologists and the cocktails they crafted. If there was ever an Alcohol A-Team, these five were it. I pointed and nodded, and they spread out and trotted away like they were going to neutralize Osama Bin Laden.

Adjacent to Skylight was The Atrium, which made for some confusion. In a lot of people's imaginary buildings, skylights and atriums kind of get lumped together for the simple reason that there is lots of natural light. But you try explaining to a production assistant that one is a type of window and the other is an entire space with glass walls and ceiling and you're bound to get a couple of dick eyes yourself.

An atrium makes a lot of sense for The Grand Prospect Hall, a venue for fancy weddings and fundraiser galas, but for an all-night dance party? Less. So we put our most nonsensical camp in this room. Kostume Kult were dedicated to costumes, art, and street theater, in the city and at Burning Man. Spend more than a few seconds in conversation with any member, and they'll have you thinking about the colors of your aura and how aliens left a bunch of eggs in the Earth while it was still cooling. It's like all the theater kids you knew from high school got together, ran away to join a circus, did a bunch of acid, decided that life was too short to be taken seriously, and started dressing like it and throwing parties. They were delightful and I looked forward to seeing them freaking out the squares. Two bartenders here would suffice.

I checked the time and somehow picked up the pace as I went up to the third floor. With its horseshoe balustrade and balcony overlooking the Grand Ballroom, this was prime space, a.k.a. bottle service area. Separated by dividers, eight groups of upper crusters, like the aforementioned owner of The Empire State Building, would lounge and drink their fancy booze here, literally looking down on the rest of the party and occasionally deigning to mingle with hoi polloi on the dance floors before coming back. I saw Juicy surrounded by eight bottle servers and hosts, each more stunning than the last, especially Krystal and Sally, in all white dresses tight enough for me to see the outline of moles and appendix surgery scars. I suspected that making sure the high rollers were treated right wasn't the only reason Juicy was handling bottle service tonight. Juicy wasn't hard on the eyes, either, in a collarless white jacket with gold accents open to reveal his flat belly shiny with gold glitter, tight low-rise golden jeans that probably set him back my week's pay, and enough gold jewelry around his neck and wrists to drown him if he fell into a body of water. As we walked past, he was going over everything one last time, and providing any info about the high profile guests that would help the staff deliver a stellar experience.

Tucked away behind a stairwell was Zoe and Sparky's room, the Theater for the Dark Arts. This would be a fun one. Picture the freak show at Coney Island minus the bearded lady, plus a buttload of BDSM-type shit. There wasn't a bar here, but I popped in just to have a peek. Velvety merlot-colored drapery covered the walls and matched the deep red sofas, and electric candles gave the space a bordello vibe. Three mannequins stood around like party hosts anxiously waiting for the first guests to arrive. One wore a black leather gimp mask with a zippered mouth and a black harness criss-crossing his chest, another had crotchless panties and electrical tape over her nipples, and the third was blindfolded with a piece of silk that matched the walls, had blood red lipstick smeared from her lips to her cheeks, and wore badly torn thigh-high fishnets. Someone had artfully attached black spray painted clothespins to her non-nipples. Whether on accident or by design, she was missing her left hand. I didn't think her holey stump was very sexy, but maybe I'm just vanilla like that.

The room was cozy, with enough space for about a hundred curious, adventurous guests. There would be performances on the small stage, our usual sideshow fare: Cross and Die smashing cinder blocks on each other, tattooed hotties swallowing swords, guys and gals shooting objects and liquids from sundry holes, etc. If you wanted something a little more hands-on, someone would gladly tie you up and/or spank you. There would be other interactive stuff from The Foreplay events at Yes House, too—less the saltshaker. Last year I really enjoyed watching people experience the room for the first time, after crossing a portal between nightclub and fetish party. One minute some bro is offering you a Grey Goose and Redbull over a boom-chick assault on your ears, the next you're (consensually) hogtied on the floor with a black stiletto on your cheek, being told that you've been a *very* naughty girl.

With a commanding view of the Ballroom, the tech booth was between two bottle service areas, right against the thick wooden banister. I saw Nasty moving between mixer boards like a zombie, mouth slack, eyes drooping. I didn't know how he was still functioning—he'd been here twice as long as me, and I was ready to lie down and sleep forever. Next to the tech booth was an unremarkable little bar decorated with cheap Christmas lights. I left two bartenders and went into a room behind the first ring over the Ballroom.

Walking in, I paused the way I did nearly every time I entered this room. I couldn't help it. Beyond the large windows Brooklyn lay before me, the lights of Gowanus and Red Hook twinkling. And there, where the Atlantic Ocean became the North Bay before splitting into the Hudson and the East River, was the Statue of Liberty, with the iconic skyline of lower Manhattan to her north. It was all so beautiful… and so worth the ten seconds of wonder, reflection, appreciation I took out of my hectic day. With the view as the centerpiece, the large room didn't need a lot of decoration. When the backdrop to your party was night time New York City, you didn't need much.

Two legendary Burner camps united to make this room their home. Everything related to Pink Mammoth, from their tents on the *playa* to their nitrous balloons, was pinker than Barbie's Corvette, and this crew was known for their day parties and top-billing DJs. Disco Knights, "...a group of likeminded souls dedicated to throwing groovy parties in interesting locations," got their groove on to old school house and disco DJ sets that bumped long after the sun came up. Together, these two camps were sure to make this room an absolute rager.

I saw Juicy in the corner talking with the head organizer of Pink Mammoth, who did not look pleased. As I watched she indicated with an angry palm the draped off area behind them and smiled sarcastically, the way some people do when they're pissed. The curtained off rectangle in her room was to be the coat check for all the bottle service VIPs. I didn't have to hear what she was saying to guess her problem. The coat check was an eyesore that fit the vibe about as well as a tax consultant's booth.

Juicy saw me and ran over. "Hey! We're moving this coat check out of here. Get rid of the bar next to the tech booth and put it there, instead. I already told Production. Make sure they're on it." He began to speed walk away.

"Wait!" I jogged after him. "What do you mean, 'get rid of it'?"

"Strike it, move it, make it disappear—I don't care." He was walking and looking at his phone.

"What about the bartenders?!" I yelled after him as a Pink Mammoth or Disco Knights DJ hit the play button.

"Move them," he said in a way that let me know the conversation was over. I stopped chasing after him and he quickly faded from view.

I shook my head and took a breath, reminding myself that on-the-fly changes were something that I had to roll with, especially as manager. Still, with twenty-three minutes left before we opened the doors, I wasn't thrilled about suddenly going off-script after months of planning.

I told Daisy and another bartender that they'd be staying in the Pink/Knights room. "Yes, sir!" Daisy snapped off a sharp salute as she brought her heels together and stuck out her chest. She smiled and half of my stress melted away. I had five bartenders left, counting the two extras I just gained. I didn't yet know what I was going to do with them, but I figured as long as I kept moving, something would happen. The cool thing about life? Something *always* happened. I ran upstairs.

The fourth floor also had the oval balcony that looked down on the Ballroom, but it was off-limits to the public. There was only one party room up here, and tonight Comfort & Joy would be holding it down.

Comfort & Joy was another gay crew famous for wild sex parties. It is said that at the Burn there is more sodomy per square foot happening at their camp than in the entire state of Nevada. Utah and Arizona, too, most likely. They turned up, every time, and New York City was lucky to have them. Their room at Palace of Gods was by no means enormous, still they elected to cordon off a good twenty per-cent of it and put up bright, neon-colored curtains to create a safe place in which they could suck and fuck one another to their hearts' content. The rest of it was a long cuddle puddle area with rainbow colored cushions and a large dance floor. There was already an unseen layer of testosterone and body odor floating in the room, and as my crew and I walked in, a shirtless dude with a hairy chest emerged from behind the curtains, sweaty and smiling wider than the Kool Aid Man. I shook my head. If a year ago you told me that my future job entailed delivering bartenders to orgies, I would not have believed you. But deliver them I did: I left three and took off.

With twenty minutes to go I was sprinting down the central stairs, hyperfocused on the steps coming up at me faster than I was comfortable with. Rolling my ankle now and arriving at the floor below in a ball of bartenders would not be a good development. I felt their impatience behind me. I'd be pretty fed up, too—they signed up to sell drinks and look pretty, not run track.

Two barbacks were breaking down the bar next to the tech booth at a speed that told me they had recently been threatened. I packed the two POS Square computers hastily in their travel cases, and took off, the two boxes slapping my legs. Running through the venue I got concerned looks. I had been fully sucked into the stress vortex and it must have shown, but I was powerless to stop it even as my rational brain was saying, "Chill, bro, you're moving two bartenders, not delivering nuclear launch codes."

I quickly set up a POS at the end of the Grand Ballroom bar and stuffed a bartender behind it. He'd figure it out. I did the same thing at the Speakeasy bar. It wasn't ideal; you wanted each bartender to have their own station, but at least these extras could help ring people up. That done and off my mind, for now, I stepped outside.

I took a deep breath and couldn't remember the last time I tasted cool, clean (relatively), outside air. I took another one. On the street everything is calm. And why wouldn't it be? Mere feet from the hurricane of activity inside and all our grand plans... was a nearly empty city sidewalk in the early evening, in a quieter part of Brooklyn. There wasn't a line of dressed up guests jostling each other to get into the biggest event of *my* year. Shit, there wasn't a single person there who didn't work for us. I felt my heart rate drop as I remembered that Halloween and New Year's Eve were totally different animals. On Halloween, folks rolled in between ten and midnight, some of them totally sober, even. On December thirty-first, those same people are banging down the door at nine-oh-one, pupils the size of nickels, chewing their second pill of ecstasy and chasing it with nips from a flask.

Crius was in front of the main entrance, ringed by ten of his security guys. They were just shooting the shit, laughing, and smoking. They knew their jobs better than anyone, and with Crius at the helm, there was nothing they couldn't handle or weren't prepared for. Just seeing the big man dropped my stress levels by a few points. I sent up a prayer of gratitude: *Thank fuck this guy is here.* You want your top people at an event this big, and Crius's was one of the names highest on that list. We all breathed easier when he was around, and even though Yes House in Bushwick would be having big events, too, not having our head of security at Palace of Gods was unthinkable. Yes House would survive without him. Would we, out here with six thousand people? I wasn't sure.

With a couple of minutes remaining, I checked on the doors. Destiny, who came out of retirement for the weekend, was all set up with a crew of five to man one of the two entrances. She and her team all wore fake furs and had electronic scanners in hand. Spread out around them were half a dozen security guys, with the shortest one a hulking six and a half feet tall. Not one looked equipped with the necessary facial musculature to form a smile. Beyond them, inside the courtyard, was general coat check. One-hundred rolling racks, thousands of tagged hangers, and a staff of six.

The open robe let the fall air cool my sweaty skin and spin the manager tag hanging from a lanyard around my neck. I went around to the garden area on the other side of the Victorian building to see how the team at the other entrance was doing. The setup here was identical to the first: five people with scanners and faux furs, behind them another coat check. Five stony-faced black clad security guards were posted here, too, and I saw another one further up the block. The loner would be making sure our guests weren't doing drugs on residential stoops. I nodded at everybody, pleased that we were ready for the masses, and went inside.

While guests would be walking through this space on their way in, the glassed-in passage on the other side of the entrance was largely a behind the scenes staff-only and staging area. Cora sat on a folding chair, posture perfect, typing on a laptop in a curtained off production "office." Sammy Saves and his five EMT's were sitting in a semicircle, their square shoulder bags in the middle. The Modern Gypsies, a production company specializing in gargantuan puppets and spectacle acts, were assembling a fifty-foot dragon that they would dance through the larger rooms, Chinese-New-Year style. Various technicians moved through the space, grabbing stuff from a dozen tool boxes. Everybody was moving fast, and with five minutes left before we opened the doors, there was a look of dead-tired determination on people's faces, mixed with a dash of, "Stay the fuck out of my way and don't touch my coffee cup." Sammy was the exception. As always, he looked as serene and happy as Thich Nhat Hanh. I guess if you spent the first half of your professional life bandaging stab wounds on the streets of South Brooklyn, helping dehydrated or bad-tripping party girls and boys wasn't that big of a deal. I stood off to the side and made myself be still and take it all in.

Remember this, I told myself.

I heard a cheerful but urgent voice.

"Performers! All performers to the green room, quick like a bunny!" Zoe was skipping through the space like a kid on Saturday morning, smiling ear to ear. Seeing her, I became aware of what my own face was doing, and for the first time in many hours I allowed my eyebrows to soften and my scalp and jaw to relax. I smiled, too.

Just then the music began to pound. Not a sound check. I didn't need my phone to tell me that Palace of Gods would be live in one minute. The hairs on my arms stood. There was no drug in the world that could give me the electric anticipation that I felt then. Everything slowed down the way it does in a modern war movie after a mortar round hits close to the protagonist and he goes deaf. I saw a clown sprinting, ridiculous and ungainly in his enormous shoes, his painted-on smile belying the stress in his eyes. A stilt walker, her muscular legs shining with sweat, nearly collided with the dragon. A production grunt spun a roll of black tape in his hands, desperately looking for the end. Cora, typing, a deranged little smile on her face. And all the while the cardiac *thump thump thump* of the music.

Despite no one being in line yet, I unclipped the walkie from my belt, selected the channel reserved for security and door staff, held it in front of my mouth and pressed the button on the side.

"Open the doors."

I got a series of "copy," and just like that, it began.

~~~

Guests began to trickle in at half past the hour, wearing costumes that they had been preparing for weeks or months. Quickly it became difficult to discern the partiers from the paid performers. A man in a golden corset strode past me. Golden snakes were uncoiling themselves from his headpiece and a solitary golden serpent wound its way down his right arm. He carried a golden staff as tall as him, topped with a hissing cobra ready to strike. His body (as well as the Nike Airs on his feet) was spray painted gold, and his lips were a rich purple. His contacts transformed his eyes into those of a nocturnal wildcat, the irises ringed in gold.

I strolled around the first floor (ah, to *stroll* once more!) observing the people in their costumes; allowing myself to forget, if for just a moment, just how many moving parts needed to operate in concert *at all times* for things to go off without a hitch, and just marveling. For now all the action was on the first floor because it was the only one open. At ten we'd open the second, and the third and fourth at eleven.

A tall woman that carried herself like royalty walked past me. A full head taller than me in six-inch heels, her pitch-black hair matched her wings, neatly folded against her beautiful bare back. Each feather shone with a near-blue gleam and I wondered if they were real and, if so, if there was a pile of plucked dead crows somewhere. She was magnificent in a please-do-not-ferry-my-soul-to-the-Underworld kind of way. Black feather armbands cinched her upper arms and accentuated her vinyasa triceps, and a solitary ruby-colored stone in the center of her feather choker was the only non-black touch, apart from her crimson lips. She was wearing what looked like a black one-piece bathing suit and black thigh-highs with a solid black stitch running down the backs of her legs to disappear into the heels. She glided through the crowd, turning heads and causing people to slap their friends' arms so they could see her too. I watched a woman slap a man's arm, none too lightly, after catching him checking out the risqué raven's tail feathers.

As more people arrived and everybody became desensitized to outrageous costumes (also, I saw at least five more medusas and a murder's worth of crows, magpies, and grackles), it took a lot more to catch people's attention—not for lack of trying! It was immediately clear that this was no Midtown halloween party full of slutty nuns and nurses and the bro's who loved them. These were dress-up aficionados who spared no effort or expense to ensure they showed up as the costume *gods* they were.

Just before ten o'clock I was happy to see that everything was off to a smooth start. People were exploring and finishing up their first rounds of drinks. The bartenders were animated and engaged, and all the POS systems were holding up. For now, anyway.

I was catching up with a consenticorn I once made hot love to on my desk at YES when I took out my phone and saw something on its screen that made me disengage and walk away. Phone still in hand I hopped up the main stairs and stood at the edge of the nearly empty Ballroom. Nearly empty and *silent.* I knew Security would start letting guests up at ten on the dot, music or no music, and people walking into a silent ballroom on the biggest party night of the year was the last thing I wanted. Not only a party foul (three years running), but some bush league shit, to boot. Fucking Leche. Seeing no sign of him, I found his name in recent messages then told the phone to call him. He picked up after five rings, each one raising my blood pressure several points.

"Yo, Lokes," he said, sounding about as stressed as a picknicker on half a Xanax in Prospect Park. Was that *chewing* I heard?

"Leche! We're about to open the second floor. Where are you? Why is there no music in the Ballroom?" I was trying to keep my voice, as well as panic and frustration, down.

"Yeah, I'm in my car, just eating a burrito, but don't worry, everything is ready to go. Just tell the DJ to start his set."

I wished that I was talking into a corded handset of an old-timey telephone so I could slam it down hard enough on its cradle to rupture Leche's eardrum. I hit the red icon on my screen, instead, hoping that he felt all the anger in my index finger, and ran full out to the stage on the other side of the room while thinking, *Burrito in his fucking car? Now?* and leaped on it, nearly tripping and sliding headfirst into the DJ booth. There was a young man behind the decks wearing a cycling cap that said Brooklyn on the upturned brim. The fuck was he supposed to be? He noticed me but didn't look up, or make any attempts to hide his Tinder swiping.

"Hey, hi, are you the opening DJ?" I asked, out of breath.

"Yep," he said, still not looking up. His *yep* sounded foreign, but I couldn't recall if he was one of the Berlin superstars we stole from Berghain for the weekend.

"I'm Loki, the manager. We're going to open the floor."

Neither of these facts seemed to impress him. He swiped right on a chunky Asian girl with a septum ring and a lot of eyeliner.

"So, uh, can you start playing now?" I said, trying to sound both chill and authoritative.

"Sure," the DJ calmly responded, swiped left on a stunning blonde (sand at the beach, for him, I guess?), gave me a winsome smile, and put his phone into the back pocket of his European-cut black jeans. He hit a single button on the decks and electronic drums poured out of possibly the biggest sound system in the borough (the generator it relied on for power, humming away in the farthest corner of the parking lot, was the size of a Chinatown apartment). With the music playing I felt more at peace. I gave the DJ, now with one fancy headphone pressed between his shoulder and ear, a nod of gratitude and he returned it by bobbing his head a bit more enthusiastically to his own beat. I sat on one of the steps to the stage, my ass heavy as a full beer keg. Breathing my parasympathetic nervous system into action, I watched people pour into the Ballroom. I let my head hang and tracked my chin to one shoulder then the other, trying to stretch some of the tension out of my neck and upper back. To think that we were one Tinder match away from silence greeting the most fabulously decked out people at *the* costume dance party of the year… Unbelievable.

Just add it to the notes and keep moving, I thought. *It ain't nothin', not a thing. It's ten o'clock—if you keep letting things going awry derail you, you got a* long *night ahead.*

My phone vibrated. A text from Juicy. "Meet me. Third floor."

I sent him an "omw," pressed myself off the step with far too much arm strength required, and hustled out of there.

Juicy was by one of the VIP areas, pacing and talking on the phone. I hung out for a minute until he hung up.

"So out of all the fucking nights, the fire department chose to do a *random* inspection of Yes House *tonight*. Birdy is handling it, but Amar is on his way over there now because it's better if an owner is on the premises for this kind of thing." He paused to light a cigarette. I knew that whatever he said next would translate into more stress for me. I wasn't wrong.

"With the bottle service groups already arriving, I'm pretty much stuck here, which means you're on your own. I mean, of course you can come get me in an emergency… but it would be a lot better if you didn't." He laughed even as we both knew he wasn't kidding.

I wiped a film of sweat off my forehead. "It just keeps getting better, huh?"

"You got this!" Juicy said before putting his hand on the side of my neck and smiling, then he turned and split, leaving me in a haze of cigarette smoke, wondering if it had been there at all.

With nothing pressing or requiring my immediate attention, I decided to see what was happening on the fourth floor. The performers' green room was hair-sprayed entropy (predictable, of course—put more than two performers into one space and within minutes they would have made a colossal mess of it). I watched, fascinated, as fifty or sixty of them moved about the long space. The room was lit with drop lights and the bulbs framing the thirty or so mirrors we had lugged up four flights of stairs for them. Purses, totes, rucksacks, and garment bags were piled everywhere. Colorful pieces of costume- and street clothing were literally flying through the air, a piece of performance art, in and of itself. There was a self-serve hospitality bar with enough Red Bull, rosé, and top-shelf booze to energize and intoxicate a platoon of Russian soldiers, and everybody took frequent breaks from putting on wigs and makeup to avail themselves of its chilled libations. Apart from the free booze and liquid speed, the most dangerous thing in the room were four performers putting on stilts.

Zoe was standing in the middle of the fray with a sheet of paper in her left hand and a Juul in her right. She let out a thick cloud of fruity vapor, her eyes moving back and forth as she perused what I assumed was a call sheet, the all-important document that told every single performer where to be and when. She appeared focused and calm, and I silently commended her for how far she'd come. In the not too distant past, she would've been having a meltdown during an event half as big as this.

I thought of Zoe and Lada, a couple of eighteen-year-olds from upstate New York, standing shoulder to shoulder in a Brooklyn loft, heads full of plans and dreams of orchestrating performances that defied everything from gender roles to what it meant to be a working artist. Looking at Zoe now, coolly at the stern of an entire cast, I smiled, then left the room.

Vibration in my pocket. From a bartender: "Need you at Speakeasy now."

I couldn't tell if I was becoming a better runner or my joints and muscles were simply going numb. The Adderall certainly wasn't hurting things. I felt people stare at me as I firmly pushed through the crowd. Someone at a party moving fast, purposeful and unsmiling, is generally a sign of something gone wrong.

The first thing I noticed when I ran behind the bar was that every bulb in the chandelier was out, making the Speakeasy even darker than it was before. This might have been bad. In front of me were two hundred people lined up to get drinks. This was good, but also in front of me were five black POS screens. This was very bad; the type of *very-bad* that was costing us three hundred bucks a minute. A manager's nightmare, second only to someone dying on the dancefloor. In that moment, though, I would have much rather been performing CPR than facing a sea of thirsty people whose drugs were kicking in.

Like most people, my tech troubleshooting amounted to holding down the power button on whichever device isn't working. After doing this on two POS and getting nowhere, then once again considering the chandelier, I knew that the problem was power.

Juicy promised me an intimate knowledge of the venue, and he didn't disappoint. In an instant I ran across the room to where I knew the fuse box was and immediately found our electricity issue. A guy dressed up as a dragon or monitor lizard or whatever, with carefully painted on scales and an actual tail, had the fuse box door open and was flicking switches as if he were DJing. Suddenly furious, I grabbed his arm tighter than was strictly necessary and yanked him away from the wall.

"What in the actual *fuck,* dude?" I yelled in his face, all the stress and tiredness transmogrified into easy, objectified anger that I was able to focus on one person. He looked back at me uncomprehendingly and I saw at once that he was higher than all seventeen Apollo missions combined. With the hand that wasn't holding the unperturbed lizard man (he may have even been enjoying my firm grip on his sweaty, scaly forearm) I went down the row of black switches, flicking any that were on "0" back to "1." The chandelier went on and I looked at the bartenders, who gave me thumbs up. My fury cooled. I perp-walked my willing prisoner to a security guy at the nearest exit.

"Make sure he takes a time-out, but let him back in twenty minutes," I said to the giant at the door. "And, ask someone to duct tape that fuze box closed." To lizard man, who was finally realizing that he fucked up, I said, "Walk around the block, get some water from the bodega, whatever, then come back. If you pull that shit again, you'll be out for good and banned from Yes House for a year, okay?"

"I... I... it was just so *bright* in there." His eyes were wide and wet. "I just wanted to turn some lights off. I'm sorry." With the *sorry* he began to cry. I sighed.

"Okay," I said, as gently as possible while still being heard over the music. "It's okay. Just chill for a few and come back." I exchanged a look with the security guy and left.

The waves of anger had all but dissipated, leaving behind the still, dark waters of exhaustion. I looked at my phone. Not even midnight, but I was struggling to keep my eyes open and focused. My stomach felt like I took a shot of off-brand battery acid. The pills took care of my appetite, but provided no nutrients. I couldn't remember the last time I ate. That morning? The day before? I wasn't sure and it didn't matter. I had to keep moving. Thoughts of food were both distracting and futile.

The first floor was packed. In the baroque space the costumed guests looked like they were at a modern masquerade ball. The Grand Prospect Hall that night was as much a character as any of them; a spectacle of architecture and design. Few people were aware of this anachronistic gem hiding on an unremarkable Brooklyn block, let alone having ever partied here. Both lifelong New Yorkers and visitors explored the venue, wandering its labyrinthine hallways and stairwells in wonder.

The drugs certainly didn't make the palatial building any less fairy-tale-like. Guests wandered around in a state of perpetual awe, their pupils the size of manhole covers, letting the visual reality stream in uninterrupted. Bulging jaw muscles and eyelids squeezed shut during too-long hugs told me whose molly had kicked in. Walking into previously unexplored rooms people's heads swiveled around to take it all in, lips parting involuntarily.

I watched two girls in sexyfied white togas and elaborate headpieces that looked like birds' nests woven out of gold holding hands like children in a magical forest. They had just walked into the Oak Room and stopped. I was close enough to see the sweat shining on their bare skin, from dancing in another room and the drugs, probably. They clenched their hands tighter and pulled each other closer. Shoulder to shoulder they stood for a full ten seconds, not dancing or moving. I'm sure they had never been to a party like this. I wanted to be inside their minds just then, to experience it all with them.

When Kate Cummings began to sing just a few feet in front of them, shining, lit up like a celestial vision, the spell only deepened. They smiled dreamily… and closed their eyes. I left them there like that and kept moving, only to see the same pair fifteen minutes later in the Oak Room Lounge. "Do you think they're *real*?" one asked the other as they watched a tattoo artist in black latex gloves ink a tiny wave onto the inner wrist of a half naked minotaur.

I saw them one more time that night, taking photos and videos of each other walking up and down the grand staircase with exaggerated grace, princesses making their way to a ballroom of guests just waiting to greet them. At the top of the stairs they hugged for a selfie.

I smiled. *Amateurs*, I thought, not unkindly, then laughed at myself, a twenty-five-year-old nightlife veteran.

In the Grand Ballroom the Modern Gypsies began their dragon show. Fifteen members of the troupe, dressed in all black and all but hidden under the long, colorful body, used metal poles to make the enormous beast writhe and dance through the crowd. A thousand smartphones popped up like we were at a Harry Styles concert. There were lights inside the body of the dragon, making the mythical creature glow as it slithered and snapped its jaw playfully at people dancing. Suddenly, the dragon reared back, raised its whiskered snout to the ceiling, and blew a stream of smoke as long as a city bus. It did this several more times from various points on the dance floor. Sober or high, people lost their shit.

I melted into the crowd, and for just a moment I was one of them: mouth open in amazement, colorful flashes reflecting in my retinas. It lasted a few seconds, but in that magical time I wasn't a manager, an employee, or Juicy's henchman… I was just another dude at the party. I snapped out of it too quickly, remembering that I had to keep moving, checking up, observing, fixing. I wondered if I would ever experience Palace of Gods as a guest, and felt a deep sadness. This was what I wanted. This was why I drove to New York City, right? This, here, on this autumn night, was the wildest dream of the boy—and let's face it, then I was but a *boy*—scraping gum off a dance floor, occasionally looking up and wondering what it felt like to be a part of the inner circle. Wasn't it? And if it was the dream and I the dreamer woken to discover it's real, why did I feel like I sold my soul to the devil, only to work these parties for all eternity; to never again enjoy that very specific lightness and freedom that comes from knowing that for the next several hours, "real life" was utterly irrelevant, occluded by the music… the dancing… the drugs… the sweat… the breath…

I pushed those thoughts away, promising myself to give them the space they deserved… when I didn't have a job to do, and left the Ballroom.

On the third floor, while weaving between the people dancing, my vision blurred and suddenly the horizon of bobbing heads tilted radically. One second I was squeezing past a sweaty guy wearing antlers and a codpiece, the next I was on the floor, tangled up in my robe, my right shoulder pressed against the sticky floor. Some dude floated into my line of sight like a purple ghost and offered me a hand. His mouth moved but I didn't hear him. I lay there long enough for real concern to spread across his face. It felt so good to just give up. With resolve I didn't realize I had, I got my hands under me and pressed myself up to a cross-legged position, then got to my feet. I gave my would-be savior a nod and stumbled off, nodding my head forcefully to the beat. I was officially done, my motor sucking fumes from an empty, polluted tank. I had no idea how I was supposed to make it through the night.

On the third floor everything was going as expected, if not altogether smoothly. The bottle service tables were mingling with their neighbors, either newly united in their elitism or because of existing friendships, and people were jumping between them like kids at a sleepaway camp slumber party. By my count each VIP had brought up at least two random but very attractive normies from general admission, disregarding the established table capacity by a wide margin. This resulted in very expensive bottles emptying at a much faster rate, which I'm sure Juicy wasn't mad about. The servers couldn't possibly keep track of who was drinking whose bottles anymore, though, so they just kept bringing them out by the crate and doing their best to not under- or overcharge any one table disproportionately to the others. They also did their best to fulfill requests and answer questions.

"We need more Don Julio 1942 here."

"Can you get me some molly? I'll take blow, too, if you can get that."

"Can you walk us onto the DJ stage so we can dance?"

"We can smoke up here, right?" (At least ten people had cigarettes lit).

"Is there, like, a food menu?"

There were still a couple of them forcing smiles, but most of the servers looked ready to walk out at any minute (after inflicting bodily harm to one or more of the VIPs, perhaps). It came as no surprise that they were drinking, and not lightly, in the server area. The situation was just too stressful to handle sober.

To my surprise, there were two NYPD officers by the banister, which would have alarmed me, had I not been thoroughly depleted and incapable of strong emotions. Evidently the cops were doing a walkthrough and saw the guests were leaning too far over the banister and getting too close to the enormous projector shooting lasers toward the main stage. The guests paid no more attention to the cops than they did their servers when they told them to keep away from the railing. This was going to be a problem, I sensed, but made no move to intervene, instead choosing to observe with removed and mild interest.

Juicy appeared before me like a jack in the box, cutting through my haze with his excited commands.

"Two things!" he said. "First, one of the tables wants to close out early. They spent seven grand. Go help Sally with that, on the double. Two, I ordered fifty pizzas and they're here. Meet Cora out front and bring them up. Now, please."

Before I could ask which came first, *now* or *on the double*, Juicy turned to an attractive sweaty guy in full Centurion get-up.

"Now look," he yelled over the music. His blue eyes shone with anger. "I'm trying my best to accommodate you guys, okay? But I made a deal with Zach for a table of six. Now there are twenty people at the table and you want to bring more? No. That's it!"

I had never seen him snap at anybody like this. I backed away, not interested in seeing how the situation would play out. I was suddenly glad to be getting the pizzas instead of dealing with something like this.

I made my way downstairs, fighting against the tide of bodies rising up from the first floor. The pounding music went well with the shoulders driving into me. What should have been a one minute walk took ten. The air conditioning, even going at full blast, was no match for six thousand dancing people. The whole building was a bog of hot bodies, and I tried not to think about how much of other people's sweat I was absorbing as I maneuvered through the crowd.

I walked out a staff-only door to immediately be slapped with a "Hey! Stop!"

I whirled to face a large security guard, my manager's badge held out as far as the black lanyard would allow to aggressively show him I wasn't just some tripping hippie stumbling through a restricted area. He inspected the laminated card with my name on it for a couple of seconds before nodding me on my way. I had never seen the guy before, and he, me. The event was so big he couldn't tell a manager from a guest.

I closed my eyes and took a deep breath. *God, it's so fucking good to be outside,* I thought. The tiny moment of blissful peace would not last, though.

"Yoo-hoo, hello?" said a voice beside me.

I opened my eyes and noticed Cora several feet away, guarding more pizza boxes than I have ever seen together in one place, stacked on the hood of a blue Honda Accord flashing its hazard lights. I saw immediately that this was gonna take at least two trips.

I grabbed ten pies, which required one hand under the boxes at waist level and the other on top, over my head. Cora, shorter, took fewer. I let my cheek press against the warm cardboard. Cheesy steam kissed my skin as it wafted out of the slots in the boxes.

This is gonna be fun, I thought to myself. *Not.*

I peeked around the pizzas so I could see where I was going (and so the same security guard would see my face and not tackle me to the ground). The security guard held the door for us. As I passed him I gestured with my chin towards the Honda and remaining pies. "If somebody tries to take those," I said, "kill them."

We walked in. I knew that the sight and smell of fifteen pizzas at a party of this magnitude could be enough to incite a riot—we would have to tread cautiously. I decided to say as much to Cora.

"Hey, wait," I said. "I think we should go—"

"Pizza! They have pizza!"

The shout was louder than the music. All the people in our vicinity stopped dancing and heads began to turn towards us, slowly, like zombies who just smelled fresh brains.

I froze as glazed eyes found us. A mermaid with milky white contact lenses licked her chapped lips slowly. Then all hell broke loose.

"Pizza! Oh, my fucking sweet Jesus I will give you a hundred dollars for one of those!"

"Two hundred, I swear I will Venmo it to you right now!"

Fuck. I turned to Cora. "Run, Cora, run for your life!" I yelled behind me, then abandoned her to her fate and ran for the stairs.

Unless you know something I don't, there is no graceful way to hurry up a grand staircase with ten hot pizzas in your hands. We did our best to escape the ravenous hordes without falling and making a cheesy mess.

On the third floor we shoved our way through the crowd, using the boxes as a battering ram. After bumping into people they turned to give us the dick eye, only to immediately change their tune when they saw the pizza boxes. Several tried to help clear a path for us, hoping that we would reward them with a hot slice or two.

"Go, Cora, go!" I urged. "Don't make eye contact, just keep moving!"

Finally, we made it to the servers' station and dropped our cargo. It was no longer our problem. Juicy told us to take the remaining pies waiting outside to the production office, which was far easier because it was on the first floor, in a staff-only area. Who knew being the manager of a festival entailed being a pizza boy.

Behind the black curtains of the production office I sat down for the first time that day (if you don't count my short but sweet dance floor faint). I bit into a slice of pizza, warm on my palm, and my heart melted like fresh mozzarella. It may have been the only thing I ate that whole day, I could no longer remember. As I tasted the delightfully tart tomato sauce, chewy cheese, a hint of oregano; as the subtle crunch of the crust traveled up my jawbone and vibrated my eardrums, it was like my mouth was relearning to chew. Actual tears formed in my eyes. I'll tell you now, that pizza was absolutely mediocre, barely adequate, as far as these things go—remember, this was Brooklyn, after all, not Dearborn fucking Michigan—and *the most delicious food I had ever eaten*. I chewed slowly, not because I was trying to savor the experience but because the act of masticating each bite into a swallowable mass was arduous. I closed my eyes and felt like a drunk outside a kebab stand at three a.m., a too-large mouthful of food in his mouth, sauce dripping onto his unbuttoned shirt. It was bliss. I breathed and felt a deep slumber pulling me down like quicksand. The hard plastic chair I was sitting in felt like a top of the line Lazyboy. I finished a second slice, my shrunken stomach distending like a Somalian baby's.

Get up, Loki, I thought, fighting the velvety stupor of the fully sated. *Only a couple hours left. Must. Go. On…*

Come on, legs, it's now or never. Deep inside I somehow found the will and energy to send the appropriate messages to my lower extremities, and lifted myself into a standing position. The first step, as "they" say, was a doozy. Also the second and third, but soon I was walking, my body turning pizza into gasoline, and then, miraculously, running back to bottle service.

"Ready to close out?" I asked Sally.

"Yup," she said. "Five thousand." She woke up a portable POS with a touch of her manicured index finger and handed it to me.

I paused, my own finger with its sliver of dirty fingernail millimeters from the screen that was demanding a password, and looked at her. "Seven. That's what Juicy said."

"That was the original price," she responded, "but they ended up having fewer people. I told Juicy and he took two off." She looked at me placidly. How was she still so… so *nice*?!

I looked around for Juicy, but didn't see him anywhere. I sent a text, but after a minute of no reply, I put my phone away and turned back to Sally.

"Look," I said to her, "Juicy told me seven thousand, and that's what we have to charge them."

Her calm began to drain from her face, replaced by a deepening blush. The perpetually chipper, lighter-than-air girl I knew suddenly went away.

"Dude!" she snapped, "It's five, I'm telling you."

I shook my head, patiently, condescendingly. It didn't matter that *I* could barely think straight. Sally was tired, high, drunk, and confused, clearly. But I had to make the call, and if I blew two thousand bucks by undercharging a table, after Juicy specifically told me how much they owed, I'd end up being the second person laying in front of that Kebab cart.

By now Sally was furious, and looked it. Her eyes flashed a sharp blue and she stuck out her chin as her voice rose.

"Why don't you believe me?"

It was then that I lost it. I just couldn't keep it together anymore. Everything—the stress, the tiredness, the uppers' nasty edge—exploded out of me in the next sentence. I wheeled on her and raised my voice.

"Look, you're wrong, okay? It's just a fact!" The dog was off the chain and sprinting towards traffic. "*I'm* the fucking boss. We're running seven and that's final, got it!?"

There were no longer just roses blooming on the tall blonde's cheekbones: her face turned red as a field of blooming poppies.

"*You*," Sally hissed, "are not the fucking boss of *me*, you understand that? And if you think you can talk to me like that, boy, are you in for a fucking shock." She stormed off, her golden heels flashing, and out of my sight in several strides of her long legs.

As I stood there, POS in hand, my phone vibrated. Inside Juicy's blue speech bubble: "Sorry. Yes, it's five thousand."

"Fuck," I said, to an audience of just me, as shame and remorse eclipsed the anger of a minute ago. Not only did I lose my cool, but I snapped at Sally, of all people—a model employee *and* Oliver's girlfriend—and I was completely in the wrong, to boot. I was sure to get a talking to after the dust settled, if not sooner. I tried to find her so I could apologize, but after a few minutes of looking I had to give up and go back to work.

The final hours of the party flew by "uneventfully." There were no fires, broken bones, or foamy-mouthed overdoses. The EMTs, largely idle all night, were downright bored. Though I did see a very large, very sweaty, barely dressed man hugging Sammy Saves, pressing the helpless medic's face into his furry glistening cleavage.

Finally, the last of the guests piled onto the sidewalk; a merry mob cackling in a way only possible at six in the morning on a pre-dawn Brooklyn morning, when you're with your crew.

"Have a good night!" I yelled after them, expending the last drop of cheer in my soul, and closed the door. I breathed a sigh of relief. It was done. The first night was in the bag. Almost. All that was left was for me to collect the cash and toss it into a heavy duty black garbage bag.

We did it, and I knew I should feel a sense of accomplishment, but it never came. I felt ground down to a nub, my body at once utterly drained and humming in an attempt to reestablish homeostasis. Sixty em-gees of Adderall were still coursing through me and it felt like my skull was no longer an exact fit for my brain. I was feeling emotional, erratic in the peaks and valleys that traded off with increasing frequency.

At seven a.m. Xavier, Juicy, and I were the only people left in the enormous venue. I wish I could tell you that we sat in a cozy corner somewhere, smoking cigarettes and trading stories from the night, laughing like schoolboys, but that's not how it ended. We were absolutely depleted. Saturday dawned gray, to match our collective moroseness. Xavier, silent, gloomy, drove the three of us back to Bushwick. On the Brooklyn-Queens Expressway over DUMBO I stared at the scuffed metal guardrail flying past my window and wondered how he kept the car from veering into it. Juicy sat in the front, palms flat on his legs, eyes closing for seconds at a time. "I'm so *hungry*," he kept saying. "I think I just need a *banana*, man. Xavier, are you hungry? Oh man. *Banana...*"

His brother didn't acknowledge him, just stared through the windshield. I was sprawled out on the back seat like the last noodle in a colander, two duffle bags of cash to keep me company.

We arrived at mine as the sun was rising over the neighboring buildings. I shed clothing and shoes piece by piece on the way to my bed. Overcome with mental, physical, and emotional exhaustion I closed my eyes and felt them swell with tears, before a dreamless sleep overtook me.

~~~

I woke up at noon. Not bad, a solid five hours of rest. A hot shower brought me most of the way back to fully functioning human. I forced myself to eat a banana from the dappled bunch hanging from the hook on the kitchen counter, got dressed, and walked to the L train. It was time for Round Two.

Mayhem before doors—again. A DJ scrolling on his phone in a silent room—again. Then we ran out of water and had to switch to sparkling—again.

I was stressed and exhausted. Again.

The night was a blur and I have little recollection of the party. It's almost like the mind needs to make it that way to protect itself and the nervous system from serious dysregulation. Noise, lasers, smoke, flesh and fabric; leather and lights. Behind it all, a beat, shaking everything and body. I tried to dance with Zoe and some other staff in the Mayan Warrior room. They were celebrating, exuberant in their collective achievement, and pulled me in. I so badly wanted to share in their high spirits, but just couldn't get into it. I looked around from under a heavy brow, almost resentful; a curmudgeon begrudging their joy.

I was grateful when the music stopped at six, starting a countdown in my mind: soon I would be free.

It was up to me to collect all the cash, cut bartenders, and put away the expensive POS and wifi devices. I went from bar to bar, sending people home and throwing the cash into a gym bag.

Some guests were shuffling out, while others still swayed and stepped to the music. *Just break down and get out of here,* I told myself, as I emptied literal buckets of cash tips into a separate duffle. I wobbled through the dancing zombies, clenching the handles of the bags. At that point I didn't know how many tens of thousands of dollars I was carrying, but the weight was getting heavier by the second. My legs ached and my shoulders felt like the bones would just rip from their sockets. Every step was a battle won against gravity; a victory of resolve and stamina.

In our temporary office I dropped the cash in a safe, glad to be free of the literal and figurative burden. It was time to get the POS and mini router rentals. My last task of the night, but it had to be done perfectly. I would use the last of my strength to not fuck this up. Juicy and I planned this for weeks; I had to make sure they all wound up in the right box, in the correct place, with all the hardware and wiring so they could be returned without us receiving a massive fine.

After about forty minutes I was in a good rhythm and nearly halfway done. Walking into the Oak Room Lounge, though, I saw Juicy and a production assistant at the bar, haphazardly yanking plugs from surge protectors and ripping gaffer's tape off the POS cables. The mounted tablets they were putting in random boxes, in no particular order.

At the sight of Juicy with a fistful of wires and power adapters speed walking away from the bar, the last thread keeping my emotions contained finally snapped. My brain just couldn't reconcile this with the hours of painstaking planning.

"Hey, Juicy!" I yelled as I followed him, wanting to run to catch up but managing a shambling slow jog. "Wait!"

He stopped in the middle of the now brightly lit ballroom and faced me.

"What are you doing?" I demanded, not caring that I was yelling at my boss. "I thought we had a plan. What the fuck?"

My blood was boiling. A part of me knew I was being irrational, but that part was no longer running the show. Even as I tried to calm down, I heard words flying out of my mouth, petulant, indignant, *furious*.

"Dude, first you tell me to charge a client the wrong amount—which, by the way, I got into a fight with Sally over—then you have me running around like a damn pizza delivery boy…" I was no longer in control of my mouth; the leash was totally off. "And now, after weeks of planning, you're messing up my final task? After all I've don—"

To his credit, it took Juicy that long to interject, but he finally drew a line. Quietly, coldly, he said, "Go home."

I stood there, breathing quickly, ready to yell.

"Loki," Juicy said, more gently, "You did great. Really, you were amazing all night, but right now I don't need this. Go home. Let's not end this on a sour note. You understand me?"

I was frozen to the spot, looking into Juicy's unblinking blue eyes. Suddenly my anger drained out of me, to be immediately replaced with a soul twisting melancholy. I knew I was being overly dramatic, but my heart was breaking right in the middle of that empty room, and there was nothing I could do to keep it together. It had been my dream to manage Palace of Gods, and for the last two years I worked tirelessly, pouring every fiber of my soul and body into Yes House.

My dream had come true, but now I was no longer needed, dismissed like a waiter after the check has been paid.

Juicy turned to the production assistant waiting a respectful distance away from us. "Let's hit the Oak Room next," he said, and the two walked away.

I had no words, or anyone to share them with, so I just dragged myself to the production office, chin drooping. There was a carload of people heading back to Bushwick and I hopped in with them. The rest of our crew was already at the staff after-party in a Williamsburg spa Juicy rented. I wished that I was in the mood to join them and celebrate what was by all indications a resounding success. Instead I went home and crawled into bed, too tired to cry myself to sleep.

CHAPTER NINETEEN

I woke up in a haze, my body feeling like an unoiled Tin Man. I fumbled for my phone and eventually tilted it towards my face. Ten a.m. I slept for three hours. Fuck me. I rubbed my face and rolled off the mattress and onto the parquet floor of my tiny room. Standing up to my full height was a process, but I got there eventually. I shambled to the kitchen. The intoxicating aroma of bacon hit my nostrils like I was a Looney Toons character. I filled a glass with water from the kitchen tap and chugged it in one go, then filled it again. I stood there, barefoot and disheveled, and watched Strom as he expertly flipped an omelet. Half a dozen glistening bacon strips rested on a paper towel topped plate.

"Got a little sleep, huh?" Strom asked. He was wearing a hunter green bathrobe. As always, he looked like he should have a Roman numeral after his name.

"Just three hours. I'm going back to bed. Palace of Gods fucked me up." I took another draft of water, relishing the unique New York City flavor: chlorine, rust, with a dash of expired pharmaceuticals. Strom chortled.

"Three? Try thirty—you've been hibernating since Sunday morning." He threw a pinch of salt onto the eggs, then followed it with a pinch of red chili flakes.

It took a few seconds for me to understand him.

"What are you talking about?" I asked.

"Dude," he laughed again, "it's Monday."

I put the half-filled glass in the deep stainless steel sink and ran back to my room. A closer look at my phone confirmed everything Strom said. I slept through all of Sunday and the night that followed. Not three hours, but twenty-seven.

~~~

Thirty minutes later I was up in the office at Yes House, my hair wet from the shower. While I didn't feel anywhere near great, I at least smelled clean. It took one glance at my email inbox to remember that Palace of Gods was merely the starter pistol at the beginning of the busy season. All of my unread emails were about December private events, Christmas shows, and New Year's Eve festivities. Staring into the glare of the computer screen, nausea crept up from my abdomen. I hadn't been in the building for five minutes, but already I needed a cigarette. I logged out, put on my jacket, and went outside.

Standing on the sidewalk with my back against the vestibule, I put a cig between my lips, lit it, and inhaled. As the last of the smoke snaked from my nostrils, I saw Juicy rounding the corner in black pants and a stylish motorcycle jacket, a small white coffee cup in hand.

Fuck, I thought, as my guts did a barrel roll, *Time to take my knocks.* He must have found out about the Sally incident. And who could forget that little scene in the ballroom…

I stared at the ground like a guilty mutt and pulled on the cigarette. As I exhaled I heard his footsteps. When I couldn't hide any longer I looked up.

"My dude!" Juicy said as he walked up to me. Smiling, he squeezed my left shoulder. Leaving his hand where it was he looked me in the eye.

"How you feeling? Back at it, already? Man, you don't even rest," Juicy added.

I was thoroughly confused. This was not the dressing down I expected. Also, he must have guessed that I just woke up.

"Uh, yeah, well, neither do you," I replied, just to make conversation.

A breeze picked up, making the cloudy day a degree or two colder. A white plastic bag drifted out of the open dumpster in front of the club. Juicy and I zipped up our jackets.

Juicy was animated and alert, with his shoulders open and gaze clear—my complete opposite. The edges of my vision blurred and swam into focus (probably due to my mini coma), I could barely keep my eyes open, and after standing on the street for just a couple of minutes my legs hurt. I was still exhausted, somehow, with a layer of spaciness superimposed on my tiredness. It is entirely possible that this interaction wasn't even happening.

"You're a fucking legend—and that's what I love about ya!" Juicy continued. "I'm actually glad you're here. I wanted to talk about something with you."

Here it comes. I took a preparatory breath he didn't even notice.

"I got lots of stuff coming down the pike, some you've heard about," he said. His eyes flicked to my cigarette and he gave his hip pockets a quick pat. I took out my pack of Camels, opened it, and flicked my wrist. I held the blue and white packet out to him, one cigarette jutting out ahead of its mates. Juicy put it between his lips and I cupped my hand around the lighter as I flicked it, and he leaned in to light up. He thanked me, smokily.

"I'm moving the falafel shop down the block," he continued. "'It will be a proper restaurant—the grand opening is in a couple of weeks!"

I smiled. I loved watching Juicy get excited about new projects and visions come to fruition. It was contagious. Even in my depleted state I felt a spark of his energy as my own.

"Yes House is expanding, too," he said. "We're in talks with a bougie hotel down in Mexico, maybe opening another YES here in the city... Shit, we might even partner with a cruise line!" He laughed, his eyes glimmering. "Can you imagine some Middle America shlubs in sandals and socks crunching on snow crab legs as our aerialists swing overhead in thongs?! Ha! They're gonna lose their fucking shit." He was thoroughly entertained by the thought.

I couldn't help but smile more at the image, myself. The sun peeked out from behind a wispy strip of cumulus cloud, and we instinctively turned our faces up to it and smoked in silence for a few seconds. I was beginning to allow for the possibility of this not being the chewing-out I expected. My neck, shoulders, and the muscles between my scapulae were softening. Either my transgressions at Palace of Gods were not as grave as I imagined, or Juicy had simply chosen to let them slide. Still, what he said next made me cough hot cigarette smoke until my eyes teared.

"The point is, I'm gonna be pretty busy and will need some extra help around here. That's why I want you to manage Yes House; you'd be the first-ever GM."

After I recovered and my breath returned to normal I was finally able to talk, however hoarsely.

"GM?" I blurted, "I thought I was about to get a serious talking-to—or worse!"

This only added to Juicy's bonhomie. "A 'talking-to'?" he chuckled. "For what, the other night? I mean, okay, that wasn't great…" He got serious. "The truth is, though, I know what it takes to work that event, how much it takes out of you. Towards the end there you were kinda at the end of your rope. I get it. You and me, we're good."

All the sadness and worries of the previous night receded, allowing the sweet light of relief to shine inside my chest. It felt like somebody took off of me a heavy pack, like one of those giant trekking rucksacks with the muddy boots hanging off the back. I furtively pinched the tender skin in the webbing of my left thumb to make sure this was real.

"I… I don't know what to say," I said, just to fill the silence, as thoughts bounced inside my skull like a pinball. "First of all, thank you." I felt warmth on my cheeks even though the sun had retreated behind another cloud.

"General Manager," I said, tasting the words like an exotic dish. "What does that even entail?"

"Some of the stuff, you already do," said Juicy. "Like making the staff schedule and managing some night events and parties. In that way you're pretty much halfway there. In addition you'd be taking over some of my duties."

"Say more."

"Well, first off, you'd be the one dealing with city and state shit. The fire department wants to schedule an inspection of the sprinkler system? You'd be the one opening the letter and setting it up. The State Liquor Authority needs ten grand to renew our license, you write the check and make sure they get it and I don't get shut down. You know what I'm saying?"

"Yeah, I get it," I told him. And I did. There were any number of things to take care of, details large and small, without which the club would grind to a halt.

"You'd also take on more of the business development side of things. You see an email from some hotshot who wants to throw himself a birthday party or a TV production that wants to shoot a scene in the Theater—you start that conversation, provide quotes, etc."

"Okay," I said.

"But most important," Juicy said and paused meaningfully. "When something goes wrong, it's your phone that would ring first, not mine."

I tried to imagine the details of this new life, down to the phone ringing in the middle of the night with god knows what disaster waiting for me on the other end. My workload already felt enormous some days. Could I take all of this on, from the tedious extra hours on the computer to putting out fires (literal ones, quite possibly)?

I nodded, more in understanding than commitment. "Right," I said slowly. "Okay, cool, and I am assuming…"

"More money," Juicy said. "Of course."

"Go on," I smiled.

"Well, let's see. You get thirteen hundred a week now and you manage three to four nights. As GM you'd be on the floor less, two or three nights a week, let's say, but have all those extra things to take care of." Juicy turned his head to look down the block, as if he was doing mental math, but I knew that he had an exact number in mind before he even laid eyes on me that day. He turned back to me.

"I'd be willing to go as high as fifteen hundred," he said, then, having made his offer, looked at me in silence.

An extra thirty bucks a day. Not even. To be the first line of defense against any number of shits hitting all types of fans, among other things. On the other hand, money had little to do with what was essentially a dream come true, an opportunity for which I would have killed for a year ago.

A gust of cool wind flipped several wavy strands of hair across my face. I didn't bother to move them as Juicy and I continued looking at each other.

This was what I was hoping for, wasn't it? So much more than that, even! I had never even conceived of a universe in which *I would be second-in-command under Juicy!*

So why was there a voice inside my screaming, "Say 'no'! Don't do it!"

Juicy smoked without using his hands as he took out his phone and squinted through messages and emails. Apparently there was nothing too urgent and he put the phone back in his pocket, took the Camel from his mouth and flicked ash into the wind. His eyes found mine, the question floating between us amid the cigarette smoke. I'm sure that after two years of my jumping at every opportunity he gave me, my hesitation now was surprising to him.

"I, uh," I broke the silence. The "YES!" was on the tip of my tongue but something kept me from spitting it out. "I'll get back to you by Friday," I finally said.

Juicy pulled on the cigarette and the ember flared and rushed towards the filter. He flicked the butt towards the street behind him without looking.

"Okay," he nodded. "Let me know soon." He went into the club, leaving me to stand there feeling cold and empty, inside and out.

~~~

I wake up on Friday, shirtless but still wearing my pants from the night before. I could sleep another three hours, easy. I still haven't recovered from Palace of Gods and worked the last three shifts in a row. I check the time and see that I have thirty minutes before I have to go to work. I roll out of bed and give myself the pat-down usually done before undressing, usually before going to bed. In my pockets I find: four drink tickets, seven rubber bands in varying degrees of griminess, seventeen dollars, three empty baggies with a pinkish residue, a crumpled credit card receipt, and glitter.

I've yet to give Juicy an answer. I haven't even had time to think on it, to say nothing of quietly sitting long enough to allow guidance to rise from the settled sand of my psyche. And I'm working again tonight. Love House. Not exactly an event conducive to quiet reflection.

But you already know how the night went. The belligerent fence shaker, the behemoth in a k-hole, Daisy's champagne shower. Fast forward to a brightly lit Theater, and me, finishing up closing duties.

Apart from Licky hard at work in the dishwashing station (and Tristan passed out in the costume container), Juicy and I are the only people left in the whole building. He's leaning on the bar, iPhone in hand, cigarette between his lips. He exhales and the glowing screen illuminates the cloud of smoke.

"You're still here," I say as I walk across the room, not wanting to startle him. The bright lights cut my eyes but don't seem to bother him. After a few seconds, Juicy thumbs the display to sleep and looks up at me, a tired smile on his face.

"You ready to run this place, or what?" he asks, as I put my elbows on the bar beside him.

I take a breath, nodding slowly. "Let's talk," I say.

As we stand there, leaning on the bar nearly shoulder to shoulder, the last three years flash through my mind in a collage of light and darkness. Bright and beautiful, at first, here I am meeting Xavier in San Francisco, then Juicy and the rest of the crew at Burning Man. Here's me driving across the country with a head full of hopes and dreams and a heart full of joy. Amar, coaching me on how to properly insert a urinal cake; and the not-entirely-jocular abuse from the Spanish guys. Begging for and getting the bookkeeper job; getting a saltshaker fastened to my cock. Dancing. So much dancing. Ecstasy; sweating and smiling so wide I nearly broke my cheek muscles. I smile now at these images.

The joy in my heart and on my face doesn't last, though. As I revisit shiny memories, the clouds roll in to obscure the light. The look on Sparky's face right after he was fired; Fox fighting back tears; Dan Rockies the day before he left. The endless nights of stress and exhaustion. The fights with Clea. Snapping at Sally. Juicy sending me home after I lost it in the ballroom…

Am I ready to run the place?

I might be ready to run, full stop.

As I struggle to give Juicy an answer, as my mind swings back and forth like an out of balance pendulum, I think of something I heard earlier in the night.

"Are you really gonna open a spot in Williamsburg just to make a pile of money?" I ask. I immediately realize that what was meant to be a question now hangs between us like an accusation.

Juicy stops smiling. "Who told you that?"

His eyes narrow and he blinks a couple of times. I hit a nerve.

"I just heard—" I begin to say, but he quickly cuts me off.

"It's a viable option—" It's my turn to interrupt.

"I thought Yes House was all about community, freedom of expression, art," I say, hearing the condemnation in my voice.

"And what about the money, Loki? Or do you think that art is free? That I can keep the lights on and the rent paid with radical self expression and drunken dancing?" His voice takes on the uniquely sharp edge of defensiveness and condescension.

"It just seems like this Williamsburg thing is out of character," I say quietly.

"Let me explain something to you," he says. "I am a businessman, one. Two, I have three brothers, an aging mother, and—oh yeah!—a *community* of people who depend on me." He pauses to let that sink in as he glares at me. This is the angriest I have ever seen him. "And three, you think I don't know what's best for my fucking club?"

In the lit up empty theater I suddenly feel like a kid made to stay after class. The room feels warmer, even though I personally shut off the thermostat an hour ago. I feel Juicy's anger charging the air molecules between us.

The message is loud and clear: Drop this and back off, you're out of your league.

But now that I am expressing what has been on my mind, I can't stop. And I don't want to.

"Think about what Yes House is, man!" I raise my voice. I realize that for the second time in as many days I am challenging my boss, and still I continue. "A club in Williamsburg? Come the fuck on—that is a sellout move!"

At the word *sellout*, Juicy's mouth tightens into a tense sliver. He looks older, harder, meaner. He shakes his head and takes a deep breath. He's this close to his edge and I am the one that took him there. Mouth barely open, in hardly louder than a whisper, he says, "I have dedicated every goddamn minute of every day of the last five years to building this place up, literally and figuratively; to creating a space then filling it with the right people—I think the word you used before was 'community'?—then taking care of those people... *Me*. Now, after managing a handful of events *you* want to talk about 'sellout moves'?" He stares at me. We both know he's not expecting an answer, yet he has it, nonetheless.

I can't look away from his bloodshot blue eyes as he says evenly, "Well, then, fuck you."

Boom.

I don't even remember the last time anyone said that to me, let alone anyone at Yes House. An *owner*, of all people, and someone I considered a best friend.

I feel faint, yet enraged. I can't bring myself to move. I don't know how long we stay like that, anger and hurt linking our gazes together. With every second the silence pushes us further apart.

"Fine," I respond, shaking my head. I don't want Juicy to know how much he hurt me, so I look at the floor as I try to will away the tears forming on my lower eyelids. I might as well try to keep a cut from bleeding. After the first two drops hit the dancefloor between us, I look up and once again make eye contact with my friend and mentor of the last two years.

"I resign," I say, voice steadier than I expected.

Juicy slowly nods his head, his lips pressed together. He looks older than his thirty-eight years just then, and I clearly see the price he has paid for the life I so envy. *Envied*. Without another word he turns away and walks to the exit behind the performers' changing room. I hear the push bar and the slamming of the door. I stand alone in the echoing silence under the bright lights, motionless as the tears slowly roll down my cheeks.

Ten minutes later I'm walking up Yefferson Street. Head down, utterly defeated, I am aware that the sun is rising to my left, somewhere over Ridgewood. Birdsong begins to fill the air all around me, a constant but unsynchronized chorus that lightens my step; the simple melodies lifting my soul. By the time I startle the family of rats cavorting on the sidewalk in front of my house and walk through the door, I feel okay.

CHAPTER TWENTY

When I wake up after eleven hours of dreamless sleep, everything is different. It feels like while I was unconscious my very life was rewoven from a different fabric, using lighter colored thread. I shower and dress with a smile on my face. I even put on tunes and bring my Bluetooth speaker to the bathroom—when was the last time I did that?

Feeling energized and carefree as a kid on the first day of summer vacation, I nearly skip down the littered street to Wycliff Star for my morning coffee (at six p.m.)

As I wait for the pouty cutie to make my cappuccino I let my eyes run over all the Twin Peaks shit on the walls. When was the last time I just waited patiently for something as I let my mind and eyes wander, free of thoughts and stress?

I had no clue how unhappy I was, or where that misery was coming from; how I was using Yes House as both the anchor in my life and the chains of self-imprisonment, all the while sinking deeper. Standing there in that gloomy little coffee shop I realized that I was addicted to YES, to the same stress that was so detrimental to my mental and emotional stability.

But the cycle was broken, and now… I'm free.

After sitting at the single black table on the sidewalk and enjoying my coffee, I meet Juicy to hash out the details of my resignation. He's surprised that I harbor no hard feelings, and the tension from just twelve hours before has gone from me. In fact, I am joyous and smiling, happier to see him than ever. And why wouldn't I be? Once again, he's a good friend. Just a friend. Or at least he will be after my last shift at the end of December. I can't say he shares my enthusiasm, but what can you do?

~~~

Word at the club travels fast. By the time my next shift rolls around, everyone knows my days are numbered. Half of the staff are shocked, while the other half aren't surprised in the slightest.

"Leaving us, huh?" Amar says when I walk into the Front Room. He's sitting in front of the bar, scrolling through smoke machines on Amazon. I am not sure if his smoking makes it ironic or simply a fun coincidence that I enjoy very much in that moment.

"Well, I saw that coming," he says without looking away from the screen of his MacBook Air.

Ouch. I try to not take it personally. Nobody understands nightlife better than him. How it eats through people, leaving behind a trail of disillusioned burnouts. Still, that hurts. I thought we were close. Then again, Amar was close to Dan Rockies, too.

The next six weeks fly by. Between my regular work shifts, training the new manager—Yessica, if you can believe that—and the occasional silks workout, I spend most of my time at Yes House. I don't mind, though. Like it, even. Now that I know there's an expiration date on this part of my life, I appreciate it much more.

Before I know it, I'm on the way to YES for my final shift. It feels surreal and somehow momentous, the ten-minute walk down Yefferson Street from my house, no different from hundreds except that it's the last one. I feel a bit sad, but as I put my hand on the cold metal of the front door I'm looking forward to the night, going through the managerial motions one last time, and, of course, any farewell surprises in store for me.

I go through the last couple of items on the pre-opening checklist: flick the switch that sets the disco balls in the Front Room spinning, grab a walkie and earpiece, and put cash in the registers. Walking around the club in black jeans and a black blazer, I keep expecting people to run up to me and take me in their arms, and with tears in their eyes say, "Loki, no, don't do this to us. Pleaaaase! I'm going to miss you so much. I love you!"

An hour before doors, this has happened a total of zero times. Weird.

In the Theater I see Lada sitting on the catwalk jutting from the stage surrounded by a mess of green and red fabric. She's using a black pair of scissors with steel blades as long as my forearm to make last-minute costume modifications. There is a hot glue gun a couple of feet away from her, plugged into an orange extension cord snaking its way across the wooden dance floor. I smile at the familiar sight.

"Hey Lada," I say after walking up to her, unnoticed. "Final alterations for the X-Mas Spectacle?" I ask, unnecessarily.

"Mmhmm," she replies without looking up. She lops off a small green triangle of fabric from what looks like a skirt that didn't have much to lose to start with. The X-Mas Spectacle has been the biggest and best theater production pretty much since the club opened. Critically touted—it even got a write up in the New York Times—it runs for seven magical nights starting mid-December, and as usual, is completely sold out.

Lada lays the scissors down and holds the skirt in front of her, inspecting it at arm's length. "Can you pass me that glue gun?" she says. She still hasn't looked at me, and the last of my hope for her acknowledgement of why this night is important to me fades away.

No longer smiling, I pick up the warm glue gun and place it next to her leg on the platform.

"Thanks," she mutters. She puts the skirt in her lap and hunches over it, back rounded, nose inches from the fabric, and applies a dollop of glue. Feeling sad, I watch her carefully put a sparkly snowflake on the green material, then I walk away. I'm sure she will have no recollection of our brief exchange. I shake it off and move on.

The next time I am in the Theater, Lada is gone. The production crew is sweeping the floor, setting up ruler-straight rows of black folding chairs, and rigging various props and aerial apparatuses that will descend from the ceiling during the show. The guys in the tech booth are running through all the sound and lighting cues. Performers in diverse states of undress are running around like they just vacated a clown car.

All that is to say: nobody even gives me a second glance.

That's alright, I console myself. *They're all saving it for after the show.*

At six I pop out. More than an hour after sunset, outside it's full dark. Brisk, too; can't be more than a few degrees above freezing. A line of about fifty people is waiting along the colorful wall of the club. Some are wearing heavy winter coats, some miniskirts that bare legs so cold they look like poultry stuffed into high heels, and others have on a combination of the two. I know from experience that these extreme optimists are hoping to get tickets to the show. It's my job to give them a realistic amount of hope.

I walk up to Crius, who looks extra sharp in his black suit, black single breasted wool coat, and red tie. I know we're a striking pair standing next to the vestibule in the glow of the giant lit up YES and arrow on the wall above us. I look at the line of people and the plumes of their exhales in the chilly evening and make sure Crius knows the drill: tell them the show is sold out, but invite them to grab a drink in the Front Room while they wait to see if there are any no-shows. Between you and me, the likelihood of this was incredibly small, but don't tell the people now streaming inside, cold, full of hope, and thirsty.

Less than thirty minutes pass before 250 people flood the entrance. 150 of them are ticket holders, and the rest are without tickets: 35 Yes House regulars, 15 old staff members, and 50 randoms.

We will have no seats or legal capacity for anyone after the 150 ticket holders. I'm just supposed to say, "no" to everyone else.

This is going to suck, I think.

Since the Theater is still closed to the guests, the Front Room is packed like a sardine cocktail party and about a hundred people are out shivering in the Patio.

Before the Theater doors open, I announce in both the Front Room and Patio that, "sorry, but if you don't have a ticket then you will not be admitted!"

The fifty randoms instantly leave, disappointed. *Thank God,* I think.

Some forty-five minutes later I am standing next to the usher when he opens the Theater doors. The stampede of well-dressed people with their YES-stamped wrists held high nearly flattens us both, and within a few minutes the ticket holders occupy every seat and booth.

After the literal dust (and feathers) has settled, I look out at a still-full Front Room. I generally have no compunction about turning people away—a full house is a full house, after all, and I legally can't let more than one hundred and fifty people in—but some of the expectant faces I see belong to ex-staff, friends, and customers who come so regularly I know the name of their pets. This is a part of the job that sucks, and I sure won't miss it.

As I take a breath and get ready to ruin their night, I see in front of me Daisy, smiling ear to ear; Lesh (Arc's girlfriend), pink nipples poking/showing through her skin-tight white top, a white leather dog collar around her throat; and, connected neck to neck with Lesh by a silver chain is another stunner in an identical outfit. Behind them is the guy who played Jesus in last year's Xmas Spectacle. Great: one of my favorite colleagues, a girl who has used my cock as a coke mirror, and the figurative son of god.

Sighing, I mutter "ah, fuck it," then say, "You guys, the first ten in line, follow me. The rest of you, hang tight, we're gonna squeeze everybody in."

They're overjoyed and I feel like a hero. I lead the first ten along the back of the full Theater, past the rearmost VIP booth and the bar, and cram them into the space in front of the black curtains that obscure the kitchen hallway. I come back and grab another ten and stuff them in another corner of the Theater, pretty much plastered against the black emergency doors. The remaining thirty I Tetris all over the place, even sending a few handfuls up the steel ladder to hang out in the tech booth, where the sound and lighting guys look at me like I've lost the small remainder of my steadily declining marbles. The production staff all over the theater, having less room to maneuver, give me the dick eye, also. I pretend not to notice and take my place next to Lesh as the Theater lights go down.

The Yes House X-Spectacle in a nutshell. Pluto, the bookish nephew of the renegade, Karl Karlson, is hosting a Christmas dinner for the whole family. In no time at all, the dysfunctional relatives are at each other's throats and the scene descends into mayhem. Everyone storms out, leaving only a heartbroken Pluto and his uncle, Karl, who attempts to raise his nephew's spirits with the gift of a time machine. In short order, he talks the timid boy into going for a little interdimensional spin, during which the two: flee from an underground strip club in 1970s New York City, crooked cops hot on their heels; watch the Virgin Mary give birth to both Jesus *and* a disco ball; and stage a coup d'état in Santa's workshop, freeing all the enslaved elves but nearly getting captured by the tyrannical ho-ho-hoer after snorting some of "Santa's snow," which they thought would help them run faster but actually plunged them into an icy K-hole.

All pretty basic plot devices, admittedly, but things get outlandish in the second act, when lizard people show up and attempt to steal the time machine to further their goal of world domination. The show reaches its climax when Pluto, Karl, a gaggle of 1970s strippers, and several newly-emancipated elves battle the lizard people, and win.

With order restored across the multiverses, Karl and Pluto travel back to their timeline. Home again, they destroy the time machine, having learned that the greatest present we can give ourselves and others, is *presence*, exactly where we are. The end.

When the curtain reopens, the cast comes out on stage and cavorts to Mariah Carey's "All I Want for Christmas is You" and a standing ovation from the audience. They take a collective bow. As I stand and clap, my face warm and tingly from smiling, I experience a rush of sensations and emotions. This is really happening: it's my last shift with these beautiful weirdos.

As the performers celebrate a successful show and embrace each other, the production crew gently ushers the audience out of the theater. I should start moving, too, checking to make sure the rest of the club is ready for the flip, but I just stand there, taking it all in.

I hear my name and turn to see three performers—Evil Santa, Liberated Elf Number Two, and Pluto—walking purposefully my way and smiling. *Here we go!* I think as a pleasant warmth spreads through my belly and my heart beats irregularly.

"Hey, what's up?" I say, playing it cool.

"You got some drink tickets for us?" Pluto asks.

"Uh, yeah, sure, here." I smile lightly as I take out a small stack of drink tickets and peel off a few for each of them. Behind the smile, I want to cry with disappointment. The threesome runs to the Front Room. They didn't want a tearful hug, just free booze.

This interaction is repeated throughout the night: I hear my name shouted excitedly only to spin around and have my hopes dashed by increasingly more inebriated performers, friends, and VIPs looking for drink tickets. Of course this is an integral part of managing, but tonight (for me, at least) is different.

As all around me people are having fun and getting looser, my mood darkens.

I let my mind take me to a place of isolation and self-pity. *I gave these people, this place, my heart and soul for what feels like a decade, and now all I'm good for is a free drink or two. Nobody's shown me love in weeks. And tonight, of all nights?*

I feel so foolish for believing I meant something to them; for letting them mean everything *to me.*

The theme of tonight's party ("House of No") is darkness, and it matches my mental and emotional landscape to a tee. Dark like a Berlin techno basement on a February night, tonight there are no colorful lights and trippy video-mapping in the Theater nor performers in neon leotards.

I escape to the Patio, feeling pushed, ejected, by the unfriendly bass thump. The cold breeze instantly finds its way up my sleeves, chilling my bare arms and throat. It's refreshing and helps clear my thoughts. There's a handful of people outside, and as I relish this moment of quiet and clarity, one of them walks up to me and starts complaining. I compose my face into a neutral expression and listen, all the while mentally repeating the mantra, *This is your last shift.* The critic, a young person of unclear gender identity (someone I recognize as being contentedly cis-hetero six months ago) goes through a list of grievances that prove Yes House doesn't care about our community. Around the time they wrap up about the unsatisfactory number of bathrooms and move on to the outrageously expensive drinks, my earpiece comes to life with Crius's voice, effectively saving me from the suicide I am about to commit.

"Loki, come in. Repeat: Loki to the front."

Equally excited by the *Goodbye, Loki* moment as I am to extricate myself from this conversation, I hold down the microphone button and respond, maybe a bit too happily, "Copy. Coming to you." I give the complainer a look of deep regret. "I hope I can hear the rest of your ideas in a bit, but for now," I point an index finger to my earpiece, all too aware of the pistol-to-temple pantomime, "gotta run!" and with that I blast through the gold doors.

In the Front Room Fidel is by the cash register. "Harlequin had to run to the bathroom," the big man says, his eyes as easy as always. "Can you cover the register so we can keep getting people in?"

"Sure," I say and plop onto Harlequin's padded stool, shoulders drooping, just as the crowd in the Theater explodes in cheers and whistles. Must be the Midnight Moment. *When's the* Loki *Moment?* I think as I take forty bucks from a starved-model type and stamp the inside of her pale wrist with a black YES.

I watch from the tech booth as the one a.m. moment comes and goes. Two o'clock, the final performance, brings Lada and Meloza in black sparkly leotards swooping through the air on a lyra, hands locked onto the other's wrist… but no hugs or champagne for me.

I storm out of the Theater like a preteen who's been sent to bed without supper, shouldering people out of my way with unprofessional force, stomp across the Patio, punch in the lock code and burst into the costume closet, slamming the door behind me. Half relieved, half disappointed to find the shipping container empty of people, I sit heavily on the beat up carpet and let my back fall against a clear plastic bin full of feather boas, tiaras, and Venetian-style eye masks. I cross my arms over my knees and let my forehead fall onto them. No longer wanting or able to hold it in, I release a shuddering exhale wrapped around an anguished sigh which preludes the flow of hot tears that fall onto the crotch of my black pants. The drops shine darker than the fabric for a few seconds, then blend in.

Alone in a shipping container converted into a costume closet, I cry and accept my seemingly crumbling world. What I thought was my family was nothing but a business; and for me, business hours were over. Like Dan Rockies before me, I was now on the other side of it: drained, wrung out, snapping at coworkers, discarded like a towel at a bathhouse. Juicy told me to go fuck myself, and now that I'm leaving, nobody gives a shit.

The truth is, nothing could have made a *company* love me back—not the unpaid hours, backbreaking labor, or pushing my mind and body beyond limits I didn't even know I had. When I met Amar in that box truck in the desert all those years ago he told me the business came first. It was my fault for not taking those words to heart.

I chased a dream across the country, only to find myself just as alone as before, only on the opposite coast.

These maudlin thoughts crowd my mind as I stare at the starkly lit metal ceiling. I am considering a gently swaying spider web in the corner when my earpiece jars me. Crius's voice comes through, tiny and huge at the same time.

"Loki. Loke, come in. I need you at the front."

As I unclip the radio from my waist and begin to turn down the volume knob until it clicks and shuts off the device, I hear Crius again, more urgently.

"Loki, repeat: need you at the front. It's an emergency."

I reluctantly take my fingers off the ridged power knob. *What now?*

I cough to clear my throat and snuffle up two nostrils' worth of snot. I hold down the button and mutter, "On my way."

I lean forward and push off the ground, briefly wondering if I have the strength to get up. I somehow make it, shove my hand into a bin behind me without looking and grab the first thing I touch, a pair of sequined ruby undies. I guess I got the *Bedazzled Panties* bin. I wipe my face with little success of absorption and put them back.

Gonna take care of whatever bullshit this is, then go home. Fuck it.

In the Front Room four of our biggest security guards are looking in all directions like they're trying to catch a dancefloor pervert.

"Loki," Crius says, coming out of nowhere. This is the most concerned I have seen him. "We got a situation. Come on, let's go," he says then begins to push his way through the crowd.

Just as I start following in his wake, I feel my body hoisted off the ground. In the blink of an eye I am above the crowd, face up towards the disco ball. Just as I realize what is happening, the four guards throw me on their shoulders like a bag of laundry and charge through the crowd, yelling, "Move, move, move!" It not only looks like I am getting forcibly ejected, but like I am getting kicked out of the club for sexually assaulting one of the owner's mothers.

They split the partiers like bowling pins on our way to the front of the Theater, where they deposit me, none too gently, onto the stage. I wobble, then turn around and look at the crowd. It's the view of a lifetime.

In addition to the hundred patrons cheering and whistling (for no *actual* reason) are: barbacks chanting in Spanish, performers twerking on the bar, Romeo and Krystal dancing with bottles of champagne held up in all four fists, Carlos Surfista leaning on the bar and smirking boozily at me from behind his pointy mustache and personal bottle of rum, Dan and Meloza dancing in front, mouths open, Lada, Juul between her red lips, headbanging and hopping, Amar under the tech booth, still as an Easter Island figure, makeup smeared across his face, my roommates, Strom and Macaw, fingers in their mouths, whistling, Nasty and Whiskers fist pumping in the tech booth, Sauce, the meat in a supermodel sandwich, Clay Stone and Tristan in cupcake outfits, Xavier and Oliver behind the bar cocktails raised high, Grandma in full clown regalia, and most of my Chewbacca campmates. Everybody is applauding and screaming my name.

For a moment I am utterly nonplussed. I have never experienced this kind of attention. The literal spotlight. Then I just raise my arms and absorb the love, like a flower turning towards a late-May sunrise.

The stage shakes as Dreams and Vish jump up on it. They're wearing nothing but pink booty shorts, and the crowd, utterly unsure of where this is going, cheers louder. The two performers grab me and strip me of everything but my tighty-whiteys (gray Calvins). I put up little resistance as the crowd roars.

Dreams struts around me, hips swaying, chin held high. I continue to stand there with my hands in the air like a kid at his first concert. She suddenly stops in front of me and slowly wiggles out of her shorts, never breaking eye contact with me. Her long uncircumcised penis hangs between us for a moment before she spins around and faces the crowd (the penis arrives a split second later).

Before I have the opportunity to adjust to these latest developments, Dreams faces me again and swan dives to the stage and pops up into a perfect handstand. She parts her legs until they are in an upside down straddle. Now her waxed anus and taint are inches from my chest. She begins to topple towards me, almost surely on purpose, and I have no choice but to support her thick muscular thighs with my sweaty hands. I feel heat rush to my face and know it's red as a stoplight.

I don't even pretend to know what to do at this point, apart from keeping Dreams and her ballsack from falling into me.

Vish appears with a foot-long candlestick in one hand and a can of whipped cream in the other. He's the star of the show—Dreams and I are just sharing his spotlight—and it's the final act. He spits on the base of the candle twice, and in one practiced motion stuffs it halfway into Dreams's ass, smooth as you please. The audience gasps and goes "ooooh" like you do right before biting your own knuckle; I flinch but don't let go of the legs. I can barely do a handstand under the best circumstances, and here she is making it look easy as pie while taking a candle in her ass. Vish winks at me then empties the entire can of whipped cream around the base of the candle. With a flourish he produces a lighter and lights the wick. The crowd oooohs.

Offstage I hear someone yell, "Have your cake and eat it, too, Loki!" and I begin to giggle uncontrollably. Juicy is right in front of the stage, practically jumping up and down with excitement.

I've never tossed a dude's salad, but you know what they say: when in Rome…

I close my eyes and begin the face-first dive to new depths…

…only to open them a second later and find Dreams out of the handstand. I missed eating my first man-ass by millimeters.

The crowd sighs a collective "awwww." I do not share their disappointment.

Having enjoyed my moment, filled with gratitude and much-delayed gratification, I put my hands together and bow towards the room a couple of times. Just as I'm ready to jump off the stage and join the party, though, yards of pink silk descend from the ceiling, and for a moment I am lost in the fabric. I look up and see Koochy twenty feet above me, balanced on the thin catwalk, smiling like the Cheshire Cat as he gives the silks a couple of tugs to assure himself that the rigging is secure.

I suddenly understand that Dreams's candle sodomy was not the final act—I am. It's time to show everyone what I've been training for during all those lunch hours.

I disentangle myself and bunch the silks up in one hand. Holding them away from me I give the crowd a showman's smile, then start climbing. They go bananas: this, they did not expect. Every audience loves a surprise (and the potential for either a funny fail or a horrific spinal injury).

When I'm fifteen feet above the hundreds of upturned faces of my friends, coworkers, and complete strangers I separate the two silks, make sure my feet are secure in each one, and slowly scissor my legs apart until I am in a split. One voice cuts through the crowd's cheering, and it's in my head. *Point your toes,* Lada commands, *channel your inner ballerina!*

I pull myself up and out of the split and climb higher. Near the truss, at the very top of the silks, I hook a leg around them and wrap the tail end about my waist. I stay like this, the spotlight and all eyes on me, the music bumping. Holding on with one hand I hold the other towards the audience in a come-here gesture. They respond in exactly the way I wanted. When the applause and cheering can't get any louder, I release the silks from my hand and start to freefall.

It takes no more than a second for me to roll and spin to within a half a foot of the stage. Before my face is smashed beyond recognition, the silk tightens around my waist and I hang suspended like a Mission: Impossible character, legs and arms out straight (and toes pointed).

After a few moments I do a nifty pull-up, unwrap myself, and land my feet on the stage. I am immediately showered with the loudest applause I have ever heard. As I take big whooping breaths I feel my sweaty face shining brighter than all the stage lights combined.

I jump off the stage and land next to Juicy, hands shaking and legs unsteady under me. He holds his arms out and I fall into them. I squeeze him to me and breathe him in: coffee and cigarette smoke. "Love you, man," I say into his ear.

"Love you, too," he says as he hugs me back.

The performance is over, the stage goes dark, colorful beams slice up the atmosphere, the music goes up, and the dance party continues. For what feels like ten minutes I am passed from one set of arms to the next as my friends all wait their turn to hug me. My heart is melting.

As it does every night, the music eventually stops and the lights go on. The people shuffle out, having created memories they may not remember; having left sweat and their inhibitions on the dancefloor. The rest of what they left will be routinely gathered up by the cleaning staff, some of it secreted away in the Lost and Found outside the office door.

After finishing my rounds and barring the golden doors with a two-by-four, I stand in the Front Room and take it all in one last time: the enormous eyeballs slowly blinking out of rhythm, the black and white tiles of the floor, scuffed and littered with baggies, paper straws, tinsel, and condom wrappers; the sticky bar with a lonely bedraggled drink ticket swimming in a tiny brown pool… then walk back through the Theater and out onto the pre-dawn street.

CHAPTER TWENTY-ONE

Unlike after Palace of Gods, this time the beach wasn't a figment of my wishful imagination. The fine sand between my fingers and toes was warm as I looked at the towering granite cliffs jutting out of the Gulf of Thailand. The crystal blue water off of Koh Phangan twinkled and invited like an easy lover, but for now I was content to just sit in the sun. I pressed my lips to the machete-cut opening and tilted my head along with a green coconut. The cold sweet water poured down my throat.

I couldn't be farther from Bushwick (that may even be geographically true). I traded the rat-infested pile of garbage that was Yefferson Street for the pristine beach upon which I now sat.

A few days after my last shift at Yes House I fled the country with no plans to come back for at least a year. The idea was to keep traveling, but I had been in Thailand for two months when the world was brought to its knees by the Covid pandemic. Planes were grounded, the trains stood still in their depots, and buses sat long enough for their tires to flatten. Borders closed and fear reigned supreme.

Some of my performer friends back in New York packed their bags and left the city. What was New York to them, without a stage to perform on? What's a concrete jungle if all the monkeys have been caged? The ones who stayed gamely danced and sang and fisted each other via Zoom, but they all agreed: it just wasn't the same.

Yes House still threw parties, held community meetings, and hosted classes, all on the internet. To YES's great credit, many people in the city said they wouldn't have made it through those first months of solitude and uncertainty without that connective piece.

Early pandemic was a time of reflection for me. I didn't envy my New York or California friends. It was easier for me living on a faraway beach. I'd rise with the sun, go for a beach walk and swim, have some fruit and a coco, then just think.

I thought of my journey of the last three years. Yes House. The man I became, and the manager I grew into. I thought of my faults and shortcomings. Of these I had plenty.

I recalled those early feelings of resentment every time Sable yelled at me or Amar made me feel like a nameless slave. I finally understood that Sable was a lot like me: she had a big heart and a lot of ambition. It's not that she was mean or ill-tempered, but years of nightlife wore her down and soured her. Amar, on the other hand, I don't know. I am not even sure that guy is made of the same parts as other humans.

I thought of all the people I made deep connections with—Dan Rockies, Clea, Sally and Juicy, just to name a few. With the benefit of twenty-twenty hindsight, I considered all the decisions I made, and how I would do it differently now. Even though my unbelievable Yes House experience had ended just a few months ago, it now felt like a faraway dream. On more than one occasion I questioned if any of it happened at all.

When I could no longer contain it, I began to write.

The first page of words left my mind and body through my fingertips and wound up in a Google Doc. Then two pages. Then five. Then I had two hundred.

Juicy called me that June. I had been living in Thailand for six months. We chatted for two hours, catching each other up on our very different pandemic experiences. That winter and spring in New York were hell, but he read a lot and enjoyed the stark beauty of empty avenues and subway cars. I had my beach and writing. Just before we said goodbye he told me that YES was about to reopen as an outdoor bar, and that if I wanted to come back, he'd love to have me. He sounded excited, and I was, too.

I missed my family. After being away from them for what seemed like ages—and writing and reliving everything we'd been through together—I just wanted it back. All of it. The good times and the bad. The party and the emotional breakdown.

Minutes after we hung up I clicked the "book now" button on a Google Flights page.

I went back to New York City, but that was the only part of the plan that didn't fizzle out like a poor video call connection. Juicy & Co. did manage to reopen that summer as an outdoor venue, only to be shut down almost immediately when the State Liquor Authority raided the joint. Evidently they violated one or more of the many strict regulations placed on restaurants and bars during the pandemic.

I kicked around for a couple of weeks, but without the momentum and purpose of Yes House—not to mention pay—I felt like a Slinky in a one-story apartment. This was not the triumphant return I envisioned. Before I knew it I was on more planes: New York to Mexico City, Mexico City to Puerto Escondido.

For seven months I lived in the small beach town on the Pacific coast of southern Mexico. Every day I worked on this book and played volleyball. I excavated every memory (a much easier feat when you don't drink) and relived some of my more colorful Yes House experiences. Like a lucid dream, the more time passed, the less real it seemed.

Pass, it did, but time doesn't rush blindly ahead when you're living amongst surfers and hippies (and digital nomads—eww) in "the Hidden Port." The summer of 2021 took forever to arrive, it seemed, but when it did, it brought with it a vaccine for the CoronaVirus. As the US vaccination rate went up, the authorities were getting ready to give restaurants, bars, and clubs the green light to open. After what felt like a decade of loneliness, we were this close to once again experiencing the joy of social gatherings… and the magic of The Party. The owners and managers at Yes House were planning a grand reopening, and the entire community, myself included, were shaking with excitement.

Rested and rejuvenated after my time in Mexico, I flew back to New York City. For the third time, I was ready to give my heart and soul (and maybe a couple other parts of my anatomy) to Yes House.

I met Juicy at Sararina, a chic Italian restaurant in Bed-Stuy. Bed-Stuy was still hood as fuck, but white girls were walking around under murals of Biggie in this part of Brooklyn, and you could get a thirty-dollar plate of macaroni. Go figure. We sat in what was supposed to be a temporary outdoor dining structure, but it had been there long enough for all the wooden blue planters to be spilling out great bushes of climbing ivy.

Juicy was wearing dark blue jeans and a white t-shirt with a rainbow heart sewn over the place where his own heart would be beneath the layers of skin and bone. Sitting on the plain bench and leaning his back against the ivy-covered plywood wall of the structure, he was smoking a cigarette. He looked good: relaxed and like he hadn't aged a day.

"Ah, man, it's great to see you!" I said, and it really was. It felt so good to be back home, in the city. "I can't believe everything is finally opening again," I said.

"It's great to see you, too," Juicy said. "And I know, man, it's crazy! The pandemic is basically over." He took a drag of his cigarette.

"When are you guys planning to reopen?" I asked, not even trying to keep the excitement out of my voice.

"Soon," Juicy smiled. "Very soon."

"Oh, man. I am pumped. I can't *wait* to go back to work. I'm ready to give you and YES my all for years to come." It felt like every word tumbled out faster than the one before it.

"Yeah, so, uh, here's the thing," Juicy said. He appeared to be looking at the second story of the brownstone next to the restaurant. When he lowered his gaze and looked at me my stomach clenched like a ballsack in an ice bath. In an instant I knew what he was going to say, and I wished there was some way for me to not hear the words. Still, he continued.

"The other partners and I have been talking a lot over the last six months about the future of the club. Ideas, different directions to explore, goals, plans… and staffing. Your name came up." Juicy paused to take a sip from his glass of water. I ignored mine and sat perfectly still.

"Zoe doesn't want you back," he finally said, "and when one of the partners is a complete no-go on something, well, that's just the way it's gotta be. Amar and I really tried to go to bat for you, but she put her foot down. I'm sorry, Loki."

Juicy's delivery was casual without coming off callous.

I tried to swallow but the air got caught halfway down my too-tight throat. My mind pulsed with sadness, anger, and confusion.

"But..." I finally managed, leaning across the table, "What did I do? You said you wanted me back?" I couldn't help but wince at the sound of my voice, the abandoned lover pleading.

As they tend to do, the waitress showed up at the tensest possible moment of the conversation. I pulled back and smiled like I just farted and shat a little. She placed a margherita pizza and a bowl of meatballs between us. Her bare arms were toned and utterly unmarked by tattoos. Anomalous in this day and age (and neighborhood). She wore a simple black tank top and jeans to match. She wished us a pleasant meal and walked back inside the restaurant.

Juicy and I watched the steaming food in front of us, smelling the tomatoey tang of the sauce and baked dough. He finally reached for his silverware.

"Look," Juicy said, unwrapping the napkin from a polished fork and knife, "The truth is, after you left some people came forward and said that over the years you upset them or made them uncomfortable, or whatever. I don't even know who or when, it just got back to me."

For a moment I was speechless with shock. I mean, there was that tiny thing with Sally, but...

"What did I do? Who was it?" I said. "I'll call them and apologize right now. I mean, I was a manager, after all, and I couldn't always be everyone's best friend!" My chest felt tight as I heard myself getting defensive. This was like when we fired Fox, except now I was the one pleading.

Juicy used his knife to carve through tendrils of gooey cheese and the last bit of dough that the pizza wheel didn't cut, then he picked up the small slice, folded it between his fingers and thumb, and bit off half of it. Still chewing he said, "Seriously, I don't know. Supposedly it was never a specific thing or some egregious act, just a general vibe you gave over the years." In two big bites he finished the slice, leaving a thin crescent moon of blackened crust on his plate.

I couldn't eat. I was still reeling from his vague third-hand accusations, and what they meant. I wouldn't be coming back to the Yes House. I wouldn't be coming home to my family, after all.

"So there's nothing I can do?" I asked.

"Nah, man," he responded. "I'm sorry. I have an owner who's blackballing you, current staff that you've rubbed the wrong way—I can't. Maybe it won't be forever, but right now I can't rehire you." Juicy speared a meatball with his fork and shook off some of the thick red sauce. Before bringing it to his mouth he said, "Who knows, maybe you'll work somewhere else for a bit, get a whole different experience, and come back. You don't know how this thing will shake out. Stay positive."

As he chewed heartily, I felt like the meatball, with one important difference: I was being spat back out.

The rest of the meal was understandably strained. I ate a few slices of pizza, hardly tasting any of it. We ate in silence; shooting the shit seemed pointless.

I took the train to Chinatown, where I was staying at a friend's apartment in a building too derelict to be historic. After walking up five flights of stairs, I kicked off my sneakers and lay on the couch. Beyond the hanging plants and the window was the blue gray steel of the Manhattan Bridge. I briefly watched a guy on a blue Citibike struggle up the steep incline. I closed my eyes as a train rattled towards Brooklyn. I felt as low as I did on my last shift, back in the costume closet. Except this time there would be no surprise celebration.

~~~

The next couple of weeks felt like the time after a difficult breakup. I would see an Instagram post about the YES reopening celebration and die a little inside. A friend I hadn't seen in a while would ask, casually, "Hey, you gonna be working at Yes House again now that you're back? That first party is gonna be *sick*," and I would try my best to be nonchalant: "Nah, that's all in the past—it's time to move on and expand my horizons." I was too ashamed to say that I wasn't wanted, that I got kicked out of the family.

I started waiting tables at Cafe Mogador on St. Marks. An East Village gem, the Moroccan bistro is world renowned and has been around for forty years. It also belongs to Juicy's Aunt, so I had an in.

These days I ask Broadway actors and NYU students if they want oat or coconut milk in their latte, and whether they'd like merguez with their eggs… instead of asking celebrity DJs if they preferred Dom Pérignon or Veuve Clicquot during their set (the real ones chose Dom, everytime).

With every passing day, Yes House and my time there seem more distant. I think soon I'll have to dig up photos just to prove to myself that it wasn't a surreal fairytale or fever dream.

Speaking of coffee and Eggs Benedict… I have to wrap this up. It's Saturday morning and I'm about to work one of the busiest brunches in the city. I check myself in the mirror. Dark blue shorts and a black tee, a plain black apron. I do kind of miss the leather pants, fishnet belly shirt, and feather boa, but man, am I more comfortable these days—and it takes far less time to get ready.

I look at my face in the mirror and I am content with the man looking back at me. There's no glamor in selling challah French toast, but that doesn't diminish my smile one bit. I reach into my back pocket and fish out a black hairband. There was a time when I'd have to dig around and make sure I wasn't about to inadvertently whip out a handful of baggies. I pull my hair back into a bun, then turn my head this way and that when I notice something.

I bring my face closer to the looking glass, and sure enough, there it is, between my right eyebrow and hairline.

A tiny spark; a lost little star far from its home constellation. *Glitter.*

Thank you, really, for reading

Special shoutout to everyone who works and understands the nightlife industry. I hope you related to the story in one way or another.

If you enjoyed the book or just want to chat, please reach out on Instagram to me @yeslokiyes or the book @Yes_to_the_Night

Made in the USA
Las Vegas, NV
25 May 2024

90323486R00204